The Cry of the Renegade

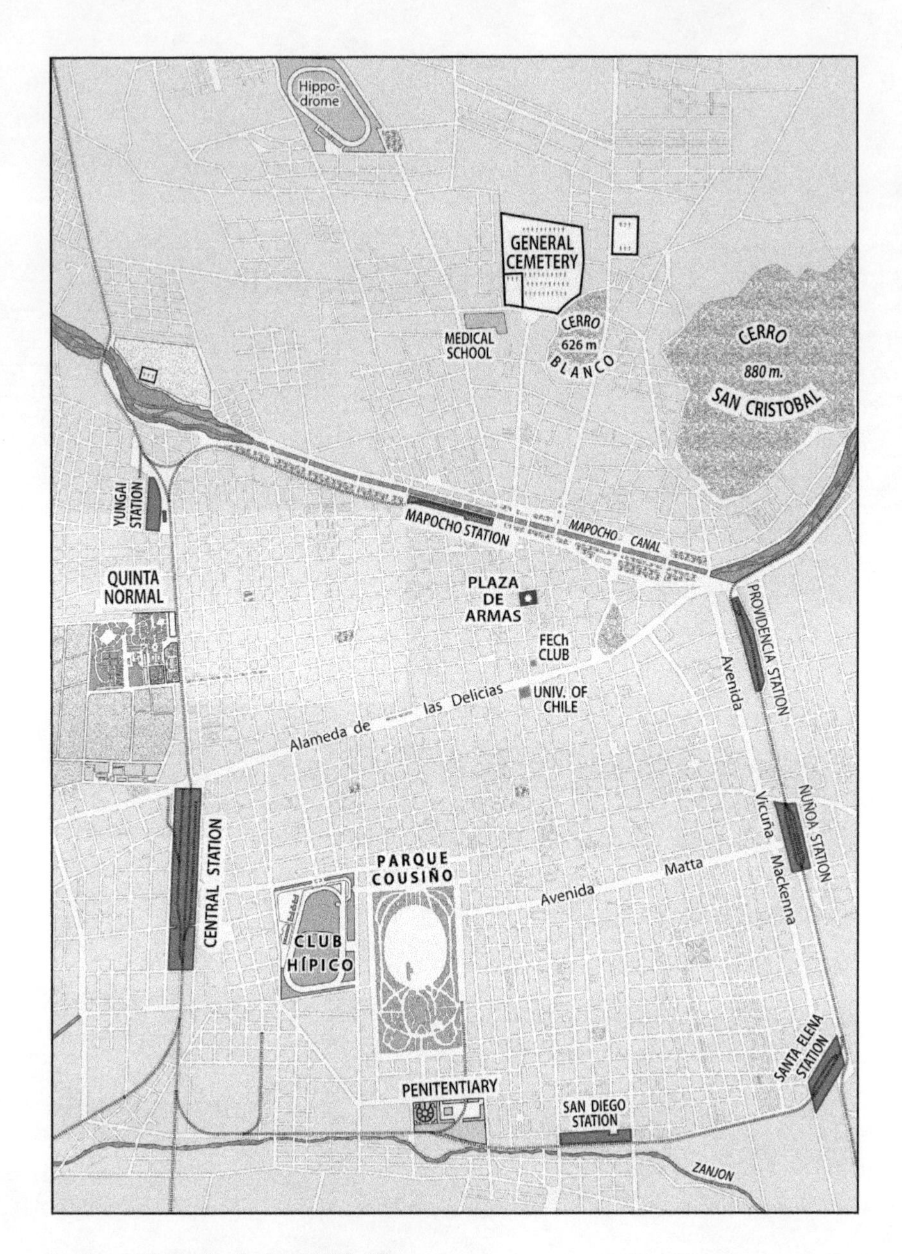

Santiago, 1920. Map by David Ethridge

The Cry of the Renegade

Politics and Poetry in Interwar Chile

Raymond B. Craib

OXFORD
UNIVERSITY PRESS

Oxford University Press is a department of the University of Oxford. It furthers the University's objective of excellence in research, scholarship, and education by publishing worldwide. Oxford is a registered trade mark of Oxford University Press in the UK and certain other countries.

Published in the United States of America by Oxford University Press
198 Madison Avenue, New York, NY 10016, United States of America.

First issued as an Oxford University Press paperback, 2019

Library of Congress Cataloging-in-Publication Data
Names: Craib, Raymond B., author.
Title: The cry of the renegade: politics and poetry in interwar Chile /
Raymond B. Craib.
Description: New York, NY: Oxford University Press, 2016. |
Includes bibliographical references and index.
Identifiers: LCCN 2015042158 | ISBN 978-0-19-024135-3 (hardcover: alk. paper) |
ISBN 978-0-19-005378-9 (paperback: alk. paper) | ISBN 978-0-19-024137-7 (epub)
Subjects: LCSH: Chile—Politics and government—1920-1970. |
Political violence—Chile—History—20th century. |
Anarchists—Chile—History—20th century. |
Anarchism—History—20th century. |
Gómez Rojas, José Domingo, 1896-1920.
Classification: LCC F3099.C76 2016 | DDC 983.06/4—dc23
LC record available at http://lccn.loc.gov/2015042158

It is evident that the broadest outlines of the historical process are the product of factors outside our grasp and control, which we can come to know only after an imperfect, fragmentary fashion. But it is no less evident that the character, and even in certain cases the direction, of historical facts depends to a very large extent on the caliber of individual human beings.

~ Victor Serge, *Memoirs of a Revolutionary*

CONTENTS

ACKNOWLEDGMENTS

This book has been a long time in the making. I received important financial support from the Cornell College of Arts & Sciences Dean's Fund, the American Philosophical Society Franklin Grant, and the Cornell Institute for the Social Sciences and its then-director Ken Roberts.

Portions of chapter 1 appeared in "Anarchism and Alterity: The Expulsion of Casimiro Barrios from Chile in 1920," in Barry Maxwell and Raymond Craib, eds., *No Gods No Masters No Peripheries: Global Anarchisms* (PM Press, 2015), which was republished in slightly altered form in Geoffroy de Laforcade and Kirk Shaffer, eds., *In Defiance of Boundaries: Anarchism in Latin American History* (University of Florida Press). Early portions of chapter 2 appeared as "Students, Anarchists and Categories of Persecution in Chile, 1920," in *A Contracorriente* 8: 1 (Fall 2010). The translation of Gómez Rojas's "Renegación" ("Cry of the Renegade") first appeared in "The Death of the Firecracker Poet: Three Poems of José Domingo Gómez Rojas," in *New Letters: A Magazine of Writing & Art* 78:1 (Fall 2011). All the translations of Gómez Rojas's poetry in this book are my own, but I received substantial and generous guidance and help from Michael Kidd and Jeannine Suzanne Routier-Pucci. I am deeply grateful to them both. Any errors are my own.

Many colleagues and friends have contributed to this project by reading chapters, listening to presentations, having unplanned conversations, sharing archival finds, or recommending readings: my thanks (in no particular order) to Alice Michtom, Mary Roldán, Bert Altena, Constance Bantman, Rebecca Tally, Dalia Muller, Camilo Trumper, Hal Langfur, Jonathan Ablard, Ricardo Brodsky, Roberto Brodsky, Robert Travers, Nancy Appelbaum, Nilay Özok-Gündogan, Barry Carr, Bruno Bosteels, Durba Ghosh, Karen Benzara, Gil Joseph, Claudia Verhoeven, Emilia Viotti da Costa, Tom Klubock, Barry Maxwell, Camille Robcis, Lessie Jo Frazier, Jeff Gould, Kyle Harvey, Duane Corpis, Pablo Silva, Silvia Federici, Jim Scott, Danny James, Ryan Edwards, Josh Savala, Jennifer Jolly, María Cristina García, José Luis Gutiérrez Molina, Salah Hassan, Fouad Makki, Susana Romero Sánchez, Shelly Wong,

Paul Nadasdy, Leonardo Vargas-Méndez, Neema Kudva, Bill Goldsmith, Ernesto Bassi, Alfonso Salgado, Marianne González le Saux, José Moya, Susan Gauss, Viranjani Munasinghe, David Ethridge, Guillermina Seri, Kirk Shaffer, Martin Oyata, Geoffroy de Laforcade, Heidi Tinsman, Consuelo Figueroa, Steve Hirsch, Ramsey Kanaan, Mark Overmyer-Velázquez, Charles Walker, Tori Langland, Marian Schlotterbeck, Lina del Castillo, Thom Rath, Andrej Grubačić, Federico Finchelstein, Carlos Forment, Jessica Stites-Mor, Shawn McDaniel, and Kari Soriano. I also received excellent feedback from audiences at Cornell's International Planning Series in the College of Art, Architecture, and Planning; the Department of History at the University of Connecticut; the 2012 European Social Science History Conference in Glasgow; the Hemispheric Institute of the Americas at the University of California at Davis; the *No Gods No Masters No Peripheries* conference at Cornell University; the Institute for Comparative Modernities at Cornell University; the Latin American Studies Program at the University of Miami; the Department of History at Binghamton University; the Transnational Americas Working Group at the University of Buffalo; the *Desencuentros* workshop at Indiana University; the Janey Latin American Studies Program at the New School for Social Research; the New York State Latin American History Workshop; the History Department at the University of British Columbia-Okanagan; and the Latin American Studies Program at the University of Bergen. The opportunity to present part of this work at the Cátedra de la Memoria at the Museo de la Memoria y los Derechos Humanos in Santiago in 2014 was an honor. I thank Ricardo Brodsky, Carlos Peña, and Marc Chiernek for the kind invitation and Consuelo Figueroa for her comments.

I am particularly indebted to a number of scholars in Chile working on similar themes. Víctor Muñoz Cortés, Mario Araya, Santiago Aránguiz, Alberto Harambour, Pablo Abufom Silva, and Eduardo Godoy Sepúlveda are the epitome of mutual aid. I never would have found the large file of interrogation records pertaining to Pedro Gandulfo if not for Víctor's and Mario's help. The family members of a number of the main subjects of this book were extraordinarily gracious and supportive. I thank Teresa Lonis, Jorge Andrés Barrios Pulgar, Odette Benavente, María Peñaranda Barrios, Graciela Gandulfo, and Quena Blanco. My special thanks to Juan Luis Gandulfo and his family, Victoria and Juan Pablo, who kindly hosted me at their home. Juan Luis answered my many questions, sent me an array of material, and gently prodded me forward with his kind letters and emails. Others who kindly answered questions include William Sater, Rudolf de Jong, Melissa Sepúlveda, Sergio Grez, Mieke Izjermans, Oscar Ortíz, Miguel Silva, Rafael Sagredo and Fabian Pávez. Tomás Ireland and Juan Humberto Vera I have never met, but their emails of inquiry and support kept me motivated. I had excellent research assistance from Ryan Edwards, Josh Savala, Jorell Meléndez-Badillo, and Claudia Gilardona. My thanks to Kyle Harvey who rescued me from image-failure at the last minute.

Excellent intellectual and political spaces for the study of anarchism have been created in Chile by the Grupo de Estudios José Domingo Gómez Rojas, the Archivo la Revuelta, the Librería Proyección, and *El Surco*. I am indebted to the archivists at the Archivo Nacional, the Archivo Nacional de la Administración, the Biblioteca Nacional del Congreso, the archive of the Ministry of Foreign Relations in Chile, the Fundación Pablo Neruda, and the International Institute for Social History in Amsterdam. Particular thanks to Claudia Tapia (at the Archivo del Escritor in the Biblioteca Nacional) and José Huenupi (at the Archivo Nacional).

The entire manuscript was read by Karin Rosemblatt, Paulo Drinot, Sasha Lilly, and readers for Oxford University Press, all of whom offered extensive and excellent commentary. I have not taken all of their advice, but I hope they see their efforts reflected here. David Ethridge made the stellar maps despite an abbreviated timeline. Susan Ferber has been an ideal editor. She has listened, patiently, to me talk about this project for years. When it came time to bring it to fruition, she remembered those many conversations and helped me get it to where I wanted it to be. I am very grateful to Maya Bringe for overseeing the book's production with such diligence.

Cornell University continues to be a very productive and rewarding place to work, not least of all because of my wonderful colleagues in History and around the campus. My thanks especially to intellectual comrades Eric Tagliacozzo, Wendy Wolford, Barry Maxwell, Fouad Makki, Derek Chang, Chuck Geisler, Paul Nadasdy, Steven Wolf, Neema Kudva, Ernesto Bassi, Durba Ghosh, Suman Seth, and Robert Travers. I am grateful to the staff in the History Department (Katie Kristof, Barb Donnell, Judy Yonkin, and Kay Stickane) and the Institute for the Social Sciences (Anneliese Truame and Lori Sonken). I have learned much from our graduate students over the years, and I need to particularly thank Ryan Edwards, Josh Savala, Kyle Harvey, Susana Romero Sánchez, Rebecca Tally, Mónica Salas Landa, and Daegan Miller, for offering me a wide array of comments and suggestions. I am especially indebted to my former colleague Mary Roldán with whom I had many formative conversations about this project, and to Rick López and Mark Overmyer-Velázquez for some two decades of friendship and intellectual exchange. I have significant debts to three very special people: Thomas Kennedy, whose work has been inspiring and support unwavering and who noticed the stars trembling in the clear black night; Leonardo Vargas-Méndez with whom I have shared so many conversations about Chile, the Left, and the future; and Tamara Loos—a sterling intellectual and the epitome of friendship and humanity. Thank you.

As has been the case for more than two decades now, my family has supported my obsessions. My deepest thanks to Mary Brock and to my sister Linda. Cynthia Brock has graciously dealt with my research absences and writing habits with a remarkable degree of patience and love. Moreover, her own example as a constant sentinel (see chapter 1) has been consistently inspiring. This book is dedicated to my parents—in my sixteenth year of parenting, I realize how much I owe them—and to my kids, Connor and Alana, who have lived with this book from the beginning; and to Anthony, who joined us along the way. I hope this book resonates across these generations.

A final acknowledgment: at the International Institute for Social History in Amsterdam, I found an impressive collection of materials related to the subject of this book in the archive of an historian who, in the wake of Chile's 1973 coup d'état, had been imprisoned, tortured, and eventually exiled from his home in Santiago. He had diligently collected this material for his own work—work, and a world, cut short by a ruthless dictatorship. Every folder I opened and every page I turned, I felt Marcelo Segall Rosenmann there. His work remained unfinished, but hopefully this book will serve to bear witness to his labors and to the fact that no archive is made in vain.

ABBREVIATIONS

AN	Archivo Naciónal de Chile
IS	Intendente de Santiago
FCAP	Fondo Colecciones y Archivos Particulares
JS	Judicial de Santiago, Criminal
ARNAD	Archivo Nacional de la Administración de Chile
MI	Ministerio del Interior
MJ	Ministerio de Justicia
BN	Biblioteca Nacional de Chile
AE	Archivo del Escritor
MRE	Ministerio de Relaciones Exteriores de Chile
AGH	Archivo General Histórico
IISH	International Institute for Social History (Netherlands)
MSR	Marcelo Segall Rosenmann collection
DAS	Diego Abad de Santillán collection
leg.	legajo (file)
f.	folio

The Cry of the Renegade

Introduction

FRIDAY, OCTOBER 1, 1920

The body of the firecracker poet wound its way through central Santiago. The funeral cortage extended some fifteen city blocks and numbered in the tens of thousands, a sizeable number for any funeral procession. But for a twenty-four-year-old poet, university student, and clerk in a municipal office?[1]

The funeral procession had begun at the entrance to the club of the Chilean Student Federation (FECh), where José Domingo Gómez Rojas's friend and defender Pedro León Ugalde bade him farewell. Residents of the tony homes that lined Ahumada Street watched from windows and balconies as the cortage proceeded south to the Alameda, Santiago's central boulevard, which soon echoed with the music played by musicians accompanying the procession. On what would usually have been a busy Friday afternoon, central Santiago had come to a halt. Cars—increasingly common on the city's streets in recent years—circulated, but trams, the most accessible and widely used form of transport in the city, remained in their stations. They would not return to operation until the following morning. Tram workers, upon the news of Gómez Rojas's death, had called a work stoppage in order to attend the funeral.[2] They joined other workers—printers and typesetters, carpenters and painters, shoe-workers and glassworkers, members of the Chilean Workers Federation (the FOCh), the Socialist Workers Party (the POS), and, clandestinely, the Industrial Workers of the World (IWW, or Wobblies), among others—to march side by side, as they had done repeatedly over the previous months and years, with students from the FECh. Wobblies unable to attend because they remained imprisoned in Valparaíso's jail sent a floral bouquet to decorate Gómez Rojas's coffin, while their counterparts in Santiago's penitentiary

Figure I.1
Farewell to the firecracker poet: the funeral cortage of José Domingo Gómez Rojas in central Santiago, October 1, 1920. *Sucesos* (October 7, 1920).

raised funds to benefit the poet's family. The mood among students in the FECh, who usually would have been raucously preparing for the annual spring festival of poetry, theater, and arts in the streets of Santiago, was subdued.

From the Alameda the procession turned north and passed the Presidential Palace where, only months earlier, on the eve of what would become a three-month repression of purported subversives that would culminate with Gómez Rojas's death, a senator had stood and stoked the patriotic passions of a crowd, hurling invective and heaping accusations at the FECh. Its leaders were anarchists and subversives, he would claim. It was a hotbed of pro-Peruvian sentiment; it sought the destruction of the social order; its leadership had the insolence and temerity to question national policy. The crowd, some three thousand strong, had then descended on the FECh club and laid waste to its interior, destroying the cantina, smashing the billiards table, ransacking the library, and torching its literary collections and archives. The funeral procession's route, in other words, was a succession of symbolic spaces, the significance of which was lost on no one, least of all the nervous soldiers manning the two tripod-mounted machines guns pointed at the marchers from the ground floor of the presidential palace.[3]

From the Moneda the procession continued toward the Plaza de Armas, Santiago's central plaza, where the son of a prominent conservative politician had been shot and killed only hours after the assault on the FECh. Anarchists would be blamed for the murder and Santiago's intendent (governor), whose offices looked out across the plaza, would help oversee the state's response. Continuing north, the mass of mourners approached the Mapocho canal, passing four blocks to the east of the public jail where Gómez Rojas, one of the hundreds of individuals who would be accused of and detained for subversion, had been held in isolation, malnourished, mistreated, and tortured.

After crossing the canal, mourners continued along Independencia Avenue and its numerous student boarding houses, toward the University of Chile's medical school and past the asylum where Gómez Rojas had spent his final days, in a meningitis-induced delirium, before arriving at the city cemetery. Once at the cemetery, numerous orators stepped forward to eulogize the poet. They included Alfredo Demaría, president of the FECh; Rigoberto Soto Rengifo, another student, arrested in July and released from prison only hours prior to the funeral; Carlos Vicuña Fuentes, attorney for many of those who had been detained and an outspoken critic of Chile's parliamentary republic; and Roberto Meza Fuentes, director of the literary and sociological journal *Juventud* (Youth), the entire archive of which had been set alight in the attacks of July. Other speakers included prominent labor leaders and members of Parliament.

Just as notable by their absence were a host of poets, students, and workers who considered Gómez Rojas a friend and comrade. These included medical student and well-known agitator Juan Gandulfo and typographer Julio Valiente, both of whom remained in the penitentiary, along with dozens of others arrested in the last weeks of July. Valiente had been an early casualty, detained on July 19, whereas Gandulfo had been in hiding and only recently captured. Still others, such as future literary luminary José Santos González Vera, remained on the run. González Vera had fled the capital during the repression, making his way south to Temuco where he would meet up with an aspiring poet and FECh correspondent named Pablo Neruda, who would not soon forget the killing of a fellow poet. Others found themselves in places of even further exile: men such as Casimiro Barrios, who had been expelled from the country under a recently passed residency law and who, by the time of the funeral, was busy organizing workers in the Peruvian port of Callao. And then there were Adolfo Hernández and Evaristo Lagos, two young men whose fates

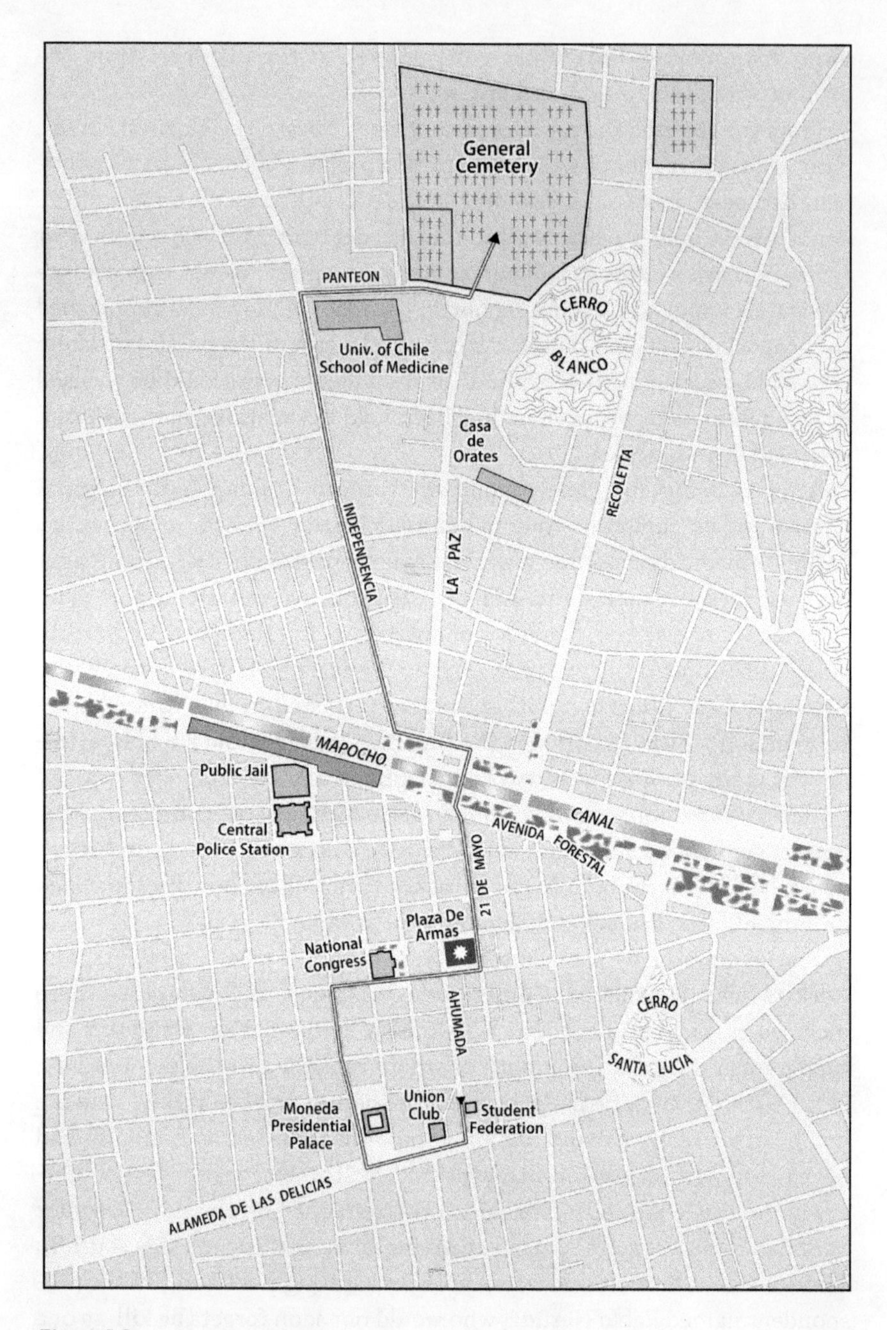

Figure I.2
Final passage: the funeral route of José Domingo Gómez Rojas. Map by David Ethridge.

seemed destined to follow that of Gómez Rojas. Detained indefinitely in Santiago's asylum, their psychological states deteriorated while only blocks away the body of a poet and comrade was interred.[4]

Why and how did José Domingo Gómez Rojas—twenty-four years old, "still a child," in the words of his friend and future literary luminary Manuel Rojas, and the young hope of Chilean poetry, as Pablo Neruda would recall—end up in a prison, an asylum, and a cemetery?[5] This book is an effort to answer that question. It is not a biography of José Domingo Gómez Rojas, although he figures prominently in its pages. It is, rather, a book about the context within which his arrest, imprisonment, and death unfolded and about the experiences of a number of the men he counted as friends and comrades. Covering a four-month period of 1920 in Santiago, it is a book about anarchists and aristocrats, students and teachers, poets and prosecutors, and cops and Wobblies.

THE LONELINESS OF MARTYRDOM

"There are lives caught like dried flowers between the pages of a book," writes anthropologist and historian Greg Dening, in a lovely meditation on history, elaborated through the life and death of a young shipman, William Gooch. "I would not like this life of William Gooch to be like that—exemplary, still. Now that I have found him, I wish him resurrection for who he was, not just for how I would use him. But his life has no monument other than this book, and by that it is joined to my purposes, my artificial curiosities."[6] Such is the blessing and the curse of History.

Unlike that of Gooch, the abbreviated life of Gómez Rojas has its memorials and monuments. In the aftermath of his death, students and workers ensured he was not forgotten. His personality and poetry pepper the pages of the writings of his friends Manuel Rojas and José Santos González Vera—both anarchists and both future winners of Chile's most prestigious national literary prize.[7] Decades later Pablo Neruda, who had arrived in Santiago only months after the young poet's funeral, memorialized the killing of Gómez Rojas in his *Memoirs*, remarking that "within the national context of a small country, the repercussions of this crime were as profound and far-reaching as those of Federico García Lorca's assassination in Granada later."[8] In 1983, a university student movement against the dictatorship of Augusto Pinochet named itself the José Domingo Gómez Rojas Group. Across the decades of the twentieth century Gómez Rojas's name has appeared with regularity in the Chilean press, in novels within and beyond Chile, and on anarchist websites.[9] He has also been the subject of a recent critical biography.[10] There is, as well, a literal monument to him: a park on the edge of Santiago's bohemian Bellavista neighborhood, not far from Pablo Neruda's home *La Chascona*, is named after him with a small plaque dedicated to his memory.

There is, then, little need to rescue Gómez Rojas from oblivion. He has been remembered. But he should be rescued from a historiographical fate as equally lonely: martyrdom. This requires not only situating Gómez Rojas in his historical context but expanding beyond biography to allow others whose lives intertwined with his, who were themselves pursued and persecuted, or were pursuers and prosecutors, to also determine the trajectory and character of historical facts. This includes men such as Casimiro Barrios, an eloquent, fiery, white-collar organizer deported from the country just as the repression began to unfold (the subject of chapter 1); Juan Gandulfo, university student, Wobblie, surgeon, and inspiration to a generation of political activists, including Pablo Neruda and Salvador Allende (along with his younger brother Pedro, the subject of chapter 2); and the judge José Astorquiza, appointed to oversee the prosecution of purported subversives and the man long held responsible for Gómez Rojas's death (and, with long-time anarchist agitator and printer Julio Valiente, subject of chapter 3). Then there is Gómez Rojas himself, poet, student, dramatist, mystic, and Wobblie (subject again of chapter 4). Their individual stories convey a collective reality of life in Santiago in the late 1910s. They draw attention to the everyday forms of violence—hunger, illness, dislocation, exploitation, poverty, police truncheons—that characterized Santiago (and cities elsewhere) and against which these individuals set themselves, often at significant personal risk. Just as importantly for my purposes, they are a reminder of the daily labor of organizing and the daily work of mediating between theory and practice that is at the heart of emancipatory politics. These are histories of militancy defined not by bomb-throwing or assassination but by the hard grind of organizing, protesting, communicating, and laboring at resistance, over months and years. It is their stories together that open up the event known as "the prosecution of the subversives" and reveal, behind a history of repression and a story of individual tragedy, a collective history of struggle, militancy, and hope.[11]

The histories herein are also a reminder that Chile's experience with repression, illiberalism, and violence is hardly restricted to the infamous coup d'état of 1973.[12] The immediate post-World War I era was one in which the social and economic tensions that had previously been held at least partially in check threatened to burst, an impression furthered by the political rise of an amorphous middle class and the political entrance of the working class. Given the context, "the country can no longer be governed as a fiefdom of a few fortunate families," proclaimed one deputy on the floor of the Parliament.[13] As in much of the world at the time—from Barcelona to Peking, from Sydney to Atlanta—the combination of postwar recession, political crisis, and revolutionary inspiration created a heady mix of possibility for some and fear for others.[14] Violence ensued. Despite the repeated efforts by many to criminalize oppositional voices and to caricature anarchists and others as the progenitors of violence, it was Chile's ruling class who chose force over law. There was also the long-standing structural violence of a radically unequal system: the violence of the state, of capitalism, and of the wage system, on full display in the postwar years. In the midst of the tumult, upstart candidate Arturo Alessandri assumed the presidency, ushering in a half-hearted period of labor and social reform capped by a military coup d'état and the drafting of a new constitution in 1925. Despite the collective efforts of workers, students, professors, and white-collar employees to assert their political agency as citizens and to shape the country's future, Alessandri's reforms and the 1925 constitution were imposed from above, short-circuiting hopes for radical change in a moribund system.[15] A half-century later, Augusto Pinochet would look back on that constitution as the beginning of Chile's decline, and he and his coconspirators would initiate a much more ruthless and lasting persecution of so-called subversives. In the meantime, students and workers would recuperate and invoke the name of José Domingo Gómez Rojas as they sought to escape the confines of the dictatorship and its efforts to obliterate memory.[16]

ARTIFICIAL CURIOSITIES

As there are monuments, there are also "artificial curiosities": artificial in that historians have little choice but to recognize their own interests in the lives they choose to narrate, the questions that bring them to their subject, the curiosities that draw them to archives, and the contexts within which they write. There are a multitude of curiosities addressed in the following chapters, but two guiding interests deserve at least brief mention here: the histories of students and anarchists.

Anyone who has picked up a newspaper in the past decade has at some point come across an article about student politics in Chile. From the 2001 "mochilazo" (backpack uprising) to the "penguin revolution" of 2006 to the student insurgencies in 2011, the past two decades have seen high school and university students in Chile dramatically shape the political contours of national life and debate and inspire others well beyond the bounds of Chile. These movements were often filtered through, but not dependent on, Chile's student federation (FECh). Despite such movements and despite the highly politicized atmosphere at most public universities throughout Latin America, university students and their political activities have been infrequent subjects of systematic study, particularly among US and Europe-based scholars of Latin America. When they have been studied, it is usually in relationship to the uprisings of the 1960s and after, implicitly linking student politics to the new social movement literature that characterizes the era.[17] Neither 1968 nor the recent and ongoing mobilizations were unprecedented. Students have had a long tradition of political organizing and agitation, one inadvertently obscured by the language of and focus on "new social movements" and the more recent past.[18] For much of the twentieth century public universities throughout Latin America have served as the primary sites for the political formation of future civilian leaders, intellectuals, and political activists around the continent. They have also served as sites for radical challenges to such inherited formations. In Chile, it was the University of Chile where future leaders and intellectuals often cut their political teeth in organizations such as the FECh; others learned their politics from the working people with whom they interacted daily on the streets of Santiago or in cafes, meeting halls, and clubs, including that of the FECh itself.

By 1919 and 1920 the FECh had become an organization, and its club a physical space, within which not only increasingly radicalized university students but also former students, workers, and worker-intellectuals gathered, talked, read, and found common cause. Such alliances generated trepidation among many in the halls of the presidential palace and the Parliament. Across the city, one exiled attorney recalled, students, poets, workers, young intellectuals, and others "got together, discussed, wrote, prognosticated, and organized themselves into an apocalyptic tide that filled the dithery aristocracy with dread."[19] In a world transformed by a world war and a socialist revolution, and in a country experiencing a crisis in political legitimacy, such interactions appeared increasingly threatening and constituted a challenge to the prevailing logic of social identities and social relations.[20] They were, in a word, subversive.

Subversion, like "terror," is rarely well-defined, least of all by those who use it to justify repressive and illiberal policies. Its exculpatory ambiguity is its attraction. In turn-of-the-century Chile, as in much of Europe during the same period, subversion was largely equated with an equally ill-defined anarchism.[21] Those in power used terms such as "subversive" and "anarchist" as a means to delegitimate a range of oppositional political voices, from the mildly reformist to the adamantly revolutionary, and as a means to legitimate their own repeated contraventions of the law.

Anarchism has experienced, both as a political praxis and as a subject of academic inquiry, a well-deserved resurgence in recent years, although one could argue that it has never gone away but simply not been recognized as such.[22] This has been as true for Chile as elsewhere.[23] Indeed, in Chile in recent years anarchist politics and organizing has been at the forefront of social protest and has suffered, not surprisingly, distortions and caricatures at the hands of the political and media establishment.[24] Beyond Chile, caricatures and distortions linger. Commentators across the political spectrum persist in promoting images of anarchists as little more than an inarticulate concatenation of bomb-throwing nihilists, disorganized and incoherent radicals, and middle-class kids suffering from bourgeois ennui. Liberal political theory itself sets the bounds within which anarchism can only be imagined as an aberration or a fantasy.[25] Fellow travelers on the Left have been no kinder: the twentieth-century profile of Marxism has cast a long shadow over the history of the Left and in retrospect anarchism appears, if it appears at all, as an immature stepchild in the Marxian tradition.[26] Immature, impatient, incoherent, its only theoretical contribution seems to be to dispense with the theoretical. Yet anarchism was, and remains, much more than either of those perspectives permit. For one, it was a powerful intellectual and political force in the late nineteenth and early twentieth centuries. None other than British Marxist historian Eric Hobsbawm, a less-than-sympathetic commentator, would note that the revolutionary Left of the early twentieth century was driven largely by anarchists and anarcho-syndicalists.[27] Some of the world's foremost scientific thinkers and intellectuals were also anarchist theorists and practitioners: men such as Peter Kropotkin, Elisee Reclus, and I. Mechnikov, and, if we were to be slightly more capacious, Oscar Wilde and Henrik Ibsen, among many others.[28] Anarchism resonated among a wide-range of political, social and cultural radicals: anti-colonialists, transcendentalists, and labor organizers, among a multitude of others.[29] It also had its limitations. One looks in vain, for example, for any mention of the struggles and persecution of Mapuche people in the writings and speeches of the Chilean anarchists in what follows.

A word of caution is in order here: in what follows I take a broad perspective on anarchism. The fact is some of the individuals who populate the pages of this book—Armando Triviño, Manuel Silva, Juan Gandulfo, and others—described themselves as anarchists, anarcho-syndicalists, or anarcho-communists. They opposed what they perceived to be the cruel fictions of representative democracy and party politics; they refused to vote; they advocated for worker control of the means of production; and they fought for the abolition of the state, forms of hierarchy, and the wage system. Others—Casimiro Barrios and Pedro Gandulfo, among them—neither embraced nor rejected the term, but instead understood it as part of a broader orientation or struggle toward emancipation and equality. They read anarchist works, organized alongside anarchists, and at times described themselves in terms reminiscent of anarchist politics and yet belonged to organizations that defined themselves as socialist; they envisioned revolutionary change but were not averse to pushing for reform within the existing political system; they could be politically eclectic without devolving into ideological incoherence. In retrospect it might be argued there was little "anarchist" in their politics, but that is both too narrow and too anachronistic a perspective. Anarchism was, for them, a fundamental part of their political vocabulary and ideological horizon. At the minimum they were anarchists by affinity, seeing it as a critical part of a broader Left tradition that emphasized, first and foremost, a common enemy in the old aristocracy, the new bourgeoisie, and the state upon which both relied for their wealth and power. They might best be understood by invoking a well-known quote from anarchist Gustav Landauer: "The state is not something that can be destroyed by a revolution, but is a condition, a certain relationship between human beings, a mode of human behavior; we destroy it by contracting other relationships, by behaving differently."[30] The revolutionary politics they espoused must be taken seriously, but so too should the relationships they created and their mode of human behavior.

At times "anarchism" was the most resonant term available to describe a longing, an aspiration—something almost, as life-long anarchist Manuel Rojas would write, "poetic."

> It is an ideal, something that one hopes will happen or come to exist, a world in which all would be for all, in which private ownership of land or goods would not exist, in which case the first thing that has to happen when the revolution comes is to burn the Property Archives; in which love would be free love, not constrained by laws; without the police, because they would not be necessary; without an army, because there would be no wars; without churches, because love between human beings would already have been born and all of us would be one. Other things also, but these are the essentials.[31]

Thus the protagonists in this book embraced a range of anarchist positions, from individualist perspectives associated with Max Stirner and Friedrich Nietzsche to the anarcho-communism of Peter Kropotkin to the syndicalism of the IWW. Such perspectives were not seen as mutually exclusive, nor did they differ substantially in their desired outcome: an end to capitalism and the state and the achievement of individual freedom and collective equality simultaneously (rather than sequentially).

The idea of an existing orthodox Left in the early 1900s is problematic, and a range of orientations intersected in ways that belie any easy assignation of a particular "-ism."[32] In Chile, at least, there existed a "capacious left": inclusive, anti-categorical, and pluralistic, within which the distinctions of doctrine frequently were blurred.[33] This is not to erase differences but to argue that they were neither as well-defined nor as inflexible as they are read to be after the fact: that is as true now as it was in the interwar period. Too often terminologies constitute a linguistic shorthand that does little justice to the complexity and range of political praxis. Agitators and organizers on the Left frequently repudiated ideological rigidity and orthodoxy without ever abandoning a commitment to a socialist commons characterized by ideals of individual freedom and social equality. Rather than taxonomies—as if people's dreams, practices, and ideals could be as easily catalogued and tagged as dead butterflies or beetles—contingent, contradictory, compelling, and human histories are needed. If that all sounds too poetic, then a more prosaic proposition: anarchist or not, what did those accused of anarchist activities and subversive affiliations do? What ideas did they espouse? What deeds, if any, landed them in prison in 1920?

In its focus on Santiago—a single city—this work would appear to go against the grain of the recent turn toward the transnational. Yet a study of a single city can be just as transnational as a study of multiple locations spanning the globe or of an individual's cosmopolitan travels. The synchronic reality of modernity—birthed by dramatic transformations in transportation, financial, and communications technologies—and capitalist production ushered in a recognizably globalized era from which few regions remained untouched.[34] That very reality birthed the forms of anarchism and anarcho-syndicalism embraced by the subjects of this book. In fact, some of the earliest and most persistent questioners of the nation-state form were anarchists, including those in Santiago, Chile.[35] They were inspired and challenged by ideas from an array of places; they were shaped by the structural forces of global finance, trade, and extraction; they were linked by transnational bonds of solidarity and by an empathy with anti-imperialism. They were, as anarchist geographer and theorist Peter Kropotkin claimed, all too aware of the "immense likeness, which exists among the laboring classes of all nationalities."[36] The places they inhabited were shaped by and filled with influences and ideas from far and wide. The world was, in other words, there in Santiago.

But *Santiago* was also there, in Santiago. The specificities of production, industry, social relations, urban planning, economic policy, and urbanization profoundly shaped the forms politics took and the militant particularisms, as well as universalisms, that developed.[37] The particularities of friendships and antagonisms, petty histories and profound solidarities, personal affection and class hatred, impacted the course of history here. To understand how people come to be radicalized requires being attentive to the specificity of their surroundings. The majority of the subjects of this book were not peripatetic, transnational radicals: they were, I argue in chapter 1, sedentary radicals. They saw themselves as citizens of the world, loyal to humanity rather than the nation-state, but they also understood themselves to be members of a social and political world on a much more immediate scale: a scale in which self-governance, association, autonomy, and federation could be practiced and realized even as inter- and transnational solidarities were forged and imagined. So just as they fostered translocal linkages and connections with counterparts in Lima and Callao, La Paz, Buenos Aires, Panama City, New York, Sydney, and Barcelona, and regional relationships in Chile's north and south, they also created and nurtured very local ones in Santiago's streets, plazas, and neighborhoods.[38] There they established practices, habits, routines, memories. Through their social relations and interactions, they helped create the space of Santiago.[39] "Geography," the anarchist geographer Elisee Reclus wrote, "is not an immutable thing; it is made and remade everyday." It was not remade from scratch but rather through the accretions of relationships and interactions of comrades and friends, the antagonisms of managers and laborers, and the quotidian itineraries of the city's denizens.

Despite appearances, this is not a history *of* Chile. It spends little time examining the persecution of purported subversives that took place beyond Santiago, in places such as Valparaíso, Antofagasta, Lota, and the Magallanes. Rather, it is a history of the collective and personal experiences and struggles of a number of men—few women were arrested and targeted, despite their prominent presence in Santiago's industrial sector and labor agitation—who made their lives in the city of Santiago. Their history should not be appropriated to tell a national story.[40] They had little interest in such nationalist perspectives. At the same time their history cannot remain placeless, nor can it simply wish the nation-state away. It is, in this sense, a *Chilean* history. This is a history, after all, that would look very different if it had occurred elsewhere.[41] Moreover, the subjects of this book may have embraced a common humanity and dreamed a utopian future, but they knew all too well that they lived in a dystopic present and thus they perceived the state—its institutions, legal regime, and political structure—at times as an immediate means through which to struggle against labor exploitation, social inequality, and a lingering colonialism. Similarly, they had little choice but to submit to capitalist labor systems and housing markets, despite the fact that such activities could appear to legitimate or reinforce the existing system.[42] This does not make them faux anarchists or closet liberals. It makes them human beings living in a social world not entirely of their making and articulating ideas and aspirations that cannot be reduced to bullet-points culled from a textbook on political theory.[43] Regardless of the categories deployed and the labels ascribed, this is a story of individuals and the collective struggles they waged, futures they imagined, and worlds they occupied.

Beginnings are invariably arbitrary. But some are better than others. This history begins on July 19, 1920. And it begins, as so many histories of a place do, far away, at one of its distant peripheries: in this instance, the contested borderlands between Chile and Peru.

CHAPTER 1

A Constant Sentinel

JULY 19, 1920

In early twentieth-century Chile, state authorities—prefects, intendents, police agents, spies, and congressmen—hassled, harangued, persecuted, prosecuted, framed, caricatured, criticized, arrested, and expelled men and women they did not want in the country. One of those individuals was Casimiro Barrios Fernández.

On July 19, 1920, Chilean security personnel escorted Barrios to the borderlands between Chile and Peru and expelled him from the country. This is Barrios that same year: almost thirty years old, balding, well-dressed, married, and a father. He was, by all accounts, a proud and fearless man, characteristics captured by the directness of his gaze and the hint of a smile in what is a mug shot. The paper that published the photograph got his name wrong, but many readers would have recognized him: some eighteen months earlier he had experienced a moment in the reading public's eye when, after becoming the first person ordered expelled under Chile's 1918 Residency Law, the popular weekly *Zig-Zag* published an interview with him and photographs of him and his family. A year and a half later, Barrios departed Chile under threat of force, labeled a foreigner, an anarchist, and a subversive.

ERRANT SWALLOWS

Casimiro Barrios Fernández arrived in Chile in 1906 at the age of sixteen.[1] He was one in a wave of young immigrants from the sierra of

Figure 1.1
A constant sentinel. Casimiro Barrios Fernández, c. July 1920. Courtesy of the International Institute for Social History.

Cameros in La Rioja, Spain, to set his sights on South America. His hometown of Nieva de Cameros was characteristic of many of the small villages that clung to the mountainsides of the sierra, where the population had traditionally devoted itself to sheep herding. Transhumant paths coursed across old Castile to the edges of Extremadura, while the wool cloth from the sierra made its way to many of the commercial centers of the plateau and as far south as Andalucia in the eighteenth century.[2] The sierra had seen an outmigration of its young population in the late nineteenth century, prior to a larger outflux from the Ebro valley regions of La Rioja, as the herding and wool industry declined and a phylloxera plague devastated the region.[3] Initially many of these adolescents migrated south, either to Extremadura or to Andalucía, following centuries-old pathways.[4] Gradually, and especially by the late nineteenth century, the migration shifted toward South America with young migrants leaving directly from their villages and towns in the sierra.[5] Most were in their teens, opting to leave upon finishing their basic schooling at thirteen or certainly prior to mandatory military service upon turning twenty-one.[6]

Transportation changes facilitated this shift toward transatlantic migration, as did the increased existence of agents actively recruiting migrants. The Chilean Colonization Agency had representatives in various towns in La Rioja, promising free travel for those willing to make the trek.[7] Although migrants had to be wary—stories circulated of phony agents and fake companies, such as the Spanish American Iron Company, whose agents promised passage to Cuba on a ship that in reality sailed for the Transvaal—many found their way to South America via Barcelona, Santander, and A Coruña.[8]

The Barrios family was no exception. Four of the five Barrios brothers left the slowly contracting village of Nieva de Cameros around the turn of the century.[9] While Eleuterio Barrios, like most of his fellow *neveros* and most European migrants more generally, headed for Buenos Aires, the eldest brother, Ciriaco, traveled to Taltal, in northern Chile, followed shortly thereafter by his brothers Rogelio and Casimiro.[10] Taltal was a dusty port town of 15,000 souls but growing quickly as the demand for nitrates mined from the surrounding Atacama desert expanded rapidly for export to North America and Europe. The tax revenues and profits derived from nitrate exports, the motor of Chile's economic growth between 1880 and 1915, stimulated a boom in manufacturing, transportation, and industry. Cities such as Santiago and towns such as Taltal grew, as did the service sectors needed to provision a veritable army of itinerant laborers working in the nitrate fields, the railroads and the ports. Barrios and his brothers sought out Taltal because they had an uncle, Julián, who had settled there and become proprietor of two general goods stores: "El Sol" and "Las Novedades."[11]

Barrios would not stay long in Taltal. With the death of his brother Rogelio in 1905, and then Ciriaco in 1908, he may have had little reason to remain.[12] By 1911 he had relocated to the capital city of Santiago, where one of the first tasks he set for himself was to have Ciriaco's poetry published.[13] Ciriaco was six years Casimiro's senior. In Taltal, he had established a reputation for himself, under the pen-name Gil Güero, as a poet and a correspondent with Santiago's *El Heraldo de España*.[14] His poems revealed an attention to social inequalities. Some evoked the plight of La Rioja's peasants while others, such as "Nostalgia," reflected the difficulties of migration:

> Poor errant swallow!
> not well tested in flight
> for a land remote
> I left my warm nest.[15]

Just how much he had established himself as an ally of working people is suggested by the editorial that appeared in *La Voz del Obrero* upon notification of his death: "The cause of social justice has suffered an irreplaceable loss: with the death of señor Barrios it has lost one of its next apostles."[16]

How much of an ideological influence Ciriaco had on his younger brother is unclear, but Casimiro clearly shared his brother's sympathies for the plight of workers in Chile's burgeoning industries. This perhaps is not surprising. As well as the influence of his brother, Barrios must also have been impacted by the massacre at the nearby Escuela Santa María de Iquique in 1907, in which state forces under the authority of Silva Renard killed hundreds of striking workers, their wives, and their children.

At some point after arriving in Santiago, Barrios married a *chilena* with whom he raised a number of children. He had saved enough money to establish his wife with a *cigarerría* (tobacconist stall) while he worked as a clerk in a garment shop—La Buena Compra—on San Diego Street just south of the city center.[17] But the Great War (or, as Barrios put it, "the goddamn war") put an end to his wife's business, although he later was able to set her up with a small milk stand. The couple and their children lived only minutes from Barrios's work place on San Diego street. This was an area of the city in which politics was in the streets and this street particularly was a vein of political militancy: A world in which barbers who had affiliated with "the idea" (anarchism) would hang a sign advertising cheap books: *Soldier, Don't Kill, Worker, Don't Vote; Evolution and Revolution; The Conquest of Bread; In the Coffee Shop*; and the like.[18] On the streets of his neighborhood Barrios would have repeatedly encountered a number of anarchist and socialist organizers who also lived in the immediate vicinity. Just to take a few examples: Barrios lived on the same block as anarchist militant and carpenter José Tránsito del Ybarra; Zacarías Soto Riquelme, a young painter and future founder of the Socialist Party in Chile, lived close by as did Octavio Palmero, a Cuban chauffer who would be deported in 1920 for subversion. Barrios's shop was on the same block as the *Zapatería El Soviét* (The Soviet Shoestore) owned by Eduardo Bunster, one of the leaders of the FOCh with close relations to the anarchists.[19] Moreover, numerous stores and workspaces along San Diego served as nodes of distribution for FOCh and other Left publications.

Barrios's home, only minutes away, sat on the northern edge of what was the center of Left cultural and political life—the "barrio Latino."[20] If there was a "radical Santiago," this was it. Here amidst a mix of conventillos, boarding houses, and middle class residences, lived many of the men arrested in late July of 1920 for membership in the Industrial Workers of the World (IWW). It was here that university students with

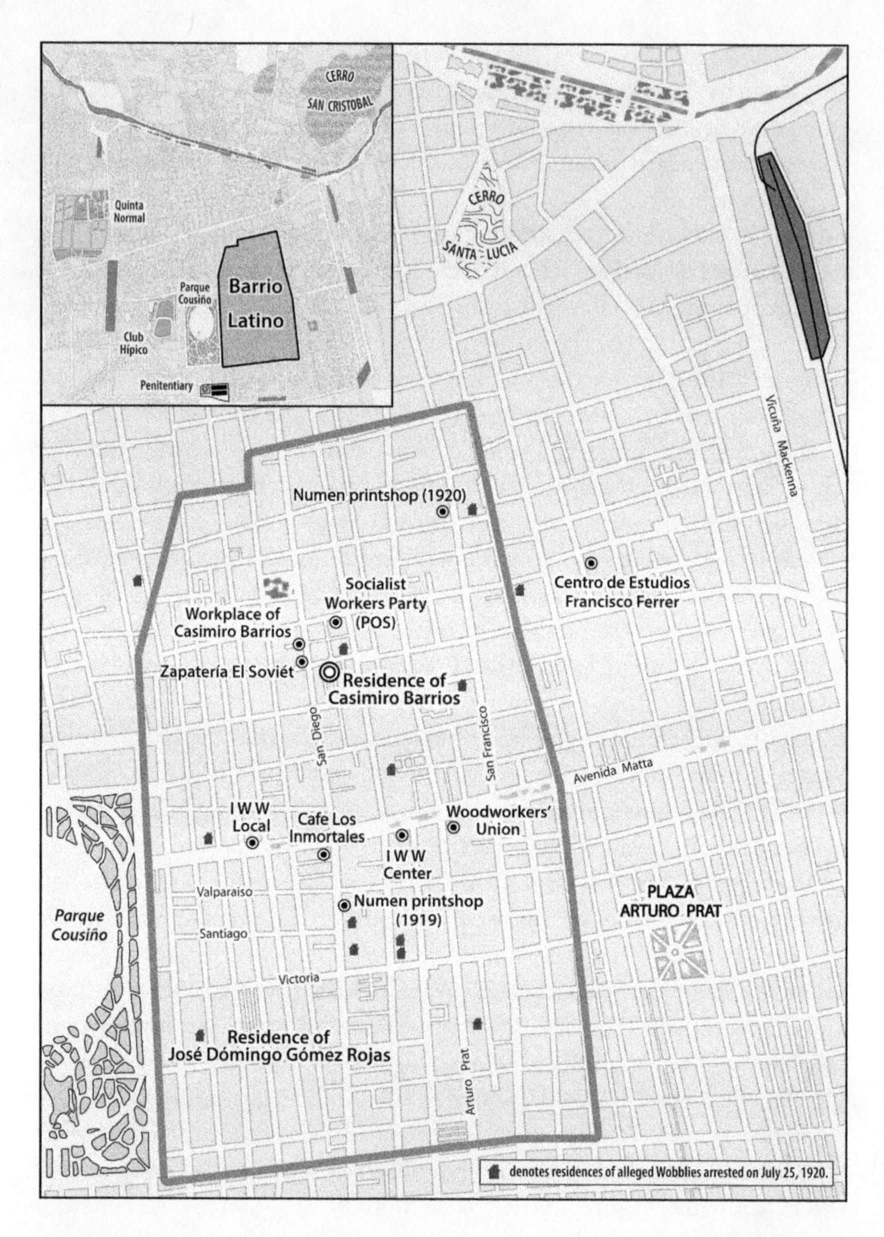

Figure 1.2
Social city: the local world of Casimiro Barrios and the general area of the Barrrio Latino, centered around the intersection of Avenida Matta and calle San Diego. Map by David Ethridge.

strong anarchist proclivities—the brothers Juan and Pedro Gandulfo, Santiago Labarca, José Domingo Gómez Rojas, and others—would gather with working men at the Cafe Inmortales or the Centro de Estudios Francisco Ferrer to read poetry, share texts, and talk politics. It was here that students and workers gathered, under the watchful eyes of infiltrators and spies, to organize protests or argue strategy or to propose a theatrical performance to raise money for the families of imprisoned comrades. It was here, and along streets just to the south, where one would find the glass and shoe factories, the leather workshops, the metalworks, and the furniture assemblies in which many of Santiago's working men and women labored. Here the spatial, the social, and the political were mutually reinforcing.[21]

By the second half of the decade Barrios had become, with his energy and eloquence, a prominent figure in the political Left of Santiago.[22] From his counter, Barrios would watch the happenings on the busy street outside. When a demonstration arose in the streets nearby Barrios would leave his post for an hour—with the permission of his employer, Artemio Bustos—and unleash "a torrent of fiery (inciting) words and then return to selling cloth."[23] He acquired a reputation for being particularly outspoken regarding the lack of enforcement of existing labor laws, such as the 1914 "chair law," requiring employers to provide a chair for each of their clerical workers, and the 1907 "ley dominical," which provided for a day of rest each week.[24] Although on the books, these laws were rarely enforced. In other instances he spoke openly and frequently about the need for new legislation: for a minimum wage, a limit to the number of hours one could work, and a reduction in the interest lending houses could charge.[25] He also spoke out against alcohol: like many working men at the time, he saw alcohol as profit-making poison intended to keep the workers docile and to retake the money they had been paid.[26] Eloquent and well-informed, living and working in the heart of one of Santiago's busiest commercial districts and politically radical neighborhoods, Casimiro Barrios would feel the wrath of the business owners who feared the enforcement of such measures.

TEN WHO SHOUT

A phrase from the era: "Ten who shout achieve more than 10,000 who stay quiet."[27] And if 100,000 shouted?

On November 22, 1918, upward of 100,000 people took to the main thoroughfare of Santiago, the Alameda, to protest skyrocketing food prices and inflation. The demonstration had been organized by the Asamblea Obrera de Alimentación Nacional (Workers' Assembly on National Nutrition, or AOAN), created in 1917 by the labor movement, in conjunction with university students from the FECh, to address the

Figure 1.3
Food for thought: the gathering on the Alameda de las Delicias organized by the AOAN, November 22, 1918. Courtesy of the International Institute for Social History.

scarcity and rapidly escalating costs of basic foodstuffs and staples at a time when the major growers were increasing their exports. This was not the first time Chile's populace had taken to the streets en masse to protest the cost of living. In 1905 some 30,000 *santiaguenos* had marched on La Moneda.[28]

Hunger can be a powerful organizer. For many it had been and continued to be a pervasive presence in their lives. One of the most persistent themes running through the semiautobiographical works of Manuel Rojas—a contemporary of Casimiro Barrios—is the perpetual, stuctural violence of hunger. His most famous short story "The Glass of Milk" (*El vaso de leche*) is a meditation on hunger, dignity and solidarity. An opening sequence of his novel *La oscura vida radiante* is emphatic on this point:

> —And what are we to do now?
> —You wait a bit.
> —It's just that my wife and kids and I are hungry.
> —We are all hungry.
> —We have always been hungry.
> —What's new?[29]

But hunger can incapacitate as much as it can motivate. Given that hunger rarely left working families in peace, it is in and of itself an insufficient explanation for the protests in 1918, particularly if historians wish to avoid reducing working peoples' politics to a mere reflex generated by the severity of their material conditions. Scarcity shivers in the shadow of abundance. Maurice Maeterlinck's Nobel Prize-winning play *The Blue Bird*, published in 1908, was a huge success and popular among many of Santiago's renegade intellectuals. The book opens with poor protagonists looking from their windows at the wealthy across the street whose plates are filled with food. They are stunned that the wealthy are not yet eating because they are not hungry. "Not hungry? . . .Why not?" It was inconceivable that they ate well everyday.[30] Santiago's working people generated their own popular refrains that used food as a means to critique greed and accumulation: "They are pigs who don't give lard;" "To avoid breaking the shells they don't eat eggs."[31] It was not scarcity alone that drew tens of thousands in to the streets of Santiago, but rather the fact of abundance and the patterns of profit-making in a system of ill-repute.

The cost of living—and there was a price to life—was high in the 1910s for most working people. World War I wrought havoc on much of Europe, but for some in Chile it was an opportunity: sales of nitrate to the allied forces initially boomed and commerce and industry prospered.[32] Little of this wealth trickled down to working people. Worse still, agriculture confronted its own problems. In 1914 Chile had begun to import wheat from California and Australia due to bad harvests, substantially pushing up the price of bread.[33] Many understood that agricultural speculation, as much as bad harvests, were at the root of the pricing. Little relief was to be found at the municipally owned Vega Central, where wholesalers would buy large quantities of food from producers and then resell at inflated costs to small retailers, who passed on the costs to consumers.[34] Confronted with rapidly rising prices and discontent in 1914, the administration of Ramón Barros Luco read the political winds and responded to help consumers, but when such issues returned in 1918 the administration of Luis Sanfuentes would respond with a tin ear.[35] Prices had already doubled between 1900 and 1910, and they did so again between 1910 and 1920, such that by 1918 a wage-worker would have had to devote close to 75 percent of his or her earnings on basic subsistence.[36] Chile was not unique in this regard. The last years of the 1910s saw nation-states throughout much of the world saddled with inflation, poor harvests and food shortages.[37] As social mobilizations erupted, statesmen and elites found themselves in precarious circumstances. The crisis was due in part to global issues—war and weather, for sure—but many in Chile also honed in on the fact that major growers, despite the crises, continued to export much of their harvest. Even then, some asserted that Chile was exceptional. "Not even in countries at war, in the midst of freight crises and submarine campaigns," wrote one editorialist in 1918, "has the cost of bread, sugar, milk, butter, coal, etc., been so high as in Chile, a country of agriculturalists, of wheat, of beans, of cows and forests, and mineral coal."[38] Food quality proved an issue too: sellers frequently cut corners by adding sawdust to coffee grounds or passing horse meat off as pork sausages.[39] The availability of meat after the war had dropped to the degree that some commentators began to identify caribou and other game as new sources.[40] The purity of milk and the freshness of fish were constant concerns.[41] High prices and low quality were exacerbated by rising inflation as large landowners engaged in monetary tactics that reduced the value of paper money, a situation that only worsened after the end of the war in Europe.[42] Salaried employees and wage workers both suffered as speculation on money meant radical fluctuations in the value of the Chilean peso on any given day.[43]

As prices for foodstuffs rose, with no effort on the part of the government to limit food exports, the FOCh, in conjunction with university students in the FECh, the National Association of Catholic Students, and others, organized the AOAN.[44] A remarkably inclusive organization, the AOAN was composed of workers from various industries, *empleados* of both sexes, university students, and middle-class professionals.[45] The alliance they forged is indicative of how deep the crisis had become. What little legitimacy Chile's ruling class had now evaporated. The curse of hunger and spectre of speculation had crossed from Santiago's most marginal populations to its middle-class professionals and petty proprietors. They surely recognized themselves in another refrain from the period: "We are all mule drivers and we walk the same road/ Fools we would be not to help one another."[46]

Indeed, the AOAN established a formal precedent for what would become a powerful alliance across social and ideological lines. Meetings, for example, were held in the FECh student club on Ahumada Street in central Santiago, with some seventy or eighty people—students, laborers, and white-collar employees, as well as one or two police infiltrators—usually in attendance.[47] The AOAN leadership was itself reflective of this inclusivity: Santiago Labarca, then-president of the FECh; militants Carlos Alberto Martínez and Evaristo Rios from the Socialist Workers Party (POS); Francisco Pezoa, delegate and anarchist from the Casa del Pueblo; and Moises Montoya, from the Woodworkers' Resistance Society, all served in organizing roles.[48] Other prominent members included Julio

Valiente, an anarchist militant and owner of the *Numen* printing press that played an important role in the circulation of political ideas and social knowledge in the late 1910s, and Casimiro Barrios, who, by this point, was a prominent militant in the Santiago branch of the POS as well as the AOAN.[49] He spoke frequently at meetings and demonstrations protesting the cost of food and basic necessities and demanding that the government crack down on the "abuses of speculators."[50]

The AOAN addressed many issues, including monetary policy, identification of culprits engaged in price-gouging, petitions to allow the owners of street-stands in the open markets to sleep in their stands, and improved means of bringing foodstuffs such as vegetables, beans, and milk to market.[51] "We do not want the closing of markets," wrote the authors of one letter. "We want to see more and more open, such that free competition will put an end to the excesses that harm the people."[52] But this was hardly an embrace of some unfettered free market. The key issues around which many mobilized in November were that the government reduce or stop exports of cereals and that farmers be permitted to sell directly to consumers.

To push these demands the AOAN organized the November 22 demonstration.[53] News of the scheduled demonstration traveled widely—more widely than expected, perhaps—when a pilot flew flights over Santiago dropping leaflets announcing the demonstration.[54] That Friday somewhere between 60,000 and 100,000 people descended on Santiago's center for the protests, a "human sea," wrote *El Mercurio*, occupying the entire length of Santiago's main artery, the Alameda.[55] They came carrying signs that left little doubt as to their purpose: "We ask for the cancellation of the juridical personality of the Stock Exchanges who are responsible for the high cost of living"; "Ban the export of foodstuffs"; "The tax on Argentine beef must be suspended."[56]

The wave of hungry humanity was, for the administration, food for thought. In the immediate wake of the demonstrations, Sanfuentes's administration issued an order suspending a variety of food exports for the remainder of 1918 and for much of 1919.[57] In early December, the Senate suspended tariffs on Argentine beef; decreed that taxes on rice and tea would go to repair roads in order to expedite the transport of foodstuffs from the countryside to the cities; created a state fund for warehouses to sell basic necessities to the public at cost; declared an end to a variety of middleman monopolies; and advocated for the creation of open markets in various Santiago barrios.[58]

The government also responded by organizing patriotic rallies in Santiago, ratcheting up repression against labor and its allies, and circulating alarmist claims of Peruvian plots to take back the northern districts of Tacna and Arica, captured by Chile in the War of the Pacific (1879–1883). Such claims were largely hyperbolic responses to Peruvian attacks on a number of Chilean consulates in Peru earlier in the month, but combined with the powerful appearance of the AOAN, they provided a strategic opportunity for the regime to push again for the enactment of a residency law.[59] Calls for the enactment of such a law were not entirely new and had increased in recent years as officials battled strikers who threatened to cripple the ports of Valparaíso and Iquique.[60] They also battled Australian officials who had adopted Chile as a convenient destination for agitators they wished to deport: three times over the course of 1918 Australian authorities marched their unwanted Wobblies—English, Irish, Danish, American, and Spanish—on to ships bound for Valparaíso.[61] Such deportations led to moments of diplomatic strife and eventually, according to British Ambassador Francis Stronge, a "hope that the incident would serve as a lever for bringing about prohibitive or restrictive legislation" within Chile.[62]

It did. While the imagined plots brewing in Peru were the stuff of fantasy, the Residency Law soon became reality. Enacted in December 1918, the law prohibited entrance into, or residency in, Chile by "undesireable elements."[63] Like other exclusionary laws, this one also noted that entrance would be prohibited for foreigners condemned or currently under prosecution for common crimes, those without employment, individuals engaged in illicit activities, and those with certain illnesses. The law also gave power to intendents (governors) to force foreigners to register with local officials and to obtain personal identity cards. But the impetus for the law was to prohibit immigration to, and residence in, Chile by people with political ideals that challenged the status quo. Just as crucially, it set in place mechanisms for the expulsion of non-Chileans who were perceived to be creating problems for the administration and its allies. If much of Santiago's populace had organized against speculators, the administration responded by targeting purported agitators.

Although cast as a defense of the nation against those who practiced or preached the overthrow of the social order through violence or those who propagated doctrines incompatible with the "unity or individuality of the Nation," the case of Casimiro Barrios reveals how the law was in many respects designed as part of a larger effort to silence and undercut labor and its allies.[64] In an increasingly repressive atmosphere in which advocating specific ideas was tantamount to practicing them, Barrios's activities and outspokenness led to an expulsion order being issued against him on December 18, 1918, for "preaching the violent overthrow of the social and political order and provoking protests against the existing order."[65] Fourteen years after emigrating to Chile, enticed perhaps by Chilean colonization agents scattered in and around La Rioja, Barrios found himself the first person to be ordered expelled under the new law.

SEDENTARY ANARCHISTS AND UNDOCUMENTED IDEAS

Barrios was not expelled. At least, not immediately. The authorities stayed his expulsion order in early January 1919.[66] In part, it resulted from an intense campaign on the part of some POS members in Santiago and of organizers in the AOAN.[67] Barrios had established himself as a powerful and admired presence among Santiago's working sectors, and various organs of the POS—*La Aurora* and *La Bandera Roja*—published editorials condemning the Residency Law and the order for Barrios's expulsion.[68] His colleagues in the POS as well as many in the AOAN rallied around Barrios, raising money for his defense and for his family, organizing information campaigns, and roundly condemning the new Residency Law, or "the law of the machete," as they called it.[69] But Barrios had defenders in other quarters.

Only two days after the issuance of the initial expulsion decree, deputies and senators from the Liberal Alliance (composed of Liberal, Liberal Democrat, and Radical party members) in the Parliament voiced concerns on the floor of their respective chambers.[70] Over the course of two weeks, from December 18 to January 4, they returned repeatedly to the case of Barrios, debating at great length and with great intensity. While complicated, the issues raised by his defenders can be distilled down: first, why was the law applied to Barrios? Second, was the retroactive application of the law legal? Third, on what basis were decrees of expulsion founded? And fourth, could ideas, rather than actions, serve as the basis for expulsion and other forms of persecution?

The latter three questions were raised at various points by various officials. One deputy in particular, Antonio Pinto Durán, raised multiple questions related to evidence and applicability. He critiqued everything from the manner in which the Residency Law had been passed ("in the middle of the night when I was preparing for travel in Antofagasta") to the nature of the evidence upon which his expulsion was based ("I wouldn't trust the Security Section's methods as far as I could spit").[71] Deputies questioned whether the law could be applied retroactively and made sure to note that "whenever people have preached new ideas they have been accused of being subversives and of disturbing the social order."[72] Finally, others questioned the applicability of such a law to an individual who had come to Chile at a young age and had married a Chilean woman with whom he had children of Chilean nationality.

Some of the strongest arguments made repeatedly in defense of Barrios were that he was not an individual to whom such a law ought to be applied. For one, they argued, Barrios was doing little more than demanding the law be upheld. Indeed, in retrospect, Barrios's efforts may strike some as reformist, even liberal, and squarely outside of revolutionary politics. Not that advocating for—and struggling to ensure—the enforcement of existing national labor laws is necessarily exclusive of a more revolutionary program. Rosa Luxemburg, a decade earlier, had argued that reform and revolution were not mutually exclusive, that the daily struggle for economic and political reform was part of the struggle for revolution itself.[73] If one were to locate Barrios on an anarchist spectrum he might be closer to English anarchist and educator Colin Ward than Russian firebrand and revolutionary Mikhail Bakunin; that is to say, he was a "quiet revolutionary" who did not see efforts at reform as mutually exclusive from revolutionary politics and whose relentless, daily labors in Santiago contributed to "a long series of small liberations that have lifted a huge load of human misery."[74]

Indeed this is worth stressing, because it was precisely such efforts that appear to have compelled Senator Agustín Torrealba Zenón to take the floor of the Parliament and speak at length in defense of Barrios, even while emphasizing that Barrios was a member of a party "that calls itself the Socialist Worker" and not Torrealba's own Democratic Party.[75] Torrealba, a former gasfitter, had a reputation for intensely defending workers' rights and pushing for various labor and housing legislation. He was also an outspoken nativist, opposing the government's efforts to bring immigrants to Chile because of the labor competition it would create. There are also hints that he viewed such immigration as degenerative of the Chilean "race."[76] Such positions might make it surprising that Torrealba so staunchly defended Barrios, who was himself an immigrant. Regardless, Torrealba rose to Barrios's defense. He had interacted with Barrios while president of a Santiago artisan society. Barrios, he noted, had joined the Sociedad de Empleados de Comercio (Business Employees' Society) and had campaigned hard before the government and congress for the passage of the Sunday Rest Law.[77] To ensure compliance and enforcement of this law, and others that had been passed for the benefit of working people, Barrios had organized demonstrations and meetings. He spoke out repeatedly against the sale and consumption of alcohol, joining his voice with those of well-known anarchists such as Armando

Triviño and Manuel Antonio Silva, members of the FOCh, and members of temperance societies who saw alcohol as the source of much working class misery and as profit-making poison intended to keep workers docile and poor.[78] It also kept them incarcerated: of the approximately 229,000 individuals arrested by the police in a given year in the 1910s, 162,000 (or 70 percent) of those were for drunkenness.[79] Those imprisoned for drunkenness were required to labor in public works on behalf of the municipality.[80] Anti-alcohol campaigns became commonplace. The National League against Alcoholism requested, optimistically, that the owners of commercial and industrial factories post the following: "Alcohol destroys one's health, saps one's will, and in the end leads to misery."[81] These efforts, combined with the government's own concerns regarding alcohol sales and consumption as well as the debates around Prohibition in the United States that were followed closely in Chile, worried the major wine growers and manufacturers who soon formed the League for the Defense of the Wine Industry.[82] This was big business, dominated by some of Chile's most prominent families and politicians, with surnames such as Urrejola, Errázuriz, Subercaseaux, Tocornal, Ochagavia, and Salas Edwards.[83] According to some statistics, over 300,000 Chileans at the time worked in some form in the wine industry and capital invested in the industry was estimated to range anywhere between 300 million and 900 million pesos.[84] Barrios's agitation was thus one more thorn in the business's side, as Senator Torrealba fully understood:

> For these reasons, I imagine that this man has attracted persecution from the business owners and distributors of alcoholic beverages, above all those who have their businesses in the barrio of San Diego, who do not want to see him continue his campaign. He has been, in effect, *a constant sentinel* who has forced them to close their shops on the days required by the law. I imagine that these businessmen, tired of putting up with the continuous vigiliance of this citizen, would have denounced him to the Santiago intendent, accusing him of being an anarchist and a dangerous man. I believe this to be the real motive behind the accusation that, without a doubt, they have made against him. . . . The fact is this man has followed the relevant authorities around demanding the enforcement of the laws. In the criminal courts there is proof that he has made repeated claims against the business owners who did not close their stores or businesses, in violation of the Sunday rest law. To this he dedicated all of the free time he could spare.[85]

Had the intendent been swayed by such commercial interests, Torrealba asked, particularly given that the government had nothing more than a report from a Security Section agent upon which to base the decree of expulsion? Regardless of how outspoken Barrios might be, that did not make him a threat to the internal security of the nation, he argued.[86]

Similar arguments were presented in the Chamber of Deputies, where Barrios was lauded as a "gentleman" and a "modest worker," one concerned with those who were less well-off (to which another deputy responded: "Then let him go preach in his own land! There is a lot more misery there than in Chile").[87] The well-off, one deputy noted, see the principles that structure society as naturally indisputable, but if one were to see through the eyes of those who work ten or twelve hours per day and still cannot earn enough to feed themselves and their children, the world would look quite different. The comment provoked a heated and revealing response from another deputy: there was plenty of work in the *campos* at good pay, he claimed, but workers in the city did not want it and instead chose to pass their time in the taverns.[88] He and other *agricultores*, many of whom over the previous decades had planted deep agricultural roots in the central valley surrounding Santiago, offered four or five pesos a day for work in the fields plus room and board but still could not find workers. The root cause of the high prices of foodstuffs, he argued in a revealing shift, was the fact that the labor force was poorly distributed.[89]

All of these comments—whether from defenders or accusers of Barrios—are revealing of why a significant group of Parliamentarians spoke in favor of a residency law and the expulsion of Barrios: large landowners and growers had just watched, in Sanfuentes's response to the AOAN demonstrations, their export possibilities and profit margins radically curtailed, while businessmen in the central commercial district of Santiago had to suffer Barrios's constant efforts to get labor laws enforced and alcohol laws implemented. They would have preferred not to admit that such was the case. Instead, they embraced the canard of the foreign agitator. They did this in two ways: by emphasizing the alleged foreignness of certain ideas and by emphasizing the alleged foreign-ness of certain individuals. Both tactics were mobilized against Barrios.

For example, despite the fact that the majority of Chile's anarchists, anarcho-syndicalists, and revolutionary organizers had been organizing and agitating for decades in Chile, editorialists and politicians repeatedly blamed foreign ideas for the supposed agitation of the otherwise content Chilean worker.[90] In his interview with Barrios, a reporter from *Zig-Zag* concluded with a predictable insult: "He is a victim of the criminal propaganda that circulates among workers in old Europe who, through the university or through books, are imbued with utopian theories which, if they don't fit there, are even less appropriate here in Chile where currently our greatest evil is an excess of liberties."[91] Such efforts to assert the presence of "misplaced ideas" were obvious to many at the time.[92] In a revealing exchange during a meeting of the central committee of the AOAN immediately following the expulsion decree, Enrique Huerta noted the following: "It is not possible that they can claim that Barrios came to Chile as a foreigner to preach subversive ideas: I have known this man for nine years and his principles *were taught to him by Chileans*. First he was an anarchist and then a socialist." Evaristo Rios agreed, remarking that Barrios had learned his ideas in Chile and that his only "crime" was to be a foreigner.[93]

In other words, neither anarchism nor socialism were somehow "alien" or "mis-placed" ideas, and immigrants could discover them in the societies in which they landed rather than necessarily importing them from whence they came. Such ideas—and the practices through which they evolved—were simultaneously universal and particular. Such arguments deserve attention, if only to counter the persistence of perspectives that continue to marginalize the context of non-European spaces and leave room only for ideological mimicry.[94] In 1920, Chilean militants and organizers bristled at the repeated and patronizing suggestions that the ideals they held dear were somehow foreign or imported. This does not mean that Barrios's ideas were necessarily from Chile in some simplistic anti-Eurocentric inversion, but rather that it should not be assumed that they were from someplace else. Workers and intellectuals pondered the point with some intensity and with good reason. "There is not even a thought, or an invention," wrote Kropotkin, "which is not common property, born of the past and the present."[95] In an era of nationalist excess and proprietary patriotism, there is something subversive in the undocumented idea.

Neither officials nor the press were content with stressing that Barrios's ideas were somehow foreign. They also sought to remind the public that Barrios himself was not Chilean, that he was, for all intents and purposes, a foreign agitator. Juan Gandulfo, a medical student and prominent member of the FECh, seemed to have Barrios in mind when he scathingly remarked that "Chilean journalists, among whom there are two or three who really understand the social question, have chileanized the 'professional agitator,' in order to satisfy their bosses and the commercial businesses which advertise in this country's newspapers."[96] What such "Chileanization" looked like is apparent from an image that appeared on the cover of the popular weekly *Sucesos* in January 1919 and intended to convey support for the newly enacted Residency Law. President Sanfuentes sits astride a white stallion, a knight in shining armor protected by a shield in the colors of the Chilean flag. He raises his sword and bids farewell to the subversive: "Get the hell out of here and do not even think to come back to these shores. Understand that the Chilean does not put up with plots and will cut you to the quick."[97] The target of the knight-in-shining-amour's wrath is an amalgamation of orientalist prejudice: swarthy and glowering behind a bushy beard, the subversive holds smoking bombs in each hand; through his belt are tucked a bloodied scimitar and a large pistol; on his head is perched an oversized *ushanka*. To be sure the association with Russia and its recent revolution was not lost on the viewer, "maximalista" (Bolshevik "terrorist") is written across the front of the ushanka.[98] The image is saturated with stereotypes regarding agitators: a conflation of anarchist bomb-throwers and Russian revolutionaries; an overarching assertion that agitators and subversives were foreign, male, and dark-skinned; a visual suggestion that such individuals were little more than sociopaths bent on destructive violence.

Yet authorities clearly understood that in Barrios they had someone who hardly fit the image of the peripatetic, foreign agitator. As Barrios himself noted in an interview with *Zig-Zag*, having arrived in Chile at the age of fourteen he had lived there for half of his life.[99] In fact, Barrios filed a writ of habeas corpus with the courts, based on two arguments: that the Residency Law could not be applied retroactively and that the law could not be applied to someone who had resided for as long as he had in Chile.[100] The latter argument is revealing in its implicit critique of the categories of "foreign" and "domestic" and its emphasis on residency in place. Barrios was indeed an immigrant to Chile, and had kept his Spanish citizenship. Yet the repeated accusations of foreign-ness directed at him by nervous officials and indignant aristocrats rung strange. After all, he had settled in Santiago as an adolescent and been a resident of the city his entire adult life. He had married a Chilean with whom he had children. He had over the course of the previous decade become a prominent and important figure in the local and regional labor movement and had developed close relationships with members of Chile's political class. If anything, he was a consistent fixture—a "constant sentinel," as Senator Torrealba put it—in Santiago's political, social, and commercial life. An agitator he may have been, but he was hardly peripatetic. He was a sedentary anarchist.

There is the rub: it was precisely his sedentariness—which brought with it a knowledge of national labor laws; deep relationships with neighbors and employers; a rootedness in the specificity of Santiago and its neighborhoods; his ability to be a constant sentinel—that made him such a formidable opponent. Insurrections and protests are rarely organized from afar. They depend on careful, patient, extensive organizing carried out by individuals in situ. For every Errico Malatesta, there were a hundred Casimiro Barrios. The fact is peripatetic radicals made good press but it was sedentary ones whom industrialists and employers feared most.[101]

Figure 1.4
The imagined anarchist. The cover of *Sucesos*, January 1919, which appeared a month after the passage of the Residency Law, portrayed a subversive saturated in orientalist imagery. Courtesy of the International Institute for Social History.

A CAPACIOUS LEFT

By the time the image of Sanfuentes and the "subversive" appeared on the cover of *Sucesos*, Barrios's expulsion order had in fact been rescinded. Despite deep opposition from many in the Parliament and a Supreme Court rejection of Barrios's own petition, Sanfuentes himself stayed the expulsion order after meeting personally with Barrios.[102] The minister of the interior was called to the Parliament to explain himself and the fact that the administration had made a mockery of the law.[103] Minister Quezada did indeed show up and argued that the government was within its rights to suspend the order of expulsion, explaining that Barrios was given clemency in part because he had lived in Chile for many years and was married to a *chilena* with Chilean children. Such acts created complications for authorities who on the one hand wanted little more than an easy path toward expulsion for these individuals, but on the other hand did not want to undermine one of the central tenets of the bourgeois social order they sought to defend: marriage. In an effort to stem the immediate flood of criticism, Quezada noted that Barrios had agreed to abstain from all political activity.[104]

Conservative deputies were not persuaded, and they accused the government of acting out of fear. Blanlot Holley, a champion of the Residency Law and an ardent supporter of the right-wing Patriotic Leagues that had reformed again, argued that the administration was not a monarchy free to give clemency as it wished.[105] Another advocated for preemptive expulsion of men such as Barrios who led others to the "thicket of social disorganization, of disorder, and in the end, the utopia of men without country and without possessions."[106]

Did Barrios in fact embrace such a utopia, one of men without country and without possessions? The answer is as unclear now as it was then. Over the years Casimiro Barrios has appeared repeatedly, if briefly, in various essays and books of Chilean history, the Chilean Left, anarchism, and labor history. How he appears in those texts varies considerably and the ambivalence is telling. Some have categorized him as an ardent anarchist; others as a socialist. The same was true in 1919.

The stigma of being accused an anarchist could be hard to shake and worrisome. An incident at a POS meeting in March of 1919, only weeks after the suspension of Barrios's order of expulsion, is revealing. Víctor Roa Medina, long-time POS militant and the Party secretary, hosted a gathering at his home at which he suggested that the name of a weekly publication, *La Bandera Roja*, most likely modeled after the publication of the same name in Buenos Aires, be changed. Barrios was in attendance and took offense at the suggestion, observing that the title gave the paper its identity in both Chile and Argentina. He also may have bristled at the suggestion because *La Bandera Roja* had been organized in response to the expulsion order directed at him. Regardless, he responded to Medina's suggestion with sharp words, calling Roa a coward and ridiculing his knowledge of socialist doctrine.[107] What is especially striking is the response by Roa Medina and his allies: they argued that Barrios was in fact not a socialist but an anarchist and that his subversive ideas were going to get him expelled from the country and ruin the socialist party.[108] A vote was taken on whether or not to expel Barrios: he survived the vote, Roa Medina stepped down, and Barrios took over the publication of *La Bandera Roja*.

This dispute between Roa Medina and Barrios occurred at a particular juncture: shortly after Barrios's expulsion order was stayed, tram operators in Santiago went on strike. Meanwhile, the AOAN pushed to capitalize on the momentum by calling for nationwide demonstrations in early February 1919. Having been caught off guard by the size of the November demonstrations, and reeling from both the tram strike and congressional criticism of cancelling Barrios's expulsion order, Sanfuentes's ministers and party stalwarts saw such mobilizations as an opportunity to regain ground and to move against labor movements under the pretense of a subversive threat.[109] Deputies warned of "reckless agitators preaching sedition" and the spread of "the red flu." "International anarchism takes on a very dangerous form in countries of incipient organization," railed Deputy Urrutia Ibáñez. "It no longer throws bombs at the heads of government; it provokes the rebellious mass to rise up against work, discipline, and the social morality that exists, has existed, and always will exist in all States."[110] Sanfuentes was granted powers of martial law. Throughout the months of February and March the police shut down presses, detained union leaders, beat workers, arrested a multitude of others under false pretenses, and circulated claims of maximalist conspiracies.[111] One paper reported that the military presence sent to the northern pampas to suppress the AOAN organizers was of a magnitude not seen since the civil war of 1891.[112] Meanwhile, in Santiago, under the threat of violence the leadership of the AOAN cancelled a set of demonstrations, an act that angered many, particularly those who were anarchist in orientation, including shoemakers, tailors, and typesetters.[113] New confederations appeared, including a Gran Confederación de Trabajo that began to meet regularly on Wednesdays at the offices of the FECh.[114] It was in this context—of heightened repression combined with internal divisions over strategy—that the dispute between Roa Medina and Barrios unfolded.

While at first glance the dispute appears to be yet another dismal example of the kind of sectarian division that has allegedly pervaded the Left, it could also be seen as an example of the various ideological threads that made up the POS. Barrios was someone hard to pin down and in this he was not exceptional for the time. As one colleague noted, Barrios began as an anarchist and became a socialist, and yet a POS militant accused Barrios of being an anarchist and other POS militants defended Barrios and noted that he served as the secretary of the Santiago branch of the

POS. Such efforts to rigidly situate Barrios highlight the differences of opinion regarding strategy, tactics, and so forth, but they also suggest that there was a capaciousness to the Left. Anarchists and socialist could at times be indistinguishable from each other, and at other times significantly overlap on many, even most, issues. Was Barrios an anarchist? A socialist? Both, or something else entirely? Barrios himself avoided too rigid a label: at various points in an interview with *Zig-Zag* he referred to himself as a socialist, a radical, a free-thinker, and a "militant in the most advanced parties," while also noting that he had mellowed over the years.[115]

As was the case in many parts of the globe at the time, in Chile the line between anarchists and socialists could be relatively fluid. Socialists and anarchists attended each other's rallies and, at times, meetings; they met, mingled, and discussed ideas regularly at workers' centers, union halls, and the FECh's club; and they were at their root united by their opposition to the bourgeoisie and wage labor system. When a young José Santos González Vera was introduced to a number of anarchist workers, one asked: "Is he an anarchist?" González Vera's friend responded: "No. He is just a sympathizer." "That too is good," responded the worker. "Young men arrive where they wish. He will have plenty of time to become a good comrade!"[116] University students espoused anarchist ideas as they sold copies of Trotsky's writings recently translated in to Spanish; others sustained a relationship with the Radical Party, yet similarly embraced anarchist ideas and writings. Meanwhile, contributors to *Verba Roja*, who self-identified strongly as anarchists, warmly embraced Lenin and the Bolshevik Revolution as a welcome "prologue" to a communo-anarchist future.[117] In the hours following the June 25 election in Santiago, anarchist Armando Triviño stood alongside socialist Luis Lipperguer and addressed a crowd of some two thousand. He argued that Alessandri's victory should be respected and that workers should not remain satisfied until a regime akin to that created by Lenin in Russia had been formed.[118]

Not all anarchists were convinced, least of all Juan Gandulfo, who proved to be one of the earliest critics of the Bolshevik Revolution. In 1918 he predicted tyranny by "Soviet Russia's most astute and audacious political group, the Bolsheviks, who in short time will drown any genuinely popular initiative in blood. The lesson they will leave us for future generations will be deplorable and horrific."[119] Gandulfo's critiques and his calls for the creation of a Latin American committee in solidarity with anarchist prisoners in Russia's prisons would eventually lead, by the early 1920s, to a break between him and many of the working men who identified as anarchists, anarcho-syndicalists, and anarcho-communists who continued to see in Bolshevism not an enemy but an ally. "The maximalist program [and] our anarchist program" are not different, claimed a pamphlet distributed by one radical in late 1918 and early 1919.[120] Titled "Maximalist program! To the workers," it called for workers to garner a better understanding of the Russian Revolution and laid out points of correspondence: the implantation of a communist system; bread and freedom for all through economic equality; land and agrarian implements to the peasant; factories and workshops, their machinery and tools of labor, as well as all means of transport, to the city worker; abolition of private property; expropriation of the rich and other hoarders of social wealth in favor of all; no more authorities, politicians or governors; no more bosses, capitalists, or landlords; no more parasites of any social class; and disarmament and the suppression of militarism. This is in essence an anarcho-communist program, not surprisingly given that along with anarcho-syndicalism, it was the prominent position held by many on the Left at the time. "I am a communist anarchist, not an individualist," recalled one of the characters in Rojas's highly autobiographical novel *Sombras contra el muro*. "I believe in the group, in the mass, in the people; the lone man is fucked."[121]

SOCIAL ACCOUNTING

Given that they had gathered largely to coordinate their efforts to track and arrest purported anarchists, the attendees at the International Police Conference in Buenos Aires must have relished the irony of their Argentine host opening the proceedings by invoking the concept of "mutual aid."[122] It was February 1920, and representatives from Peru, Chile, Bolivia, Paraguay, Uruguay, Brazil, and Argentina met to forge an agreement that would facilitate policing across and within the borders of the various signatories and encourage them to coordinate their police efforts to suppress subversion. In the war for survival, cooperation, not competition, was key, as all the attendees well knew. Throughout the proceedings hovered a pervasive whiff of self-preservation, with grumbles regarding anarchists and agitators being expelled with little concern for the consequences in the receiving country. The practice was common enough: the previous year the Argentine police had rounded up a number of anarchists implicated in a recent and bloody strike in Buenos Aires and had deposited them on the border with Chile, high in the Andes. Prevented from entering the country, they were also unable to return to Argentina and thus, *El Mercurio* reported, doomed to "wander the highlands waiting perhaps for a propitious opportunity or police mistake" that would allow them to move one way or the other. What was needed, the editors claimed, was some kind of agreement that would in the future allow the countries to "avoid this type of 'football.'"[123] This was precisely what the Buenos Aires convention was intended to address. Police efforts would be transnational as, in theory at least, information and agents would flow more freely across political borders, expelled radicals would no longer simply take up in a new location where they had left off in the previous one, and methods of identification would be standardized.[124] Such forms of what French criminologist Alphonse Bertillon called "social accounting," officials agreed, were necessary to defend workers throughout the region from dangerous theories and theorists of revolution.[125] Only by working collectively could respective national governments ensure their own survival.

This was not the first such efforts at coordination, but by early 1920 it seemed essential to political survival as the Chilean delegate suggested:

> Social problems or the social question, as it has also been called, which have long preoccupied thinkers and the governments of all countries, have now acquired, almost suddenly, due to the war, an extremely serious character because it is frankly revolutionary.[126]

He then continued with a long disquisition on the Russian Revolution. With some disgust he observed: "The wave of the underclass, with no political or social culture, filled with prejudices and base passions, now governs, and is the lord and master of its former lords."[127]

In 1919 and 1920, Russia was never far from the minds of those eager to keep their property and their heads. French Prime Minister Clemenceau, in an effort the previous year to shore up support for a policy of economically and politically isolating the Bolsheviks, had reminded the Chilean Legation in Paris, "The declared hostility of the Bolsheviks toward all governments and the international program of revolution that they propagate constitutes a danger to the national security of all nations."[128] Fears and accusations of "maximalism" circulated widely as did translated critiques and analyses of the revolution by Russian opponents of Bolshevism.[129] The revolution had clearly given succor to the working men and women of many parts of Chile. One young worker at the time, later interviewed, recalled how the revolution "awoke a tremendous enthusiasm" among working men and that, while some among the anarchist community were dubious, the majority were in support of the Bolsheviks.[130] Workers devoured the daily news of the revolution. Sanfuentes and his ministers only had to look from their windows on any given day to see how much of an inspiration it proved to be to many: the POS and the FOCh organized demonstrations daily, in nearly all parts of Santiago, linking support for the revolution with their own demands regarding controls on the prices for basic staples, the reduction of rents, and the raising of salaries.[131] Chilean officials could not help but take notice, particularly given similar circumstances appeared to be threatening other European countries such as Spain. A member of the Chilean legation in Spain wrote a lengthy letter to the newly appointed Chilean Minister of the Interior in late 1919. In it he identified two causes for the dramatic increase in sindicalism, direct action, and conflicts between labor and capital: the inspiring example of the Russian revolution and the increased cost of living associated, in part, with "speculative manipulations" that had enriched a small segment of Spanish society. "The workers have not seen in this the fulfillment of inexorable economic laws; they see only that while they feel more intensely each day the cost of living, there are others rapidly improving their position by hoarding basic necessities in order to sell them at monopolistic prices or in order to export them abroad."[132] He understood he just as easily could have been discussing Chile.[133]

The Bolshevik revolution and the end of the Great War in Europe brought new urgency to finding answers to the "social question." Indeed, until then Chile's political classes had generally refused to acknowledge that there was any question to answer, that the ramifications of industrialization and urbanization required little change in policy. "The social question does not exist," claimed Enrique MacIver, a wealthy spokesman for the Radical Party. "Workers don't have ideas; they have needs."[134] The war and the revolution dramatically challenged, and ultimately killed, such perspectives. By 1920 political "rationalism" and economic liberalism were open to question, political and economic crises were commonplace, and workers were generating and articulating plenty of ideas.[135] For writers, officials, bureaucrats, and organizers at the time—even if they too could be susceptible to exaggeration—such issues were foremost on their minds. If Baldomero Lillo's realist fiction on the difficulty of life in Chile's mines had been somewhat exceptional in its focus at the turn of the century, by 1917 the contradictions of Chilean society, liberalism and capitalism were too obvious to ignore. Hunger and suffering were perennial subjects in plays, fiction, and film. Popular culture—particularly plays, such as Armando Moock's *Penitas de amor* (1916), Antonio Acevedo Hernández's *Almas perdidas* (1917), and Víctor Domingo Silva's *Viento Negro* (1919)—took up such questions as the basis for their dramas.[136] Moock's play *Los Perros* (The Dogs) opened in Santiago in December of 1918. Police were in attendance and described to their superiors a play on the difficult situation of the working class in Chile, due to low daily wages paid to them by their bosses. Although a parody, it was clear the play was rooted in a common sense about the times. "In the play's three acts are presented scenes of misery: children in rags, half-naked, mothers who cry at the foot of a cradle in which a creature has died because it lacked food, and medicine, etc."[137] Ever wary of parody gone too far, the agent noted that at no moment in the play were there attacks on public officials. In 1920 Joaquín Edwards Bello published *El Roto*, his novel of life in Santiago with a plot organized around a brothel near the Central Station and peppered with statistical insertions such as the following:

> The statistics are frightening: in seven years, smallpox has consumed more than 30,000 Chileans and tuberculosis, in its various manifestations, more than 60,000. Syphilis is making greater inroads. In 1908, the Republic's police round up off the streets some 58,000 drunkards; in 1911 they round up 130,000! Alcoholism is worse than a hundred earthquakes: it is a constant cataclism which annihilates the country and against which the moralists can do nothing because the powerful families are wine-makers.[138]

Uncertainty reigned as to whether it was typhus or Spanish influenza that plagued the city between 1918 and 1920, but regardless, the mortality rates were high.[139] The epidemic only worsened Chile's already abysmal rates of infant mortality, some of the highest in the world.[140] Working-class children who lived beyond the age of one were often stricken with rickets, congenital syphilis, or tuburculosis.[141] Among the population more generally, deaths exceeded births in Santiago in 1920 and average life expectancy hovered around thirty.[142] No wonder that young anarchist and FECh affiliate José Santos González Vera would suggest that "an impoverished Chilean who reaches old age should be given a retirement benefit."[143] Even the otherwise sanguine mainstream press began to pay attention and articles and editorials on "alcoholism, infant mortality, prostitution, the misery of the slums and the unhealthy conditions of the majority of the inhabited areas" became commonplace.[144]

Housing access and conditions, despite parliamentary efforts at reform such as the 1906 Workers' Housing Law that attempted to improve the quality of and access to housing for workers and their families, continued to be a problem. With the contraction in the nitrate industry and the subsequent influx of unemployed workers from beyond Santiago in 1919, the government resorted to the creation of *albergues*, temporary housing in tents, former warehouses, and offices—such as those of the Antigua Empresa de Tranvías Urbanos on Chacabuco—to house workers until they and their families could be transported to other parts of the country to particular work sites.[145] Conditions could be grim, as reporters from *El*

Mercurio found when they visited an albergue on Chacabuco: the building's western and eastern walls were gone, and the roof was in terrible condition. The unit housed some 150 people. The reporters concluded that "the Government agencies for social welfare are almost non-existent" and that only private charity could at this point help.[146] Yet private charity had long been assigned such tasks. The relative absence of the state—and the realm of social services, armed with sociological theories and statistical methodologies—was harshly felt and not soon forgotten.

For workers and families not awaiting transportation to places south, housing often meant a simple room in one of the proliferating *conventillos* (tenement houses) that increasingly filled the Santiago landscape. Conventillos could be found throughout the city but tended to be concentrated in industrial zones, such as near the Mapocho tram station, where many inhabitants lived in the shadows of the tram company's towering and belching chimneys.[147] In some parts of the city entire city blocks were made up of conventillos, their interiors often connected by a network of doors and passageways.[148] González Vera passed much of his adolescence in Santiago's conventillos. A young anarchist, he approached his subject with an unromanticized yet tender appreciation:

> The house has an almost bourgeois exterior. Its façade, which belongs to no particular style, is uneven and crude. The wall, painted like the sky, serves as a canvas for the neighborhood kids who have decorated it with ribald and scandalous phrases and images.
>
> The middle door lets one see all the way to the patio. The corridor is nearly blocked by troughs, braziers, pots with leftovers and an array of decorative objects along walls blackened by the smoke.
>
> In a corner of the patio is a stack of deteriorating furniture, lying there either through the negligence or foresight of its owners. On a table, imprisoned by pots and boxes, bushes of ivy, carnations and roses lift their multiform arms up in an irresistable impulse of ascension. The green tone of the plants emphasizes the bland and shapeless mass of everything else.[149]

In many instances, a family often occupied a single room in a conventillo. Rooms were small—on average under sixty square feet in 1907—and often lacked windows, running water, and electricity.[150] Typical was a property publicly auctioned on San Francisco Street, in one of Santiago's prominent working class districts, in September of 1920: it measured roughly 6,400 square feet, which contained three homes facing the street and twenty-seven interior *casitas*, essentially rooms.[151] Rooms were crowded, with a family frequently renting the bed out during the day while the male head

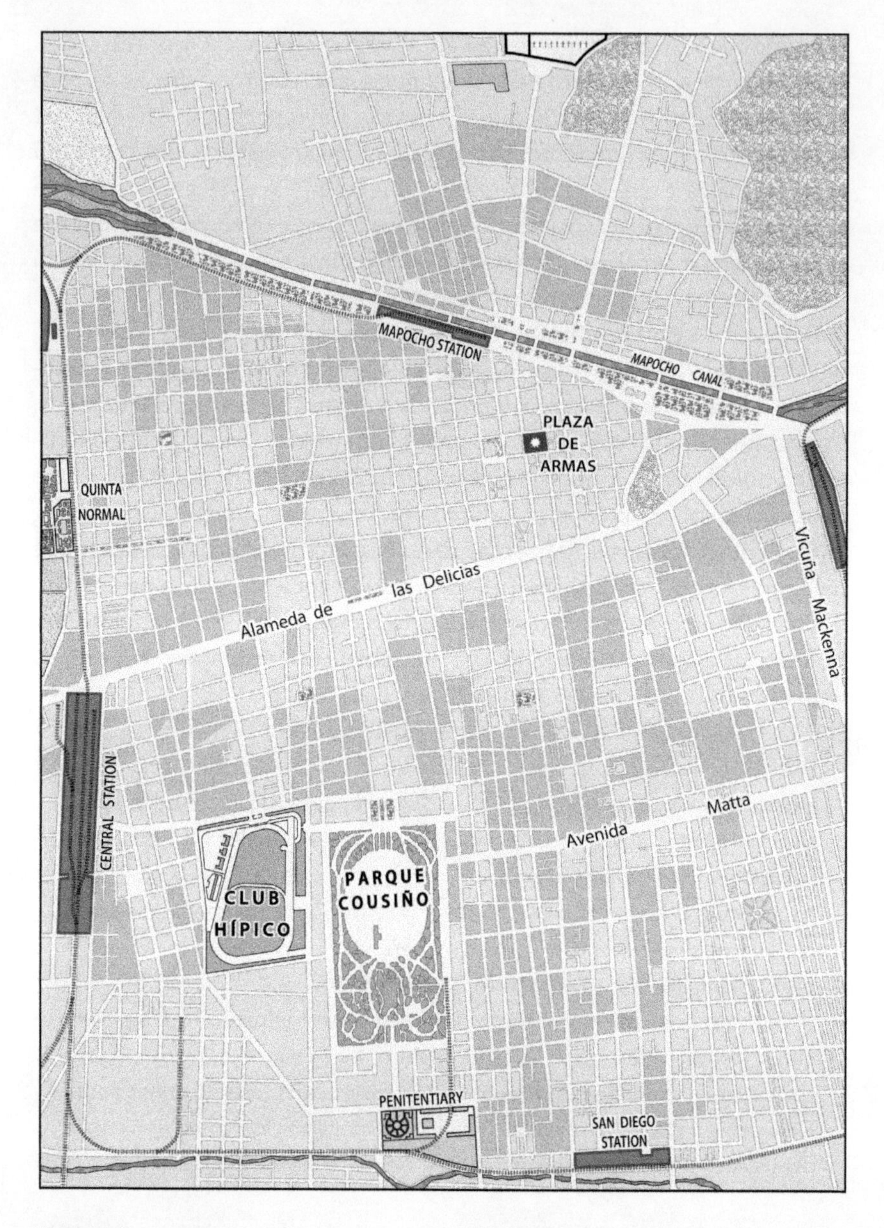

Figure 1.5
Tenement city: Gray squares indicate city blocks on which conventillos existed for the years 1900–1923. Note their prevalence north of the Mapocho canal and to the west and south of the city center. Map by David Ethridge, based on Isabel Torres Dujisin, "Los conventillos de Santiago (1900–1930)," *Cuadernos de Historia* 6 (July 1986).

of household was at work, or being occupied by a large number of single men who would rotate rights to the bed. The quality of housing for working people—particularly in Valparaíso and Santiago—had been an issue confronting the government for decades. Political candidates and parties included housing issues in their platforms as far back as the 1880s, and Alessandri wrote his law school thesis on working class housing. Some in the government saw affordable and safe worker housing, as well as access to credit and mortgage instruments, as key to offsetting the attractiveness of anarchism. But initiatives such as those included in the 1906 Workers' Housing Law seemed to have limited reach—the state made little progress on housing during the nineteen years the law was in effect—and regulation and oversight were at times seemingly nonexistent and by the end of the 1910s housing remained a major issue.[152]

An already inadequate housing situation in Santiago was exacerbated by an influx of workers and their families, particularly from the north. As postwar depression hit, mine owners closed or curtailed operations with alarming frequency. In 1918 the nitrate industry alone employed some 57,000 workers. By 1919 that figure had declined to about 45,000 workers and, one year later, nearly halved to 23,500.[153] The end to the war in Europe meant a dramatic decrease in nitrate demand for the making of ammunition. Moreover, both the United States and European countries had enough surplus for agricultural purposes.[154] In 1919 alone Chile's revenue plummetted some 93 million gold pesos, the vast majority of the losses due to the collapse of nitrate.[155] Mine closures and firings pushed workers to the cities, primarily Valparaíso and Santiago. The numbers were staggering: In a two-week period in January 1919, some 1,900 workers—not including their families—lost their jobs in Tarapacá and were transported south to other parts of the country.[156] In late 1919 *El Mercurio* interviewed Antofagasta's intendent, Alberto Cabero, who estimated that over the previous two years some 40,000 people had left the north in search of work, constituting a veritable "exodus to the south."[157]

EXODUS AND EXPULSION

There was, at the same time, an exodus to the north. Thousands of workers perceived to be Peruvian nationals were fired from their positions and expelled from the country.[158] As the AOAN stepped up its efforts to force the government to reduce exports of foodstuffs and deal with the realities of working peoples' lives in Santiago, the government expanded its Chileanization campaigns in the north. While geographically distant from the center of political power in Santiago, the Chilean–Peruvian borderlands and the status of Peruvians in Chile were central to the unfolding discourse about and persecution of subversives, and Chileanization campaigns would have dramatic consequences for Chilean–Peruvian relations in 1919 and 1920 and for organizers and agitators in Chile.

Since the end of the War of the Pacific (1879–1883), which pitted Chile against Peru and Bolivia, many residents in the occupied borderlands between Chile and Peru had lived an ambiguous existence, at least in official eyes.[159] In the aftermath of the war, a victorious Chile annexed both the Bolivian coastline with its port of Antofagasta and the Peruvian province of Tarapacá, an annexation sanctioned by Article Two of the Treaty of Ancón (1883). The treaty also dictated that the status of the Peruvian provinces of Tacna and Arica—occupied by Chile—would remain indeterminate until a popular plebiscite, scheduled for March 1894, would decide if those territories would permanently transfer to Chile or be returned to Peru.[160] But who would vote in the plebiscite was not made clear, and the ambiguous language of the document fomented problems.[161] Part of the issue revolved around whether Chile had full sovereignty in Tacna and Arica (as Chile would claim) or was solely an occupying force for ten years (as Peru claimed).[162] In the meantime, authorities in both Peru and Chile sought to gauge their chances of success in any plebiscite by gathering reams of statistical information on the national origins of populations in the provinces and the likely outcome of any plebiscite.[163] The census data consistently indicated that Peruvians outnumbered Chileans in the disputed provinces by a significant margin, not surprising given that the region only years earlier had been under Peruvian and Bolivian jurisdiction. Chilean statistics reveal the magnitude of this territorial expansion: a total of 802 Peruvians were resident in Chile in 1875, four years prior to the war. A decade later, that number was 34,901.[164] Chile had embarked in the 1890s on a strenuous campaign of Chileanization of the border region, but with little success.[165] Although Peruvians in the provinces of Tacna and Arica had had to cope with violence and discrimination directed against them, the magnitude of such persecution increased dramatically around 1910—the time of the centennial celebrations and of a more aggressive push to Chileanize the northern provinces—as *ligas patrióticas* persecuted Peruvians in the region.[166] Waves of violence swept the borderlands and racist depictions of Peruvians—as childlike black terrorists—were commonplace. Insinuations of Peruvian anarchist conspiracies abounded. Cartoonists fused racism and reaction when they slyly invoked the legendary Black Hand (Mano Negra)—an anarchist cabal in Spain that was later determined to be a police fabrication, but only after numerous organizers and agitators had been executed—by drawing a literally black (and allegedly Peruvian) hand lighting a bomb.

Chileanization meant colonizing not only the place, but the past of the greater north or borderlands through archaeology and scientific appropriation. Scientists exhumed the dead while prefects expelled the living; the

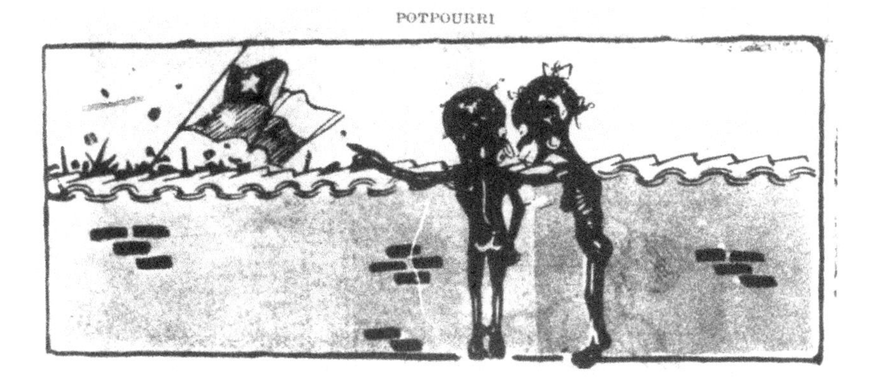

Figure 1.6
Race war: Peruvians racialized as black enemies. *Sucesos* (July 29, 1920).

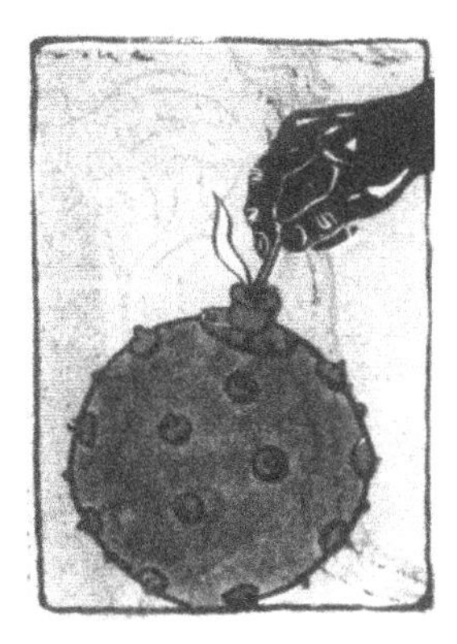

Figure 1.7
Peru's black hand. Playing on the notion of the black hand—or Mano Negra, the name given to an alleged group of anarchist conspirators in Andalucia, Spain, in the 1890s—the artist here brings an array of stereotypes and prejudices together: Peruvians as anarchist, bomb-throwing blacks. *Sucesos* (July 29, 1920).

teaching of history and geography came under scrutiny and Chile closed schools perceived to be engaging in pro-Peruvian propaganda.[167] By 1918 hostilities between the Peruvian and Chilean governments worsened as the recession in the nitrate industry led to increased conflict around unemployment and nationality in the north, with accusations by Peru of Chilean expulsions of Peruvians from the borderlands.[168]

In the midst of such animosity, the passage of the Residency Law appeared as yet another component of an ongoing "policy of terrorism" of which Peruvian officials accused their Chilean counterparts.[169] While not perhaps intended as a means to further expulsion efforts in the borderlands, the Residency Law did open the possibility for renewed "legal" expulsions of a substantial part of the Peruvian population, and particularly in the north.[170] In such a volatile situation, the status of individuals born in Tacna/Arica after the war proved complicated. Some fled to Peru; others sought to either garner, or confirm, their Chilean nationality. Particularly difficult cases were those of individuals born in these provinces after 1883. The language in the treaty of Ancona had never specified what the formal citizenship of children born in Tacna and Arica after 1883 would be.[171] With the passage of the Residency Law, individuals and families sought to confirm their nationality. Regardless of where they lived, borderlands inhabitants found themselves living an unexpected double identity, unable to prove their nationality and thus finding themselves at the whim of officials. The Residency Law pushed Peruvians who had long resided in Chile to seek a change in citizenship. Others whose status had never been determined sought such determinations. Unless well-connected, their efforts were rarely successful. But the rationale used by officials to deny their requests is telling. Nicanor Palza, a fifty-year-old mechanic in Iquique, recently married to a Chilean widow, had his petition denied because, as the Comisario put it in October 1919, "one cannot know his feelings toward the Nation [*patria*]."[172] To this breezy dismissal Palza responded with a barely subdued anger:

> It is very difficult, frankly impossible, to know or understand a person's feelings. . . . I have affection for the country where I have been raised and have lived all my life; I am aware that I have never committed an act against the honor and good name of the country; I want to be a Chilean citizen because this is my second homeland and one from which I do not plan to leave and where I have made my home.[173]

What became of Palza's case is unknown. But it was not exceptional. Petitioners with long histories of having worked and lived in various parts of Chile, of having served in the military, with letters from neighbors and employers attesting to their qualities, and whose status was effectively that of a Chilean national, still confronted an exclusionary and suspicious state.[174] These letters attest to the relationships forged by and between individuals of Peruvian and Chilean descent, and by and between individuals of seemingly unfixed nationalities and backgrounds.[175] For Chilean authorities such ambiguities must have been frustrating. Moreover, the authorities clearly wanted the process of Chileanization to be undertaken by colonizers from the center and south of the country rather than by conquered subjects with some original attachment to the region.

To ensure such an outcome, Chilean officials repeatedly resorted to vague allusions of threats to the social order as a rationale for denying petitioners citizenship or continued residency. For example, Anjel Pacheco, a baker born in Tacna in 1883, sent a letter to officials and enclosed both his marriage certificate and the birth certificate of his son, in order to demonstrate that he was Chilean. His own birth and baptisimal record had been taken by Peruvian priests when they fled north after the war.[176] Officials denied Pacheco's petition. "I believe," remarked the presiding official, "it would be too risky to grant said petition in light of the fact that, contrary to that expressed by the petitioner, once his naturalization is granted he can, with much greater ease, undermine the established order."[177]

EXPULSION

The established order was the problem. This made it difficult for Casimiro Barrios, despite his brush with expulsion, to steer clear of politics. Through the winter of 1919 he worked closely with what remained of the AOAN, organizing to get lending houses to reduce their interest rates.[178] Intendent reports identified Barrios as one of the main instigators of a September 1919 general strike when beer workers struck in Santiago, followed immediately by tram workers, chauffeurs, and shoeworkers, in response to a police assault on the local office of the FOCh in Limache.[179] The Santiago intendent ordered Barrios brought to his office to remind him of his promise to avoid political activity. Barrios kept a low profile, but in June of 1920 the intendent accused him of issuing threats against individuals involved with the passage of the Residency Law and ordered him again to his office.[180] "With his characteristic mode of innocence," reported the intendent, Barrios denied the accusations and assured the intendent that "as a foreigner, he would not intervene in workers movements nor preach his ideas in public."[181] A short time after this appearance, he returned of his own accord and suggested to the intendent that the police be more proactive in enforcing the law requiring Sunday as a day of rest, concluding his piece of unsolicited advice by "threatening" the intendent that if this did not happen he would "raise the issue with workers' societies."[182]

Whether any of these claims by the intendent can be trusted is perhaps not as important as the mere fact that Barrios was again coming under intense scrutiny. As the presidential elections scheduled for June 1920 approached, those in power turned again to the Residency Law and applied it with full force. It had not been uncommon for the occasional ruffian or pimp to be expelled under the law, but by March of 1920 the law began to be applied to individuals perceived to be propagating doctrines incompatible with the established order.[183] Such was the case, in March, for Ecuadorian-born Lisandro Paladines and, in May, for Peruvian-born Nicolás Gutarra Ramos.[184] In response, the leadership of the FOCh, at a gathering in Santiago in early July, demanded the government revoke the Residency Law because it impeded free speech and was applied capriciously.[185] The demand fell on deaf ears. Even worse, the government attempted to enforce more strictly the order that all foreigners resident in Chile register with the intendent in their zone of residence. The requirement that foreigners register and acquire identity cards had been a part of the 1918 Residency Law but had been only minimally enforced. Barrios received such an order in March.[186] The Santiago intendent in early July 1920 was asking that the registration bureaucracy be better financed and restructured.[187] His request came in part as a result of increased efforts to register, identify, and track foreign nationals living in Chile. He issued an order, simultaneous with his request for increased funding, that all foreigners resident in Santiago sign in to a special registry overseen by Santiago's police prefect and obtain a government-issued identity card.[188] To facilitate the registration process, foreign residents were to make their way to the local offices on specific dates according to their country of origin, gender, and age. Young men from Russia and Spain—associated with Bolshevism and anarchism, respectively—found themselves near the top of the list. But not the very top. That sad privilege went to Peruvian men between the ages of fourteen and twenty-five.[189]

On July 7, after months of being superintended, surveilled, spied on, and registered, Barrios was summoned to the offices of Santiago's police commissioner of investigations, Fidel Araneda Luco, for distribution of subversive propaganda.[190] There are also tantalizing hints suggesting that Barrios was the victim of accusations made by aspiring playwright Carlos Cariola, who would become one of Chile's important twentieth-century dramatists. Both Barrios, in 1918, and Juan Egaña and Pablo de Rokha, editors of *Numen* and young poets, in 1920, suggested Cariola in some way bore responsibility for the intendent's efforts to expel Barrios. [191] What also seemed to hasten Barrios's case was that he had been "insolent" toward the Santiago intendent who reported that he "had to force him to leave the room."[192] Such things made it evident, the intendent reported, that Barrios was "a dangerous foreigner ... who did not respect the authorities, and [was] a danger to public tranquility."[193] One cannot help but suspect that what made Barrios dangerous was not any purported violent tendencies. Barrios was in many respects the opposite of what the authorities wished to portray: sedentary, not peripatetic; a patient and savvy organizer rather than a rash and wild-eyed agitator; a man with deep roots in his barrio rather than a "foreign" mischief maker. Rather, his alleged insolence was highlighted. Insolence—an anti-authoritarian position, an unwillingness to be submissive, an intolerance for hierarchy, an inclination toward "taking liberties," a sneer, a smirk, a smile, a refusal—would tellingly reappear in official documents and missives, as if it were itself a criminal act.

Briefed on the case, Araneda rescinded Barrios's stay of expulsion and had him sent to Valparaíso for deportation. Escorted by a senior police official from Santiago, he arrived in Valparaíso where the government's efforts soon ran into problems. The steamship company refused to take Barrios because he had no passport; Chilean authorities could not grant him one as he was considered a Spanish citizen. Such complications were commonplace. The intendent of Valparaíso had previously warned his Santiago counterpart that "the difficulties that arise in each case regarding the application of the Residency Law have not been few. It would be convenient if the authorities throughout the country were to explain these circumstances to the Government so that they can resolve them."[194] Exporting radicals was tricky: where would they be sent? How would they

Figure 1.8
Expulsion: Casimiro Barrios being escorted by Security Section agents on to a ship in Valparaíso harbor. He would be taken north to Arica, where he would disembark and be forced across the land border with Peru. *Sucesos* (July 22, 1920).

be tracked? Moreover, the paradox of documentary regimes is that they cannot be controlled solely for repressive means: it is fitting that an individual accused of being an anarchist reveals the paradoxes to be found in systems of nationalist identification.

The Valparaíso intendent suggested having Barrios taken by ship as far as Arica, where he would then disembark and be transported overland to either the Peruvian frontier or Bolivian border.[195] Such a suggestion contravened the spirit of mutual aid to which the Chilean government had been party only months earlier at the police convention in Buenos Aires. Regardless, when the steamship *Palena* left port for places north on July 9, Barrios and a Santiago Security Section agent were aboard.[196] After being granted permission to withdraw funds from the National Savings Bank for his family, Barrios was transferred to the custody of the police in Tacna.[197] He was taken to the border with Peru, to the Sama River, and expelled.[198]

It was July 19, and the atmosphere in Santiago was turning volatile.

CHAPTER 2

The Brothers Gandulfo

JULY 19, 1920

It was a cold Monday evening in central Santiago when hundreds of young patriots came looking for the head of Juan Gandulfo. They came angry and wearing *la mirada milagrosa*, the "miraculous gaze" inspired by too much whiskey. Tumbling along Ahumada, one of Santiago's busiest downtown streets, they soon reached the entrance to the club of the FECh. The patriots forced their way in and up the stairs, where one of their party vomited on the piano and then wiped his mouth on the corner of a Chilean flag draped in the hands of a colleague. Meanwhile, another stepped forward, pointed at a young man and exclaimed: "That's Gandulfo, friend of the *rotos* and opponent of the war!" Gandulfo not only knew his accuser but had also played an important role in his life. He was Iván Pra Balmaceda, a young man from a politically prominent family who a year earlier had been admitted to Santiago's asylum, the Casa de Orates, at his father's insistence. It was a rare thing to be released—common wisdom held that one never left the cemetery, the morgue, and the asylum—but Balmaceda beat the odds, thanks to a medical opinion provided to his father by one of the asylum's interns: none other than Juan Gandulfo.[1]

Now they met again. Earlier that evening, as a chilly July rain swept the city, Balmaceda and his companions—most of them students at the Catholic University and children (the "golden youth") of the aristocracy—had attended a patriotic banquet to honor the first battallions of Chilean reservists, mobilized under orders from President

Figure 2.1
Synonomous with revolution: Juan Gandulfo. From *Juan Gandulfo Guerra: Homenaje de sus amigos* (1957).

Sanfuentes due to purported threats from Peru, who were preparing to depart Santiago for the northern borderlands. As the festivities drew to a close, a group of the young men proceeded to the Olimpia café where they joined a number of military officers for drinks.[2] The conversation soon turned to Juan Gandulfo and another young man, Santiago Labarca. One officer informed the recent arrivals that Gandulfo, Labarca and others in the FECh had spoken out against the mobilizations. At a meeting the previous night, he explained, Gandulfo and his colleagues had demanded that the government provide a rationale for such movements. Just as insulting, they then had the temerity to suggest that the troop mobilizations had more to do with internal politics than any real threat from either Peru or Bolivia.[3] This questioning of the war mobilization quickly earned Gandulfo and Labarca, among others, a prominent place on a blackboard, mounted in the nearby conservative Club de la Unión, listing the "subversives in the Federation who needed to be 'punished.'"[4]

Balmaceda and his peers, fortified by whiskey, took up the call. An opportunity for punishing the offenders presented itself immediately upon their leaving the Olimpia, when they encountered none other than Santiago Labarca. The angry students cornered him and his two companions in front of the Radical Club and assailed him with insults—"traitor, sell-out, anti-patriot, and coward"—and fists.[5] Labarca managed to find refuge in the club and escape their wrath. Emboldened, his assailants proceeded to the FECh, only blocks away, looking for Juan Gandulfo.

They found him, along with his friend and writer González Vera, and a number of others. A brawl ensued. González Vera was soon pinned to the ground; another defender of the premises found himself being strangled with his own tie. One assailant suggested they lynch Gandulfo and the others, a suggestion that prompted Gandulfo to muse that perhaps the young man had recently returned from the United States.[6] Gandulfo grabbed a bottle and wielded it threateningly above the heads around him.[7] The patriots tumbled over one another to beat a hasty retreat down the stairs. Soon after, police Inspector Ismael Moreno arrived on the scene with four other officers. Before long the police ventured up to the room and dragged Gandulfo out to the street, where the inebriated assailants peppered him with threats, all the while following the police to the stationhouse.[8] Once at the station, Gandulfo as well as a small number of the students who assaulted him were taken into a room and confronted by an official. One officer spoke to the official:

> This Peruvian youth named Juan Gandulfo incited the people to revolt, from the balconies of the Student Club, suggesting that rather than go to war now was the time to unseat the President of the Republic and proclaim social revolution. Some distinguished young patriots who were peacefully passing by, became indignant upon hearing this Peruvian spy and obliged him to be quiet, reproving him as he deserved. I, in representation of the authorities, took him out of there to save his life.

Gandulfo attempted to contest this account but was silenced by a guard "with the face of a bulldog." When he asked that eyewitnesses be examined, the police brought in the young men who had assaulted him, including Pra Balmaceda.[9] One of them recounted the meeting at the Olimpia and the discussion about the FECh, Labarca and Gandulfo, and anti-patriotism.[10] One of the officials, he continued, "invited us to give them [Labarca, Gandulfo and Diez] a deadly beating."[11] According to Gandulfo, one of the policemen proceeded to angrily tell the young men that if he were to take down their report as given, they would be imprisoned for assault and for violation of private property. However, he continued, "if you were to declare that this Peruvian spy was speaking to the crowd, inciting it to revolution, the joke will be on him and you all will be free." At that point Pra Balmaceda drunkenly stepped forward and said he would sign such an affirmation.[12]

On the verge of being placed in a cell, Gandulfo's luck changed. A friend who happened to be a captain in the military, along with Gandulfo's brother Pedro and a number of other students, teachers, and officials, arrived and gave their version of events. A new document was drawn up and Gandulfo was freed.[13] As Gandulfo left the station, a group of workers approached him: "We waited for you, compañero Gandulfo, in order to show you that you are not alone. We know that the troop mobilization is pure nonsense: be patient, the light will come and the truth will shine and each will get what he deserves."[14] With that, the workers and the students walked to their homes in the rain.

SYNONYMOUS WITH REVOLUTION

That Labarca and Gandulfo would incur the wrath of the Golden Youth is not surprising. Labarca was a prominent public figure who had recently finished a term as president of the FECh, during which it had made a shift to the political Left. Born in modest circumstances in the provincial town of Chillán, Labarca had arrived in Santiago to study at the engineering school. He had worked as an organizer in the AOAN, had affliated with the FOCh, and had served as a coeditor of the prominent anarchist journal *Numen*, which had landed him in jail on at least one previous occasion and ensured continued police surveillance.[15] He had also been at the forefront of attempting to forge an alliance between workers and students.

Of all the FECh affiliates of the period Gandulfo was, according to his friend Pablo Neruda, the "most formidable of all," a man admired and feared for his political daring and courage.[16] Born in 1895 in the port town of Los Vilos, north of Valparaíso, Gandulfo was one of six children of Salvatore Gandulfo and Sofia Guerra. Salvatore had emigrated from Sardinia in 1866 with the intention of going to the United States, but ended up in Buenos Aires and soon made his way to Valparaíso, Chile. There he acquired a reputation for being an excellent mason. The family—including four sons—lived in Valparaíso until 1906 when an earthquake leveled much of the city, at which point they moved to Viña del Mar. Shortly thereafter, Salvatore died from tetanus contracted while at work on Chile's National Library in Santiago.[17] Juan Gandulfo attended schools in Viña del Mar and Valparaíso before going on to study medicine at the University of Chile with the intentions of becoming a surgeon. He was a top-rate student at the university and interned at the Casa de Orates and at the Public Assistance office. He was also a well-known writer and artist, and his engravings, drawings, and scientific sketches were highly regarded. His skill as a surgeon was legendary. His friend Manuel Rojas etched his own portrait of that skill: "He is a surgeon not because he likes blood but because it is precise and serious work and because someone is suffering and needs, quickly, relief and protection."[18] Rojas understood he could just as easily have been discussing Gandulfo's political activities also. He was widely known and praised among many in Santiago for his political work. He taught classes at night schools, at the Universidad Popular Lastarria (UPL) and in union halls. He had helped coordinate, between 1915 and 1917, the Council for the Liberty of Conscience and its successful nonviolent, direct action efforts to stave off a parliamentary attempt to criminalize atheism and agnosticism. He had been involved, like Labarca and Barrios, in the AOAN. He was a tireless organizer in the Chilean branch of the Industrial Workers of the World.[19] He was an anarchist *de linea* (hard line), recalled his brother Pedro, refusing the entire premises of electoral politics, representative democracy, and capitalism.[20]

Gandulfo was also, by all accounts, a relentless agitator and a powerful orator.[21] Men spoke of his ability to hypnotize or magnetize his audience when he spoke. He was the "most dangerous of all popular orators," one individual recalled.[22] In March 1920, while president of the Medical Students club, he was imprisoned for purportedly subversive statements and for "offenses against the President of the Republic."[23] In a speech to a

Figure 2.2
Free radical: Juan Gandulfo (center, front) surrounded by students in front of the Security Section, after his release from six days in jail, March 1920. Courtesy of the International Institute for Social History.

gathering of the membership of the Wood Workers Federation, Gandulfo had remarked that the President of the Republic was incapable of solving the conflicts between capital and labor, in part because he simply lacked the intelligence and in part because it was impossible for him to betray his own class or personal interests.[24] For this the police roughed him up and jailed him. As Manuel Rojas would observe, "if the president is incapable of doing something, the police agents are not. We live in a democracy, but it is a bourgeois one."[25] Threatened with a general strike by various working men's organizations affiliated with the IWW, as well as students in the FECh, the administration ordered his release after six days.[26]

Gandulfo had an impressive intellectual and political resume. Little wonder that by the time the patriotic students descended on the FECh, the twenty-five-year-old had become "a symbol for students, a hero for workers, and an agitator and dangerous anarchist for the government."[27] The name Gandulfo, one of his friends summarized, "was synonymous with revolution."[28]

LUCIFER OR LENIN?

Chile's President Juan Luis Sanfuentes had revolutions on his mind. By mid-July 1920, it seemed as if something revolutionary came from every direction. For one, there were the disruptions—bedeviling many leaders around the globe—to international trade and finance wrought by the Great War, as well as the social and political reverberations of the revolution unfolding in Russia. At home, Sanfuentes confronted a political convulsion of serious proportions. Two years earlier the Liberal Alliance, a coalition of political parties, had garnered, for the first time, a majority in the Parliament and on a platform of social reform. Despite having little subsequent success implementing such reforms, the Liberal Alliance seemed on the cusp of presidential victory when, in late June, 1920, the small percentage of the populace entitled to vote had gone to the polls to elect the next president of the Republic. Liberal Alliance candidate and upstart Arturo Alessandri had mounted an impressive challenge to the more conservative, National Union candidate Barros Borgoño. Alessandri seemingly represented a shift away from the traditional aristocratic politics that had held sway for nearly three decades.

A senator from the northern state of Tarapacá, Alessandri had quickly acquired a reputation as a populist—either "Lucifer or Lenin"—to many, leading the author of a document from the Bank of Chile to refer to Alessandri as "the rabble's candidate."[29] The insult backfired: when the document became public, Alessandri embraced the label and opened his public addresses to roaring crowds with "My dear rabble." He was an otherwordly figure to many. Ventura Maturana, a senior official in Santiago's Security Section from 1920 to 1931, may have only slightly exaggerated when he claimed that the balconies and doors of Alessandri's house bore scars from having been "clawed at by the fingernails of the virtuous ones looking for relics to take to their ranchos."[30] Alessandri attracted a significant following: students and workers, military reservists and even a good portion of the "pacos" (beat cops), a worrisome mix for many in power.[31] Not all were persuaded. Backers of Barros Borgoño of course were dubious, but so too were some working men and women who had long since lost patience with the vapid promises of limited electoral, parliamentary politics and the incestuous political reproduction of Chile's oligarchs. González Vera spoke for many of them when he observed that both men were candidates of a status quo, the only difference being "Barros Borgoño is the soul of the smart set [and] Alessandri is the caudillo of the anonymous bourgeoisie."[32]

In any case, the election proved too close to call.[33] A tribunal was convened to review the results and determine the outcome, which stoked controversy, conspiracy theories, and conflict among the candidates' respective supporters and ratcheted up the tension throughout the country in July. The tension even prior to the election had been palpable on the streets of Santiago and elsewhere. On June 14 a policeman had fired shots in front of Alessandri's home. He claimed it was in self-defense from an attack by a group in front of the home; others claimed it was no less than an assassination attempt against the presidential aspirant.[34] As the elections approached, the main political parties were called to the intendent's office to discuss concerns over street demonstrations.[35] Members of both parties, over the course of the next weeks, would claim to be victims of assaults by supporters of their opposition.[36]

Social, economic, and political questions converged in a heady and, for those in power, worrisome mix. The government confronted social crises of serious proportions. By July 1920, fears mounted that bread would be unavailable due to a shortage of flour.[37] Unemployment persisted and the number of workers with their families arriving daily at the offices of the Worker's Federation in Santiago reached at times into the hundreds.[38] In Santiago work could be hard to find, especially given that many factories had temporarily closed due to a lack of coal, as stevedores went on strike at the ports.[39] Coal production plummeted in early July and members of the Parliament voiced concerns that Santiago would be plunged into darkness.[40] Strikes nationwide soared: official statistics, prone to underestimate strike activity, show a steady increase from 30 in 1918, to 66 in 1919, to 105 in 1920.[41] Maturana claimed the number of strikes in 1919 alone was close to three hundred.[42] In the city strikes had become, by July 1920, a daily reality, particularly in the manufacturing industries (shoes and furniture, among others) that by this time employed more workers than the mines.[43] Protestors publicly critiqued the authorities and rumors circulated of unknown individuals looking to print five thousand copies of pamphlets calling for the populace to rise up in revolt.[44] Minister of Justice Lorenzo Montt, concerned with "tumultuous gatherings" around the country, demanded that public order be enforced by whatever means necessary.[45]

Matters for Sanfuentes were further complicated in early July by a coup d'état in neighboring Bolivia. Insinuations of Peruvian involvement in the coup soon circulated, rumors some in the deposed Bolivian administration did little to quell, confirming for many that Peru's irredentist aims persisted and new plots were afoot.[46] Chilean diplomats had long been tracking Peru's every move and were particularly attuned to any acquisition of weaponry. For example, the Chilean legation in Boliva reported in May 1920 that Peru had acquired a variety of planes, munitions, and asphyxiant gases.[47] With Alessandri's support among students, workers, and reservists in Santiago's regiments, Sanfuentes and his advisers—in particular War Minister Ladislao Errázuriz—used the coup in Bolivia as an excuse to mobilize troops on the border with Peru and Bolivia, question Alessandri's patriotism, and suppress a broader movement of dissent.[48] In other words, a general atmosphere of belligerent suspicion combined with both political necessity and opportunity to create what would become known, with derision, as Don Ladislao's war. In the wake of the coup and rumors of Peruvian involvement, the Chilean government would look to acquire weaponry as quick as possible, engaging in discussions with the Italian and Japanese governments for the immediate acquisition of arms.[49] The Senate, meanwhile, sought to approve a five-million peso emergency fund to cover the costs of "mobilization, provisioning, wages, and other necessities related to support of the military."[50] Some commentators would later recall that Sanfuentes delayed announcement of the possibility of war so as to permit the Chilean aristocracy with mining interests in Peru and Bolivia to sell high, although US consul George Makinson would note in 1924 that "the majority of the big tin and silver mining companies operating in Bolivia are incorporated under Chilean law for they were originally organized and financed in this country [Chile] and Chilean citizens still hold controlling capital-share interests."[51] Meanwhile, minister of war Ladislao Errázuriz ensured his business friends lucrative contracts for outfitting and feeding the troops. Accusations would proliferate that various companies were "speculating on the soldier's stomach," increasing their profit margins by sending spoiled beans and potatoes to the front.[52]

Regardless, the rush to war generated an intensely patriotic response around Chile. But not everyone was persuaded. In particular, Sanfuentes and his ministers confronted a vocal and very public critique of their policy from student leaders in the FECh.

BEYOND REFORM

By the 1910s university students were becoming a powerful political and social force in many countries in Latin America, Chile included. Throughout the nineteenth century the University of Chile, and subsequently the Catholic University (founded in 1888 by the Santiago archdiocese), reproduced elite power. Faculty were often drawn from a number of prominent families and hiring reflected a structural nepotism. Universities, in contrast to their colonial predecessors, ran on a Napoleonic model, meaning they had a largely utilitarian function: to train the next generation of professionals drawn from the oligarchy.[53] Such a model of higher education came increasingly under assault after the turn of the century as children of a developing middle class sought access to higher education, as urbanization and immigration transformed forms of association and challenged the traditional patronage networks that characterized power and mobility in the nineteenth century, and as societies' elites lost legitimacy in the waves of economic crises caused by boom and bust cycles of global capitalism.

The most well-known confrontation with the traditional model of university education arose in 1918 with the university reform movement in Córdoba, in neighboring Argentina.[54] There, provoked by university authorities' efforts to control the city's intellectual climate, students organized protests and issued a manifesto. "The universities," it declared, "have been, until now, the secular refuge of the mediocre, the rental property of the ignorant . . . and worse still, the place in which all forms of tyranny and insensitivity found a lecture room within which to be taught."[55] Students clamored for an array of changes in the university, addressing everything from transformations in its social and cultural functions to the need for students to be able to self-govern.[56] Not surprisingly, the calls for university reform quickly surpassed the bounds of the university itself and demands for social change more broadly blossomed. "The university," the students claimed, was nothing more than the mirror image of the "decadent society" in which it existed, "a senile man who will neither retire nor die."[57]

University reform clearly resonated in Argentina and Peru. In Chile the FECh, under the leadership of Labarca and Gandulfo in 1918, created a working group to study university reform while a student delegation visited counterparts in Argentina.[58] But university reform was, at best, a marginal issue for the leadership of the FECh in the postwar period.[59] For one, university student activism and organizing was hardly new in Chile by 1918. A pivotal moment came with the founding of the FECh in 1906, a result of students having been snubbed by government officials at a ceremony intended to honor students for their labor in combatting epidemics in Valparaíso.[60] Upon arriving at the Teatro Municipal, students and their families found themselves relegated to the upper and rear sections of the Theatre while invited officials and dignitaries, who most likely had contributed little to the anti-epidemic effort, claimed the best seats in the house. In protest, medical students jeered and threw paper down onto state dignitaries. Soon after, in August, they formed the FECh, headed by a medical student, José Ducci, with the support of the rector.

Such a formative start set a combative precedent and over the next decade university students became frequent voices in city and, increasingly, national politics. Their politics on occasion took on a kind of public ridicule of the established order. In 1913 members of the FECh ridiculed an unpopular papal nuncio "by snatching his monsignorial hat and parading it on a donkey down the Alameda the following day."[61] Despite the existence of a fairly robust anti-clericalism in Santiago at the time, such behavior was still perceived as scandalous. Anarchist printer and agitator Julio Valiente recalled with some indignancy the "overpowering . . . influence of clericalism over the masses and in all of Chilean society."

> That influence reached to such an extreme that when a priest passed by on the street it was essential that each man remove his hat in front of the priest and pay his respects. If the priest were carrying the Holy Sacrament, accompanied by a sexton, then the pedestrian should remove his hat and kneel immediately.
>
> If one, through neglect or willful intention, did not fulfill this obligation, he was immediately abused by any person who might be passing by, or by the sexton who accompanied the priest, in the most ruthless fashion, because such an attitude was considered sacriligious, stigmatizing one as barbaric.[62]

The infamous ex-priest Pope Julio (aka Juan José Julio y Elizalde) was persecuted for his ribald attacks on the church and insinuations of sexual activity among priests and nuns.[63] When he visited Quillota to speak in

1917 the local priest had the bells rung for the entire speech so no one could hear his words.[64] Three years after, a photograph of a corpulent Pope Julio would be included on a page dedicated to subversives expelled from the country.

But the FECh was something more than a space within which students could exercise a kind of political and social irreverence. It was a powerful mechanism through which students could engage politically, act upon the prominent political and social issues of the day, create a powerful political subjectivity, and forge alliances with other social sectors. Students in the FECh reached out beyond national borders to forge relationships with students elsewhere, attending congresses in 1910 and 1913 where they discussed the forging of a pan-American intellectual and political project. Leaders in the FECh—all male—were active in the formation of the AOAN, and medical students helped staff night clinics created for working and displaced families in Santiago.[65] Long before students at the 1921 International Student Congress in Mexico City advocated unification with the proletariat, students in Chile had been doing precisely that.[66]

These initial interventions into social and political life deepened and acquired more militant overtones in 1917 and after, in part as a new generation of leaders arose in the FECh and in part as economic crises deepened in Santiago and around the country. The leadership in the FECh by 1918—influenced by the Great War, the Russian Revolution, and dubiously justified conflicts with Perú—became increasingly internationalist in political orientation, something that helps explain the strong resonance of anarchist and socialist ideas within the FECh as well as the lukewarm reception of the Córdoba movement which tended to be more nationalist, if also continentalist, in orientation.[67] If liberal perspectives dominated the FECh's early history, by 1918 a new generation of student leaders had emerged, a generation more socially and geographically diverse and one radicalized by international, national and local events and processes. There was no rigid ideological coherence among such students—some identified with a relatively radical wing of the Radical Party, others with anarchism, and still others with some combination of liberal and anarchist perspectives. "We were members of political parties but we also maintained our own ideology," recalled Pedro Gandulfo, Juan's younger brother.[68] Two things students shared were an interest in revolutionary politics and an increasingly outspoken, skeptical position vis-à-vis their government and the existing social structure and order.

The works students read confirmed their impressions and helped them make broader sense of a decadent social order, both afar and at home. The Great War, for example, transformed how intellectuals around the world perceived Europe, long seen as the apogee of modernity. By 1917 European civilization had revealed its own barbarities and irrationalities: trench warfare, mustard gas, repeating machine guns, and the relentless slaughter of a generation of young men. Revolutionary poets wrote of the "twilight of mankind."[69] Philosophers, such as the Prussian conservative Oswald Spengler, predicted the decline and eventual collapse of Western civilization.[70] To students in parts of Latin America, Spengler appeared as a revolutionary voice, questioning the central universalisms that undergirded western European thought about itself and the world. He was, for all intents and purposes, provincializing Europe as yet one more civilizational entity destined to fall. For students and intellectuals in a place like Chile, the message was clear: if Europe was not the apex for intellectual aspirations, then Latin America could one day lead, rather than follow. And it would be a new generation of students and intellectuals who would lead in the transformation of their societies and cultures.[71] At the same time, US values were not considered an alternative ideal for Latin Americans due to US intervention in the Caribbean and Central America.[72]

With transformations in communication and publishing technologies, with the mass circulation of dailies, and with the mass publication and serialization of international works of literature, social criticism, and works of political theory, students and workers lived in a world that generated and facilitated internationalist possibilities.[73] Students read a range of writers, all of whom shaped their understandings of the realm of possibilities in their own societies and whose works they adapted to their own particular contexts. They read Peruvian Manuel González Prada, Argentine José Ingenieros, and their own Chilean comrades and poets. As well as Spengler, they read Tolstoy, Unamuno, Gorki, Dostoyevsky, and Ortega y Gasset, whose works were readily available in the FECh's substantial library, in a cheap paperback edition from one of the many bookshops that lined Ahumada street where one might show one's FECh membership card for a discount, or in translation in the pages of such journals as *Numen*.[74] FECh members also had access to an array of pamphlets and booklets sent to them via their counterparts in Buenos Aires. They read the latest in political thought and theory, such as Leon Trotsky's *El bolcheviquismo ante la guerra y la paz del mundo*, published in 1919 and made available at two pesos a copy through the efforts of *Numen* and FECH members Rigoberto Soto Rengifo and Pedro Gandulfo.[75] They read Romain Rolland and Lenin and Jaures; they read Henri Barbusse, who called for a unified front of intellectuals and workers, not unlike that of Manuel González Prada, who would shape the perspectives of Víctor Raúl Haya de la Torre and José Carlos Mariátegui in neighboring Peru. They read John

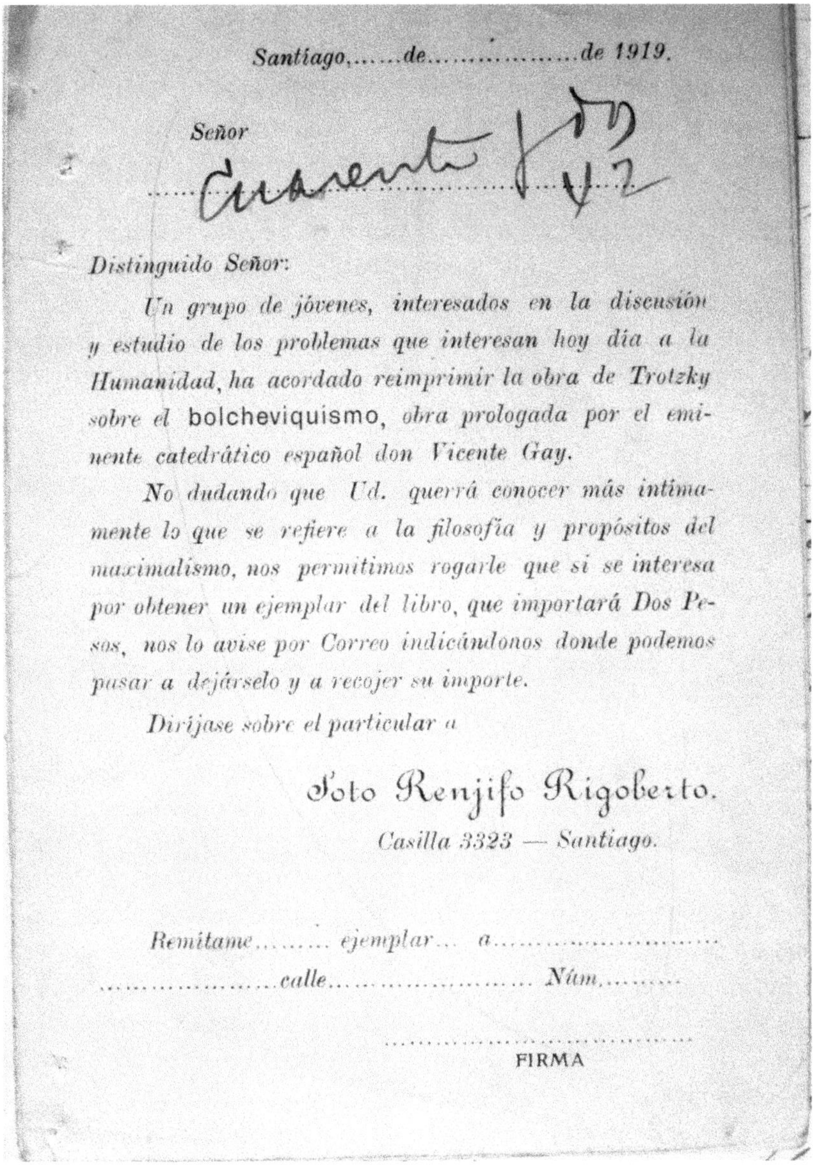

Santíago,......de..................de 1919.

Señor

....

Distinguido Señor:

Un grupo de jóvenes, interesados en la discusión y estudio de los problemas que interesan hoy día a la Humanidad, ha acordado reimprimir la obra de Trotzky sobre el bolcheviquismo, *obra prologada por el eminente catedrático español don Vicente Gay.*

No dudando que Ud. querrá conocer más intimamente lo que se refiere a la filosofía y propósitos del maximalismo, nos permitimos rogarle que si se interesa por obtener un ejemplar del libro, que importará Dos Pesos, nos lo avise por Correo indicándonos donde podemos pasar a dejárselo y a recojer su importe.

Diríjase sobre el particular a

Soto Renjifo Rigoberto.

Casilla 3323 — Santiago.

Remítame........ ejemplar... a..........................

....................calle...................... Núm.........

....

FIRMA

Figure 2.3
Trotsky for sale. Rigoberto Soto Rengifo's flyer advertising the sale of a recent translation in to Spanish of a work by Trotsky. Courtesy of the Archivo Nacional de Chile.

Dewey, Henrik Ibsen, and Maeterlinck. And they read the core of the revolutionary Left: Peter Kropotkin, Mikhail Bakunin, Errico Malatesta, Karl Marx, and Max Stirner. It was a capacious Left to whom students looked for inspiration. Stirner—arch-individualist and target of Marx's wrath in the latter portion of *The German Ideology*—sat comfortably with Malatesta and Bakunin.[76] Brothers and friends, Juan and Pedro Gandulfo personified the experimental and inclusive climate of political thought: while Juan situated himself squarely in the anarcho-syndicalist IWW, Pedro and friend Rigoberto Soto Rengifo established a reading group devoted to Stirner. "We were nihilists," he recalled.[77]

Students were not doctrinaire, but they were increasingly radicalized. They were inspired by and followed closely the unfolding revolution in Russia (Mexico's revolution received little attention) and adopted pen names such as Pravda, Ivan, and Sachka Yegulev. Liberal democracy appeared to no longer be the only political possibility. In fact, it appeared to many as the problem rather than the solution to the world's and the country's social ills. Look what a century of liberalism had produced: severe economic distortions; an extremely skewed form of democratic politics that mocked the very concept of representation; persistent poverty, inequality, and underemployment; the continued subjugation of Latin Americans' economies and political life to the interests of the United States and Europe; repeated massacres of workers and their families and the passage of "social defense laws" which permitted the police to determine what constituted "subversive ideas." Liberal democracy, in other words, appeared neither liberal nor democratic.

Santiago's social and physical structure confirmed these theses. It was outside the bounds of books and universities that many students learned the most profound of lessons. Their interactions with Santiago's urban poor and working classes, who had little access to adequate health care and treatment, who went hungry, and who lacked housing, dramatically shaped their political perspectives, as did the glaring inequalities of the city. In a period of rampant hunger, a typhus epidemic, a housing crisis, the persistent threat of disease, and runaway inflation, Santiago's inhabitants watched the city's elite prepare to occupy the city's first modern skyscraper, complete with a luxury restaurant on the first floor and built at the cost of some $3,500,000.[78] Truffles for the few, tuburculosis for the many: the cruel irony of conspicuous consumption.

PATRIOTS AND PROFESSORS

As the University of Chile expanded—enrollment had reached close to four thousand students by 1918—students increasingly came from more diverse geographic and social backgrounds.[79] A number of the prominent leaders in the FECh—Santiago Labarca and Juan Gandulfo among them—were from the provinces (Chillán and Viña del Mar, respectively). Their social backgrounds too were increasingly diverse as a growing middle class—for lack of a better word—sought access to higher education, new opportunities, new political structures, and new areas of study.[80] While such students were part of a growing middle class, few lived—in terms of their physical proximity and financial precarity—far from the working class.[81] University education was not synonomous with membership in the owning class. The middle class itself—schoolteachers, journalists, shopkeepers and clerks, and public employees (over 27,000 by 1919 as the state bureaucracy expanded)—lived a tenuous existence of "genteel poverty" in the 1910s, constantly struggling with relatively meager incomes and rampant inflation.[82] Not surprisingly, intellectuals, artists, poets, writers, and critics could rarely make their livings by writing. "Literary activities have not yet become lucrative professions," Víctor Domingo Silva would recall in 1923. "We have had great poets dressed in a robe and serving a provincial parish; critics and intellectuals tucked in their odontological offices, in their legal offices or in their medical consultancies, and novelists, at times unpublished, in military or police uniform."[83]

Students' social and geographic origins dictated where they lived. While students from elite families continued to live in the city center, and to an increasing degree in developing suburbs such as Providencia to the east, students from more modest backgrounds, often from the provinces, found affordable room and board in working-class and quasi-middle-class parts of the city. Most prominently this included the district around the University's School of Medicine north of the Mapocho. Here students roomed in pensiones on Independencia, Olivos, O'Higgins, Recoleta, Carrión, and Maruri next to the school and the Casa de Orates and Santiago's morgue.[84] Reflecting their financial circumstances, two or three students—at times from the same province—would share a single room, which they would furnish sparingly with beds, desks, and a wash basin purchased from one of the neighborhood's many pawnshops.[85] This was also an area populated by workers in many of Santiago's industries, including some in the anarcho-syndicalist movement at the time.[86] These were homes and workshops students passed on any given day walking in the street, to or from the city center, the School of Medicine, or one of the gambling houses along Recoleta that caused occasional consternation among neighbors.[87] Other students lived in the Barrio Latino, near the home and workplace of Casimiro Barrios, south of the Alameda and east of the Parque Cousiño. Places abounded where university students, intellectuals, and workers talked, drank, and smoked together. They met at the Francisco Ferrer Social Studies Center, a working men's club named after Spain's well-known anarchist educational theorist executed by the Spanish government in 1909; or at Los Inmortales, a café prominently situated at the intersection of Avenida Matta and San Diego and only doors away from the IWW offices; or at the Casa del Pueblo's main offices, where self-defined anarchist workers would give poetry readings.[88] This was a neighborhood with a strong working-class and anarchist presence. Indeed, if one were to map an "anarchist Santiago," this would be its center: with the offices of the woodworkers' union, the carpenters' union, the shoeworkers' and painters' unions, the printing shop of Julio Valiente where he published *Numen* with Santiago Labarca and *Verba Roja* with Armando Triviño, and small artisan shops all mixed in with bars, cafes, and hotels that rented rooms by the night, the hour, or simply for "a little bit of time."[89] Pedro Gandulfo lived here with two others students on San Ignacio Street, not far from the printer Florencio Rozas Ortega, a founder of Chile's socialist party in the 1930s, who would be arrested in the sweeps in late July. This was where Casimiro Barrios lived and worked, as did many of the workers and intellectuals accused of being anarchists and targeted by the Security Section during police raids in the last week of July. So too did José Domingo Gómez Rojas.

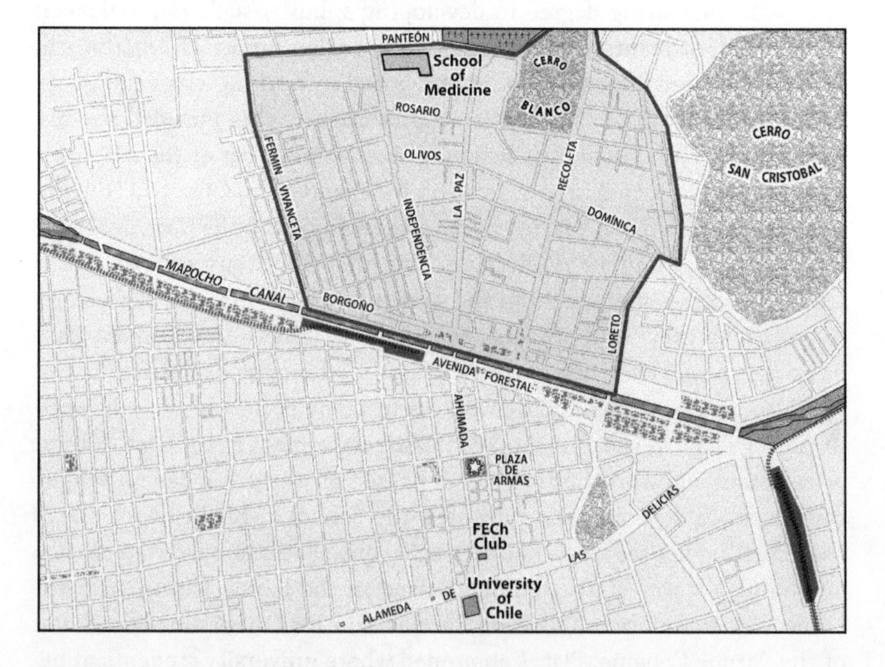

Figure 2.4
Student city: major area of student boarding houses as well as location of the University of Chile, its Medical School, and its Club. Map by David Ethridge.

Whether inspired by the revolution in Russia, appalled by the persistent disparities of Santiago, or moved by their quotidian experiences in the city streets, students increasingly took aim at social and political issues and they found in the FECh an organizational and institutional space within which to do so. Indeed, this is precisely one of the reasons why the response to the rhetoric and activities of the FECh would be so intense: it breached the boundaries of acceptable opposition. As long as students talked like students—limiting themselves to university reform, questions of faculty positions, funding, and the like—there was little threat. But by 1918 it appeared that the leadership of the FECh was becoming increasingly immersed in social issues and national politics, much to the chagrin of many. Students were asserting a right to speak on common affairs.

As such, they were regarded with increased suspicion. In late 1918, in the midst of the AOAN demonstrations in Santiago and the Sanfuentes administration's efforts to push through a residency law, repeated accusations of anti-patriotism were directed at the FECh because its members had been in contact with their student counterparts in Peru.[90] The moment was a tense one: only weeks earlier Deputy Nicolás Cárdenas had been censured in an extraordinary congressional session. In a moment of political courage, Cárdenas had effectively questioned blind patriotism. His comments—judicious and measured—scandalized the Parliament and Chilean high society and resulted in his censure and removal from the post of vice president of the chamber.[91] The resulting political climate proved oppressive. One of Cárdenas's colleagues observed, with more than a hint of dismay, "after that negation of patriotism, nothing else would do but an energetic, enthusiastic and vehement afirmation of patriotism . . . From that moment, all patriotic displays were not only useful but indispensable."[92] Little wonder that when FECh member Rigoberto Soto Rengifo appeared on the floor of the Parliament to defend the student organization, he invoked patriotism but attempted to shift how it was perceived. There were, he argued, two kinds of patriotism: one, heroic and characterized by blind sacrifice during international crises; and then a second kind, the patriotism of daily work on behalf of one's compatriots. It was this latter form, Soto Rengifo argued, that could be found amongst the membership of the FECh: students who after their classes go teach in night schools, who provide free legal and medical services for the poor, and who helped found the UPL so workers could get an education (although working men and women had long been collectively educating themselves).[93]

Despite Soto Rengifo's efforts, the FECh and the UPL became repeated targets of popular and official invective. Rumors circulated of anarchist ideas and anti-patriotic discourses predominating among the faculty and students of the UPL. Accusations flew that "foreign adventurers" had established a foothold in there, that its professors and students were defending Deputy Cárdenas's comments, and that the student leadership of the FECh had engaged in anti-patriotic behavior.[94] Deputies and senators wrung their hands over the state of the university. They expressed exasperation at student strikes, arguing that such behavior was typically "Russian" or "Araucanian."[95] The university exists, argued one senator, in order "to awake in the heart of the child, and subsequently of the youth, an endless love of country and an equally endless spirit of sacrifice when called to fullful his civic duties."[96] Another invoked the example of Germany as a country in which schools were committed to patriotism. "Germany has lost this war," he proclaimed, "but no one can deny that with her elevated teachings she knows how to form a generation of patriots who have drawn the world's admiration."[97] In their Santiago, no less than in Wilhelm von Humboldt's Berlin, the university was a means to protect national culture, police its boundaries, and create a new generation of rulers.

It was not only politicians who found grounds for critique. Other students and professors spoke out. The sudden and very public denunciation of the FECh by Pedro León Loyola—a philosophy professor at the University of Chile, a director of the UPL, and an honorary member of the FECh—exemplifies that shift. As early as 1916 he had evidenced a growing frustration with the political and intellectual direction of the FECh, criticizing students for protesting and critiquing without offering a positive program of their own. Loyola was more inclined to seek reform within the system than to challenge it and in his attention to "the spirit," and his critique of scientism, industrialism and materialism, he shared the ethos of Mexican intellectuals Antonio Caso and José Vasconcelos.[98] By 1919 his patience with the FECh ended. There was, he wrote, "an abyss between certain current doctrines of the Federation and some of my most cherished ideals."[99] He lamented that increasingly it appeared as if intellectual and political life had become polarized into "two extremes that do not understand me and which I do not understand: the theorists of reactionary brutality and the theorists of revolutionary brutality."[100] He resigned his position at the UPL, a university he had helped found and which he now saw as an institution largely directed by an insurrectionary FECh.[101]

Nor was the shift in the FECh leadership in 1918 welcomed by all students. Not all students in the FECh necessarily shared the same political persuasion. The FECh itself became a site of struggle, and as the FECh's leadership shifted to a more oppositional position, strong frictions developed among and between members. Already in 1917 then-president of the FECh Agustín Vigorena Rivera, a militant in the Radical Youth and strongly anti-anarchist, made clear that he did not want the FECh "confused with a resistance society," suggesting in the process that such confusion may already have happened.[102] The student population was ideologically and social heterogeneous, increasingly so by 1918. The fact is one cannot speak of university students as if they formed a unified or homogeneous group, or attribute to them a kind of political or social coherence. González Vera recalled later the ideological heterogeneity that existed in the student population at the time: "Among the students there were radicals, masons, anarchists, vegetarians, liberals, some socialists, collectivists, nietzcheans, stirnerians, spiritists, catholics, nationalists, schemers y almost wild kids."[103] Moreover, students had other potential incentives for joining the FECh and thus were not necessarily declaring a particular political position when doing so. With a FECh membership one could have breakfast, lunch, tea or dinner for a very modest price, or get a haircut and a shave, or take boxing lessons on weekday evenings.[104] With a FECh membership card one could get discounts at various bookstores, tailors, shoe stores, and tie shops.[105]

The fact of the matter was that by 1918, with Labarca and Gandulfo as president and vice president respectively of the FECh, there was little doubt as to the orientation of the organization, and their focus on forging alliances with workers and agitating openly for social transformation heightened the tensions with and around the FECh. By this time the group had committed itself to principles of continuous critique of existing institutions and social life, advocated the right of both students and workers to be heard, and endorsed the organized action of the proletariat. In 1920, as the presidential elections approached, tensions escalated rapidly. In late June leaders of the FECh held a convention at which they issued a number of public statements regarding contemporary political and social issues, including a call for the abolition of militaries, loyalty to humanity, a suspicion of nationalism, and a demand that mobilizations on the Peruvian border be justified.[106] The popular response was immediate and intense. An editorial in *El Mercurio* provided a typical reaction, lambasting the students for issuing statements on things outside of their purview and that "wound the feelings of the Chilean people."[107] *Zig-Zag* responded similarly, sarcastically commenting that a new executive power had been born with students demanding explanations from the government on issues related to international affairs.[108] Moreover, criticisms of the mobilizations were taken as clear indications of one's "Peruvian" sympathies; indeed, as one young writer recalled, even to criticize "war" in the abstract was to invite attacks on one's physical person.[109]

Just as important was the convention's statement of principles regarding the social question.

> The Federation . . . considers that the solution to the social problem can never be definitive and that the transitory solutions to which one can aspire presuppose a permanent critique of the existing social organizations. The critique should be directed at the economic regime and the moral and intellectual life of the society. . . . Before the real necessities of the current moment, [the Federation] feels that the social problem should resolve itself through the substitution of the principle of cooperation for that of competition, the socialization of the forces of production and the consequent equal redistribution of the product of communal labor, and by the effective recognition of the right of each person to live fully his intellectual and moral life.[110]

Such ideas—referred to with suspicion in the press as "advanced tendencies"—raised concerns with much of the reading public and pushed the press to interview FECh president Alfredo Demaria.[111] If readers were looking to be assuaged of their concerns, they would be disappointed. The point of the FECh, Demaría argued, was that "students should not come together only for their own benefit; rather, they should come together especially for the collective welfare."[112]

MUTUAL AID

A profound and powerful anger was directed at students and workers who seemed not to respect their mutual boundaries, nor to know their place. Increasingly students, particularly those involved in the FECh, found themselves demonstrating, working, and organizing alongside sectors of Santiago's working class. Such interactions were not altogether unprecedented. Take, for example, a signal event—not only in Santiago, or Chile, but the world over—that occurred in 1909. On October Francisco Ferrer, the highly respected and internationally renowned Catalan educator, founder of the progressive Modern School of education, and political organizer, was executed by the Spanish government, having been accused of anarchist agitation and, falsely, for a recent wave of bombings against civil and ecclesiastical authorities. No evidence linked him to such activities but he was executed nonetheless, setting off a wave of international protest and indignation.[113] In Santiago thousands gathered in a central plaza to protest Ferrer's execution, university students sharing the plaza, the soapbox, and their indignation with a multitude of workers. To the dismay of governments around the world Ferrer's execution forged new—or deepened existing—relationships between workers and students and furthered the dissemination of, and interest in, anarchist ideas.

Relationships, even if on occasion antagonistic and tenuous, between workers and students persisted over the coming decade.[114] Students offered legal consultation to workers, as well as medical services, and opened an evening dispensary. They helped create and sustain a number of *universidades populares*, the most famous of which was the UPL, founded in 1910, which offered workers free courses in fields as diverse as Spanish language and literature, history, philosophy, geometry and physics.[115] Here working men could expand upon—and also convey—what they had learned in what Manuel Rojas called the Universidad de Chanco (School of Hard Knocks).[116] By 1916 students were staffing eleven study centers across the city. Over the course of 1919 and in to the early months of 1920, worker and student alliances took shape, in part as the leadership of the FECh moved ideologically closer to Santiago's changing labor context and in part as both groups suffered the increasingly heavy hand of police repression. Already by October 1919 a number of Santiago newspapers were accusing the FECh of instigating or provoking workers movements—by which they meant protests and demonstrations and strikes.[117] In 1920 such forms of mutual aid would persist and would appear to many in power as a breach of the social order and a threat to Chile itself.

Forging such solidarity did not come easy. Workers were understandably skeptical, if not suspicious. Santiago Labarca, when he presided over the FECh, worked to generate strong bonds between the FECh and various workers' unions. Yet the membership of the Shoemakers Federation suspected Labarca was a government agent. Moreover, Labarca's discourse could at times be patronizing, such as when he declared that workers without intellectuals could not carry out work of real benefit and that it was time for "brawn and brain" to march together.[118] In other cases, workers viewed repression of students with little sympathy. When Juan Gandulfo was detained in March 1920, the FECh and FOCh both called for meetings to protest his detention. Members of Antofagasta's Employees' Federation were bemused at best: "What would one protest? And why?" they asked. "We have already seen many things worse than that . . . especially in Antofagasta, the imprisonment of Gandulfo seems to us like no big deal."[119] More broadly, the abyss that divided a worker's future from that of a student was obvious to many. "Students?" Manuel Rojas would recall, his memory filtered through the voice of his fictional character, Aniceto Hevía. "They are inconsequential beings, almost celestial, who arrive, speak or shout for a time and then leave: the student becomes a doctor, an engineer, an architect or an attorney, he marries and disappears, while the carpenter, even if he marries, will always be a carpenter and a shoemaker a shoemaker."[120]

With a century of distance it is all too easy to chuckle at the suggestion that middle-class students and working-class men somehow made common cause or could speak to one another in the language of class or of politics or of a common future. Yet while awkward interactions, misunderstandings, and suspicion were commonplace, it is also the case that meaningful alliances were forged by and between students and workers. Listen, for example, to González Vera, who, in the midst of the great strike of September 1919, said: "Before, the student youth spent its energies in shouting, laughing and worshiping the cult of the superficial. Then the bourgeoisie were on their side; but today, somewhat suprisingly, that youth that shouted, laughed and worshipped has begun to see itself in the real world."[121] Manuel Rojas counted both Juan Gandulfo and José Domingo Gómez Rojas among his closer friends and found inspiration in their work. In March 1920, the editors of *Verba Roja* would note in a front page editorial that students and workers had put aside past differences and come together to work for their common interest and to campaign in defense of individual rights and freedom of thought.[122] *Verba Roja* had in fact been publishing excerpts from the recently created organization, *Clarté*, which called for manual and intellectual laborers to unite—broadly for social ends but also, in specific instances, to halt the efforts by European powers to intervene in the unfolding revolution in Russia.[123] Writers for *Numen* noted approvingly that the French CGT had recognized the importance of affiliations between workers and intellectuals and that the only workers who opposed such alliances in Chile were "the most backward" of all.[124] Already in 1905, Peruvian intellectual and anarchist Manuel Prada had made a similar call in his "The Intellectual and the Worker" and, more recently, French veteran, pacifist, and intellectual Henri Barbusse had issued calls for intellectuals to engage politically alongside working people.[125] Such unity was clearly happening. Student leaders in the FECh—Labarca, Gandulfo, and Pedro León Ugalde, among others—were increasingly in attendance at meetings not only of the AOAN (which they helped found) but also of the FOCh and the POS. At times they attended to seek the support of workers, such as when León Ugalde requested the support of the FOCh in protesting the government's denial of student requests for occupying public rights of way for the spring festival.[126] The FOCh delegates agreed to work in solidarity with the students by organizing and participating in a work stoppage on a date to be established.[127] In other cases workers, such as those from the Federation of Shoemakers, supported the FECh in its campaign to ensure freedom for the press, which had been violated repeatedly by some magistrates.[128] Meanwhile, law students took on cases for working people, including León Ugalde, who represented itinerant merchants who were fighting the municipality's efforts to impose fines on them.[129]

Perhaps most crucially of all, the space of the FECh itself became the frequent home to multiple worker organizations in need of a place to meet. Students stopping in at Ahumada 73—to shoot billiards, have a whiskey or a beer, get a haircut, or grab lunch from the cafeteria—would have frequently encountered more than students. Many of those who assembled with regularity at the club, including González Vera himself, were not university students but former FECh presidents, artisans, laborers, and young worker-intellectuals employed outside the bounds of the university. It was a space in which students, former students, labor organizers, and workers met and organized and talked. In 1918, under the leadership of Labarca, the student club had become one of the main meeting locations for the leadership of the AOAN, which included Labarca and Gandulfo, Carlos Alberto Martínez of the POS, Julio Valiente of *Numen*, and Moises Montoya of the Woodworkers Resistance Society.[130] In February 1919, as the conflict between labor and Sanfuentes's government ratcheted up, the syndicalist committee for the AOAN, composed of twenty-four delegates, gathered for a late meeting at the FECh club. The very first order of business was approval of a request by workers on strike against the major department store Gath y Chaves to use the offices of the FECh for their meetings. The request was approved.[131] Indeed, various committees of the AOAN met frequently at the FECh, as did a group of Santiago anarchists—Julio Valiente, Manuel Zamorano, Moisés Montoya, Armando Triviño, and others.[132]

In other words, the FECh had become much more than a student federation. Put another way, the leadership of the FECh had expanded what it meant to be a student, what the role of the FECh could and should be, the idea of who could engage in politics, and the very meaning of politics itself. Spaces such as the FECh club, as well as the streets of Santiago themselves, became places students and workers together inhabited and appropriated, making them their own. These were spaces that fostered the creation of alliances, coalitions, and friendships as the distance—both social and physical—between workers and students diminished.[133] This is not to suggest that they forged perfectly egalitarian configurations, but rather to stress that such political and social solidarity was both possible and real. In a way heretofore uncommon, some workers and some students came to occupy the same city.[134]

Little wonder then that a group of laboring men waited patiently outside of the police station that July 19 evening to ensure Juan Gandulfo's release and to accompany him home. And, in the wake of the attack on the student club, workers joined with students at the club to protect it from more assaults.

THE DESCENT OF THE GOLDEN YOUTH

On the morning of July 20, the day after his arrest and release, Juan Gandulfo woke to a steady, cold rain. It was reason enough to not venture outside but the rain did not stop thousands of city residents—"a river of people," as one journalist put it—from gathering along Matucana to send off the reservists making their way to the Central Station to ship out to Valparaíso and points north. Along the avenue the crowd unfurled Chilean flags while from the balconies above celebrants showered the troops with flowers. Over the din of the crowd could be heard the refrains of patriotic songs echoing off the walls of a nearby girls' school. A veteran of the War of the Pacific could be heard celebrating: "And now, there are no alessandrists or barrists. There are only Chileans. Very beautiful . . . Very beautiful."[135]

The patriotic send-offs continued the next day throughout the country as well as in Santiago. Officials from all parts of the country commented on the extraordinary size of the daily demonstrations in support of the troop mobilizations and, on occasion, for the definitive annexation of the disputed territories in the north.[136] Among those attending the patriotic rallies were large contingents of university students. These were students from various disciplines, schools, and social backgrounds: some were former members of the FECh angry at the political shift it had taken but most were the sons of Santiago's well-to-do, or *canalla dorada* ("gilded swine"). Sons of Chile's most prominent families, they resided in the city center, mostly attended the Catholic University, were intensely patriotic, and had responded to the FECh's leanings with the creation of their own organization. Their targets were not only the FECh itself—both the organization and its premises would bear the weight of their wrath—but also a particular group of individuals associated with the leadership of the FECh, including Juan Gandulfo, Santiago Labarca, and Alfredo Demaría.[137]

On July 21, another group of patriots came looking for the head of a Gandulfo. This crowd—having initially assembled at the Mapocho Station to send off in grand style the next batch of reservists heading for the northern frontier—numbered not in the dozens, nor the hundreds, but the thousands. They were drunk not on whiskey but on words; it was not the insinuations of military personnel in the Club de la Unión but the inflammatory accusations of Senator Enrique Zañartu, issued no less from the balcony of the presidential palace La Moneda, which sanctioned their actions. The students in the FECh had questioned the government; they had had the temerity to suggest a different strategy in international affairs; they had preached pacifism; they were funded by Peruvian gold; they were sell-outs; they had spoken out of place; they were traitors. Each accusation, each charge, stoked the fires further and the crowd marched from La Moneda, down Bandera, to Ahumada and the offices of the FECh, only blocks away. If the first assault had been spontaneous, this one was decidedly not.[138] It was not Juan Gandulfo they would find this time, but his younger brother Pedro.[139]

Pedro was twenty years old at the time and enrolled in the university studying law. Unlike his brother Juan he was not active in the IWW, and while he expressed an avid admiration for the writings of Stirner, he did

Figure 2.5
Stirnerian man: Pedro Gandulfo c. 1920. Avid reader of Stirner, younger brother of Juan Gandulfo, and law student, Pedro Gandulfo would bear much of the crowd's wrath on July 21 at the FECh. Courtesy of Juan Luis Gandulfo.

not identify as an anarchist. Like many young men at the time, he was eclectic intellectually and politically, averse neither to party politics (he supported Alessandri) nor feelings of nationalism, and interested in an array of oppositional and progressive ideas and texts. Unbeknownst to him at the time, he would have to forgo his career in law due to the events that would unfold that afternoon. Unsettled by the attacks on the FECh and his brother on July 19, Pedro had come to the FECh club the next day with his colleagues and friends, including González Vera and at least six Wobblies armed with chisels, to defend it from further assaults. On July 20 there was in fact a brief scuffle in the FECh club when a dozen or so young patriots entered and lingered briefly.[140]

July 21 would be a different encounter altogether. That day's issue of *El Mercurio* contained an article criticizing the FECh for its July 18 resolution and claiming that the earlier assault on the club had been a result of Juan Gandulfo's purportedly inflammatory speech to the crowd.[141] In the meantime, various "respectable persons" had called for the cancellation of the FECh's juridical personality, and students affiliated with the Agronomy Center withdrew from FECh membership.[142] Indeed, tensions ran high enough that FECh members had at least one pistol on the premises for self-defense. At around 1:30 p.m. Pedro Gandulfo was eating lunch with a number of others—including Soto Rengifo and Roberto Meza Fuentes—when the phone rang. The voice on the line warned Pedro that a large group, numbering in the thousands, was marching down Bandera to the FECh. Pedro immediately put in a call to the prefect, then the intendent, and then the Ministry of the Interior, all to no effect.

By the time he realized that no help would be forthcoming, the crowd had arrived. Its composition was heterogeneous, but the core of those who would be identified as the primary assailants were "Catholic youth," referring subtly to both their social status and their status as students at the Universidad Católica, and a number of military personnel. Prominent faces in the crowd included Domingo Undurraga Fernández, a twenty-five-year-old former Army lieutenant; Carlos Alarcón, a former captain and an attorney; an accountant for the Santiago archbishop; the mayor of Providencia; and a significant number of Santiago's "golden youth," the children of the aristocracy, all of whom lived in the city center.[143]

Exactly what transpired is not at all clear. The claims of eye witnesses often conflict, particularly with regards to who provoked the assault, and the reliability of the police documents is questionable. But a careful examination of multiple sources suggests that the following is not wide of the mark.[144] The crowd numbered somewhere around three thousand

Figure 2.6
Mobilization: the assault on the FECh club, July 21, 1920. Note the students on the balcony. *Diario Ilustrado* (July 22, 1920). Courtesy of the Archivo Nacional de Chile.

people. They arrived at the FECh and pulled up stones from the street, hurling them at the windows and eventually storming the premises.[145] Once inside the protestors approached the stairs, where they stopped as the club's manager threatened them with a pistol which he then passed to Pedro Gandulfo who, by his own admission, fired a shot into the air. The bullet passed through the hand of a flag-wielding man and lodged itself in to a mirror on the opposing wall.[146] While some of the protestors retreated, others found their way in through neighboring buildings, at which point Gandulfo fled to the dining hall and fired three more shots in the air. One of the bullets apparently pierced the hat of Alfonso Casanova Vicuña, the son of well-known painter Álvaro Casanova. The assailants retreated for cover again, although one young man managed to reach Gandulfo and inform him that he had come to the FECh not as an assailant but "to save us and he advised me [Gandulfo] to flee because they were coming to kill me."[147] Gandulfo, Lafuente, Zuñiga, and Soto Rengifo fled to the fourth floor of the club, where they made their way across to a neighboring house, breaking the cupola with the butt of the pistol in order to enter.

They could hardly have chosen a less amenable place to flee. The home belonged to Arturo Lyon, a conservative party member and prominent landowner whose brother-in-law happened to be visiting that day. The brother-in-law was none other than Raúl Edwards MacClure, a prominent businessman and conservative politician whose citizenship status had recently been reinstated after he served, without prior permission, in the English military during the war.[148] He also happened to be a relative of Enrique Zañartu, the senator who an hour earlier had stoked the crowd's passions from the balcony of La Moneda. Exactly what transpired next is contested, and there are significant disparities in the sources. Gandulfo and his colleagues entered the house and hid in an upstairs room. Time must have passed excruciatingly slowly but soon noises were heard on the stairs and a group of men—including Edwards MacClure and Undurraga—burst into the room. Threats ensued, and Gandulfo was eventually persuaded to drop the gun. One of the men with Edwards MacClure then demanded the students kiss the Chilean flag. Gandulfo replied that while not opposed, neither he nor his comrades would do so by force. The police soon arrived and arrested the four students. The police report claimed that when searched the agents found, among other things, a portrait of Trotsky—which, if true, was a undoubtedly a copy of the card announcing the Spanish translation of Trotsky's most recent book, for which Soto Rengifo had been collecting orders.[149]

Meanwhile, on Ahumada and in the student club, the crowd vented its anger as the police looked on.[150] They entered the club's library and gathered many of the books, as well as the entire run of *Juventud* magazine, threw them to the street below, and burned them. Some three thousand published volumes, as well as innumerable manuscripts and letters, were destroyed.[151] Individuals sacked whatever they could: they pulled out lightbulbs, ripped keys from the piano, and dismantled chairs. They destroyed the billiards table, the entire cantina, and a large portrait of former University Rector Valentín Letelier, whom they apparently mistook for Peruvian President Leguía. (Such dismally humorous episodes abound: Astorquiza would issue an arrest warrant for none other than Italian anarchist Errico Malatesta, believing him to be a member of the FECh because he found a copy of one of Malatesta's texts, published in Chile, on the premises of the Student Club.)[152] Meanwhile, a senior police official raided the federation's archives, making off with a vast store of letters, receipts, and documents, many of which would be used for further arrests and prosecutions.[153] Another group of men pried the two bronze plaques that had been made for the FECh, by students in the Arts and Crafts School, from the wall in front of the club and paraded them, along with other assorted items from the club, through the downtown streets of Santiago, eventually ending up near the offices of *El Mercurio* where they posed for a photographer with their trophies in hand.[154] A member of Parliament who witnessed the procession drily remarked that the young students acted as if they had captured "weapons, standards or flags from the enemy on the field of battle."[155] Indeed, by now, for many, the FECh had become an internal enemy. Little wonder no arrests were made and the police commander on the scene noted that none of his personnel were able "to take the name of any of the assailants."[156]

The scene that confronted some of the Parliamentarians was shocking enough to move them to emotional discourses on the floor that very afternoon. In a heated exchange only hours after he had witnessed the golden youth parading the remains of the club around central Santiago, Deputy Gallardo Nieto questioned the rhetoric of war that had seemed to spur such action. Even the Minister of War, he noted, "has not said, nor could he have said, with justice, at any time that Chile finds itself seriously threatened." The population, he continued, had an obligation "to not sully the sentiment of patriotism, putting it at the service of interests or causes or purposes that are not inspired exclusively by a sincere and clear understanding of the interests of the country."[157] This apparently created a stir in the gallery, where the public could observe the proceedings. No wonder

Figure 2.7
Scenes of destruction: Remnants of the FECh cantina after the mob subsided. *Diario Ilustrado* (July 22, 1920). Courtesy of the Archivo Nacional de Chile.

Figure 2.8
Scenes of destruction: The billiards table destroyed. *Diario Ilustrado* (July 22, 1920). Courtesy of the Archivo Nacional de Chile.

Figure 2.9
Burning books. Students and police watch the papers of the FECh burn. Notice the police officer at the left with a large stick, and the two in the center right: all would claim they were unable to identify and arrest the assailants. *El Mercurio* (July 28, 1920). Reproduced in *Sucesos* (July 29, 1920). Courtesy of the Archivo Nacional de Chile.

Figure 2.10
The Golden Youth with a bronze trophy. Participants in the attacks on the FECh posed for a photograph outside the offices of *El Mercurio*, with bronze plaques ripped from the club's walls in hand. Note the excision of the face in the back row, center left. *El Mercurio* (July 28, 1920). Courtesy of the Archivo Nacional de Chile.

as the implication was as obvious as it was sharp: that patriotism and the mobilization itself was being manipulated for political ends in the midst of an electoral controversy. His point was proven when deputies from the opposition accused him of being a Peruvian agent.[158]

Perhaps the most damning indictment of the assault was made by Héctor Arancibia Laso. He laid the blame for the attacks at the feet of Zañartu, suggesting that he provoked the crowd from the balcony of La Moneda and accused the FECh of being financed by Peru. The public authorities, moreover, could not have been surprised by what occurred next. In fact the police gathered at the FECh and watched with their arms crossed. One beat cop would later tell his wife he had been ordered not to intervene by his superiors.[159] Arancibia Laso's own experience confirmed this accusation. At 2:30 p.m. he had passed by Ahumada and saw more than one hundred guards standing around as people entered the FECh and walked out with a wide array of things. He had entered the club and found the policeman in charge upstairs with another six guards watching as a group of young men threw furniture off the balcony and took a hammer to the piano.[160] Arancibia Laso made his point clear: "It was this golden youth, which calls Santiago's workers or the voting public 'la chusma' [the rabble], who destroyed everything, who committed these acts of vandalism, and who completely dismantled a large part of the building and who stole the objects it did not destroy in its crazy rage."[161] As others in the room choked back their bile, he questioned who were the real subversives in such moments: "We—accused of being bolsheviks, maximalists and rebels—are the ones who are defending law and order."[162]

CHAPTER 3

Subversive Santiago

JULY 19, 1920

Ashes and flags took to the air. In the aftermath of the assault on the FECh club the embers of its immolated library glowed, an abundance of words reduced to detritic ash drifting along Ahumada Street. If carried on the wind some blocks north, to the Plaza de Armas, the fragments would have floated through a dense clutch of Chilean national flags, flapping overhead. A punitive sky. The air quickened with political turbulence as a mass of young men celebrated the attacks on the FECh, roaming the plaza and infiltrating nearby streets. This was not the traditional early evening ritual of the era's elite youth who would gather near the Plaza de Armas "to watch the young ladies go by."[1] It was a late-night hunt for anti-patriots whom they could force to kiss the flag, the favored demonstration of patriotic submission. A young locksmith, on his way to the theater with his girlfriend, caught their attention. Things unraveled quickly. He refused their demand he kiss the flag, less out of some anti-patriotic sentiment—he apparently had been a participant in the patriotic manifestations earlier that day—than the manner in which the demand had been posed. In the ensuing scuffle, shots were fired and a flag-bearer fell. Julio Covarrubias Freire, son of Conservative Party stalwart Manuel Alejandro Covarrubias Ortúzar, lay dying in front of the Gamboa pharmacy.[2]

Over the following days, Covarrubias would be eulogized by much of Santiago's high society. The Santiago Tennis Club, to which he had

Figure 3.1
Patriotism's first martyr: Julio Covarrubias Freire was shot and killed hours after the attack on the FECh club on July 21, 1920. His death—responsibility for which was never determined—stoked the flames of patriotism and repression. From *Coronas fúnebres* (Santiago: Imprenta Cervantes, 1921).

belonged, canceled all tournaments for a month, hung Covarrubias's portrait in its main hall, and donated a substantial sum in his name to the Red Cross.[3] The conservative Union Club commissioned a bronze crown inscribed with the words "To the First Martyr of patriotism, Julio Covarrubias Freire." Ministers of the Interior, Treasury, and War, as well as the President of the Republic himself, turned out for the funeral and joined the procession as it made its way, over the course of two hours, through the city center to the cemetery.[4] Here numerous speakers—including Minister of War Ladislao Errázuriz, Senator Héctor Zañartu

Figure 3.2
The Gamboa pharmacy. Julio Covarrubias Freire died outside the pharmacy's doors. From Chiléctrica S.A.'s *Transeléctrica: 75 años* (Santiago: Colofón, 1996), 32.

Prieto, and Domingo Undurraga Fernández, the young lieutenant who would soon be identified as one of the main perpetrators of the July 21 assault on the FECh—arose to simultaneously extoll the virtues of the young man, rally the crowd to the defense of the Chilean flag, and heap scorn upon the assassins.[5]

Who shot Covarrubias remained a mystery, although the police arrested the locksmith, Carlos López Marchant.[6] He spent the next six months in a Santiago cell, despite the uncertainties surrounding Covarrubias's death and the fact that many placed the blame on subversives and anarchists. It was "from a group of subversives," wrote one reporter, that the shots came.[7] *Zig-Zag* accused "maximalists" of committing the act while the *Diaro Ilustrado* labeled them the Red Gang and "the nation-less."[8] Covarrubias was "the first victim of those without a country!" clamored one editorialist.[9] Members of Parliament made similar accusations. "These events, Mr. President, which we all deplore," spoke one deputy, "reveal with sad eloquence the absolute necessity for the authorities to labor with bravery and energy to prevent individuals with neither God nor law from continuing to profane the father land."[10] Others demanded the government "extirpate this cancer" eating away at the nation's soul.[11] Another editorial explicitly linked the event to the FECh: the assailant, the writer claimed, had shouted "Viva Peru! Viva Gandulfo!" as he fired his shots.[12]

All of these assertions were unfounded: an assassin was never arrested, nor tried in a court of law, and at least one commentator suggested that Covarrubias's death resulted from the accidental discharge of a weapon in the hands of one of his own friends. The evidence linking anarchists to the young man's death was the same as that connecting López Marchant: none. For the accusers, living through a period of persistent economic and political crisis, of unsettling urban change and dislocation, subversion seemed to be lurking in every corner. Leaders of the FECh, labor organizers, supporters of Alessandri, all became suspects. Evidence enough was to be found in the ideas they professed, in the words they wrote, in the publications they printed and circulated, and, not least of all, in the demonstrations they organized in the city's streets, streets the city's well-to-do had long thought their own.

THE CITY AND THE CITY

The events of July 21 left many of Santiago's residents on edge. Deputies argued that the police should have forseen the violence, and that they needed to use adequate force to prevent such events in the neighborhoods where they lived.[13] They were unable to fathom that such chaos had occurred outside their very doors in broad daylight. "I could understand," expressed one deputy, "if these events had happened on the outskirts of the city, where there is not sufficient surveillance; but I cannot explain to myself how it is that they happened in the very Plaza de Armas or in the most central streets of the city."[14] There was in effect a geographical hierarchy that mapped onto the social hierarchy. Although some of Santiago's patricians and *rastacueros* (nouveau riche) had begun to decamp to Providencia, Nuñoa, and developing suburbs east of the city center where they could, along with upper class foreign residents, seek relief from the congested city center and recreate on the trimmed grass of the Los Leones Lawn Tennis Club, many continued to live where the center of power had always resided: in the city center.[15]

Although something of a colonial backwater during Spanish rule, with independence from Spain in 1818 Chile's fortunes gradually changed, as did its seat of power, Santiago. With political consolidation under Diego Portales, beginning in 1830, and with newfound wealth generated by mineral discoveries of copper and silver in the north, Santiago hosted a rapidly growing population of agriculturalists, merchants, artisans, military men, and capitalists.[16] As the economy grew—with the Californian and then Australian gold rush, increased exports of wheat and minerals

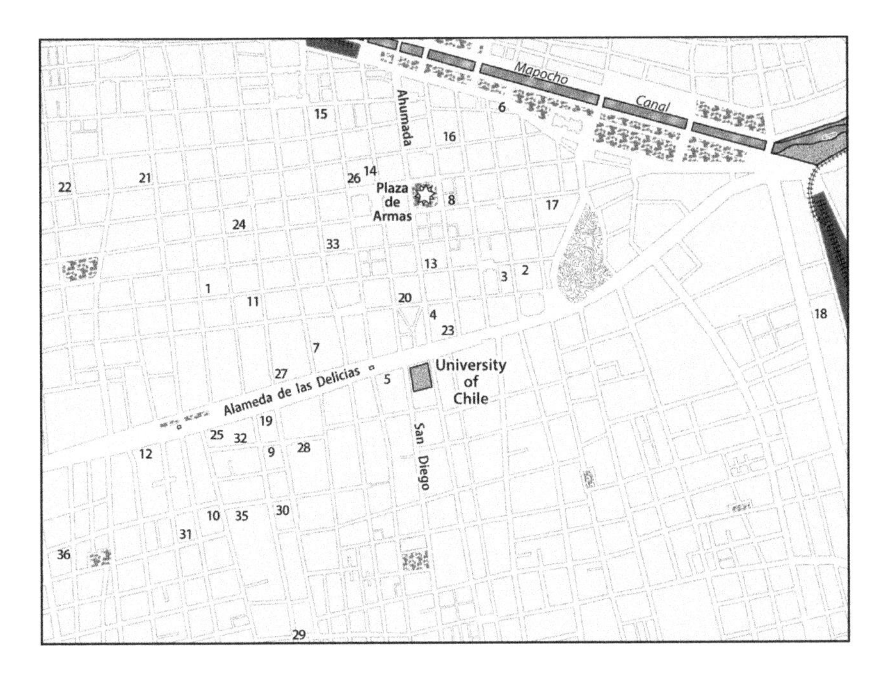

Figure 3.3
Aristocratic city: central Santiago in the early 1920s was still largely populated by the city's elite and many of the students who later would be identified as having led or participated in the attacks on the FECh club. This map locates residencies of prominent Chileans, based on the *Diccionario Personal de Chile*, published in 1924. Numbers correspond as follows: 1. José Astorquiza (special prosecutor and judge); 2. Raúl Edwards (a prominent Santiago patrician); 3. Francisco Subercaseaux; 4. Arturo Lyon; 5. Arturo Alessandri (liberal presidential candidate in 1920); 6. Pedro Aguirre Cerda; 7. Luis Barros Borgoño (conservative presidential candidate in 1920); 8; Senator Luis Claro Solar; 9. Manuel A. Covarrubias (father of Julio Covarrubias Freire); 10. Joaquin Echeñique (one of the founders of the *Diario Ilustrado*); 11. Guillermo and Ismael Edwards Matte; 12. Ladislao Errázuriz Lazcano (Minister of War); 13. Deputy Galvarino Gallardo Nieto; 14. Minister of the Interior Pedro García de la Huerta; 15. Deputy and Director of *Diario Ilustrado* Rafael Luis Gumucio; 16. Deputy Ramón Herrera Lira; 17. Senator Enrique Mac-Iver; 18.Minister of Justice Lorenzo Montt; 19. Senator and wine producer Silvestre Ochagavía Echaurren; 20. Writer and Director of the Cámara Industrial de Chile Carlos Pinto Durán; 21. Attorney General Julio Plaza Ferrand; 22. Senator Armando Quezada; 23. The Undurraga family residence (Palacio Undurraga); 24. Deputy Tomás Ramírez; 25. Deputy Carlos Alberto Ruíz; 26. Former president Juan Luis Sanfuentes; 27. Deputy and Minister of Hacienda Guillermo Subercaseaux; 28. Police prefect Rafael Toledo Tagle; 29. Deputy Oscar Urzua Jaramillo; 30. Deputy Claudio Vicuña Subercaseaux; 31. Senator Enrique Zañartu Prieto; 32. Senator (and son-in-law of Juan Luis Sanfuentes) Héctor Zañartu Prieto; 33. Senator Carlos Aldunate Solar; 34. Member of the presidential tribunal Ramón Briones Luco; 35. Consul General to the U.S. and senior official in the Bank of Chile Carlos Castro Ruíz; 36. Deputy Víctor Celis Maturana. Map by David Ethridge.

with Chile's incorporation into a global economy, and the rapid mineral expansion with the capture of the nitrate-rich northern provinces during the War of the Pacific—the city solidified itself not only as the bureaucratic seat of power but also as the cultural and social center for Chile's aristocracy and nouveau riche as well as its foreign industrialists and capitalists. As the city expanded, they continued to populate the colonial center and ranged to locations just south of the Alameda, building homes inspired by an eclectic mix of influences from Paris, Moorish Spain, and Renaissance Italy.[17] The aristocratic pomp persisted well in to the first decades of the twentieth century with, among others, the completion in 1920 of the Palacio Undurraga, built at the request and expense of Domingo Undurraga Fernández's father. Meanwhile, the areas further south of the Alameda and west of the parque Brasil were populated by working people in larger and larger numbers, a phenomenon which had, as early as the 1870s, raised increasing concerns about vice, crime, and disease. Intendent Benjamin Vicuña Mackenna (1872–1875) formalized the spatial distinctions with a Hausmann-inspired reconstruction of parts of Santiago, establishing a *cordón sanitaire* between the city center (or what he termed the "ciudad propia")—with its new efforts at potable water, sanitation, commercial activity, macadam-laid streets, tree-lined avenues, and the like—and the marginal areas (or suburbs) inhabited by working people. As with most social engineering projects, Mackenna's were marginally successful at best and the paramount "social question" persisted into the new century.[18]

Figure 3.4
The Palacio Undurraga, finished in 1915, was built for Luis Undurraga Fernández, a conservative party politician whose son was one of the leaders of the attacks on the FECh. From Chiléctrica S.A.'s *Transeléctrica: 75 años* (Santiago: Colofón, 1996), 63.

In the wake of the War of the Pacific, and flush with earnings from export taxes on nitrates mined in the captured northern borderlands, Chile's governing elite invested in infrastructure. The government, and Santiago itself, grew rapidly. By the early 1900s, for residents Santiago must have been an experience both exhilirating and unsettling, a dizzying world in flux (one captured with poetic force in Pablo Neruda's early poems such as "Galope Muerto" and "Walking Around" in which the form and content is one of juxtaposition, disorientation, and contingency combined with a feeling overwhelmingly melancholic and fragmentary).[19] The early 1900s were, in Chile as elsewhere, years in which men and women felt as if they lived on the cusp of a new world. They would have marveled at the changing urban physiognomy. For the 1910 *centenario*, Santiago seemed to be in perpetual transformation with new buildings and parks taking shape in the urban landscape. The Palace of Fine Arts and the Tribunales de Justicia were being built, the Moneda underwent expansion, the Parque Forestal was created, and the cerro San Cristobal reforested and integrated into the city with a zoo and a funicular to take residents to the top.[20] Consumer culture rose to new heights in the form of the multistory British-owned Gath y Chaves department store, built one block from the Plaza de Armas in 1910.[21] Shoppers could admire the latest in fashion and then take an elevator to the fourth floor for tea.[22]

Residents saw the arrival of Hudson, Dodge, and Ford motorcars, as well as Indian motorcycles, particularly after 1912 when the luxury tax of 60 percent which had previously been applied to the importation of automobiles was reduced to 15 percent.[23] While the number of motorized cars in Santiago in 1911 could have been counted on two hands, in 1917 alone nearly four thousand such vehicles arrived on Chilean shores, more than half of which were destined for the capital.[24] Cars initially had a hard time circulating in the city and their cost made them an elite item, although there was a suprisingly robust rental car market by 1918.[25] Taxicabs became commonplace too and questions arose around how best to make fares uniform.[26] Even so, for most in the city the main source of public transportation remained the tram which expanded rapidly as electric lines, introduced in 1900, replaced the draft animal as a power source.[27] Conflicts over fares between the streetcar company and the Municipality of Santiago reveal just how much Santiago's public depended on streetcar transportation.[28]

Even the skies were not immune to change: airplanes, though rare, left the press clamoring for photographs of pilots once back on earth.[29] Wires and cables criss-crossed the pedestrian's horizon, a kind of thin scaffolding upon which the density of the modern city was draped, as electric

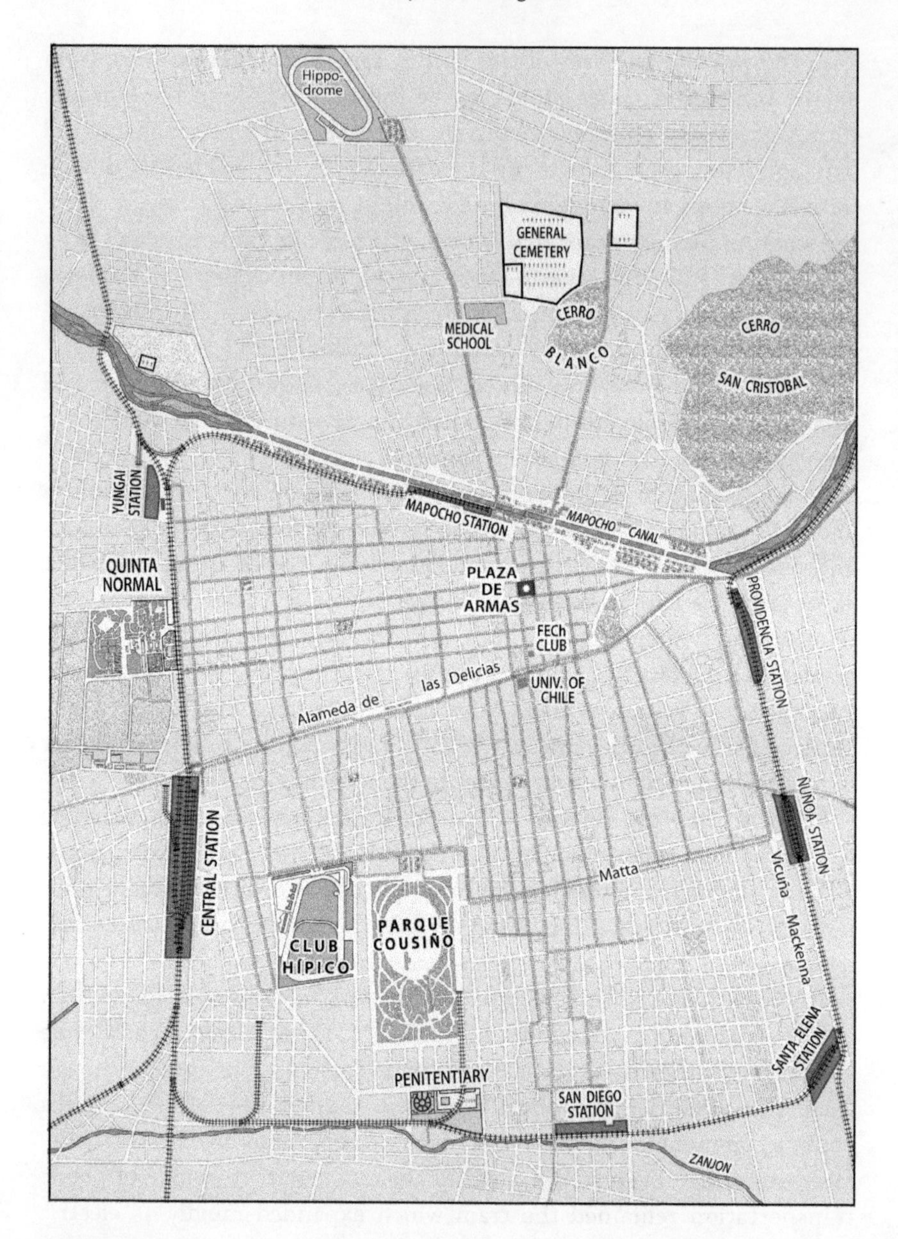

Figure 3.5
Mobile city. The major tram and train lines that increasingly facilitated travel across and around neighborhoods. Map by David Ethridge.

streetlights lit the downtown, replacing gas and parafin lamps.[30] Cinemas appeared, dazzling viewers who lined up to watch films such as *La agonia de Arauco* (1917), one of the first films to be directed by a woman, as well as the array of imports from Hollywood studios such as Fox, Paramount, and Goldwyn.[31] A proliferation of newspapers and magazines, filled with images and articles of far-flung places, brought the world to the pedestrian in kiosks on street corners while others oriented the newcomer to the growing metropolis.[32]

As well as excitement there was anxiety. The dizzying array of technological changes that pumped elite self-confidence also primed consternation. Mass culture could appear threatening, and not "culture" at all. In the new world of the cinemas, social classes mixed. New forms of association between workers and students created feelings of disassociation among others accustomed to more rigid class boundaries. The "death of God" and the crisis in artistic representation had its corollary in the rise of a politics that questioned the very possibility of representation. The continuous influx of migrants from the north, the concomitant growth of the city, and the networks of mobility within it meant that Santiago's neighborhoods were increasingly traversed by a teeming raif of urban strangers. Santiago, like Balzac's Paris decades earlier, was more and more composed of "spaces without genre."[33]

New genres appeared in an effort to make sense of such changes. The avant-garde poetry of Vicente Huidobro, Pablo de Rokha, and Pablo Neruda would attempt to translate the experience of such flux in to literary form, as would that of Gómez Rojas in poems such as "Suburbs." But these served as little consolation for Santiago's well-to-do who saw only cause for further concern in such literary experimentation. They could, however, find hope, if not solace, in a different genre: the detective story. In the midst of Santiago's explosive growth, in 1914, Chile's first modern detective story appeared in *Pacífico* Magazine. The work of Alberto Edwards, the story would be the first of many published over the subsequent decade detailing the exploits of Román Calvo, "the Chilean Sherlock Holmes."[34] As were those of his British counterpart ("Like the world itself, the detective novel is controlled by the English," wrote Berthold Brecht), Calvo's feats were measured in logic, rationality, and deduction.[35] It was a comforting fiction. The literary detective came of age in an era in which police scandals—from incompetence at one end of the spectrum to criminality at the other—rocked Santiago. Calvo, an amateur detective, had little time or need for the police. Indeed, although they are not presented as criminals, they are superfluous to his investigations, thus sidestepping the entire problem of police corruption and reform. The detective novel more generally distilled the impenetrability of the city, its overwhelming strangeness, in to a discrete event—a crime. The city's pervasive opacity could thus be translated in to a finite mystery that could be solved and, with it, a reassurance that the sense of impending social crisis had itself been resolved.[36] Finally, Calvo's methodology is crucial. It is his powers of observation, combined with a tellingly photographic memory, that constantly yield success, a reassuring methodology for many of the city's residents: the truth is there to be found, and with it, order restored. All that is required is acute observation and deduction. In other words, the social order itself was not in question, despite unsettling signs to the contrary.[37]

Textual comfort was not always enough. The city's well-to-do sought other ways to cope. Some decamped for new upscale suburbs under construction to the east of the city center, even as poor and working-class suburbs grew in the city's west and south. Others urged support for institutions such as the Young Men and Young Women's Christian Associations (YMCA and YWCA), which focused on "sports, patriotic education and social service."[38] The Boy Scouts offered similar opportunities: one Chilean scoutmaster argued that the scouts should be declared a national institution, organized along military lines, and oriented toward combatting maximalism.[39] New zoning regulations were put in place to oversee the city's growth. Fears of disorderly development and subversive politics gave a new urgency to discussions of urban planning and soon efforts to develop affordable housing for workers were underway.[40] In 1910 Chile's Mortgage Bank, under the direction of Barros Borgoño (Alessandri's opponent in the 1920 presidential election), undertook low-income housing initiatives in parts of the city where workers could ostensibly purchase a home with 10 percent down and a monthly mortgage of some 8 percent, or rent for around 40 pesos per month. One of the first such projects appeared near the penitentiary and the slaughterhouse in Santiago's southern reaches.[41] Such initiatives often had overtly political objectives. For example, affordable housing plans were often intended as a means to stem the apparent popularity of anarchism.[42] They were also efforts to reestablish a sense of order in a welter of change, to issue spatial declaratives in a city that appeared increasingly written in the subjunctive.

Santiago's elites were learning that the city was no longer their own.[43] The events on Ahumada Street and in the Plaza de Armas that third week of July—the repeated assaults on the FECh, the shooting of Julio Covarrubias—seemed only to confirm for many their imminent loss of the city to a mass of agitators, subversives, and assorted rabble, even if, in many cases, the violence and turmoil had been carried out by their own sons. It was not necessarily disorder that they feared, but a change in the order of things—or, even worse, a new order, one perhaps less favorable to their interests or less recognizable. They perceived a new order coming into being around them. Nominally public spaces that had long been the purview of the city's elite—central parks and plazas, for example—appeared increasingly available to nonelites.[44] Motorcars were haphazardly being incorporated into the city's daily life—questions remained regarding which side of the road to drive on, rights of way, and speed limits—and accidents were common. The same was true for trams. While the shift to electric power did little to improve the system's reliability and its accident rate, it did have other visible effects.[45] Changes in gender roles were becoming apparent as a full quarter of the Santiago streetcar staff were women, working primarily as conductors and collectors.[46] (Factory labor shared similar gendered demographics, with nearly a third of Santiago's industrial factory labor composed of women.)[47] Public transport expanded work and leisure options for poor and wealthy alike. As migrants arrived from the provinces, housing and development expanded toward what were former peripheries and new working-class districts—such as that around the Estación Central—sprung up like "mushrooms" and were incorporated into a modern web of telegraph lines, electrical wires, trains, and the temporalities of the city, measured by a large clock mounted on the facade of the Central Station.[48] With a coin or two in their pockets, working people increasingly traveled farther through and across the city for work and leisure.[49] Even the most distant corners of the city—defined in large part by what they lacked, such as potable water, electric lighting, decent housing, paved streets—were

Figure 3.6
Mobility. Tram riders cling to the sides of the trams during peak times in Santiago. From Chiléctrica S.A.'s *Transeléctrica: 75 años* (Santiago: Colofón, 1996), 49.

connected to the city center, allowing populations to move through the city's streets more quickly and regularly than ever before. And move en masse they did. Trams powered by electricity meant that the size of the carriages and number of passengers was no longer limited by what an animal could pull. Double-decker cars—with an open-air upper deck where passengers could smoke—were soon commonplace.[50] Streetcars ran from 5:30 a.m. to 9:30 p.m. and were packed at the beginning and end of the work day and during lunch hours, with passengers and more than a few free-riders clinging to the outsides of the carriages.[51]

Figure 3.7
Vagabond radicals. A newspaper published this image with the suggestion that the man was a vagabond radical getting the latest on Lenin. Courtesy of the Institute for Social History.

Meanwhile, at every level, new officials attempted to control, monitor, and limit the movement of the wrong people. If Vicuña Mackenna's cordon sanitaire had emphasized enclosure or exclusion, by the 1910s administrations were concerned with mobility or social "traffic."[52] Increased, rapid mobility was a visible specter haunting the visions of the city's elite, concerned as they were with contact, disease, contagion, and mass politics. Circulation may have been the lifeblood of capital, but it was also the transit for infection. Santiago's mayor, during the typhus outbreak in the city in December 1919, asked the intendent to put limits on the number of riders on tram cars to avoid contagion.[53] If the well-to-do feared coming down with typhus or tuberculosis, they worried too about the health of Chilean workers who might at any moment contract "the red flu" of maximalism or the "old-world virus" of anarchism. They might catch it on trams, which had long been sites of labor activism, or in the passageways and patios of the city's numerous conventillos. Or they could catch it on streets, where books, pamphlets, and magazines of dubious origin and orientation circulated among "intellectual vagrants" and radical vagabonds. If literate, they could catch it in the places where streets and words met: a printer's shop or a bookstore.

WORDS RED AND BLACK

If there was a maker of words in red and black in Santiago, it was Julio Valiente. Valiente operated, along with former FECh president Santiago Labarca, a small but well-known printshop and press called *Numen*. A long-time organizer and anarchist as well as the typographer's union representative to the AOAN in 1918, Valiente was well known to workers and students.[54] He was also well known to the police. His print shop sat only one block east of a police station on the northern edge of the barrio Latino, and he had been in and out of jail on various charges, mostly political, over the years.

Born in 1882, Valiente had been raised by his widowed mother in a ramshackle house near the Mapocho river in Santiago.[55] Here his mother cobbled together a living to support her son and daughter. By the turn of the century he had become involved with workers' movements in Santiago. He recalled how "small groups of workers and intellectuals began to publish some anarchist newspapers, which always distinguished themselves with their attacks on political parties and their advice to the worker to believe neither bosses nor politicians and they recommended direct action by the population through its labor unions."[56] He was also attracted to such organizations for their trenchant critique of the church, which continued to exercise substantial influence over social and cultural life, and their commitment to free thinking. With a number of other young working men, Valiente helped found in 1905 Santiago's Giordano Bruno Anticlerical Propaganda Center.[57]

In 1905 Valiente had traveled north to Iquique, with anarchist and poet Francisco Pezoa, to help with the editing and printing of an anarchist weekly.[58] While there he saw first-hand the exploitative practices of the nitrate companies, including the monopolies they exercised on basic foodstuffs which they sold at elevated prices to workers, as well as the brutal treatment of workers and their families. When a smallpox epidemic struck the region in late 1905, the members of the family with whom Valiente stayed fell ill, including the children. Fearful of the spread of contagion, the authorities turned them out of their home, an act Valiente equated with outright assassination.[59]

Valiente and Pezoa evidently did not find fertile ground for their ideas in the north, and at some point returned to Santiago.[60] Valiente increasingly came under scrutiny from the police, being detained and arrested repeatedly between 1906 and 1920.[61] When not in jail, Valiente printed. By 1918 or early 1919 he had became a joint owner of the *Numen* printshop with Labarca.[62] Valiente dedicated his machinery and labor to translating ideas into words and spent his hours transmitting ideas "letter by letter, word for word, to the frames" and, eventually, to paper.[63] An array of political pamphlets and papers rolled off of the presses at *Numen*, including two of the most important anarcho-communist publications of the era: *Verba Roja*, under the direction of anarchists Armando Triviño and Manuel Silva, and the somewhat wider-ranging eponymous *Numen: Seminario de Arte, Sociología, Actualidades y Comercio*, which at various points was edited by Labarca and two young poets, Juan Egaña and Pablo de Rokha. It also counted Juan Gandulfo and José Santos González Vera among its regular contributors.[64]

With the proliferation of printing technologies, pamphlets, newspapers, and manifestos could be produced and circulated quickly. Printing presses soon became central targets of repression, to the degree that both language and the technologies that facilitated it became sites of political struggle. Papers, pamphlets, and circulars published by *Verba Roja* and *Numen* were considered instruments designed to promote the overthrow of the social order.[65] Working men and women caught distributing either of the papers faced persecution.[66] Editors, printers, and writers repeatedly confronted police persecution and censorship. Triviño, Silva, Labarca, Egaña, and Valiente all had been arrested on numerous occasions for writing or publishing articles and editorials deemed subversive by the authorities. At one point the editors of *Verba Roja*—Triviño and Silva—had written an open letter to their worker comrades pointing out that they had been arrested not for their actions, but for their words. They had published in *Verba Roja* a call for soldiers to understand that they were exploited and to make common cause with their laboring brothers.[67] For this the publication had been declared subversive, copies of the text seized, and its editors arrested and jailed. Their letter of critique from prison appeared in *Numen*, as did a stinging limerick critiquing Ismael Vicuña Subercaseaux, who had publicly affirmed the importance of freedom of the press yet remained silent when radical editors were arrested:

> This Ismael, it seems to me
> Doesn't have much in the way of brains
> As he forgets the case of "Numen"
> And that of "Verba Roja"[68]

As well as arrest and censorship, editors and printers suffered at the hands of assailants who ransacked their businesses with impunity. In January of 1919 in Iquique, patriots had laid waste to the printshop that produced the socialist *El Despertar de los Trabajadores*, destroying everything on the premises that had been purchased "penny by penny by pampean workers."[69] Other printshops suffered similar fates, as did, eventually, *Numen* on July 19, only hours after the first assault on the FECh and the arrest of Juan Gandulfo. That the FECh club and the *Numen* print shop proved to be the targets of violence on the same day was no coincidence. Both were linked by particular figures: Santiago Labarca and Juan Gandulfo (who frequently wrote under the pen-name Ivan for *Numen*) most obviously. Both the club and print shop were also seen as sites in which student leaders in the FECh and workers made common cause. It is hard not to see in the assault a destruction of possible words, a pre-emptive book burning of the kind that would in fact take place two days later in front of the FECh club. In a brief spate of fury, the assailants laid waste to the shop: they destroyed binding machines, linotypes and typographs, and composing sticks; they pilfered or damaged inks, paper, tables, and blocks. Just as his premises were criminally ransacked, Valiente was taken into police custody, as he had been on so many previous occasions, for publishing purportedly subversive material.[70] This time the claim was he had published a pamphlet containing the statutes of the IWW. He did not deny the charge. Earlier that year, he confirmed, he had printed three thousand copies of the statutes at the request of Juan Chamorro, for the sum of 350 pesos, paid by Manuel Antonio Silva. "I did not," he continued, "pay attention to the specifics of the publication, as it is not the practice in my establishment to submit the contracted publications to prior censorship." While admitting that "some twenty years earlier" he had held anarchist ideas, he denied that he continued to hold such ideas and, he added, he avoided participating in union activities and political issues.[71] The police were not convinced.

Thus on the very same day that Casimiro Barrios would make his way across the Sama River to Peru and Juan Gandulfo would walk home in the rain from a neighborhood police station, Julio Valiente found himself in a cell, detained indefinitely for purported affiliations with the IWW and for subversion. He was the first of many and his stay would be long.

WOBBLIES, ANARCHISTS, AND ANARCHO-SYNDICALISTS

Writing in defense of many of those who would be accused of subversion, attorney and parliamentarian Torrealba located the origins of their persecution in an unusual place: a bookstore. At some point in early 1920 a conservative politician, most likely Carlos Aldunate Solar, visited Santiago's Librería Hume. There he acquired a copy of US writer Paul Brissenden's large volume *The I.W.W.: A Study of American Syndicalism*, published in New York the previous year.[72] Despite the fact that Brissenden's work was in large measure a defense of the IWW "against charges of subversion and treason," the politician's attention focused on the US government's accusations against the Wobblies and its efforts to expel the Wobbly leadership as foreign agitators.[73] Before long Brissenden's hefty tome made its way to the floor of the Senate where it was marshalled as evidence in a foregone conclusion: the foreign Wobblies in Chile had to go.

The bluster was misplaced. The IWW in the "chilean region" was not led by foreign agitators but by native-born labor leaders.[74] It traced its origins to organizing efforts and strikes by various port worker federations and unions in Valparaíso. In the 1910s dock and maritime workers continued to push for an 8-hour workday with a maximum of four additional overtime hours. They also sought a reduction of the cargo weight they were expected to load or unload. Manuel Rojas would recall that dock workers were typically expected to unload barrels of carbide weighing upward of 105 kilos, and organizers sought to reduce that limit to 92 kilos.[75] Out of this experience—and the increased contacts between maritime workers along the Pacific coast, from Valparaíso to San Francisco—eventually emerged the IWW in Valparaíso in 1917.[76]

It was in many cases dockworkers, stevedores, sailors, and others associated with port labor who gravitated toward the IWW's form of industrial anarcho-syndicalism.[77] Ports were important places for the circulation of such ideas and Chile, with its coastline of some 2,500 miles, had some fifty-nine ports, fifteen of which had customs houses.[78] Of all Chile's ports, Valparaíso was the most important. Indeed, it "shined as the most active and richest of the Pacific ports" of all Latin America during its heyday from 1848 and the California Gold Rush to the 1915 opening of the Panama canal.[79] Wheat, flour, bran, alfafa hay, beans, and cattle were exported from here; vast quantities of steel, barbed wire, machinery, galvanized iron sheets, pipes and fittings, pine lumber, automobiles, sewing machines, cases of toys, print paper, linseed oil, olive oil, salmon, rice, sugar, chinaware, crockery, coffee, porcelain, glassware, cement, cotton goods, and dynamite arrived to be consumed during Chile's modernization.[80] Liverpool, Hamburg, Genoa, Callao, Hong Kong, and Panama were all linked to Valparaíso through shipping lanes. The IWW by 1919 had established itself as a major presence among working men on the docks, organizing stevedores, lightermen, sailors, and an array of others, as well as bakers. It would have successes such as when it organized stevedores to refuse to load foodstuffs onto ships in the wake of the AOAN mobilizations of 1918 and 1919.[81]

The IWW quickly expanded to other parts of the country, its ideology and tenets spread by members who were often regionally itinerant.[82] Although perhaps strongest among port workers, the IWW had success in organizing workers in other industries and trades and in places such as Santiago. Furniture workers, whose skills were in high demand, were a serious force with which to be reckoned and in early 1920 affiliated with the IWW.[83] Santiago's bricklayers, carpenters, and plasterers and others in the building trades similarly formed close bonds with the IWW, as did masons, painters, stone pavers, tailors, and breadmakers.[84] Indeed, the building trades would compose a significant component of the IWW by the early 1920s, second only to the maritime workers of Valparaíso.[85] Despite the fact that the more centralized form of organizing in the IWW did not resonate with some labor groups, such as the printers and the powerful Shoeworker's Federation (Santiago counted at the time some forty shoe factories and accounted for a large percentage of shoes made in Chile) who valued more autonomous or federalized forms of organizing, all viewed the IWW as a "natural ally."[86]

The array of individuals who would be accused of being members of the IWW were ideologically diverse and eclectic. Not all of those in the IWW were, nor did they refer to themselves as, anarchists; and many anarchists were not necessarily members or affiliates of the IWW.[87] Some were members of the IWW, others were members of various federations and unions that overlapped in ways with the organization. This was, on one level, unimportant to the police and to the businessmen and factory owners of Santiago who had, over the course of the previous three years, confronted a wave of successful organizational efforts by unions and federations. The Shoeworker's Federation had managed to organize most of Santiago's leatherworkers. Bakers, tailors, and tannery workers mobilized and organized, as did workers in the glass factories, many of whom struck their employers in July 1920. Printers, like shoeworkers, saw organizational successes during the same period, reestablishing the defunct Federation of Printing Workers.[88] Indeed, both shoeworkers and printers unions saw major growth in membership after winning serious concessions from the employers whom they struck. The FOCH had over the previous two years experienced success in organizing unskilled and female workers, and Santiago councils had been formed within the FOCh by workers in a range of other professions, including tram conductors, millers, and textile workers.[89]

As well as labor activism, efforts to undermine military discipline and commitment alarmed officials. Police spies reported that Wobblies spoke "in violent terms" against the military and distributed propaganda among young workers urging them to not show up to the barracks when summoned for duty.[90] This was an issue of repeated concern for the authorities as there had been numerous calls over the years for the abolition of obligatory military service. In 1913 José Domingo Gómez Rojas—who at the time would have been of age for obligatory service—spoke out at a public gathering against it.[91] The FOCh, among others, had spoken out against obligatory military service, in part because of the government's willingness to use military personnel as scabs when telephone workers struck in late 1919.[92] In March of 1920, the intendent sought to bring charges against *Verba Roja* for an article it published calling for "youth between the ages of 15 and 20" to not show up to the barracks when called upon to complete their military service.[93] The Sanfuentes administration by this point was concerned with the impact such calls might have on its efforts to quickly muster reservists for duty on the border with Peru and the potential for dissent in the barracks. In the meantime, rumors circulated that some of the military in parts of the country would be on the side of "the people" were serious unrest to occur.[94] "Whose side are you on, brother soldier?" asked the Revolutionary Workers Committee in one of its manifestos seized by the police. Arguing that the military was used as a means to divide the working class, the authors continued: "There are only two armies, forever enemies: that of the exploiters and that of the workers."[95] Interested readers were referred to a broad array of Left intellectuals: "Bakunine, Kropotkine, Hamon, Trotzky, Lenine, Grave, Malatesta, Malato, Ferri, etc." (Given the names and spellings, it seems likely the author of, or inspiration for, the pamphlet was French.) One could imagine it was precisely such manifestos that the Minister of the Interior worried were being distributed when he received word that various subversives were sidling up to the reservists at the train stations to discuss their "theories" and to undermine discipline.[96]

In the wake of such mobilizations, organizing, agitating, and strike activity, the IWW and anarchism served as shorthands for those concerned with the increasing strength of the labor movement, its recent organizational successes, and the momentum it seemed to be carrying in the midst of a volatile electoral and social period. Officials marshalled all of the possible stereotypes available to them, stereotypes they had already deployed in their battle against Casimiro Barrios: of anarchists, anarcho-syndicalists, and Wobblies as little more than bomb-throwers and nihilists.

While simplifications of anarchism abound perhaps no image has held sway as strongly as the image of anarchism as a murky underworld of conspiratorial bomb throwers, held together less by bonds of solidarity than by a commitment to violence. To critique such an image is not to deny the realities out of which it at times could arise, particularly in the last two decades of the nineteenth century and the first years of the twentieth. From the Russian conspirators of the 1870s to Alexander Berkman's attempt on the life of Henry Clay Frick to the bungled plot that inspired Joseph Conrad's *The Secret Agent*, the *attentat* was real enough.[97] Chile was hardly immune. In 1912 a young man—who purportedly described himself as an anarchist—assassinated two "bourgeois" as revenge for the massacre of workers in Iquique and the "catastrophe in the El Teniente mine."[98] Even so, these events account for only a small portion of anarchist activity. Indeed, it is not clear that one can even assume anarchist responsibility for many of the similar deeds that proliferated around the world. Historian Murray Bookchin, for example, has persuasively shown that in the case of fin-de-siècle Spain such deeds were often carried out by individuals with little organized commitment to or participation in anarchist movements, individuals who were "less often libertarian socialists or communists than desperate men and women who used weapons and explosives to protest the injustices and philistinism of their time, putatively in the name of 'propaganda of the deed.'"[99] Because anarchism has been so quickly equated with acts of terror, any individual act not otherwise explained has become ipso facto an anarchist act, as if the act itself was all that could be said about the ideology. This simply replicates the language of the police.

The point is not to dismiss or soft-pedal the actions and histories of such individuals: to do so would be, in the words of historian Beverly Gage, to rob "at least a few revolutionaries of their militancy—of the idea that when they spoke of dynamite and armed resistance, they sometimes meant what they said."[100] Violence rarely may have solved much, but neither did submission.[101] Visions of transforming the system through reasoned debate and appeals to man's "better nature" were often blind to the realities of class power, political practice, and the immediate and intrinsic violence of the system. From the quotidian crunch of the truncheon to the crackle of gunfire that punctuated recurrent massacres, state- and company-directed violence against working people was as pervasive as the structural violence of deprivation, exploitation and hunger. The working people and anarchists who populate the pages of Manuel Rojas's semiautobiographical novels battle many things including the police, overseers, exploitation, and a complicit government, but the violence they all confront daily is that of sheer hunger, born of an unjust system.[102] That system was rooted in wage labor. And the heart of IWW organizing and agitation was the abolition of the wage system through "revolutionary syndicalism in the street, the workshop, and [the] family."[103] This was well-known to the police and state officials, given that none of these objectives were secret. Why should they have been? The IWW was not, prior to 1920, a proscribed organization.[104] It published a monthly bulletin and numerous items relating to its work appeared in papers such as *Verba Roja* and *Numen*. Brissenden's book was hardly the first introduction to the IWW for Chilean officials. Officials had been aware of the organization's existence at least as early as 1919 when it held a large public demonstration in Santiago's barrio Latino.[105] As of April 1920, a special investigation had been underway in Iquique to determine the role of the IWW in relation to strikes and work stoppages in the region.[106] But the social and political context of the 1920 austral winter spurred the administration to look differently at the IWW and to equate it, and its objectives, with nihilistic violence.

Despite the structural and political violence inherent in the system within which they lived, Wobblies and anarchists were hesitant regarding, and wrestled intensely with, the use of violence. The conflation of anarchism and terrorism, or anarchism and nihilistic violence, unfortunately not only mirrors the language of anarchism's antagonists, but also ignores the substantial opposition to such violence voiced by multitudes of anarchist organizers and thinkers and robs militants of what was frequently a reasoned and restrained response to the pervasive institutional and officially sanctioned violence that surrounded them. Reclus and Kropotkin were deeply ambivalent regarding propaganda by the deed. Malatesta spoke consistently and vociferously against the use of violence except as a defensive reaction. Similar rejections of the equation of anarchism with violence were voiced in Chile. FECh President Alfredo Demaría, in a manifesto published in *El Mercurio*, noted that never "have we [FECh members associated with anarchism] supported violence as a means to solve social problems."[107] When a chemistry student informed González Vera that he was learning to make bombs and would provide them free of charge, the young writer informed him that anarchists trusted their convictions and rejected resorting to force.[108] Self-described anarchists sought myriad ways to agitate and organize, often preferring the "word" to the "deed." Cultural centers, literacy programs, printing presses, theater performances, and public discourses in key parts of Santiago were standard tools for organizing and for social transformation.[109] When anarchist agitator and publisher Armando Triviño wrote of "bombs," he referred to incendiary devices made of "paper and ink" rather than nitroglycerine and gunpowder.[110] His ideological comrades on the other side of the Andes shared similar sentiments, raising money and taxing bosses in order not to purchase fuses to light but a printing press to crank.[111]

Even so, Wobblies and anarchists repeatedly and not surprisingly confronted radical distortions of their aims and methods. At a 1922 congress members of the Chilean region's IWW had to yet again clarify and emphasize the meanings of direct action.

> More than in any other way, it is with respect to its methods that the IWW perhaps has been least understood. Our methods are based on direct action. Direct action is simply the opposite of indirect action which faithfully characterizes the action of official Unions. We understand direct action to mean the following: that workers act on their own behalf, rather than limiting themselves to paying a monthly sum of money to certain leaders or *caudillos* [bosses], or professional bosses, so that these can do and undo as they wish, without being accountable, in the majority of cases, to the will of the masses. This is what we call indirect action, or action carried out through representatives. Direct action, then, is the method of action adopted spontaneously by the masses in common agreement. *The term has been misinterpreted intentionally by our enemies who make it refer to assassination, arson and all that is understood as violence and destruction.*[112]

Direct action referred to boycotts, forms of sabotage, the general strike, and "labeling," primarily for the purposes of fomenting autonomy, mutual aid, and worker control.[113] In some cases forms of direct action were legal. This should come as no surprise: men and women were hardly willing to simply abandon the law or to dismiss it as a mere fiction upon which class power rested. They fought repeatedly for the creation and enforcement of laws that defended working men and women from the depredations of capitalists. At the same time some forms of direct action were illegal. How could they not be? "As if the law had ever permitted a subject class to shake off its yoke," wrote anarchist organizer and historian Rudolph Rocker.[114] Even so, unlawful is a broad category and should not be blithely equated with terrorism and planting bombs. These are hardly the only ways for people to be militant. In fact, in early twentieth-century Chile, one was much more likely to find the police planting the dynamite, in order to frame suspected anarchists.[115]

THE PROSECUTOR

Drawing from Brissenden's book, and armed with various issues of *Numen* and *Verba Roja*, officials went on the attack. They stressed the IWW's purported assaults on the "established order, fundamental institutions, and the laws of the Republic," and they noted approvingly that it "had been pursued and dissolved in all the countries of the world where it has wanted to set up camp."[116] Chile, it appeared, was to be no different.

The initial move came the day after the attacks on Valiente's printshop. In Valparaíso, the evening of July 20, the police arrested Juan Onofre Chamorro. A long-time organizer among port workers, he had also played a central role in the formation of a Valparaíso branch of the IWW.[117] The following day, July 21, police raided the Valparaíso hall of the IWW, arresting some 175 workers who were there at the time. After beating the men and clearing the hall, one of the police discovered some ten sticks of dynamite, revolvers, and other weapons.[118] These were later determined to have been planted by the police at the orders of Enrique Caballero, captain of the Valparaíso security section.[119] While the Valparaíso police detained Chamorro and planted dynamite, officials in Santiago mobilized. Their first step was to appoint a special prosecutor, with broad powers, to investigate vigorously cases of subversion. That man was José Astorquiza Líbano.

Figure 3.8
The Judge. José Astorquiza was appointed special prosecutor to oversee the pursuit and persecution of alleged subversives. Courtesy of the Institute for Social History.

On July 22, a day after the assault on the FECh club and the shooting of Julio Covarrubias, Astorquiza was summoned to La Moneda to meet with Minister Montt and attorney general Julio Plaza Ferrand, who had been involved in the repression of workers dating back to 1911.[120] José Astorquiza was born in 1866. Both of his parents were from Vizcaya, Spain. His father captained merchant vessels, including the Spanish ship on which Astorquiza himself was born while it sat anchored in the Peruvian port of Callao. The vessel made its way to Montevideo where the infant was baptized in 1868. These details of his birth and infancy would become hotly disputed as the prosecution of subversives unfolded, with some suggesting he had in fact been born in Lima and was, therefore, Peruvian. What is certain is that his family moved to Chile when he was still a child, with his father settling on a rural estate.[121] Asencio Astorquiza acquired by the early twentieth century various expanses of land in and around Linares, outside of Talca, where he raised his family, including sons José (the eldest), Eliodoro (who would go on to become a writer and literary critic), and Octavio (who would serve as a representative for Linares, intendent of the island province of Chiloé, and join the conservatives).[122] José Astorquiza moved to the University of Chile, where he earned his degree in law and political science in 1889. He returned to Talca in 1891 and soon joined a revolutionary junta opposing then-President Balmaceda.[123] After stints in various positions in Talca, he was appointed Minster of the Court of Appeals in Santiago in 1906 and served as a special judge in Taltal in 1907 investigating possible fraud in the issuance of titles to land in the nitrate zone, a controversy that for a short period of time embroiled future president Arturo Alessandri but also apparently Astorquiza himself.[124] In subsequent years, his work earned him a reputation as a man of "energy and uprightness" and someone who did not shy away from difficult cases. Nor did he shy away from strongly asserting his opinions, often at odds with his fellow judges. For example, in 1916 Astorquiza opposed the vacating of a decision against vinyard owner Gustavo Toro Concha who, along with Sara Rosa Castro, a maid employed at his home, had been found guilty of murdering his young wife. Due to an abundance of contradictory and circumstantial evidence, two of the three ministers on the appeals court overturned the previous verdict finding Toro Concha and Castro guilty. Astorquiza was the sole voice of dissent and offered a lengthy and vigorous opinion on why the original guilty verdict should stand. His opinion was shared by much of the public who had followed the case closely and were scandalized by the vacated guilty verdict. The original guilty verdict was soon upheld when the appeals court decision was itself overturned.[125]

Astorquiza's reputation influenced his being selected as the special prosecutor in 1920.[126] There may have been other reaons for his selection. According to Carlos Vicuña Fuentes, a former student leader and attorney for a number of those arrested during the prosecution, Astorquiza was a man under financial duress. He had either purchased or inherited property in Linares (as early as 1908 he owned a large property in Villa Alegre) and had incurred substantial debt to Chile's National Mortgage Bank.[127] The Mortgage Bank had been created in 1855 in order to expand credit access to landowners. The terms of the bank were such that it favored large landowners in the central valley by allowing them to borrow, at relatively low interest, up to half the value of their land. The bank garnered a reputation as another manifestation of aristocratic privilege and nepotism. At one point in time it was overseen by Luis Barros Borgoño—who would run against Alessandri in 1920—who populated the ranks of the agency with a large number of his relatives.[128] The bank's reputation apparently followed Astorquiza. According to Vicuña Fuentes, the property in Linares should have been repossessed but the authorities had looked the other way, perhaps because Astorquiza was a member of the Santiago Court of Appeals. Was Astorquiza appointed special prosecutor at the meeting at La Moneda with the implicit quid pro quo that in exchange for dealing harshly with students, workers, and others who could be accused of subversion, his debts would be forgiven? That the very candidate running against Alessandri—whose followers were deemed to be among the array of "subversives" in the city—had long-lasting and intimate ties with the bank to which Astorquiza may have been indebted is suggestive, if admittedly circumstantial. Regardless, if Vicuña Fuentes's assertion is true, it would mean that even as Astorquiza prepared to jail purported subversives, he was himself an unfree man.

This is neither a defense of, nor justification for, Astorquiza's subsequent actions. The fact is he subverted the law and bears much responsibility for the sufferings of those detained during the *proceso*. But there is some value in pointing to the context within which Astorquiza operated, if for no other reason than to avoid Old Testament narratives of good and evil which do little to advance our understanding of the past and present. Partisan narratives of the era cast Astorquiza as the Pontius Pilate to Gómez Rojas's Jesus. Astorquiza's actions should not be distilled down to single-minded anti-anarchist vengeance. Such a perspective is problematic on two fronts: first, it implies that in some ways what happened was an aberration in the democratic order of things. It was not. Repression is built in to the order of things and in such a manner as to tolerate a high degree of what would otherwise appear to be disorder. Such a point seems especially salient given that the anarchist critique of the state is that the state itself is, in some ways, disorder. Second, too much emphasis on Astorquiza relieves those around him, including some of Chile's dominant families and political elite, as well as the economic and political structure within which they operated, of responsibility for what ensued. Chile's parliamentary order was, as one early twentieth century commentator put it, akin to that of England: in both, "an aristocracy of birth and wealth has unquestioned control of social and political life."[129] Too emphatic a focus on Astorquiza—or any judge, or police chief, or bailiff, or surveyor—isolates him from the social system within which he operated and upon which he was dependent.[130] Astorquiza was no puppet, but neither was he an autonomous agent operating outside the confines of social expectations, class hierarchies, and a particular social and political order, something that holds true whether or not he was indeed in debt to the Mortgage Bank.

Regardless, Astorquiza felt pressure to move quickly. He chose to do so. Armed with reports from the Intendency and the security section, as well as copies of the IWW's monthly bulletin and issues of the weekly *Numen*,

Astorquiza ordered the detention of Santiago's known Wobblies.[131] The raids were planned for Sunday, July 25.

LA BOCA ARMADA: PROPAGANDA AS THE DEED

On Sunday morning, much of the city's populace slept. Five Security Section agents broke in to the premises of the Santiago branch of the IWW, located at the corner of Chiloé and Matta. They surprised only a caretaker, paid by the Bakers Society, but they had not come looking for individuals. Those operations would unfold elsewhere around the city throughout the day. The agents had come to collect evidence—publications, journals, documents, and hopefully weapons that would confirm the crime of illicit association.[132] The haul was large but somewhat disappointing:

- a number of framed pictures, including an allegory of the death of Francisco Ferrer, an image of a worker stepping on the Code, the church, capitalism and militarism; and a portrait of "the Red Virgin" (most like Louise Michel, from the Paris commune);
- copies of the publications *La Bandera Roja* and *La Protesta*;
- packets containing some one thousand copies of manifestos in support of political prisoners;
- packets of manifestos from the woodworkers;
- two packets of manifestos from the FECh;
- various editions of *Numen, Verba Roja, Federación Obrera, El Universitario, El Ideal Obrero,* and *Mar i Tierra*;
- and two archival boxes of accounts documents.

Yet no weapons were found, an absence one official explained away as a result of the presence of workers next door building a theater.[133]

This was a busy morning for Santiago's security agents. As their colleagues combed the IWW premises for weapons and papers, other agents rounded up suspected subversives, focusing on purported IWW members. Agents arrested carpenters, shoemakers, chauffeurs, and students over the course of the morning.[134] Others managed to avoid capture. Well-known anarchist and editor of *Verba Roja* Armando Triviño had been in and out of prison and claimed he could "smell" the coming repression in the air.[135] He fled to a Valparaíso safe house, where he stayed under an assumed name. His wife was less fortunate: she was arrested and imprisoned. His coeditor at *Verba Roja*, Manuel Antonio Silva Vergara, intially eluded agents' grasps but was captured a few days later.[136] Former FECh leaders Labarca and

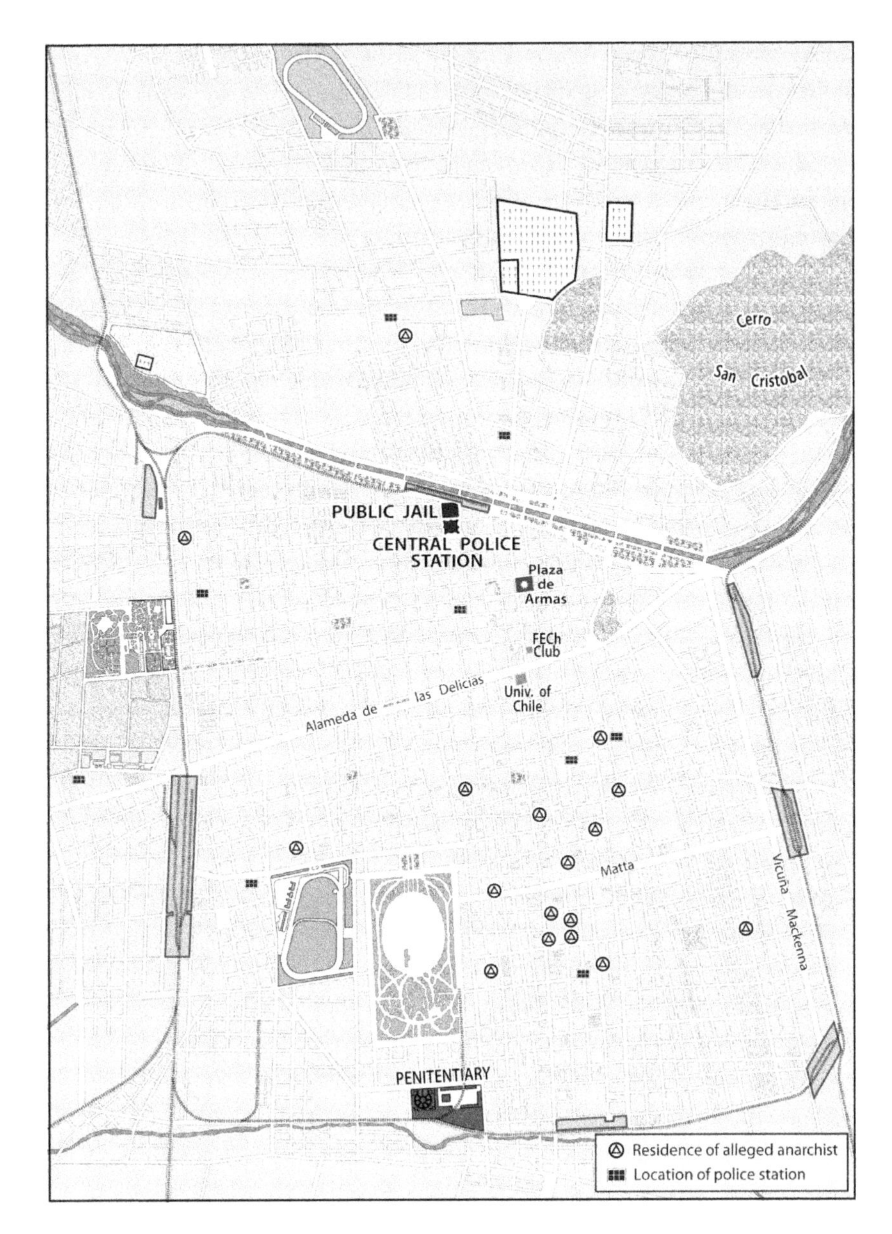

Figure 3.9
Security city: Locations of those arrested for membership in the IWW on July 25, 1920, and of Santiago's police stations. Map by David Ethridge.

Juan Gandulfo had both gone in to hiding after the second assault on the FECh and were officially deemed fugitives, as was another student, Jorge Rosemblatt. Accused of making subversive and anti-patriotic statements along with painter Roberto Salinas from the balcony of the FECh club,

Rosemblatt fled. Over the next months Security Section agents would stake out his home and interrogate his mother, all to no avail. Despite protesting his innocence, he remained on the run.[137] González Vera too fled Santiago. He bought a third class ticket for a train south, disembarking in Temuco where he met another young writer, Neftalí Ricardo Reyes Basoalto (soon to be known as Pablo Neruda.)[138]

If the agents had expected to net a cache of weapons, explosives, and the like, they were disappointed. They found three pistols and a rifle in the possession of particular individuals but in many instances they found very little or nothing at all.[139] In the home of Luis Cuadry, the agent found nothing more than a 1906 stamp from the Chilean Workers Federation. In the home of Manuel Montano, agents found nothing worth noting. At the home where José Domingo Gómez Rojas lived with his mother and where he was arrested at 10 a.m., the three agents carried out a detailed search of his residence but found nothing "connected to the subject of investigation."[140] Mostly they found pamphlets on socialism, anarchism, and the IWW, copies of a wide array of magazines related to workers' struggles (*Verba Roja, Numen, La Batalla, Germinal*, and others), occasional copies of 5 peso bonos issued by the IWW to help raise money for the building of a theater, pamphlets issued by the Committee in Support of Political Prisoners, and collections of books on anarchism, socialism, and political theory, including the texts *Influencia del anarquismo* (most likely Rufino Asenjo del Río's 1908

Nº 000129 — Tenemos un solo gran enemigo — Valor $ 5.00

Consejo Regional Administrativo

TRABAJADORES INDUSTRIALES DEL MUNDO

Formemos una sola grande unión

INTRANSFERIBLE

Bono pro-hogar común, canjeable en moneda corriente a 180 días vista, a favor José Rojas .... Santiago, 15 de Julio de 1920

RECAUDADOR — SECRETARIO GENERAL — TESORERO

Figure 3.10
Illicit association: 5 peso bonos (tickets) such as this one, designed to help the IWW raise money, were used as evidence of illicit association against the holder (in this case, José Rojas Marín). Courtesy of the Archivo Nacional de Chile.

volume published in Buenos Aires); *El Capital* (Marx's magnum opus); and a manuscript titled *A las Armas*. In other words, they found words.

Where did such words come from? With Valiente already in jail and *Numen*'s printshop destroyed, Astorquiza turned his attentions elsewhere: to the FECh. "It appears," he wrote, "that communications intended to affirm the clearly subversive aims and perturbations of public order and social tranquility that constitute the program of this association [the IWW] have emanated from the central establishment of the Student Federation."[141] Moreover, its central figures, Juan Gandulfo and Santiago Labarca, were linked to the IWW and to myriad "subversive acts."[142] If that were not enough, Astorquiza then claimed that the "nucleus" of the FECh was implicated in the death of Julio Covarrubias. This was a widely held belief at the time: an editorial in a Talca newspaper argued that the IWW and the Universidad Popular were equally complicit in the young man's death.[143] All of this speculation and hearsay amounted to evidence in the court of public opinion, and Astorquiza issued a sweeping order for the detention of FECh President Alfredo Demaria and "the members, directors and other persons of that institution," as well as searches of their homes in order to collect yet more words—books, papers and other effects.[144]

None of this likely came as a surprise to the FECh. Its leadership, and a number of its members, felt an intense animosity directed their way—from the press, the administration, and much of the public. Members of Parliament labeled them traitors; the *Diario Ilustrado* referred to them, and their teachers, as a cancer on the national body.[145] They were also targeted for harsh critique by the student federation in Valparaíso which publicly severed its affiliation with its Santiago counterpart. In the days following the attacks on its club and the death of Covarrubias, the FECh saw its juridical status revoked and its leadership and a number of its members on the run or in prison. Labarca and Juan Gandulfo were in hiding; Pedro Gandulfo, Rigoberto Soto Rengifo, and two others who had attempted to the defend the FECh club from attack were in custody; Gómez Rojas soon would be in custody too.

Even so, the FECh membership refused to submit. As Astorquiza marshalled his forces, the FECh regrouped and issued a cautionary manifesto. Given the effort to trample "freedom of thought" with "the freedom of reactionary violence," and given that "reason" cannot struggle successfully when confronted by force, the manifesto declared that the FECh would, among other things, abstain from further demonstrations but would not renounce the points it had made regarding the government's need to justify its troop mobilizations. In a pointed jab at their aristocratic counterparts at the Catholic University—some of whom had

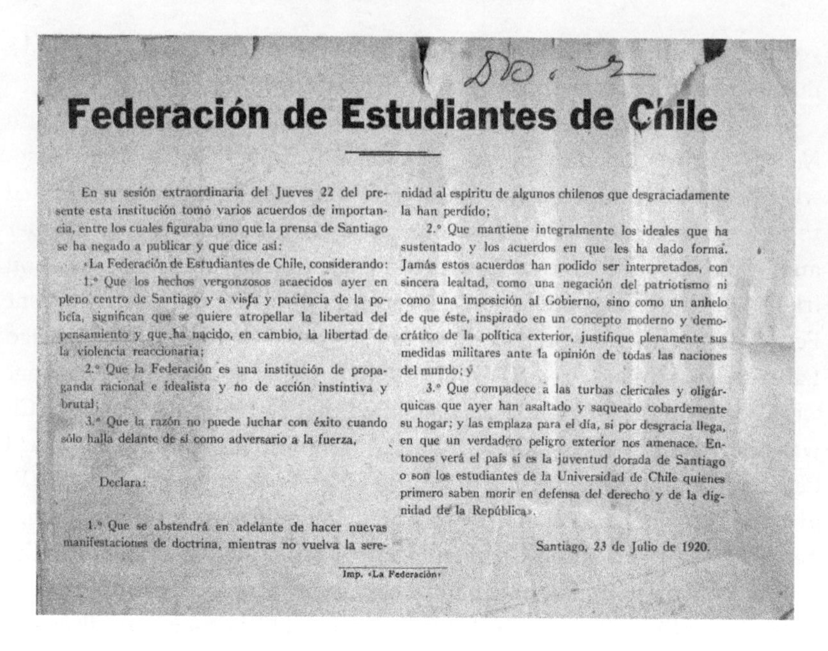

Federación de Estudiantes de Chile

En su sesión extraordinaria del Jueves 22 del presente esta institución tomó varios acuerdos de importancia, entre los cuales figuraba uno que la prensa de Santiago se ha negado a publicar y que dice así:

«La Federación de Estudiantes de Chile, considerando:

1.° Que los hechos vergonzosos acaecidos ayer en pleno centro de Santiago y a vista y paciencia de la policía, significan que se quiere atropellar la libertad del pensamiento y que ha nacido, en cambio, la libertad de la violencia reaccionaria;

2.° Que la Federación es una institución de propaganda racional e idealista y no de acción instintiva y brutal;

3.° Que la razón no puede luchar con éxito cuando sólo halla delante de sí como adversario a la fuerza,

Declara:

1.° Que se abstendrá en adelante de hacer nuevas manifestaciones de doctrina, mientras no vuelva la serenidad al espíritu de algunos chilenos que desgraciadamente la han perdído;

2.° Que mantiene integralmente los ideales que ha sustentado y los acuerdos en que les ha dado forma. Jamás estos acuerdos han podido ser interpretados, con sincera lealtad, como una negación del patriotismo ni como una imposición al Gobierno, sino como un anhelo de que éste, inspirado en un concepto moderno y democrático de la política exterior, justifique plenamente sus medidas militares ante la opinión de todas las naciones del mundo; y

3.° Que compadece a las turbas clericales y oligárquicas que ayer han asaltado y saqueado cobardemente su hogar; y las emplaza para el día, si por desgracia llega, en que un verdadero peligro exterior nos amenace. Entonces verá el país si es la juventud dorada de Santiago o son los estudiantes de la Universidad de Chile quienes primero saben morir en defensa del derecho y de la dignidad de la República».

Santiago, 23 de Julio de 1920.

Imp. «La Federación»

Figure 3.11
Student politics: the FECh issued a declaration defending itself from various charges by the government on July 23, 1920. Courtesy of the Archivo Nacional de Chile.

partaken in the sacking of the FECh club—the manifesto's authors also remarked that if a "true external danger" were to threaten the nation, everyone would then truly see who was willing to sacrifice themselves for the Republic: the "golden youth of Santiago" or "the students of the University of Chile."[146]

The language of the manifesto is quite conciliatory. While the language of patriotism is carefully avoided, the writers nonetheless invoke a defense of the nation that would seem to counter accusations of sedition and subversion.[147] Even so, the proclamation was received as an audacious insult by many in Santiago. At the same time, a group of students from the FECh declared themselves on strike as a symbol of solidarity with the four students who had attempted to defend the FECh from the assault, as well as in protest against the expulsion of Professor José Ducci Kallens from his teaching post in the school of medicine.[148] Ducci—described as one of the brilliant medical minds of his generation who would go on to found the radiology institute at the Hospital San Vicente in 1924—had been one of the original founders and first president of the FECh in 1906. Ducci was removed from his post on the grounds that he had encouraged the student convention's demands.[149]

The students had defenders. The alliance forged between the FECh leadership and workers' organizations and unions such as the POS, and that had acquired substantial force with the AOAN, was solidified in the wake of the attacks. Various labor organizations in Santiago gathered and agreed to a forty-eight-hour general strike, to begin on Monday, July 26, in order to protest the assault on, and show solidarity with, the FECh and to protest attacks on the Federación Obrero de Chile, which had also seen its juridical status questioned. The FOCh, FECh, the Shoeworkers' Federation, the Printer's Union, the IWW, and Organizations in Resistance together signed a leaflet calling for and justifying the strike due to the "outrages" committed against the FECh, the FOCh, Numen press, and students and workers, all with "the complicity or passivity of the authorities charged with maintaining order."[150]

Leaflets were printed and distributed to workers and students who would take to the streets on Sunday afternoon to circulate them. While Montano, Cuadry, Palmero, Gómez Rojas, and others found themselves hustled off to a cell, the first copies of the pamphlet calling for a strike in solidarity with the FECh were making their way into the hands of workers and students

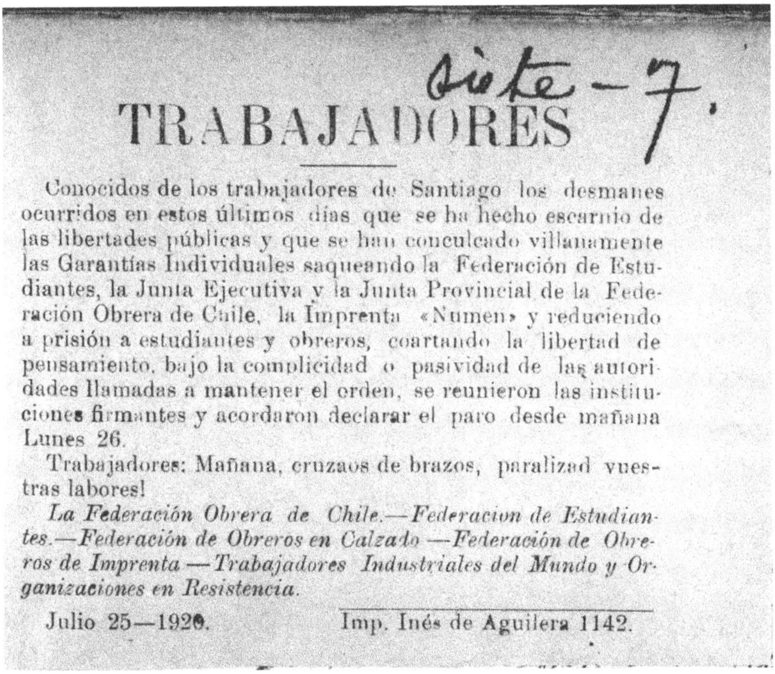

TRABAJADORES

Conocidos de los trabajadores de Santiago los desmanes ocurridos en estos últimos días que se ha hecho escarnio de las libertades públicas y que se han conculcado villanamente las Garantías Individuales saqueando la Federación de Estudiantes, la Junta Ejecutiva y la Junta Provincial de la Federación Obrera de Chile, la Imprenta «Numen» y reduciendo a prisión a estudiantes y obreros, coartando la libertad de pensamiento, bajo la complicidad o pasividad de las autoridades llamadas a mantener el orden, se reunieron las instituciones firmantes y acordaron declarar el paro desde mañana Lunes 26.

Trabajadores: Mañana, cruzaos de brazos, paralizad vuestras labores!

La Federación Obrera de Chile.—Federacion de Estudiantes.—Federación de Obreros en Calzado—Federación de Obreros de Imprenta—Trabajadores Industriales del Mundo y Organizaciones en Resistencia.

Julio 25—1920. Imp. Inés de Aguilera 1142.

Figure 3.12
Solidarity: on July 25 workers in various federations and unions called for a strike in solidarity with the FECh. Courtesy of the Archivo Nacional de Chile.

who began distributing them to a crowd some five thousand strong gathered in front of the home of presidential candidate Alessandri. The administration proclaimed the manifesto *nota non grata* and the police descended.[151]

This was only the beginning. Over the course of three days, from July 25 through July 27, the city center became a zone of running conflict between workers, FECh students, and their allies on one side, and the police and their allies on the other, as men and women took to the streets to protest the assault on the FECh and in defense of their freedom to speak and to strike.[152] They were also defending their right to be in the streets. In the midst of fairly dramatic urban transformations, questions arose regarding who had rights to the city. Who had rights to the streets (a question that had long been at the forefront of anarchist organizing)? Many of those detained the last week of July were detained not only for what they purportedly said, but for where they said it. Demonstrators filled the central corridors of Santiago, within sight and earshot of Santiago's aristocrats. With some exceptions, they saw an ally in presidential candidate—and to their minds, victor—Arturo Alessandri, whose home frequently served as a pivot around which many of the demonstrations unfolded.

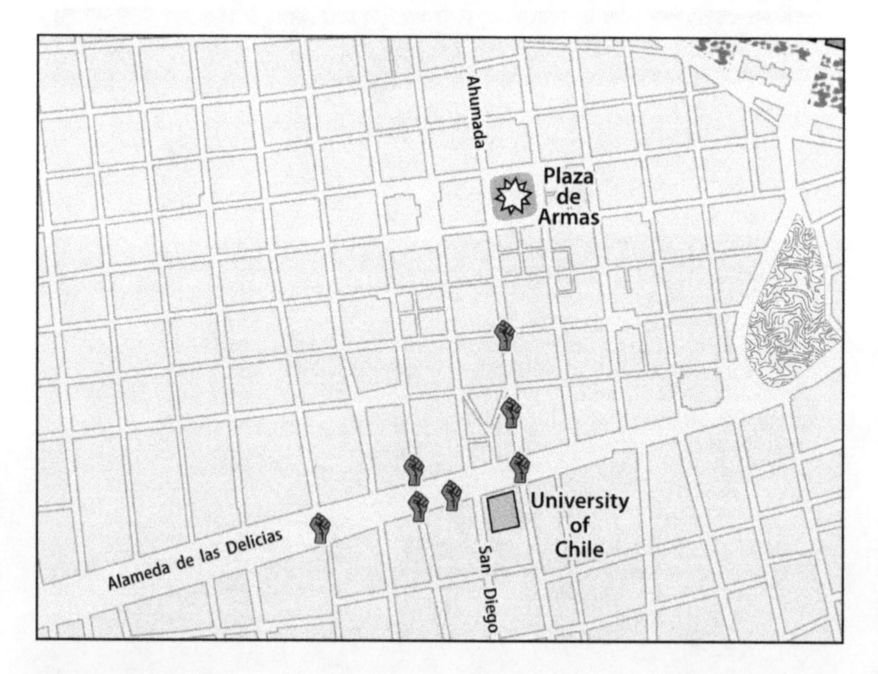

Figure 3.13
Protest city. From July 25 through July 27 downtown Santiago, particularly along the Alameda, saw repeated demonstrations in support of Alessandri, the FECh, and workers, as well as numerous clashes with the police. Map by David Ethridge.

As the protests mounted, the jail and the penitentiary filled quickly. Some, such as seamstress María Astorga Navarro, were arrested for allegedly hurling stones at the police. Astorga Navarro was one of only three women to be identified by name as an active participant in the police records related to the events of July and the prosecution of subversives. Why this was the case is not clear—female workers had been organizing and struggling both independent of, as well as alongside, men for decades and many had drawn heavily on anarchist writings and principles—but it is most likely related to the fact that both the IWW and the FECh, two of the primary targets of the authorities, were almost entirely populated by men.[153] Indeed, it is striking that the most gendered component of the *proceso* was its maleness. The most frequent appearance of women came in the form of arguments and discussions around women not as wage workers (i.e., not in the realm of production), but as wives and mothers (i.e., in the realm of reproduction).

As well as Astorga Navarro, a large group of men was arrested for allegedly impeding the passage of a tram and then attacking the police with stones, which led to a torrent of bullets being fired in the middle of the afternoon along Santiago's busiest thoroughfare.[154] Eighteen men were arrested while Deputy Héctor Arancibia protested, purportedly in "subversive terms and injurious to the Army and the Police," their detention.[155]

In most instances, however, police took men and women into custody for the pronouncements they made rather than the acts they performed. A carpenter was arrested one evening for allegedly shouting "Down with the bandits of Sanfuentes," although he claimed he shouted little more than a few "Vivas!" for Alessandri while with a large group of people.[156] Another individual was arrested for supposedly proclaiming that Switzerland was sending him money to "sustain maximalism in Chile."[157] Students and workers stood side by side on the balcony of the FECh, where, according to police reports, Roberto Salinas (a painter, treasurer of the POS in 1919, and a future founding member of the Chilean Communist Party) accused the police and the army of participating in the assault on the FECh. "True patriotism," he allegedly proclaimed, "does not consist of love for the father land but for all of humanity which knows no frontiers."[158] Men were arrested for marching with a red flag emblazoned with their union credentials and for carrying copies of the manifesto.[159] The police detained José Rojas Marín for "inciting the public to rebel against the police" and he arrived at the detention section with a wound to his head.[160] They also arrested teenager Luis Vergara Keller for supposedly shouting death to the Army and police and attempting to incite people to rise up against the authorities, although he claimed to have shouted nothing more than a "Viva!" in support of the FECh.[161] A fruitseller was arrested for shouting subversive comments based on the testimony of a passerby.[162]

Regardless of what words these various individuals shouted, they were words. Arrests and beatings were an assault not on the "mano armada" but the "boca armada," as one young attorney at the time would recall.[163] That it was dangerous words rather than dangerous weapons that spurred the repression was clear to many. A pamphlet issued by the FECh lamented the "demise of freedom of thought and the rise of freedom of reactionary violence."[164] Many must have been reminded of previous attacks on speech and the efforts by some members of Parliament to remind officials that ideas were not illegal. "In Chile," one deputy had noted in 1919, "ideas are not crimes . . . To profess such and such ideas, regardless of how strange they are, is not a crime! The fact is there is a huge difference between the republican, democratic and liberal regime that is called for in the Constitution and the law, and the regime currently in place."[165] The destruction of the *Numen* print shop, and the arrest of Julio Valiente, could be chilling in this regard. In the wake of that attack, Santiago's Typesetter's Union, which had met weekly or biweekly up to that date, did not meet again until early October.[166] Meanwhile, one of those arrested, typographer Eliodoro Ulloa, spoke for many when he offered the following defense during his interrogation: "I didn't believe that by handing out these manifestos I would be comitting a crime of such gravity."[167] Despite multiple complaints, from students and members of Parliament, that "ideas are combatted with ideas, not with the saber," the authorities were clear in their correspondence: words were subversive.[168] Propaganda *was* the deed.

"I AM THE POLICE"

Most of those arrested challenged the official version of events and the words they were said to have uttered. This could hardly come as a suprise to many. Neither the public nor public servants put much faith in the reports produced by the police. A telling case in point occurred on the floor of the Chamber of Deputies when various deputies peppered Minister of the Interior García de la Huerta and Minister of War Errázuriz with questions regarding the firing of a pistol by a policeman in a peacefully assembled crowd on the Alameda. When Errázuriz attempted to dispel their suspicions by quoting from the police report of the events, no less than three deputies responded that they had no faith in the report. Deputy Celis in fact went further, suggesting that no police reports were trustworthy, reiterating a comment made in the Parliament during the proceedings against Casimiro Barrios.[169] Subsequent Security Section investigations of alleged subversives, which included interviews with neighbors, employers, and landlords as well as searches of the accused's premises in order to determine if an individual was associated with the IWW or another illicit assocation, did little to assuage such concerns. Testimony from neighbors, employers, witnesses, and landlords pointed to police prevarication.[170]

Santiago's police force—numbering around three thousand bodies in 1920—had long had an image problem.[171] The force had acquired by the 1910s a reputation for being corrupt and dishonest, for being, in its own way, subversive. During and immediately following the centenniel celebrations of 1910, widespread criticism of the Santiago police force appeared in the press and the Parliament. Police were accused of abusing prisoners, being drunk on the job, and being corrupt.[172] The police also had a reputation for being little more than the lap-dogs of the industrialists. The Secretary of the Shoemakers Union argued that the collusion between the police and industrialists was deep and that police would accompany scabs from their homes to factories and back when workers struck.[173]

A national scandal had erupted in 1916 with serious accusations directed against the head of Santiago's Security Section, Eugenio Castro, first in the newspaper *La Opinión*, run by political economist Tancredo Pinochet, and subsequently in a book by Carlos Pinto Durán (writing under the pseudonym Roberto Mario). These authors claimed Castro hired criminals and con men—"former convicts, thieves, ruffians and vagrants"—as police agents and close confidants.[174] Mario accused Castro of having revived the practice associated with "the bandit Vidocq"—a reference to Eugene Francois Vidocq, a criminal turned police detective who served as Paris's prefect and as the model for Victor Hugo's two main protagonists in *Les Misérables*—which saw lawbreakers join the police force with predictable consequences.[175] Not only would they provide cover for their criminal associates, they also furthered the internal corruption of the force. Castro himself was not immune: evidence was offered that he extorted money from illegal gambling houses. Accusations flew that the police under Castro engaged in false claims of terrorism, exaggerating its existence or planting bombs themselves to generate panic.

All of these were actions typical of "police forces which have fallen in to disorganization and discredit."[176] The author pointed out such was the case in Europe during the height of the *attentat*, and most famously in Spain with the Mano Negra, a clandestine anarchist association that was revealed to be nothing more than a police fabrication. Indeed accusations of violence by anarchists were widespread but the evidence was thin.

The police habitually planted bombs wrapped in anarchist periodicals, which fooled no one.[177] In 1911, when the police arrested a shoemaker for possession of a book titled *Treatise on Explosives*, they found that it belonged to one Pedro Godoy, who had left it in the shoemaker's home after visiting him. Arrested and brought before a judge, Godoy freely admitted the book was his, explaining that he was studying explosives in his third year of engineering. When the judge showed him the remnants of a bomb purportedly found in the shoemaker's possession the following exchange ensued:

JUDGE: And who do you believe may have made this?
GODOY: The police.
JUDGE: How can you say this?
GODOY: Very simply because the bomb is so poorly made. I have already told you I am a student of explosives and a good student at that. Begging your pardon, that is a piece of junk [*porquería*] that couldn't do any damage, at most burning a little the fingers of the fool who handles it. A bomb is not made that way. Let me explain to you how you make one.[178]

As the AOAN prepared for more demonstrations in 1919, the police attempted to frame anarchists and agitators by exploding bombs planted next to newspaper stands in Santiago.[179]

Little wonder the police were subject to varied levels of ridicule in popular culture. In Alberto Edwards's short stories involving Román Calvo, the "Chilean Sherlock Holmes," published between 1914 and 1921, police investigators at times appeared as incompetent and thus beholden to Calvo for his abilities to solve difficult crimes.[180] Only one month before the attacks on the FECh, the film *Cuando Chaplin se enloqueció de amor* opened in Santiago. A Chaplin parody set against the backdrop of student life in Santiago during the Fiestas de Primavera, the film poked fun repeatedly at the police, with scenes of drunken cops leaving their beat. The offense led one police official to ask the Intendent to seek a resolution with the theaters.[181] The police themselves would labor under no illusions regarding how they were perceived. When Doctor Noe of the School of Medicine at the University of Chile, one of Juan Gandulfo's teachers, suggested the police create a dog-catching unit to help combat the spread of intestinal diseases and rabies in Santiago, senior police officials argued that not only did the police lack the finances and personnel for the task, but that such an undertaking would also "revive that atavistic hatred the public had for the Police, and which today has begun to disappear only after great effort."[182] The officials suggested an alternative solution: to appoint small citizen commissions, made up of "individuals of good character," to go out after midnight and poison the beasts.

Over the course of the 1910s efforts were made to professionalize the police force. This meant, in part, a militarization of the force. The military corps known as the Carabineros were, over the course of the 1910s, given increasing latitude to engage in urban and rural policing and replaced the railroad police.[183] In 1915 the Ministry of Justice issued a ruling requiring "military organization and regimen" for personnel working in penal establishments, creating a "Prisons Gendarme Corps."[184] Former military personnel increasingly populated the upper echelons of Santiago's police force, the most obvious example being Colonel Rafael Toledo Tagle, who assumed the position of prefect in the Santiago police in 1916, a position he would occupy through the early 1920s.[185] Having inherited a corps subject to substantial suspicion and opprobrium, he worked to discipline and modernize the police force, garnering a reputation as a man with an iron fist. He also initiated a benefits program for his employees—from beat cops to senior officials. Under Toledo Tagle they received a form of social security as well as dental care. He established a savings system and a mortuary fund and contracted with an attorney to defend members of the police before the law.[186] But issues remained: wages in particular were a perenniel problem with beat cops rarely earning as much as tram operators, despite working longer hours.[187]

Much of Toledo Tagle's efforts were devoted to Santiago's Security Section. The Santiago Police force was divided into an Order Section, composed of uniformed beat cops and police patrol units who worked Santiago's streets, and the Security Section that was akin to a detective unit and oversaw criminal investigations as well as issues related to the internal security of the state, including oversight of workers' movements and the Residency Law. The Security Section had long been viewed with deep skepticism: one parliamentary member claimed that "fifty of the most serious crimes that have been committed in Santiago in the last years [1910s] have been supported, defended, inspired, [and] covered up by the Security Section."[188] To oversee the reorganization of the Section, and to improve its abysmal image, Toledo Tagle appointed another former military man, Carlos Dinator, as its director.[189] Dinator, in turn, enlisted as one of his right-hand men a young, aspiring investigator named Ventura Maturana. All of this Toledo Tagle accomplished in part by centralizing power further in the office of the Prefect to the degree that, as one commentator admiringly noted, Toledo Tagle could proudly paraphrase France's Sun King: "I *am* the Police."[190]

Figure 3.14
Police labor: senior police officials sought repeatedly to improve the conditions in which their subalterns labored. This cover from a police publication in 1921 shows a beat cop under duress from various threats, including low wages. René Peri Fegerstrom, *Historia de la Función Policial en Chile: Apuntes y transcripciones, 3a parte (1900–1927)* (Santiago: Carabineros de Chile, 1982), insert between pp. 104–105.

A paraphrase that slyly conflates the state and the police is hardly coincidental. As anarchists had argued for decades, the adjective in "police state" was redundant. "Police" meant not only nightsticks, raids, arrests, and insults; it also meant the broader set of institutions that existed to structure and sustain the social order known as the state: residency laws, expulsion decrees, and forms and methods of identification, registration, and population control.[191]

ON THE SIDEWALKS OF DOUBTFUL STREETS

Tomás López Martín had inherited from his parents a special gift: x-ray eyes. He could see people "as if they were nude," and could discern the condition of their internal organs.[192] Such skills brought a steady stream of clients to his home in Valparaíso until some point in 1918, when he was arrested. He then moved to Santiago, where he began anew. He was doing quite well until he had the misfortune of attempting to divine the state of the organs of a Security Section agent, Miguel Stuven. "I see your esophagus is a little black," López Martín told him, "but that is due to nicotine. The aorta is working fine. The bladder and rectum are mildly inflamed due to some illnesses you have had in these organs."[193] Regardless of the accuracy of this diagnosis, Stuven and his partner, Ventura Maturana, organized a sting and arrested López Martín.

Of all the possible agents to have visited his premises, López Martín could not have imagined a worse one than agent Maturana. When Toledo Tagle reorganized the Security Section and appointed Carlos Dinator as its director, Dinator chose Maturana as his Secretary and right-hand man. Maturana was a young agent with big ambitions, ambitions that would come to fruition when he would go on to develop and lead Santiago's secret police under President Carlos Ibáñez in the latter half of the 1920s. In 1920, however, he was a senior member of a department seeking to improve its track—and tracking—record. A major part of the Security Section's work included identifying, registering, and tracking foreigners and purported criminals. Police had long been frustrated by an inability to adequately identify, register, and track individuals. Such concerns only multiplied with higher rates of immigration, internal migration, and urbanization. False names, aliases, and fake addresses meant accused or suspected criminals or agitators, once free on bail, could often disappear into the urban labyrinth. For example, Chile's future national literary prize winner Manuel Rojas was arrested as a young man in Valparaíso in 1914 for public disturbance, having allegedly thrown rocks at a branch of

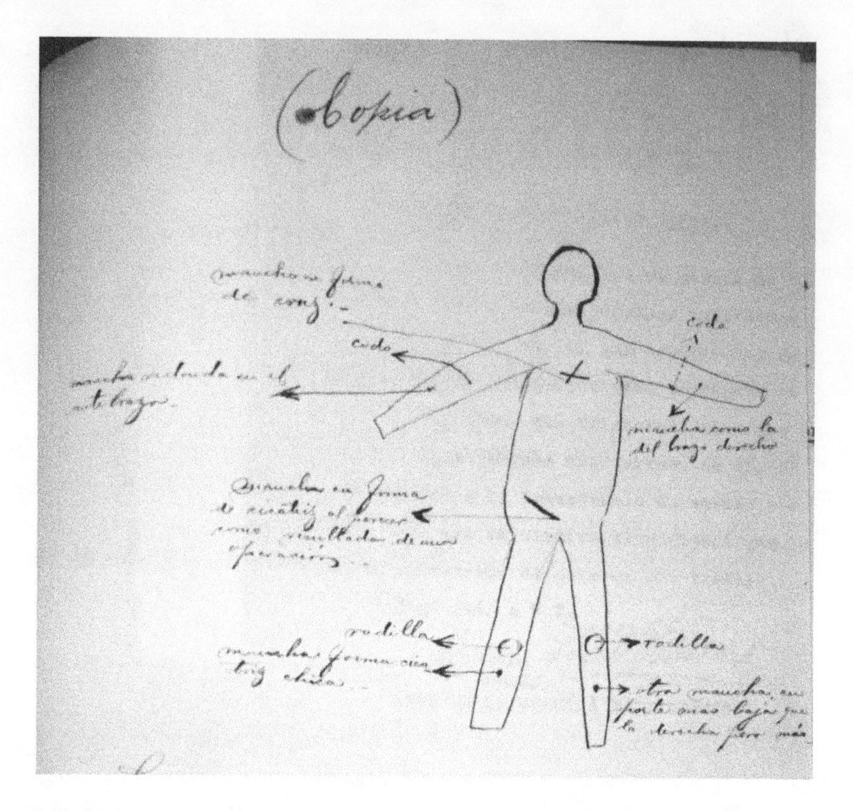

Figure 3.15
The man with the x-ray eyes. A police sketch alleges to show the manner in which Tomás López Martín scammed his clients. Courtesy of the Archivo Nacional de Chile.

the Banco Alemán Transatlántico during a demonstration protesting an increase in tram fees.[194] Rojas and the other ten or so men arrested with him were released on bail, and by 1917 had been declared fugitives from justice because they had not returned to court for their respective cases.[195] Efforts to locate them were fruitless, in part because addresses they had provided were either nonexistent or not their own.[196]

An Identification Section had been an integral part of the Security Section since the turn of the century, but its strength had waxed and waned under financial constraints. By 1917 this had changed as the administration focused its efforts. Five offices by that point had been established in the country: a main Identification office in Santiago and four smaller offices in Valparaíso, Iquique, Talca, and Concepción.[197] Such efforts were important for the professionalization of the police force. For too long the primary means of identification was through personal connections, meaning a continued proximity between police agents and delinquents.[198] The offices acquired further significance with the passage

Figure 3.16
A right-hand man. Ventura Maturana would eventually reorganize Chile's detective offices and head the secret police under President Carlos Ibáñez del Campo in the late 1920s, but he would cut his teeth as the eager right-hand man to Director Carlos Dinator in the Security Section in 1920. From *Album gráfico de la policía* (Santiago: n.p., 1923).

of the Residency Law in 1918 and subsequent efforts to compel resident foreigners to register with local police and intendencies, such that by 1920, offices in Santiago were overwhelmed by the workload. In the immediate wake of the assault on the FECh, the Minister of the Interior reiterated that article 6 of the Residency Law obliged foreigners to register themselves with police prefects and that this article was to be strictly enforced. "Police prefects throughout the republic," he stated, "will proceed to open, immediately, a registration office and take the measures necessary so that foreigners resident in their jurisdiction can fulfill the requirements demanded by the Residency Law."[199]

Registering foreigners was one thing; identifying individuals with bureaucratic reliability and systematic consistency was another. Identification and registration were part of a much broader impulse toward criminology, characteristic of many late-nineteenth century cities and societies. Efforts to improve policing and to create and theorize systems that would come to be known as criminology garnered an impetus from Santiago intendent Benjamín Vicuña Mackenna, the same official who, in the early 1870s, had developed the urban plans for Santiago that included a *cordon sanitaire*. Public order was, for Vicuña Mackenna, both a social and geographical concept. It meant predictable spaces and people knowing their place. Key to the city's success—and to the polity writ large—was circulation, a concept central to bourgeoise political economy in its privileging of the free movement of people and goods.[200] Spaces thought to slow circulation, whether due to threats of crime (dangerous quarters), disease (miasmic spaces where even the air does not properly circulate), or disorientation (winding alleyways and shortcuts), were to be destroyed or reformed. The circulation of people "out of place" was to be stemmed and movement regulated. In his semiautobiographical novel *Hijo de Ladrón*, Manuel Rojas wrote:

> We arrived in Valparaíso eager to board any ship sailing north, but we couldn't; at least, I couldn't: hundreds of individuals, police, train conductors, consuls, captains or port governors, bosses, sobrecargos and other such equally frightening beings are here, are there, are everywhere, preventing a human being from moving where and as he wished.[201]

An array of approaches and techniques had been developed over the years as a means to regulate movement, identify individuals, and to combat crime and criminal ambiguity.[202] Photography, for example, had a long history of use in police work. From the earliest days of the daguerrotype, photography appeared to offer a solution to problems of identification, a kind of visual simplicity for problems of criminal duplicity.[203] It quickly became clear that the problem of efficiency and classification would remain. As the photographic archive of delinquents grew, efficient and assured identification diminished.[204] Nor were photographs of much use when subjects altered their physiognamy so as to avoid repeated recognition. For example, IWW organizer Juan Onofre Chamorro, at every turn, fought the camera. When a 1917 law required workers in the Valparaíso area to furnish the Captain of the Port with "three photographs and a police certificate of good conduct," Chamorro led port workers in a strike, which ended only after the requirement was reduced to one image to be included on the license of the holder.[205] When journalists sought to capture his image, he willfully distorted his physiognamy. Working men and women had learned over the years how to modify their faces when confronted with the camera. Such tactics were common among prisoners to avoid being photographically documented. "Experienced prisoners have explained to me the way to fight the camera, to fool it," wrote dissident Marxist Victor Serge about his imprisonment in France from 1912 to 1917. "Some men stubbornly close their eyes, make faces, screw up their features. These are soon made to submit; and not by friendly persuasion . . . The clever ones know how to distort their features in advance, how to put on an abnormal expression, make it seem calm and natural, hold it as long as necessary."[206] Santiago's

Figure 3.17
On the sidewalks of doubtful streets: IWW organizer Onofre Chamorro screwed up his face in various ways to avoid being photographed with his "natural physionomy," part of a larger effort to escape state tracking and surveillance efforts. Courtesy of the Institute for Social History.

working men and women, organizers and agitators, immigrants and Chileans alike, were under no illusions about what efforts at photographic registration would mean for them. They knew a truth obvious to their counterparts throughout the world and powerfully articulated by Serge: "Every new registration places another creature under the power of men whose law is absolute on the sidewalks of doubtful streets."[207]

Just as worrisome for the authorities, individuals could change the photograph that appeared on a given form of identification. Quality control was key to social control. Seeing a business opportunity, Roberto Matus (who had a long history in the ministry of justice and prisons) and Humberto Ducci (the brother of the first FECh President, José Ducci) approached the intendent's chief of the Office on Identification at the end of 1919 to offer their recently patented procedure for preparing personal identity cards, a procedure they claimed prevented the doctoring or switching of the card's original photograph.[208] Too often, they contended, "we have seen that with a simple change in the picture of an identity card, which has been stolen from its rightful owner, thieves can pass for capitalists or businessmen . . . , for public employees; for diplomats; and even for Agents in the Security Section." They concluded ominously that this "could happen any day, if it hasn't already."[209] In a suggestive analogy they noted that during the war in Europe officials would falsify identity cards by changing pictures in order to gain easy access to enemy territory. Thus Matus and Ducci developed a process that used paper with a particular sheen that would disappear if tampered with: no eraser, acid, or water could be applied to change a letter or a number without negating the sheen on that part of the card.[210] It is unclear if the Intendent took them up on their offer but false identity cards continued to be a problem.[211]

Regardless, the crucial point is that the individuals subjected to various technologies of surveillance, identification, and control soon learned how to undermine, rework, or co-opt them. Enrique Prieto Lemm, author of a Chilean thesis on "identification" in 1923, understood this well. He stressed his work's significance by noting that "with the passage of time, with the material advances of modern civilization, the investigation of crimes also needs a new and powerful aid that would allow it to compete with all of the ruses that this very same civilization puts in to the hands of criminals to undermine each new advancement."[212] Con artists, criminals, and agitators subverted the promise of technology, whether it be the x-ray, photography, the printing press, or dynamite.

In a perpetual game of cat and mouse, officials and criminologists sought out new technological possibilities to identify and track criminals, foreigners and subversives. One of the first—and best-known—responses to the inadequacies of photographic archives in the 1870s had been the tripartite identification schema developed by French detective Alphonse Bertillon. The son of one of the founders of Paris's School of Anthropology, Bertillon was influenced by his father's work. The first component of his system was what he termed anthropometry, or the physical measurement of the body, especially the head and face, which in theory would allow one to establish the identity of a criminal with a prior record, an important process given criminals' efforts to obscure or dissimulate their identity. The second component was the verbal portrait, or verbal description through which a sketch artist could compose a portrait for police use. Finally, he advocated the study and notation of descriptive scars and markings as a further means to ensure proper identification.[213] He published his *Manual on Anthropometry and Iris Color* in 1885 to further diffuse his ideas, which soon made their ways to French colonies where they were used to track and identify colonial subjects and purported subversives.[214] A decade later, attendees of the International Congress in Rome (1898) adopted his "verbal portrait" as a means to combat anarchist propaganda by the deed.[215]

Bertillon's system had its limitations. It proved inefficient due to the intricate measurements involved; it could not accommodate the very real physical changes individuals experienced due to aging or illness; the equipment could be very expensive; and the system was only as good as the quality of the work carried out by technicians.[216] Over the same decades, alternative systems were developed that modified and built upon Bertillon's anthropometry. For example, the Capdevielle System involved close examination of a subject's eyes and measurement of the cornea; the Tamassia System concentrated on the study of the veins on the back of a subject's hands; the Stockis System and Wilder System analyzed and classified the lines in a subject's palm. Other systems studied the pores in a subject's fingers or measured the phalanges of the toes and fingers using x-rays.[217] But all of these systems, like Bertillon's, had limitations and suffered from inefficiency and inconsistency.

A breakthrough came with the system of dactyloscopy (fingerprint identification and classification) developed by Argentine official Juan Vucitech, who used a bloody fingerprint to solve a murder in 1892. Vucitech's innovation, historian Julia Rodríguez explains, was not accuracy, "but the efficiency with which his classification system could be married to an emerging bureaucratic archive of individual fingerprints."[218] By the turn of the century investigation units in much of Europe, the Americas, and various colonies had embraced dactyloscopy and paired it with aspects of Bertillon's anthropometrical method. Despite a very public and nasty squabble with Vucitech, Bertillon too found dactyloscopy a powerful tool in criminal forensics, using it at one point to identify members of the notorious Bonnot anarchist gang (to which Victor Serge had belonged) in France.[219] The spread of such practices was hastened by the willingness of South American governments to make their identification practices as uniform as possible in order to share information on the movements of individuals considered dangerous.

Visual technologies such as the x-ray and the photograph were deployed in order to better identify, surveil, and rule people. They were, in this sense, methods of super-vision. [220] They constituted a means to both oversee and to master the ambiguities that plagued police investigations (or, more precisely, to master the very possibility of ambiguity itself.) Not surprisingly, those being identified, tracked, and surveilled resisted. In Argentina Vucetich's efforts to have everyone fingerprinted resulted in riots and protests. Not only was the order repealed, but all fingerprint files to date were destroyed. In Chile, despite the obsession with identification, officials passed no law requiring citizens to acquire identification cards (although some professions—the military, the railroad companies, the police—and

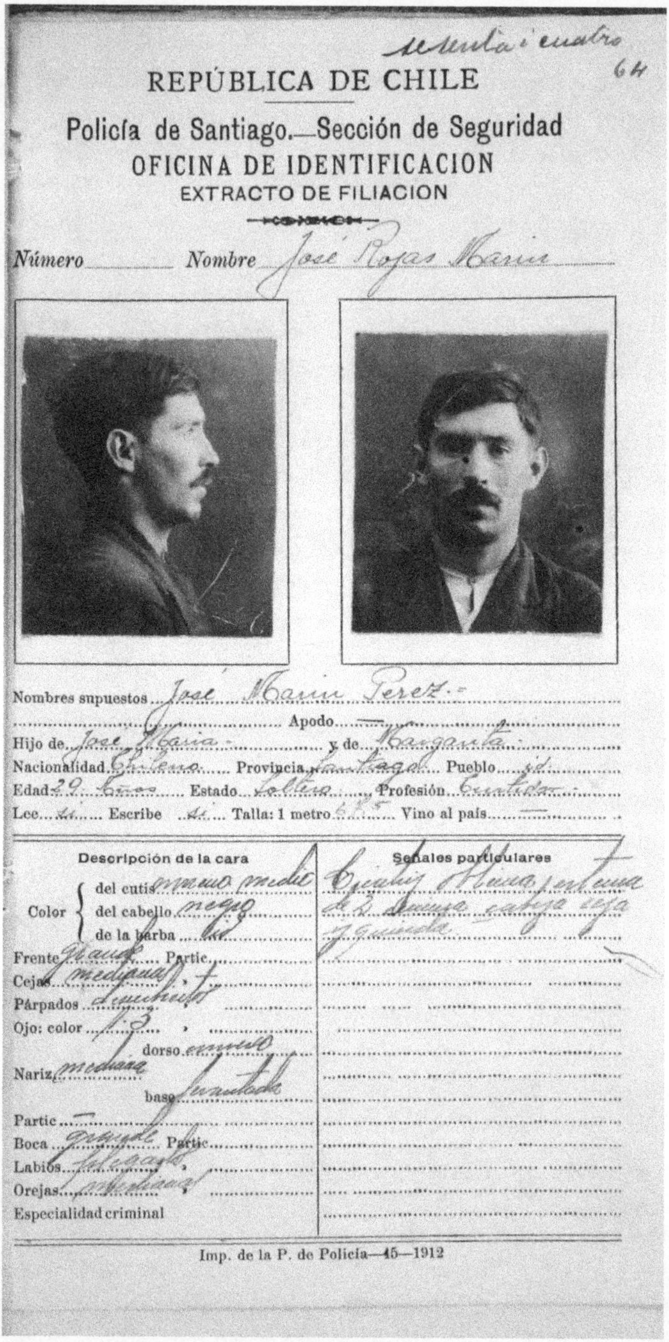

sesenta i cuatro
64

REPÚBLICA DE CHILE

Policía de Santiago.—Sección de Seguridad

OFICINA DE IDENTIFICACION

EXTRACTO DE FILIACION

Número .... Nombre José Rojas Marín

Nombres supuestos José Marín Perez.-

Apodo —

Hijo de José María- y de Margarita-

Nacionalidad Chileno Provincia Santiago Pueblo id.

Edad 29 años Estado Soltero Profesión Curtidor.-

Lee si Escribe si Talla: 1 metro 685 Vino al país —

Descripción de la cara		Señales particulares
Color	del cutis moreno medio	Cicatriz ... de 2 ... cabeza ceja izquierda
	del cabello negro	
	de la barba id	
Frente grande	Partic.	
Cejas medianas		
Párpados		
Ojo: color		
Nariz mediana	dorso	
	base levantada	
Partic. —		
Boca grande	Partic.	
Labios		
Orejas medianas		
Especialidad criminal		

Imp. de la P. de Policía—45—1912

Figure 3.18
Science and spiritism. Despite efforts to improve identification methods, police around the globe, including in Chile, continued to rely upon a mix of dubious methodologies, critiqued at one point as a mix of "science and spiritism." A police record for José Rojas Marín in 1920 uses a form created in 1912 and offers at best laconic descriptions of his physiognamy. Courtesy of the Archivo Nacional de Chile.

some municipalities did require them), most likely due to concerns over resistance.[221] Although fingerprinting was commonplace in Chile by 1920, police continued to rely on photographs and anthropometry, as can be seen in the police file for José Rojas Marín, one of those arrested on July 27 during the street demonstrations. The form, formulated in 1912, reveals Bertillon's continuing influence. Rojas Marín is photographed frontally and in profile, in such a way as to show the right earlobe, a holdover from the Bertillon system that emphasized size and proportion of that earlobe in particular. The descriptive features required on the form are from Bertillon's verbal description classification method: Rojas Marín's nose is described as "medium," his mouth as "large," and his ears as "medium." "Medium." "Large." "Small." Such laconic descriptors were almost absurdly vague. The fact is, despite its intentions and claims, and despite the 1919 founding of a National Institute for Criminology in Santiago, criminology was no hard science.[222]

Criminology was riddled with dubious assumptions and prone to manipulation. Men like López Martín—the man with the x-ray eyes—were Maturana's *bête noir* in part because his fabrications were self-interested. He claimed to see his clients' interiors as a means to prey on their fears and wallets. Yet the police themselves were prone to their own fabrications in their reports, claims, and testimony. Just as crucial, the use of measurements, descriptions, and photographs did more than identify and track particular individuals. They were deployed as a means to generate "typical" individuals: that is, not an individual at all but a composite or "statistical individual," essentially, a fiction that looked for a means to read individual features as "in conformity with a type."[223] Moreover, the specter of conjecture, not just indeterminacy, haunted police work. Bertillon's anthropometric system came to be seen as unreliable and cumbersome; his verbal portrait system was eventually assailed as a failed mix of "science and spiritism."[224] More generally, the technologies police units used were riddled with troubling metaphysical assumptions, such as physiognomy and facial morphology as predictors of criminal tendencies. It takes a leap of faith to believe that a physiognomal fact yielded a comprehensive rendition of character and that "the surface of the body . . . bore the outward signs of inner character."[225] Yet criminologists, detectives, and theorists of crime and the social body believed exactly that. Through dubious science, they had come to believe they could make one's "interior states . . . visible, legible, and governable."[226] In which case, the man with the x-ray eyes and agent Maturana—employed, fittingly enough, in the Ministry of the *Interior*—had much more in common than either would have liked to admit.

ASTORQUICISM

By early August it was clear to all that Astorquiza had moved quickly against the IWW and with remarkable success, netting at least thirteen of its allegedly central figures. In the wake of the late July street demonstrations, the jail and penitentiary were both filling fast; orders of detention had accelerated; and the police continued to raid residences in search of suspected subversives.[227] It is a measure of the pace of repression that within two weeks of starting his campaign, Astorquiza requested additional tools of his trade: paper, pens, pencils, ink, and a typewriter.[228] Some semblance of order returned to the streets of Santiago.

Astorquiza pursued his charge with missionary zeal. And zealotry has its risks. These appeared as early as July 30, on a Friday evening when two security agents approached Rosario Grecco outside of the municipal offices near the Plaza de Armas in central Santiago. They had an order to take him to Astorquiza, they claimed, although they were unable to produce the writ when Grecco demanded to see it, at which point the agents attempted to force Grecco into the back of the car. A long-term organizer, member of the chauffeurs' union, and naturalized Chilean who had served as a reservist in the Italian army, Grecco was not easy game. He managed to free himself and flee. He went to someone he knew he could trust: Arturo Alessandri, probably at his home nearby. Alessandri called the prefect, who claimed ignorance, but it soon became clear that the attempted detention of Grecco was not an anomaly. That same evening security agents had grabbed two other men—Daniel Labbé, a long-time anarchist organizer in Santiago, and Eduardo Bunster (a leftist organizer and owner of the *Zapatería El Soviét* on San Diego Street)—forced them in to a vehicle, and detained them in isolation at a local barracks. It was only as a result of Grecco's resistance that the other kidnappings came to light.[229]

The case created a crisis in the Cabinet, with ministers resigning their positions in protest over these activities and intense debates on the floor of the Parliament. A Conservative deputy accused Grecco of being one of the "worst agitators," guilty of fomenting strikes among chauffeurs.[230] Others came to Grecco's defense, arguing that responsibility for the illegal arrests lay with the Santiago Intendent Subercaseaux. The rhetoric was heated: one deputy stated that such forms of detention and imprisonment, at the Intendent's orders no less, were "almost, one could say, traitorous."[231] Subercaseaux gave a few excuses for his behavior, including the threat of a general strike, although a deputy quickly reminded him that refusing to work might be an inconvenience but it was not a crime.[232]

Absorbing the brunt of the criticism, Subercaseaux resigned his post.[233] Astorquiza, meanwhile, survived the scandal, with at least one deputy arguing that Astorquiza was a magistrate who was fastidious about the law and would never have tolerated activity "which would muddy his name."[234]

It turned out to be an overoptimistic appraisal. If anything, Astorquiza's efforts became even more single-minded. Despite a heavy snowfall on August 12 that blanketed the city, bringing down telegraph and telephone lines and halting trams in their tracks, Astorquiza persisted, his labors adding to the woes of a population trying to cope with the cold, the steady pangs of hunger, and a rapidly spreading typhus epidemic.[235] The evening of Saturday, August 14, members of the shoeworkers' union, as well as their wives and children, held an event of theater and dancing and eating in order to raise money to benefit the families of those taken prisoner over the previous three weeks. Given the context the organizers chose not to advertise the event, but Astorquiza learned of it nonetheless, most likely from one of the many *sapos* (toads or spies) employed by the police force (including, according to some, Socialist Party secretary Evaristo Rios).[236] Astorquiza, accompanied by agents from the security section as well as members of the police force, descended on the premises on the corner of Avenida Matta and Chiloé—the former IWW building—late that night and arrested some 121 men.[237]

The raid left a large number of women and children crying in the cold night air while husbands and fathers were led away. Many questioned the timing of the raid.[238] "I should tell you," one official wrote, "that when the Minister [Astorquiza] was writing the order, I allowed myself to suggest to him that it might be, perhaps, more convenient to have the raid take place from 4 to 6 pm, a time during which one could find the leaders in said locale, in order to avoid the disorder that would arise by doing it at night during a function attended by women and children."[239] Astorquiza, the official continued, responded by emphasizing that the raid had to be held at that hour—with no explanation—but that women and children were not to be detained. The subprefect went on to note that the entire raid unfolded peacefully with little of the "wails, laments, pleas, or other pathetic scenes" suggested by some people. Officials were unable to determine who among the men belonged to the associations targeted (shoeworkers, woodworkers, breadmakers, and plasterers)—everyone claimed to have wandered in from the street when they were passing by—so they arrested nearly all of the men.[240] In subsequent hours many of those detained were freed but some fifty or so men remained in custody the following day.[241]

The reaction was immediate. On August 15 upward of a thousand people, despite living in the midst of a serious repression, took to Santiago's main thoroughfare to protest the raid and the continuing detention of their family members, colleagues, and friends.[242] Students from the School of Medicine organized and spoke side by side with representatives from the FOCh and the Printer's Union. Deputies in the Parliament were not amused. As the critiques of the police and security section proliferated, the raid once again put repression on the front pages of the city's newspapers. One deputy compared the raid to something one would have expected in Tsarist Russia—an interesting choice of comparison, given the pervasive presence of Russia and its revolution in the press at the time.[243] A senator described the repeated attacks on labor and university student organizations as characteristic of a "savage State."[244] Intentionally or not, the senator's assertion would have struck a chord with many of those imprisoned and with many anarchists at the time, inverting as it did the dominant Hobbesian narrative. It is the presence, not the absence, of the state that had made life nasty, brutish, and short.

The press too grew increasingly ambivalent. By early September members of the press, who had so loudly lauded Astorquiza a month earlier,

Figure 3.19
Unlucky initials: some in the press began to question the zealous pursuit of alleged subversives. Inocencio Walton Walker found himself detained because the initials IWW were found on his clothing. Courtesy of the Institute for Social History.

Figure 3.20
The works? "Anything to not be mistaken for an anarchist and detained by Astorquiza." Courtesy of the Institute for Social History.

began to publish critiques, such as the one shown here in which one Mr. Inocencio Walton Walker is detained for a month on suspicion of illicit association with the IWW because his clothes all bear his initials. Given the efforts to improve the police force's public image and, in particular, its scientific and investigative abilities, such ridicule must have stung.

The security section and the police more generally had in fact begun to acquire a reputation for detaining and arresting individuals in the streets whose appearance or behavior struck them as suspect, giving the entire concept of "identification" an arbitrary and ominous meaning. Astorquiza himself was so closely associated with such "profiling" that one cartoonist created a shorthand for such profiling by turning Astorquiza's name in to a noun: Astorquicism. A man, unshaven and unkempt, enters a barber shop where the attendant asks him if he would like the full treatment to which the man answers: "As you wish . . . Just so that on the street they don't take me for an anarchist and I end up detained by Mr. Astorquiza."

But the act that would garner Astorquiza an ignominious place in history was his treatment of José Domingo Gómez Rojas.

CHAPTER 4

A Savage State

SEPTEMBER 1920

Gómez Rojas suffocated in shadow and murk. Little light penetrated the barred and grimed window of his cell, six strides in length and three in width. An ominous gloom rose from the gray floor, hung from the ceiling, and seeped from the damp walls. Colors were limited to muted variations on iron and unwashed rock, equal parts sinister and melancholic. A meager measure of afternoon sun was doled out on the patio, but only to those not held in solitary confinement. By 4 p.m. even they would be ordered to return to their cold rooms. For Gómez Rojas, in solitary confinement, the sun was a fiction, one more thing in motion beyond a radically truncated horizon. The fortunate were free of shackles and fed a meal of "acidic, greasy beans, and a piece of bread, black and coarse, like cow dung," but he was bound, his limbs restrained, and his diet restricted to bread and water.[1] This was Santiago's jail, a "shadowy edifice" known as the Hotel Ascui after its eponymous warden.[2] It evoked in Gómez Rojas a subversive vision of sepulture and decay: "In this jail where I have been brought/ Where the injustice of a law imprisons us:/ I thought of the tombs in which rotted/ Magistrates and judges, now dust upon the earth."

A PARADOXICAL POET

José Domingo Gómez Rojas was a child of Santiago, born August 4, 1896. Very little is known of his childhood.[3] The family moved at least three times within the city before settling on the southern margins of the barrio Latino. They lived in modest, and precarious, circumstances. A friend of his recalled one of their residences: "A poorly paved street, humble appearance, a hall down which one could see from the entrance a sunlit patio, with a grapevine in the corner in the shadow of which one could see a rough table populated with books and papers."[4] There was, at least, money for books.

By 1912 Gómez Rojas was publishing poetry. At least initially, he dedicated much of his work to his religiosity. Gómez Rojas had joined a Protestant denomination that year and proved to be something of a militant opponent of Catholicism.[5] But he also was increasingly attracted to anarchism, and in Santiago he joined in demonstrations and spoke against obligatory military service.[6] Subsequent writers and authors would ignore, or downplay, Gómez Rojas's religiosity, as if to acknowledge it would somehow diminish his political meaning or politics itself.[7] Yet the two do not sit as uncomfortably together as one might suspect. There is a rebelliousness of spirit in his rejection of Catholicism and orthodoxy and his simultaneous embrace of Protestantism and anarchism. His anarchism would never be that of an apostate.

> I have noted in my poetry a profound tendency to spiritualize life . . . To choose the supreme moment of each day, the fugitive instant in time, that makes us divine; and, as such, my poetry is only a conglomeration of culminating moments, of instances of the most forceful exaltation, as I believe that only thus is one able to disentangle the eternal verse; only thus can one achieve living a poetry of the soul; only thus can one know the feeling of the infinite and eternally original beauty of the world.[8]

Even his more visibly anarchist poems are populated with a religious vocabulary: redemption, martyrdom, the Cavalry, and Satan pepper the pages and throughout there appears, as the authors of his only biography note, "a strong identification between the son of God and the suffering of the populace."[9] This is not that surprising. For one, the church generally, despite its overarching conservatism, was not dismissive of working-class concerns in the early twentieth century. Pope Leo XIII's *Rerum novarum* encyclical of 1891 may have opposed working-class mobilization, but it hardly let employers off the hook, and Catholic action groups worked to organize workers in ways that would achieve social justice without revolution or violent agitation. While some espoused positions intensely anti-clerical (Julio Valiente, for example), others saw forms of political possibility in the church or in spirituality.

In his poem "Cristo" ("Christ"), Gómez Rojas counterposed an ideal Christ—characterized by love and utopian visions—with "hypocrits, vampires and frauds." Other writers similarly found a certain resonance between religiosity and anarchism: in anarchism's aspirations for the good for all mankind, wrote Manuel Rojas, "there is something Christian, of loving thy neighbor, but on earth without heaven."[10] There is nothing ironic or hypocritical here. The fact is religion was a deep and expansive well from which could be drawn utopian visions and social vocabularies that resonated widely. Anarchists themselves frequently recognized that there was more than a touch of religious fervor to some components of anarchist agitation, organizing and discourse at the time, despite the resounding cry of "no god, no masters."[11] Anarchism may have eschewed the institutional and hierarchical trappings of a church but it still had its own gospel, with followers at times declaring themselves "apostles." For every "everyday anarchist" or "quiet revolutionary" there was an evangelical anarchist, dogmatic and devout, even if devoid of religion's cult of personality or institutional and hierarchical foundations. Gómez Rojas, for one, saw little need for forced reconciliation. Of his attraction to both Nietzsche and Jesus Christ, he stated: "Are there contradictions? All the better. Like the world, I am a paradox."[12] This political and spiritual militancy—the anarchic and the mystic—would define Gómez Rojas throughout his short life as he sought both social and individual transcendence.

Figure 4.1
José Domingo Gómez Rojas. Courtesy of Memoria Chilena.

It would also define his poetic output, the most famous of which was his 1913 collection *Lyrical Rebellions*, published when he was only seventeen. These poems, written in the midst of Chile's centennial celebrations, were defiant and confrontational, inspired perhaps by the anarchist and labor mobilizations of the era (including the extensive protests of the execution of Spanish educator Francisco Ferrer) as well as the renewed emphasis on the social question and social inequality. They were most likely also inspired by recent sociological and literary critiques of Chile's political and economic system by authors such Alejandro Venegas, whose 1910 critique of Chile's economic system dampened the enthusiasim of the centennial, and Baldomero Lillo, whose *Sub terra* (1904) and *Sub sole* (1907) drew attention to the plight of workers in Chile's mines.[13] *Lyrical Rebellions* is a collection best described as anti-*belle époque*, a raging antithesis to the hyper-adulatory theses that fawned over a mythical Chile awash in the centennial afterbirth of its independence. The thrust of *Lyrical Rebellions* reflects the social turmoil percolating underneath the smooth facade of Chile's parliamentary republic. "Renegación" ("The Cry of the Renegade") is an excellent example.

> I, child of this century of two-faced swine,
> Forsake my century and embrace the fight
> With roars of menace and cries of rebellion
> And my songs are red, like dynamite,
> Like my pains, like my endless anguish,
> Like my eternal thirst for eternal redemption
> I would like my lines, their wings outstretched,
> to reflect my fury, my torment, my dissent;
> cries of menace, on the brink of explosion,
> And I would like my poetry of revolution
> to be the savage shriek of a reckless condor
> who takes flight, colossal, toward the sphere of the sun
> My poetry, rough and strong, does not sing of women,
> nor of false loves, nor of modern pleasures,
> nor are my crude lines mystical ballads;
> my lines are of struggle, written with skillful hand
> I hurl them daringly into the red fray;
> may my untamed lines be cries of rebellion
> My lines, course and fierce, need not be exquisite,
> they are the reflection of my self, frank and direct,
> of my love which is sublime, which is sublime passion.
> I would like my lines to run swiftly like

> steeds. My lines ring out like modest chimes,
> but at times they mimic the sound of cannon
> But, oh, on my forehead I wear a gory stain
> it is a red stain, it is a mocking affront,
> it is the legacy of the century: civilization!
> two-faced lie, ignominious outrage
> rather than civilized I would like to be savage
> to wash my forehead of all execration.
> May my fierce songs be the lyrical menace
> May my crude songs be my people's sacred book
> for I, unnamed bard, do not expect recognition
> and if I unleash my hymns it is because I now feel
> preludes to a new day
> May my lines of the dawn
> be the revolution's call to arms
> I, child of this century of two-faced swine,
> Forsake my century and embrace the fight
> With roars of menace and cries of rebellion
> And my songs are red, like dynamite,
> like my pains, like my endless anguish,
> Like my eternal thirst for eternal redemption.

A child of this century of two-faced swine—in a century barely a decade old. Gómez Rojas's anger is palpable, the stanzas unfold with a ferocious indignation. Menace, struggle, red songs, a red fray, battle, rebellion, dynamite, a gory stain, a clawed, predatory and savage condor in place of the reposed swan. There is little sonorous or dulcet in the words themselves. Take the opening line, which in its original Spanish (*Yo, hijo de este siglo hipócrata y canalla*) ends with a harsh and cacophonous indictment of the era, the hard "c's" erupting in a moment of seething invective. This is poetry as polemic, as manifesto, rousing Chile's youth, its workers, its masses.[14] "J. D. Gómez Rojas is still very young," wrote a reviewer. "Even so, he is already a rebel, a terrible rebel, a frightning rebel. He is rebelling against everything: against grammar, against literature, against poetry, against society, against civilization. . . . It is a lot of rebellion for one lone youth."[15]

Young he may have been but Gómez Rojas was not alone in seeing art, whether poetry or painting, narrative or drama, as political, oppositional, and revolutionary. Some of Chile's leading intellectual figures—poets and writers Carlos Pezoa, Víctor Domingo Silva, Manuel Rojas, González Vera, and Pablo de Rokha, among others—strongly identified as and affiliated with anarchists in particular. Moreover, during those very same years young men who would go on to become some of Chile's most innovative and experimental poets—such as de Rokha and Vicente Huidobro—would come of age. They would soon form part of a Latin American avant garde in poetry, experimenting with new forms of language, imagery, and syntax as the world came to terms with a loss of faith in both religion and science. The spell of reason appeared broken and with no reason, there would be no rhyme.[16] Language itself was no longer transparent nor adequately able to convey the depths of human experience. Increasingly, neither politics nor language seemed capable of bearing the burden of representation. Gómez Rojas's rebellion was simultaneously political and poetic.

All of this worried observers. In 1916 the Council of Public Instruction appointed Joaquín Díaz Garcés Director of the Bellas Artes school. Díaz Garcés, a former director of Chile's major daily *El Mercurio*, had a reputation for being a traditionalist, showing little patience for changing artistic currents and tendencies and convinced his task was to impose discipline among young artists who had begun to experiment with new aesthetics.[17] Conservatives made the link between the arts and politics clear: Diaz Garces was reestablishing "order and scholastic discipline" and defending nothing less than "morality and society."[18] Students in the school disagreed, lamenting his appointment in an open letter to the government, while the FECh demanded his resignation.[19] To no avail. It would be Díaz Garcés who, four years later, on the evening of July 21, would hasten to Santiago's detention section and post bail for the group of young men charged with the destruction of the *Numen* printshop.[20]

Over the course of the 1910s Gómez Rojas continued writing, filling the blank sides of forms stolen from the Commercial Telegraph Company.[21] He wrote poetry and, increasingly, dramatic pieces for the stage, inspired by Maurice Maeterlinck, Henrik Ibsen, and Paul Verlaine; by Argentine writers Alberto Ghiraldo (an anarchist to whom he dedicated his poem "El Suburbio") and Pedro Bonifacio Palacios (aka Almafuerte); and by Oscar Wilde, about whom he wrote a short work for the literary section of the daily *El Chileno*.[22] He was particularly interested in Argentine writers and poets, assembling a list of those he found inspiring and penning short essays (neither of which was published) on Leopoldo Lugones and José de Maturana.[23] He forged close friendships with and inspired many young intellectuals and writers at the time who would go on to literary fame in Chile, including Manuel Rojas, José Santos González Vera, and Antonio Acevedo Hernández, all of whom counted Gómez Rojas as a central figure in their own literary and political formations. Together, in 1913, they gave readings of their work at some of Santiago's workers' centers, including the Casa del Pueblo where they met a young agitator named Casimiro Barrios.[24] Soon after, they organized themselves into the National Drama Company, giving theatrical performances in working-class areas of the city.[25] During the same period, Gómez Rojas adopted a pseudonym, Daniel Vázquez. It was Vázquez to whom was attributed what has become, over the course of the twentieth century, one of Gómez Rojas's most well-known poems: "Miserere" ("Have Mercy").

> Youth, love, what you will,
> Has to depart with us: Have mercy!
> The beauty of the world and what it was
> Will die in the future: Have mercy!
> Earth itself slowly dies
> Along with distant stars: Have mercy!
> And perhaps even death which pursues us
> Will also have its death: Have mercy!

In 1916, death visited the family. Gómez Rojas had begun the year with wonder, hope and optimism. "This year that begins," he wrote in his diary in early 1916, "is filled with promise. Projects and hopes await only my effort to become living miracles in reality. I will intensify my life."[26] Instead he found himself writing an elegy for his brother Manuel.[27] As the family mourned, Gómez Rojas worked in a municipal office to support his mother and surviving brother. He also studied at the Pedagogical Institute at the University of Chile. In other ways, life continued as it had. He frequented Santiago's cafes, exhorted young writers to write, debated politics with intellectuals and workers alike, allied himself with workers' federations and eventually with the IWW, and continued to straddle a world both redeemingly mystical and immediately material. A world of poetry and politics.

PRISONS

Three security section agents detained Gómez Rojas at his home on July 25, 1920. The cause was suspected membership in the IWW. The basis for the accusation arose from a document that identified Gómez Rojas as one of the secretaries of the IWW.[28] How serious his commitment to the IWW was has been a long debated issue. What is certain is that his affiliation was not a police fabrication: the IWW's own bulletin, from April of that year, listed Gómez Rojas as one of the two council representatives for

Valparaíso (along with Triviño) and as a member of the IWW's board.[29] Rather than make excuses for Gómez Rojas, or try to soften his militancy and politics, the important point here is to recognize that the IWW was in fact not a proscribed organization at the time he joined it and that its appeal was not limited to workers in particular industries, but in fact ranged widely. Regardless, once identified as a member and representative, he found himself in Astorquiza's sights. He was arrested along with a number of other prominent Wobblies and anarchists and brought to the Santiago detention section and jail. "What crime brought him to the jail?" his friend González Vera would rhetorically ask. "None. But he was an anarchist."[30]

Begun in 1887 under President José Manuel Balmaceda, and built by construction crews hailing from Italy, France, and Russia as well as Chile, the Santiago jail covered some 14,000 square meters of land in a "sinister block" situated between the Mapocho Station and the main police station in the city.[31] With nearly five hundred cells, it could hold 650 prisoners at any given moment.[32] In 1919 alone, 40,990 prisoners passed through its doors, the majority for petty crimes associated with drunkenness.[33] Whether arrested for public disturbance, on one end of the spectrum, or for sedition, at the other, the multitudes arrested in late July and early August would be brought to the Detention Section, under the auspices of the Security Section, for booking and identification purposes and preliminary detention.[34]

On his arrival at the jail after his arrest, Gómez Rojas's spirits remained high. The warden assigned him cell 462, the cell where Julio Valiente had passed some period of time. Gómez Rojas admired the elder radical and experienced a deep sense of pride at occupying the very cell in which Valiente had been held.[35] He read the inscription Valiente had left on one of the cell's walls: "To be jailed for the liberty of the people is not a crime; it is a pleasure." Gómez Rojas opened his notebook and added his own aphorism: "Here men's liberty dies, but the people's freedom is born."[36] He was a week shy of his twenty-fourth birthday.

Gómez Rojas's stay in jail was brief. The sheer numbers arrested combined with the willingness of Astorquiza to hold individuals for extended periods while Security Section agents sought out evidence of affiliation with the IWW or subversion had resulted in overcrowding of the jail.[37] The fact that what constituted evidence of illicit association was broad exacerbated the problem: everything from copies of *Numen* to claims by neighbors that a suspect had "continuous meetings . . . with various people who seemed to be propagandists" was read as proof of subversion, even if witnesses and neighbors often offered contradictory testimony or retracted statements.[38] Meanwhile Astorquiza expanded the ambit of his investigations by ordering agents to investigate whether or not any of those arrested had been involved in organizing recent strikes in Santiago.[39] To cope with the demands of the *proceso* and the overcrowding at the jail, officials issued a decree allowing for those arrested to be transferred to the penitentiary, in Santiago's southern extremis and only blocks from the Gómez Rojas family home and from the factories and industries that workers had repeatedly struck in recent months.[40]

Thus by mid-August of 1920, as Astorquiza defended his mass arrests and Santiago's intendent stepped down in the wake of the scandal surrounding his arrest and detention of Grecco and others with no cause, Gómez Rojas had been transferred to Santiago's penitentiary. There he joined a number of his friends and comrades who were able to enjoy more time on the patio, walking and chatting, to receive visitors with more frequency, and to write, read, and argue. At one point in mid-August, twelve subversive apostles sat for a photograph. Gómez Rojas posed with arms folded, Pedro Gandulfo immediately to his left and Julio Valiente to his right.

One of two penitentiaries in the country, Santiago's dated from 1844 and was the second to be built in a Latin American capital, after Rio de Janeiro.[41] It was part of a larger vision of what modern societies, as well as ideas of crime and punishment, might look like and what mechanisms

Figure 4.2
Anarchist apostles. Twelve of the men detained in late July posed for a photograph in mid-August in the penitentiary. Gómez Rojas is noted by an "x," in the front row second from the left. On his right is Julio Valiente; on his left is Pedro Gandulfo. *Sucesos* (October 7, 1920).

for controlling modernity's margins should be. These projects shared certain characteristics, as historian Carlos Aguirre notes: they had "an ad hoc architectural design (inspired by the panoptic ideal of Jeremy Bentham), a highly regimented work and educational routine, a system of permanent vigilance of the prisoners, supposedly humanitarian treatment, and religious instruction of the prisoners."[42] In Santiago's penitentiary, each cell would house four men who had been convicted of perpetrating similar crimes. Ideally for criminologists and penalogists, at least one of the four cellmates would be literate and thus able to teach the others to read and write.[43] The penitentiary followed what came to be known as the Auburn system, named after the penitentiary in the upstate New York town of the same name.[44] The Auburn prison philosophy had been developed as an alternative to that of the Philadelphia penitentiary. The Philadelphia system had taken as its premise the need for isolation: men were to practice a form of monastic penitence, alone in cells for twenty-three hours of the day, reading and contemplating scripture. But the isolation drove men mad. The Auburn system advocated a different model, more in tune perhaps with modern, industrial times: isolation at night, collective labor during the day.[45]

This was the model for the Santiago penitentiary. It had workshops where prisoners worked at the behest of private industrialists who had negotiated labor contracts with the government.[46] The prisoners, in return, would earn small amounts of money that would be dedicated to partially covering the expenses of their own incarceration or to supporting their families.[47] All prisoners—whether in the jail or the penitentiary—were required to work. If work was not available within the prison walls, wardens contacted the municipal authorities who then assigned prisoners to various work projects.[48] Prisoners thus rehabilitated themselves through production rather than penitence, contemplating their crimes while laboring for others.

This was the ideal, at least. But the entire Chilean carceral complex was in need of overhaul. Over the course of the 1910s various ministries and offices issued decrees and statements regarding the need for existing penal establishments to conform to "modern concepts of the prison," to ensure the health and "moral and social rehabilitation" of those detained, and to improve food quality, hygiene, and medical care throughout the system.[49] Depite such repeated pronouncements, conditions improved only marginally and those arrested, whether students or workers, understood that prison, whether the jail or the penitentiary, was a place in which men lived in constant struggle against tuberculosis and typhus, depression, insanity, violence, and discipline.[50]

Prisoners had to cope with poor quality food, long an issue in the penal system.[51] In September 1920 prisoners in the Santiago jail refused to eat the bread they were served because it was made from "blackened flour [negruzca] of the lowest quality." Officials had complained to the supplier, Carlos Matte Eyzaguirre, and his representative, but to no avail.[52] Matte Eyzaguirre, one of Santiago's prominent patricians and identified by members of the FECh as one of the July 21 assailants, promised the minister that the situation would be resolved.[53] Prisoner frustration over food quality was significant enough that prisoners sought to cook for themselves in prison courtyards. At the penitentiary in Talca, family members brought prisoners "meat, potatoes, charcoal, firewood and other things" so that they might cook for themselves, but officials soon banned such activities on the grounds that there was no room to store the cooking utensils and prison courtyards had come to resemble "gypsy camps."[54] Even so, the practice must have continued as prohibitions had to be reiterated, suggesting a struggle between prisoners, who saw such practices as a right, and the authorities, who saw them as a privilege, at best.

Carcereal conditions took their toll on the prisoners in other ways. Typhus was a regular risk. Typhus epidemics had struck the jails in Temuco, Imperial, and Lautaro in June of 1918, and in Pitrufquen in August of 1918, killing prisoners as well as the warden. This partially explains the difficulties prisons confronted in hiring guards.[55] Tuberculosis was the most common illness and spread at such an alarming rate in prisons over the course of the 1910s that the government debated building a sanitorium to isolate and treat prisoners suffering its effects.[56] Luis Troncoso, the secretary general of the Print Workers Union and one of those imprisoned for subversion, immediately sought care, upon his release, for severe symptoms of turberculosis from medical student and FECh president Alfredo Demaría.[57] Pedro Gandulfo contracted pulmonary tuburculosis while in the penitentiary in late August. Only days before his brother Juan would himself be incarcerated, having eluded capture for nearly six weeks, Pedro was moved to the Hospital Salvador at the orders of Astorquiza, where he received treatment under "strict guard."[58] Gandulfo's plight pointed toward additional issues prisoners confronted: the penitentiary's infirmary proved inadequate for treating prisoners despite earlier promises from the Ministry of Justice that such issues would be resolved. Carceral officials continued to complain that not only was manpower wasted transporting prisoners to hospitals with limited security but that they themselves risked contracting an infectious disease by entering the hospitals.[59]

Gandulfo survived his bout with tuberculosis but lived with the aftereffects of the illness for the rest of his life.[60]

In the penitentiary, sexual violence was commonplace. Men raped other men, as well as young boys who, despite regulations otherwise, were put in with the general prison population. Prisoners sent to the infirmary were on occasion drugged and then raped. None of this was unknown to the guards, the wardens, or their superiors. Sex functioned as a currency and some prisoners worked within the prison as prostitutes, paid in cartons of cigarettes or candles. Upon Juan Gandulfo's arrival in the penitentiary in early September, he was approached by a young boy. "Sweet doctor," the boy said, "if you give me a half-kilo of sugar or a little bit of wine, I will let you 'vaccinate' me." Gandulfo gave him the sugar and refused the euphemism.

Gandulfo argued that the prison system needed to provide a means for inmates to have sexual relationships. He recounted the comments of a fellow anarchist and friend in the penitentiary:

> Listen my little bourgeois friend, I tell you this, in spite of the shame, because I know you understand. I come at night and when I soap my body while bathing. But, in spite of this, I have such an intense desire to possess another being that, even if I knew that my mate would die after I fornicated with him, I would still get together with the young man in the cell next to mine.

Such a "cry of desperation," wrote Gandulfo, should compel change in the system, but when he suggested to a prison official that prisoners be permitted to see their spouses or girlfriends (or, if unattached, a prostitute) in order to humanely address sexual needs, the official argued this would do nothing more than turn him in to a pimp. Gandulfo, always a quick wit, suggested that he already was. Prisoners thus improvised. Male prisoners married one another, a commitment respected by others in the prison just as it was "respected in bourgeois society." They held wedding ceremonies after which, during patio hours, inmates would gather and encircle the newlyweds to shield them from the guards while they consummated their vows.[61]

In theory younger prisoners were to be separated from older ones and violent criminals from nonviolent offenders, just as men and women were institutionally segregated. In fact Lafuente, arrested along with Pedro Gandulfo and Rigoberto Soto Rengifo, was released after a week because he was a minor. A leader in the Primary Instruction Student's Federation (Federación de Estudiantes de Instrucción Primaria, or Federación Chica), he was seventeen years old and serves as a reminder of the fact that student politics was not limited to university students.[62] In another instance officials had a doctor examine a young man's genitals and teeth to determine his age and, therefore, if he would be treated as an adult or a juvenile.[63] Questions of morality in the prison and fears of "moral abandon" had also led some to argue for separating those convicted of violent crimes from those whose crimes were political or petty, an issue that had also been addressed in the 1911 prison regulations.[64] But those detained for political reasons in 1920 and transferred to the penitentiary appear not to have been isolated from the general penitentiary population. Space constraints may have played a role in their placement, although Astorquiza and his superiors may also have thought putting political prisoners in with the general population might wilt the subversives' resolve. Juan Gandulfo was placed in the "Siberian patio," which would later serve as the location for firing squad executions, with at least two other reported subversives: Italian socialist Lorenzo Loggia Fratti, imprisoned for four months, a full quarter of which he spent in solitary, and Rigoberto Soto Rengifo, colleague and friend of Gandulfo's younger brother, Pedro, arrested during the attacks on the FECh club.[65] They shared the wing with a host of common prisoners whose crimes ran the gamut from the petty to the horrific: a young boy sentenced to five years and a day—the minimum sentence for the penitentiary rather than the presidio—for serving as the lookout in a robbery; a man condemned for life for the murder of eight people and the rape of an infant; a jealous husband who castrated with his bare hands the man he suspected of being his wife's lover; and two young brothers who had killed, dismembered, and cooked their grandmother in an unsuccessful effort to steal her savings and to cover up the crime.[66]

That Gandulfo shared a wing in the penitentiary with Loggia and Soto Rengifo was not uncommon. Many of those jailed for subversion were placed in patios or wings with at least some of their comrades, where they gave grammar lessons, shared news, and sat for photographs.[67] For all of the horrors of the penitentiary, it had at least some advantages over incarceration in the jail: prisoners had some access to fresh air and the patios, and the facility had a reputation for being cleaner and more spacious than the jail.[68] Not only did Gómez Rojas—who by August 12 had been transferred to the penitentiary—have regular access to the patio to walk and get fresh air, he also enjoyed visits from his mother and other writers.[69] He had pens and paper and books, as a writer items essential to his well-being; he could offer grammar courses; he could enjoy the occasional cigarette; and he could interact with his fellow comrades.[70]

DENIAL

Pedro Gandulfo and Rigoberto Soto Rengifo had been imprisoned for eighteen days when they wrote Astorquiza requesting bail. This was their second request, the first having been denied. Their argument consisted of two basic points: first, that they were innocent of the charges brought against them, and, second, that regardless of questions of innocence or guilt, the crimes for which they were being held were not so serious that they could be denied bail. To support their claims they cited the relevant articles from Chilean legal codes. In this they were not alone. Many of those detained in July and August fought vigorously for their respective rights and for bail and yet came up empty-handed.[71]

There is nothing contradictory in anarchists and anarchist sympathizers appealing to the law and the constitution. The legal system may not have lived up to its own "rhetoric of equality," but that hardly means men and women were prepared to abandon it entirely.[72] In many instances men and women accused of anarchist sympathies or affiliations were often at the forefront of attempting to ensure that laws were enacted and enforced. Despite the fact that such efforts made them targets of persecution and prosecution and despite the capriciousness with which men empowered with legal authority acted, they continued to struggle over the meaning of the law. Such was the case here: Astorquiza's response to the young men's petition for bail was a three-word phrase that would become all too common in the months of August and September: "No ha lugar."[73] Petition denied.

Such denial of bail was surely unexpected. Only six months earlier individuals arrested for various acts of subversion were either issued a warning or released within two weeks of having been detained.[74] For example, José del Tránsito Ibarra and Manuel Montano, among others, participated in a demonstration in February 1920 protesting the treatment of workers by the Franke, Jullian Company. Tránsito Ibarra spoke, declaring that "bravery was shown by joining together in public demonstrations under the red flag and not on the battlefields, fighting with weapons for unknown reasons and against one's brothers." Rather than arrest and jail, the young man was warned by a police official present to cease with "anti-patriotic expressions."[75] The political atmosphere appeared less sanguine in July, as Gandulfo and Soto Rengifo would learn.

Upon receiving the news their petition had been denied, Gandulfo and Soto Rengifo recognized they stood little chance of seeing freedom as long as Astorquiza remained in charge. They thus tried a different tactic. In a cheeky letter to Astorquiza, Gandulfo noted that it had come to his attention that Astorquiza was "Peruvian by birth." Given that his charge was to investigate anarchists and illicit societies and, in part, the connections that these might have had with Peru, the implication was that Astorquiza needed to recuse himself.[76] Calling Astorquiza "Peruvian" was wily. Everywhere a reader turned in Chile in 1920 there was yet another reference to Peruvian conspiracies, plots, or espionage. Accusations of linkages to Peru were commonplace in assertions of subversion. When the FECh club had been sacked, the assailants had posted a sign that the location was for rent. Interested parties were instructed to "inquire in Lima." Peruvian "spies" had been accused of collaborating with paid agitators, distributing subversive propaganda, and planting dynamite in mining centers.[77] A raid on the home of Armando Triviño allegedly turned up proof linking the magazine he coedited, *Verba Roja*, with Peruvian associates and money.[78] An editorial in *Sucesos* asked a rhetorical question, with no sarcasm: "How much do you want to bet that Minister Astorquiza will discover that those in the I.W.W. were receiving money from Peru for their subversive plans?"[79] Members of Parliament made similar accusations, emphasizing Peruvian membership in the IWW and conflating being Peruvian with being an agitator, an "enemy of patriotism," and Chile's eternal enemy.[80]

If working-class and poor Peruvians, especially in the north, had long felt the wrath of anti-Peruvian sentiment, by 1920 that suspicion and anger had expanded to the center of *santiagueño* political and commercial life. Throughout the month of July concerns regarding Peruvians working in sensitive industries, such as that of telegraph offices, were raised on the Senate floor, leading the head of the telegraph office to assure the government that no Peruvians were in his employ.[81] Such assurances did little to dispel images of subversive Peruvians penetrating the very heart of the Chilean bureaucracy. An editorial in Santiago's major daily suggested that all Peruvians, regardless of how long they had been in Chile, were suspect. "It is imperative that Peruvians employed in telegraph and postal offices of the Republic, in offices of cartography and architecture . . . be given notification that they will no longer find the same environment they have had up to now and that we are resolved to deny them henceforth the hospitality that they have abused."[82] These were not lone voices. Deputies spoke of Peruvian spies in the Valparaíso customs house. "They are treated better than the Chilean employees," clamored one deputy, "but, because of family connections, because they are members of the upper class, because these individuals belong to high society or because they are major shareholders in some association of brokers, they are tolerated and continue intervening in our secrets, sending communications to Peru, and offending us in our own territory . . . We want authorities willing to use an iron fist to expel these foreign citizens from our country."[83]

The call for an iron fist resonated. On the heels of such vitriol came a remarkable proposal from the Santiago intendent: "The administrative authority would look kindly upon Peruvians resident in this department leaving the country prior to August 1." This was a punitive deadline and one intended to both facilitate the expulsion of some individuals and to respond to popular calls for action against perceived traitors and infiltrators.[84] It very quickly proved problematic. Meanwhile, the consul in Iquique informed the US ambassador in Santiago that the Liga Patriotica was mistreating and expelling Peruvians and that "the actual rounding up of those to be deported was in the hands of two men well known in Iquique for their criminal records."[85] "Ninety per cent of those deported are natives of the province," he continued, "and are forced to go to Peru where they have neither homes nor interests."[86] Deportations—ethnic cleansings—persisted over the course of late August and into September with the support of Intendent Fernando Edwards, who issued "inflammatory speeches to the effect that Chile must have war with Peru and that he means personally to slaughter large numbers of Peruvians as soon as the war begins."[87]

Peruvians of various social backgrounds found themselves under assault. Chileanization campaigns and increased social crises in 1919 had led to repeated expulsions of individuals in the borderlands considered, accurately or not, Peruvian. By July and August of 1920, such campaigns had spread across geographic and class lines and internal conflicts developed within the government. Minister of the Interior Pedro García de la Huerta received complaints that the police themselves were ordering arbitrary expulsions of Peruvians.[88] He felt compelled to remind the intendent that no Peruvian citizens should be disturbed without cause and that the process of expelling "pernicious foreigners" should conform with the procedures established by the Residency Law.[89] The impetus for de la Huerta's missive derived from the fact that, despite the decades of antagonism between the two countries, personal and professional relationships between Chileans and Peruvians ran deep. Even the Santiago mayor weighed in: when an interviewer asked about him giving citizenship status to some Peruvians, he responded that one "had to take in to consideration the person's condition and one's personal knowledge of them . . . For example, I know of cases in which it was necesary to give a citizenship card to a gentleman who has lived almost all his life in Chile [and] his children and wife are Chileans; to deny them the right to live in Chile would be the same as requiring him to kill himself, because he is a true Chilean."[90]

In other words, with increased frequency the "wrong" Peruvians—those with the relevant class status and commercial connections—were being targeted and ministers in the government were forced to intervene.[91] Manuel Molina Alay, born in Tacna in 1868, had had a long career as an educator in Chile's Pedagogical Institute, teaching English and French, until he retired and opened up a small pharmacy. He had married a Chilean, with whom he had nine children, the oldest of whom was beginning his military service. Molina presented himself, along with a number of letters of support from "respectable persons" to the Minister of the Interior García de la Huerta, who wrote immediately to the Santiago intendent on Molina's behalf: "If said gentleman does not have a prior record in the Santiago police registries, please order the police to let him be and to permit him to freely go about his business, and it is especially recommended that a police guard is placed in his house as guarantee for himself and his interests, while the current situation passes."[92] Juan José Arrospide, head of the La Aguada company, drew on his relationship with Senator Enrique MacIver to get assurances he would be left alone, as did Jorge Arturo Hidalgo.[93] Carlos Botta contacted García de la Huerta directly to intervene on his behalf. The minister obliged this "Peruvian gentleman who has resided in Chile for more than thirty years, the son of Italian parents . . . and who has shown this Ministry numerous certificates from respectable commercial establishments in Santiago presenting him as a well-known gentleman from an excellent background and [they] have never seen him behave in any way hostile to Chile."[94]

Thus, when Gandulfo and Soto Rengifo asserted that Astorquiza himself was Peruvian, they did so with a seriousness of purpose laden with a heavy dose of irony. Such a tactic revealed less their nationalist proclivities or perspectives on Peru than it did their recognition that there was more than a touch of hypocrisy to the entire artifice of nationality on which a central part of the *proceso* rested. For Astorquiza the accusation struck a nerve: rather than ignore the claim, he grew angry and defensive and penned a four page response.[95] "Not a single connection of interest, nor of affection, links the undersigned [Astorquiza] to Peru," he wrote, and while the baptismal record might state he was born in Callao on February 4, 1866, family tradition held he was born on a Chilean merchant ship. His birth was registered in Montevideo in 1868, and he eventually became a naturalized Chilean in 1889.[96] The students' audacity must have rubbed raw the wound of Astorquiza's own national and class insecurities. Moreover, the documentary ambivalence could only add fuel to the fire, particularly given the persistent bureaucratic obsession with citizenship documentation when it came to working people.

Newspapers in Santiago came to Astorquiza's defense while heaping scorn on his accusers. Since being naturalized he had never once left Chile, *El Mercurio* clamored. Moreover, he wrote his thesis on the status of individuals born in transnational circumstances, a strange defense given the expulsions of inhabitants in the north that were unfolding at the very same time.[97] Writers for *Sucesos* critiqued his accusers: "These suspicions launched against his nationality are the desperate efforts of the defenders of the anarchists who, although it sounds untrue, have attorneys at the highest levels of politics."[98] While a court took up Gandulfo's and Soto Rengifo's petition that Astorquiza recuse himself, it did so only in order to quash it.[99] Shortly thereafter, the two young men began another term in solitary confinement.[100]

By the end of August, despite petitions of support from prominent politicians, Gandulfo and Soto Rengifo remained incarcerated. Pedro Aguirre Cerda, future president of Chile, wrote Astorquiza personally to note that "the Gandulfo" who had been publicly accused of subversive ideas was not *Pedro* Gandulfo (thereby conceding perhaps that Pedro's brother Juan *was* guilty of subversion), and that moreover, both he and Soto Rengifo were Radical Party "assemblyists" in frank disagreement with "anarchist ideas and even with the Socialist Party."[101] This was soft-pedaling of their ideas: Gandulfo was an admirer of Stirner and regularly attended celebrations of the anniversary of the Russian Revolution; Soto Rengifo, among other activities, helped to circulate works of Trotsky. Regardless, a letter was as far as Aguirre Cerda was willing to go and, with his finger to the political winds (he would soon be appointed Minister of the Interior in Alessandri's administration), he refused to provide legal services to any of those held in the proceso.

In the meantime, Astorquiza had begun to grant bail to at least some individuals. The criteria for his decisions is unclear. Be that as it may, Pedro León Ugalde—member of the Radical Party and who had been with Labarca when he was assaulted on July 19—was freed on bail on August 11.[102] Three days later a group of printers was freed after nearly three weeks of detention. They had submitted a lengthy letter to Astorquiza outlining their rights under the law. The government had charged them with "crimes against the internal security of the State" and "illicit association" because they had been arrested with various fliers related to the general strike in late July in solidarity with *Numen* press and the FECh, and, as such, considered them potential members of (or affiliates with) the IWW.[103] After their arrest, they were held not for the crime they had purportedly committed but rather "an infinity" of other crimes, including provoking rebellion against authority and illicit association. With careful reasoning that questioned both the logic of the process and the lack of evidence, including a reference to the fact that Santiago's own security section had been unable to find evidence of illicit association, the three men successfully argued their case.[104] The conclusion reached by the investigators from the security section confirmed their claims: "There is reason to conclude that these four detainees worked together with the organizers of the general strike . . . but there is no antecedent to establish that they are members of the Industrial Workers of the World Association [*sic*], as all of the investigations undertaken with regards to that are negative."[105] They were freed on August 14, after nearly three weeks of detention.

Why were some denied bail when others, held on the very same charges, were freed?[106] Despite being imprisoned, prisoners quickly learned who had received bail and who had not. Particularly galling to Gandulfo and Soto Rengifo, among others, must have been the news that one of the individuals who had been identified and arrested for participating in the assault on the FECh—Domingo Undurraga Fernández—had been released on bail shortly after his arrest. Undurraga, a former lieutenant in the reserves and recently returned from duties with the Chilean legation in Buenos Aires, was the son of prominent conservative party member, deputy and landowner Luis Alberto Undurraga, and his brother was a student leader in the agronomy school of the Catholic University.[107] That relative fame, combined with the fact that he was in his military uniform at the time, explains why he was repeatedly identified by eyewitnesses as having taken part in the assault.[108] The same was most likely true for another individual identified by eyewitnesses: Carlos Alarcón Ulloa. A thirty-six-year-old lawyer, Alarcón was also a former military man and a well-known horseman with a residence just off of the Plaza de Armas and across the street from the Santiago Theatre. He was well-known enough to have had his name worked in to a pun that circulated in Santiago in 1918.[109] Astorquiza interviewed Alarcón on August 11, the same day he released Undurraga on 2,000 pesos bail.[110]

Astorquiza's willingness to grant Undurraga bail came in the midst of an increasing critique that he had not pursued those who had assaulted the FECh with as much vigor as those who had been assaulted.[111] None of the assailants from the first assault on the FECh club had been arrested or questioned. In fact, Iván Pra Balmaceda, one of the main instigators of the initial assault on the FECh who sought Juan Gandulfo's head, would soon depart Chile to study at the University of Notre Dame.[112] The young men who attacked the *Numen* press that same evening had been released after a prominent Santiago conservative posted their bail, even as *Numen*'s owner Julio Valiente remained in prison. Nor had there been any concerted effort to determine who the assailants were in the photograph that had appeared in *El Mercurio* after the second assault on the FECh. Student leaders raised this issue in letters to Astorquiza, pushing him to identify the assailants who had sacked the premises, destroyed furniture, burned archives and books, and paraded around the city center with the large bronze plaque that decorated the entry to the FECh club. The plaque in particular moved to the center of the debate, given that some four dozen of the young men who appropriated it had allowed themselves, in a moment of supreme arrogance, to be photographed. Astorquiza eventually ordered security agents to investigate, and by early September they had identified fourteen of the men in the picture.

Yet other than Carlos Alarcón (identified as #3 in the photograph), none of the identified individuals was arrested or detained, and most would continue to reap the rewards of privilege as if the disorder they had wrought

Figure 4.3
The police and the Golden Youth: unlike Wobblies, Santiago's young aristocrats had little qualms about being photographed. Here a group of participants in the attack on the FECh pose with their "trophies" at the offices of *El Mercurio*. The police, eventually, were compelled to identify those in the image. Courtesy of the Archivo Nacional de Chile.

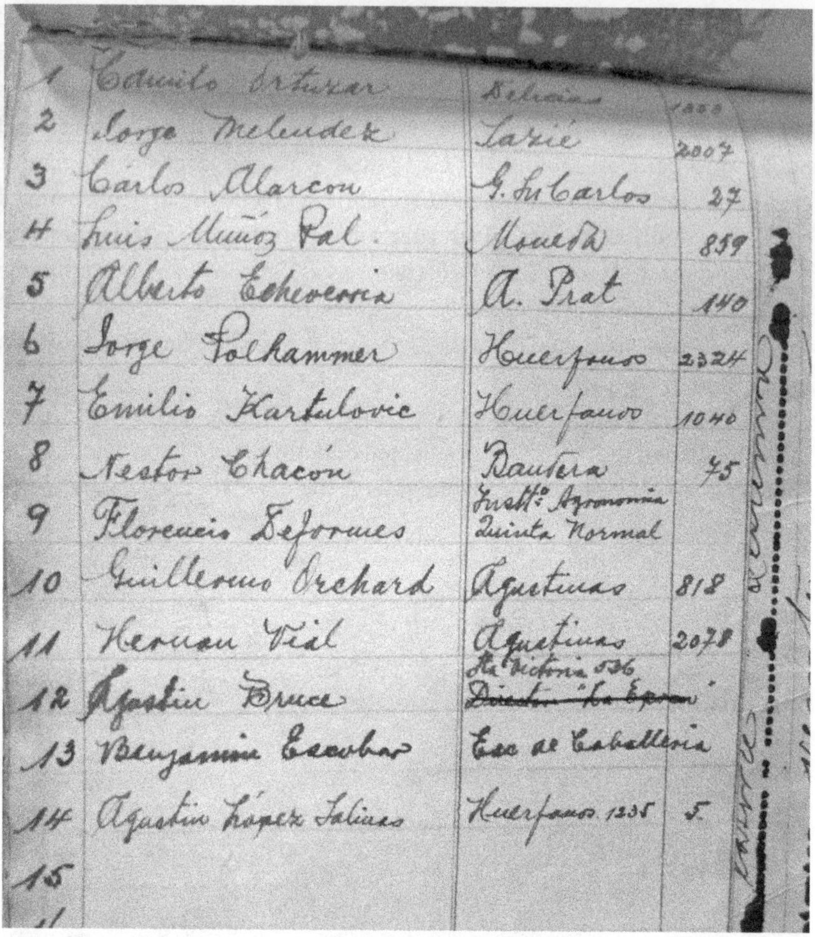

1	Camilo Ortuzar	Delicias	[illegible]
2	Jorge Melendez	Lazie	2007
3	Carlos Alarcon	G. San Carlos	27
4	Luis Muñoz Pal.	Moneda	859
5	Alberto Echeverria	A. Prat	140
6	Jorge Polhammer	Huerfanos	2324
7	Emilio Kartulovic	Huerfanos	1040
8	Nestor Chacón	Bandera	75
9	Florencio Deformes	Instº Agronomia Quinta Normal	
10	Guillermo Orchard	Agustinas	818
11	Hernan Vial	Agustinas	2078
12	Agustin Bruce	Sta Victoria 536 ~~Diario [illegible]~~	
13	Benjamin Escobar	Esc de Caballeria	
14	Agustin López Salinas	Huerfanos 1235	5.
15			

Figure 4.4
The back of the photograph offered a preliminary list of those identified. Courtesy of the Archivo Nacional de Chile.

and the criminality in which they had engaged had never occurred. Among the fourteen identified were Emilio Kartulovic (#7), known as a playboy and "sportman," and who some years later garnered fame in Argentina as a race-car driver. He also became, in time, the lover of a very young woman named Eva Perón.[113] Luis Muñoz Pal (#4), Alberto Echeverría (#5), Agustín Bruce (#12), and Agustín López Salinas (#14) would all go on to careers as attorneys, despite the fact that law careers would be prohibited for those assaulted at the FECh (such as Pedro Gandulfo). Camilo Ortúzar Cruz (#1), a son of the owner of the Hacienda Teno, near Curicó, south of Santiago, became a stockbrocker and advertised his services in the boxing programs issued by Chile's boxing federation, a member of which included

Guillermo Orchard (#10) who is squatting behind Ortúzar in the image.[114] The man wearing the mask (#13) was identified as Benjamin Escobar, a young military cadet. In 1937 he would be one of three officers sent to study in the German Wehrmacht, and two years later he would accompany Germany's National Socialist army as an observer when it invaded Poland.[115] One would remain forever unidentified because, perhaps in a moment of self-preservation, he or someone close to his family had scratched out his face from the negative.

POLITICS OF INSOLENCE

At some point in the latter part of August penitentiary officials transported Gómez Rojas, Soto Rengifo, and Manuel Montano back to the Security Section for a subsequent interrogation with Astorquiza and Minister García Vidaurre. "I met at length," Gómez Rojas recalled, "with García Vidaurre and with don Pepe."[116] Don Pepe was his irreverent form of referring to Astorquiza. It is most likely at this meeting that the subsequent exchange, recalled by attorney Carlos Vicuña Fuentes, occurred: "Are you an anarchist?" asked Astorquiza. Gómez Rojas answered: "I do not have, dear Minister, sufficient moral discipline to assume that title, which I will never merit." Astorquiza tried again. "You, young man, appear at these proceedings involved in one of the most serious crimes that can be committed in a Republic: a crime against the internal security of the State." To this charge Gómez Rojas responded with an indifferent shrug of his shoulders and a dismissive remark: "Let's not be so theatrical, dear Minister." Astorquiza, enraged, issued his order: "Take this insolent boy away immediately, put him in manacles in solitary confinement and eight days of bread and water only."[117]

It in no way diminishes the militancy and seriousness of purpose of young men such as Gómez Rojas to suggest that their purported insolence exacerbated the intensity of the persecution they experienced. In times of social uncertainty, the symbolic is sacred to the status quo. Flags and monuments, hierarchy and place, respect and manners, convention and conformity, property and propriety: these are the foundations on which rest the reassurance that all is as it should be and shall remain. To such foundations, there is little as infuriating as principled defiance. The Chilean state in the late 1910s confronted a multitude of social, economic, and political crises, as did an array of states and systems in the wake of the Great War, a global recession, and two social revolutions. In such circumstances public disturbance could be made to appear as sedition, petty transgressions could be construed as political crimes, and attitude could constitute evidence.

Political scientist James Scott has argued persuasively for the importance of forms of resistance that are characteristically quotidian, anonymous, and material. Those in positions of radical subordination will often outwardly conform and express what appears to be obedient behavior even as they understand full well the oppressiveness and injustice of the social order within which they live and find alternative means through which to express that realization.[118] Popular culture abounds with such acts, captured perhaps most eloquently in the Ethiopian proverb: "When the great lord passes the wise peasant bows deeply and silently farts."[119] Still, some choose to fart loudly. Anonymous resistance has its counterpart in public defiance, targeting not only the materiality but the symbolism of power. As such, its threat is ideological but very immediate, visceral even. History abounds with figures who openly and publicly defied a judge, a police chief, or a general: a small sampling could include the anarchist Félix Fénéon, who, with dry wit and keen insight, had the Parisian public and the jury laughing at the prosecutor who sought to put him away for purported bombings. Or the young Russian radical Bogoliubov, who refused to show General Trepov the proper respect. Trepov had him publicly beaten, which in turn provoked not only public outrage but an avenging spirit in the form of Vera Zasulich who attempted to assassinate Trepov.[120] Or take Casimiro Barrios, whose expulsion from Chile was preceded by an encounter with the Santiago intendent who ruffled at the young militant's alleged insolence. Or, well-known to the young intellectuals in Santiago at the time, Oscar Wilde, whose socialism was constantly paired with a commitment to individual freedom and whose work critiqued the artifice of virtue and manners behind which aristocrats and the high bourgeoisie masked their "calculating vulgarity."[121] But it was his irreverence, wit, and defiance that won him both acclaim and, when he was tried for "gross and obscence acts," prosecutorial wrath.

"To Nietzsche and to Oscar Wilde he was certainly faithful," wrote González Vera about Gómez Rojas, some years later. "Imprisoned, his attitude with respect to Judge Astorquiza was utterly faithful to the great Englishman. It surely cost him his life."[122] González Vera was an astute observer of life under hierarchy and inequality. He hardly intended to elide the role of political radicalism at the time, but his emphasis on social graces and hierarchy is important. Gómez Rojas suffered as much for his refusal to obey the protocols of social hierarchy as he did for the subversiveness of his ideas or revolutionary activities. Indeed, from the perspective of those in power at the time, the case might be made that his most subversive act was to not show proper deference to his supposed superiors—the magistrates and judges, cops and security agents—before whom he appeared. One can imagine that the impression of insolence went even deeper given Gómez Rojas was a well-known poet and intellectual, learned and respected, at the young age of twenty-four.

González Vera is not the only one to have made the comparison between Gómez Rojas and Wilde. Writer and director of *Juventud*, Roberto Meza Fuentes, noted that Gómez Rojas, "like Oscar Wilde, laughed at the judges."[123] Some in the press also made the association. A political cartoon published in *Sucesos* on August 19 shows an angry presiding judge confronting a dandy bedecked with an ascot, heeled boots, and an unruly mass of hair.[124] "Subversive!" shouts the judge, leaning across his podium for emphasis. "Do you believe in the 'queso de bola'?" The "queso de bola" (literally, cheese ball) was an expression referring to a closely shorn or bald head such as the judge's and, by extension, the law.[125] The sentiment is a sly mix of "Do you believe in anything?" and "Get a haircut, hippie!" The image, while not unprecedented in its portrayal of university students, captured the cultural concerns that underlay broader political concerns: namely, of the cultural politics of youth and the ability of style to communicate, in public and confrontational fashion, a form of disdain and defiance of public standards and morality. The figure's stance—cocky, flippant, defiant—says it all.

Everywhere they turned, Santiago's defenders of the social order saw insubordination. The Santiago intendent bristled at Barrios's insolence;

Figure 4.5
The politics of insolence. This cartoon, which appeared in *Sucesos*, portrays the subversive as a kind of Oscar Wilde dandy. *Sucesos* (August 19, 1920).

the golden youth and members of the Union Club saw it in the FECh leadership that had questioned the government's war mobilizations; sons of the aristocracy saw it in others' refusal to address them as they wished, such as when a number of young men referred to García de la Huerta's son as simply "García," dropping his full last name with all its aristocratic trappings, much to his frustration and chagrin; and employers perceived it among Alessandri's dear rabble, emboldened by his candidacy, more brazen in their attitudes and less apt to know and respect their place.[126] The alliances forged between students and workers were another example of the breach of social boundaries and categories, and young men such as Gómez Rojas, Gandulfo, and Labarca personified this breach.

Scorning convention, nonconformity, the willingness to say "no," the gesture of refusal, the shrug of the shoulders: defiant acts with powerful consequences.[127] Little wonder that accusations of insolence punctuate the documentary record with regularity, as if it were a crime. In fact, it was. At least in the nineteenth century, insolence was treated as a criminal act in the prison system where, after "disobedience," it was the most commonly punished act in the penitentiary during its first three decades of existence.[128] It may not have been adjudged a criminal act beyond the prison walls, but, judging by the price some paid in 1920, it might as well have been.

THE SHADOW OF MADNESS

"Every man," wrote Victor Serge, "who is thrown in to a cell immediately begins to live in the shadow of madness."[129] Some cells cast longer and darker shadows than others. By late August, Gómez Rojas was back in the Santiago jail. To what he owed his return is unclear. It may have been his insolent exchange with Astorquiza. Or it may have resulted from Astorquiza's visit to the penitentiary, in which he observed Gómez Rojas on the patio, out of his cell, casually smoking with his hands in his pockets, a vision of repose and comfort. It could have been any number of things, precisely because, despite the institutional and legal window-dressing, the *proceso* was an ad hoc undertaking, guided less by legal procedure or juridical precedent than by individual whim, class anxieties, and a collective will to persecute. Regardless, at some point in late August, Astorquiza had Gómez Rojas moved from the penitentiary—from the company of his comrades, time on the patio, access to books and pens and paper—to the jail.[130]

If conditions in the penitentiary had proved difficult, those in the Santiago jail were brutal. Cells were six by three, oppressive, gloomy, cold, foreboding, unventilated, and damp.[131] Both the jail and the detention section were dramatically understaffed compared to the penitentiary and in immediate need of repair.[132] The adjoining Detention Section contained a pharmacy—with very limited funds—to take care of sick prisoners, but it lacked basic heat and ventilation, so much so that one writer feared it would become inadvertently "a place of capital punishment."[133] Critiques of the jail, completed in its new location at the turn of the century, had intervened with some regularity on the public's consciousness. For example, in 1905, attorney Alvaro Lamas published his "Desde la carcel" ("From the jail"), a mix of sociological critique and searing exposé based on his experiences with the Chilean legal system and the Santiago jail. He excoriated the arbitrariness of the legal system and its victimization of the poor. More than a decade later, little had changed. In 1919 members of the Parliament voiced concerns that officials held political prisoner and anarchist Julio Rebosio "in conditions fit for the Middle Ages, in a dungeon without light and without fresh air, without food, in chains and solitary confinement."[134] Such conditions repeatedly raised concerns among members of the Parliament and the press. Many knew all too well that their nationalist forefathers, in the struggle for independence from Spanish rule, had themselves used prison conditions as a means to critique the colonial state.[135]

Solitary confinement in particular proved worrisome. A common means for punishing uncooperative defendents, solitary meant weeks shackled in "dungeons where they [prisoners] remain[ed] deprived of the basic necessities for civilized life."[136] Lengthy solitary confinement, wrote one author in an early history of the Santiago penitentiary, "engenders in the prisoner, almost always, a deadly illness which in many cases is the *tisis* (consumption) or mental alienation."[137] "This is exactly what happened," he continued, "with prisoner Benjamin Mosquera, who, fulfulling a sentence of fifteen years of solitary confinement, at the end of three years, 'lost his head' and his body was emaciated to such a degree that the other prisoners were scared to see him, saying he was a skeleton pulled from a tomb."[138] Other commentators too noted the correlation between time in solitary and eventual relocation to the asylum.[139]

This was to be Gómez Rojas's fate, despite the illegality of confining him to solitary. The penal code allowed solitary confinement and isolation only for prisoners who had been found guilty, although those indicted but not yet tried could be chained, shackled, or handcuffed, at times with iron shackles weighing some twenty to twenty-five pounds.[140] Isolation meant not solitude but loneliness and deprivation. Life was defined by what it lacked: movement, comaraderie, a sense of time, a feeling of existing. For Gómez Rojas what existed was gloom and anxiety, both exacerbated by the maddening, monotonous pounding on the wall by a prisoner in a neighboring cell. The young poet, who counted the number of times the prisoner hit the wall, recounted the experience in a poem tellingly titled "The Dead of the Jail."[141]

Gómez Rojas, at least initially, had some opportunities to seek assistance. "Co-religionists," he wrote in a letter addressed to Alberto Labarca, brother of fugitive student Santiago Labarca, "I am by order of the judge [Astorquiza] detained and strictly isolated, but do not know for what reason and without having been charged. I beg you to contact Don Roberto Parragué or another person who can work on my behalf, such as Don Héctor Arancibia or others so that they might use their influence so as to end this painful and distressing situation . . . My home now is the 'Detention Section.' "[142] He assembled a list of people who might help him, among them Pedro Aguirre Cerda ("he heard me speak once"), Arcadio Ducoing (interim director of the Pedagogical Institute at the University where the poet was enrolled), historian Pascual Venturino ("he declined"), Congressman Héctor Arancibia Lasso, and his friend Adolfo Crenovich.[143] He also reached out to Astorquiza. This time there was no shrug of the shoulders, no referring to Astorquiza as "don Pepe."[144] "With all respect," he requested a special audience with Astorquiza and his attorney to discuss the possibility of his release.[145]

Astorquiza ignored the request. Meanwhile, isolation and deprivation took their toll. Initially, Gómez Rojas continued to write, producing a number of poems that would bear witness to his time in the Santiago jail. Such activity was crucial. "In prison it is a fundamental rule of mental hygiene to work at all costs, to occupy the mind," Victor Serge recalled in his own prison memoirs. Items such as pens and paper were "prizes of inestimable value."[146] Gómez Rojas also had books to read, including Knut Hamsun's *Pan* and Maurice Maeterlinck's *The Blue Bird*. Even so, the isolation soon devoured his optimism, productivity and "mental hygiene." At one point he wrote in utter frustration of having been forgotten. "Now I understand the saying 'Don't ask anything of anyone!' " he wrote. "No one has thought to bring me, in the jail, a textbook, a book, a grammar text."[147] In isolation, the fear of having been forgotten was a terribly real one. He implored his friends to come see him, uncertain as to whether in fact such visits could even happen. "Come see me," he wrote to one friend, "I need you desperately, my spirit, my mood, my health are so bad . . . Come! I want to tell you! Come! As a man would say to a brother, come!" If they came, they did not bring those prizes of inestimable value. As the weeks passed the poet lamented he had not read a book in some twenty days, nor written a single line of poetry. "Friday is visiting day for the subversives, from 12 to 3 p.m.," he wrote hopefully to a friend. Had he been forgotten? It is difficult to tell, but his mother complained that at one point she was prohibited from seeing him due to his condition—a condition brought on, in part, by his very isolation. Many of his comrades, meanwhile, remained themselves behind bars. Gómez Rojas must have felt as if he teetered perpetually on the brink of oblivion, removed from sight and mind by an inept judicial system and an aggressive prosecutor. How easy to reduce a man to a ghost of himself, to nothing. Of Astorquiza, with a phrase reminiscent of Jean Valjean in Hugo's *Les Misérables*, Gómez Rojas lamented: "To him I am not a student, I am not a man, I am not even a dog!"[148]

Gómez Rojas suffered not only the dismal conditions of the jail and isolation, but also illness brought on by torment. By mid-September a letter leaked out of the jail and made its way to Pedro León Ugalde. The author, most certainly a fellow prisoner, reported that Gómez Rojas had not eaten in days, had been stripped naked with both his hands and feet shackled, and been left in isolation. "For three days he has been screaming," the prisoner reported, so the guards had gagged him and subjected him to repeated dousings of water. The prisoner asked León Ugalde to intervene with Astorquiza, whom he held directly responsible for the poet's poor treatment. "Other *compañeros* are also suffering the consequences and I think some of them also are going to go mad, as some of them do not sleep at night and most are fathers."[149] The indifference of deprivation destroyed men.

Word must have circulated. A journalist for *El Mercurio* worried that the paper might soon be informing readers of "irreparable" damage to the poet's health. More disturbing indications of his deteriorating condition emerged when, on September 21, officials moved Goméz Rojas to the Casa de Orates. Students at the FECh posted a board announcing that the young poet was suffering as a result of mistreatment and abuse while incarcerated. A writer for *El Mercurio* countered that the paper's investigations found that he had suffered a series of nervous breakdowns despite various efforts to assist him by the authorities.[150] Was he sick or was he mad? After weeks of being held naked, manacled, malnourished, and in isolation, it was most likely both.[151]

Eight days later, on September 29, 1920, José Domingo Gómez Rojas died.

EPITAPH

On a spring day, a Friday, the first day of October, Gómez Rojas was buried in Santiago's cemetery. The funeral procession stretched for city blocks.

Fifteen city blocks, by some estimates. Students and workers, politicans and poets, in the tens of thousands, gathered to mourn. Even so, the absences were obvious. Many of his friends and comrades remained in prison, exile, or on the run. Casimiro Barrios had been expelled and was most likely in neighboring Peru. The Gandulfo brothers remained behinds bars, although Rigoberto Soto Rengifo was released only hours before the funeral and was thus in attendance. José Santos González Vera had fled the city and caught a train south to Temuco. Santiago Labarca, former president of the FECh and future member of Parliament, had been on the run since July 20. Living incognito for more than two months, he could not risk showing his face now.

Or could he? In an audacious moment, Labarca took the podium and euologized his comrade. Police officials monitoring the funeral did not initially recognize him behind the heavy beard he had grown during the previous months.[152] Soon enough they must have understood something had changed with the energy that swept the crowd, but by that time it was too late. The police approached the podium but the throng of workers and students together forged a human shield around him, impeding the policemen's passage and allowing the fugitive eulogy to proceed. Soon Labarca

Figure 4.6
Fugitive eulogy: A bearded Santiago Labarca bids farewell to Gómez Rojas. *Sucesos* (October 7, 1920).

concluded: "We do not bring flowers because they wither with time, nor do we shed tears because they dry in the sun; we bring only our warm affection for he who sang of beautiful ideals and died for the people's great cause."[153] Labarca then escaped in a waiting car.

Those still in prison did send flowers. Forced to mourn at a distance, enclosed and mostly alone, it was one of the few ways available to them to pay their respects and remember their friend. They were in pain. Juan Gandulfo seethed behind his bars:

> Brother, your assassination pains me like a piercing of my heart. My veins have filled with the fire of rebellion and my fists grate threateningly against the bars of my cell, which was yours also. And tears have dried themselves before reaching my eyes and a satanic idea has crossed my mind:
>
> I have wanted desparately to run to the asylum, to tear down the doors of the autopsy room and to steal your body profaned by all those pigs who have only excrement where the rest of us have a heart.[154]

He ended his letter with a final wish: "I hope, brother, that your sacrifice will not be in vain: your fecund blood has made the soil fertile and soon it will flower." A fitting epitaph perhaps, although as with monuments so with epitaphs: they rarely do justice to a life. No epitaphs, then. And no monuments. Monuments are too silent for their own good. Instead, a poem. "Poems," writes essayist and novelist John Berger, "regardless of any outcome, cross the battlefields, tending the wounded, listening to the wild monologues of the triumphant or the fearful. They bring a kind of peace. Not by anaesthesia or easy reassurance, but by recognition and the promise that what has been experienced cannot disappear as if it had never been. Yet the promise is not of a monument. . . . The promise is that language has acknowledged, has given shelter, to the experience which demanded, which cried out."[155] For a young man who himself cried out, who marshalled language to acknowledge and to shelter, to demand that what had been experienced could not disappear as if it had never been, his own poetry seems the only fitting way to conclude and to proceed. An excerpt, then, from a poem by José Domingo Gómez Rojas, written while in jail.

ELEGIES FROM JAIL

And I think that some day on the face of the earth
A new justice will shatter old rules
And an ineffable future, righteous and profound

Will impart to life new ways and new forms
In this cell I dream of a vast future,
With the tender cry that today beats in the cradles,
With the divine voices that vibrate in the pure
Sky beneath the light of virgin moons.

Epilogue

Afterlives

"Experience walks in without knocking at the door, and announces deaths, crises of subsistence, trench warfare, unemployment, inflation, genocide," writes historian E. P. Thompson. "People starve: their survivors think in new ways about the market. People are imprisoned: in prison they meditate in new ways about the law. In the face of such general experiences old conceptual systems may crumble and new problematics insist upon their presence." Such was the case in Chile and for the subjects of this book. Over the course of the 1920s, old conceptual systems crumbled. New problematics insisted upon their presence. This is as true for politics—a new constitution; new legislation to deal with worker housing, labor issues, the social question—as it is for poetry—new forms of syntax, linguistic experimentation, and a radical rupture with the content and form of previous generations. The *proceso de los subversivos* in 1920, in Chile, was central to this transformation. It was, for many of Chile's future political organizers and agitators, for its poets and its artists, a pivotal moment. It was a moment they experienced in all of its heady and dreadful fullness. The experience marked them, shaping their future political and social and creative lives and teaching them hard lessons about the limits of representation, liberalism, capitalism, and freedom.

OCTOBER 1920

In the days following Gómez Rojas's funeral, a blue sky predominated. Despite the abundant sun, a pall hung over the city and it was a somber Spring Festival.[1] The annual student festival—by then in its fifth year—was usually a raucous event, extending for days, in which university students filled the streets of downtown Santiago, theatrical performances and poetry recitals coinciding with long evenings of revelry. But not this year. "There is less organization than in previous years," one journalist noted, glossing over why this might have been the case.[2] The press went to some lengths to suggest that a period of calm and rapproachment had arrived. "One martyr is enough," a writer for *Sucesos* asserted.[3] That students and workers alike remained imprisoned and denied bail rarely made the pages of the major dailies. In the meantime, police presence in the barrio Latino doubled.[4]

The soft-pedaling of the violence and repression many had experienced, as if it were all a brief lapse in judgment, was commonplace. Journalists, in announcing Gómez Rojas's death, found themselves lamenting things such as harsh sanctions and arbitrary imprisonment. One recounted the recollections of a distinguished professor who remembered Gómez Rojas as his "best student, the most dedicated to his work and with a quick and wide mind."[5] Some, who only weeks earlier had been clamoring for crackdowns and iron fists, reassessed their positions. One writer for *Sucesos*, weeks after Gómez Rojas's death, asked of the subversives still in the Valparaíso jail: "Are these men guilty? Or has justice erred?" Although the public pendulum had apparently swung, he was still only capable of patronizing caricature and banality: "Not a single one of those detained is not a hardworking laborer and an orderly person, with a well-kept, clean and happy little house."[6] Others proffered a moral equivalence between those who supported the free exchange and articulation of ideas—even "pernicious" ones—and those who resorted to violence to combat them. "Who is right?" asked the writer. "Perhaps both."[7] Bland platitudes abounded in the search for a mythical middle ground.

Meanwhile, prison wardens and editorialists sought to defend their actions in a series of defensive letters.[8] They claimed support from an unlikely source: a letter from Gómez Rojas's own mother attesting to the good treatment her son had received while incarcerated. Yet she soon after publicly declared that in fact she was forced, under duress, to sign her name to that letter. Furthermore, the letter had been written and given to her to sign while her son was in fact still alive and in the jail.[9] In what could only have further spurred frustration, anger, and suspicions of a cover-up, the official autopsy remained secret for some time after his death, despite a member of Parliament demanding it be turned over. When finally made public, the autopsy determined the official cause of death to be viral meningitis.[10] The conclusion reached by his fellow students seems more on point: he died from the horrific treatment received while imprisoned for no other crime than an activity "inherent to man: thinking."[11]

Students in the FECh and their allies lost little time in establishing a publication that would counter the proliferating platitudes and exculpatory claims of equivalence that pervaded the press. The publication, titled *Claridad*, was for all intents and purposes a resurrection of *Numen*, which had ceased publication with the destruction of its eponymous print shop and the arrest of its owner, Julio Valiente, on July 19.[12] In renaming it as they did the students and their allies drew inspiration from Henri Barbusse, French war veteran and writer whose 1919 novel *Under Fire* had been banned in France for its pacifism and exposé of the horrors of the front. Barbusse had founded *Clarté*, an internationalist and pacifist movement calling for intellectual engagement in the political issues of the time. *Clarte*'s early members included Anatole France, Thomas Hardy, Upton Sinclair, and the secretaries of a number of Britain's most important labor unions.[13] Members of the Left Opposition after the Bolshevik Revolution—men such as Victor Serge—would find in it a space for their critiques of the increasingly bureaucratic authoritarianism they saw approaching.[14] *Clarté* also became the model for *Claridad*, which, while beginning in 1920 in Chile as a direct consequence of the death of Gómez Rojas, soon became one of the most important student publications and pan-Latin American movements of the first half of the twentieth century. As diverse a group as Chile's future Nobel prize winning poet Gabriela Mistral, Mexico's first postrevolutionary Minister of Education José Vasconcelos, and US socialist Eugene V. Debs sat on the board of directors for the Chilean *Claridad*. Versions were begun in Argentina (1926–1941) and in Peru (1923–1927), where it was directed by José Carlos Mariátegui—future founder of the Peruvian communist party—who had met Barbusse while in exile in Paris in 1919.[15]

If there was one thing some journalists and many students agreed upon, it was the role played in Gómez Rojas's death by Astorquiza, his jailers, and the police. In this turn, journalists and editorialists for *Sucesos*, *Zig-Zag*, and *El Mercurio* absolved themselves of any complicity in what had unfolded. Many of those imprisoned were "innocent victims of the malice of the judges and the police," noted an author for *Sucesos* in late October.[16] He went further, suggesting that Astorquiza had functioned as "an instrument of politicians who still dream of reprisals."[17] Students not surprisingly agreed. When they created a fictional "popular dictionary," they included not only Astorquiza but Zañartu and one of the country's predictably antagonistic newspapers:

Popular Dictionary

Astorquizar—Verb. 1a. Conj: Torture, shackle, imprison, assass . . . (here the page was ripped and we could not decipher the rest)

Subversive—Adj; can be sustantive. A man who thinks with his brain and not his stomach.

Reactionary—Adj; id; The opposite of subversive; meaning: a man who generally thinks with his stomach and always with his large intestine, seeing social problems through his belly button.

Zañartuar—Verb. 1a. Conj. From the Troglodyte dialect; meaning: To incite with impunity, to excite a pack of hounds while protected by money or coin.

Diario Ilustrado—A suspicious establishment, a very large sewer.[18]

In the wake of Gómez Rojas's funeral, Astorquiza understandably became the immediate face of a corrupt and repressive system. In the days following the burial, cards circulated through Santiago with an image of Astorquiza—alive and well—alongside the visage of the dead poet. Officials soon had him replaced as special prosecutor. He lost more than his job. One day Astorquiza's wife, Clara Parot Silva, daughter of a prominent Talca family, paid a visit to Gómez Rojas's mother. She brought her daughter with her, intending to convey her condolences. Exiting a car, elegantly dressed, the two women approached the door of the home and asked the poet's mother how she was. "How would you expect, with my son's death," she replied. "But you have to come to terms with it, to ask God for comfort," responded Parot Silva. A remarkable scene of anguish ensued: unaware of the identity of the woman at her door, Gómez Rojas's mother unleashed a torrent of invective against God, against Astorquiza, and against her son's jailers. "I will never forgive that Judge, not even at the hour of my death." Shaking and shaken, Parot Silva fled with her daughter in tears. There was no escape: Parot Silva died only months later, in an asylum south of Valparaíso.[19]

NOVEMBER 1920

In early November Pedro Gandulfo was able to gather again with comrades—Juan Egaña, Alfredo Demaría, Roberto Meza Fuentes,

Figure E.1
The living and the dead. Copies of this card, with photographs of the living judge and the dead poet, circulated widely in Santiago in the wake of Gómez Rojas's death. Loose insert in *En la tumba del estudiante poeta, Domingo Gómez Rojas* (n.p., 1921). Courtesy of Special Collections, University of Connecticut Libraries.

Santiago Labarca, Pedro León Ugalde, Pedro Godoy, and others—at a restaurant to celebrate the third anniversary of the "Maximalist Republic of Russia."[20] He most likely also attended the various events organized to aid the families of those who remained imprisoned. The FECh club held an exposition of the works of painter Roberto Salinas, still imprisoned.[21] Similiarly, on November 13, the Typographers Union Society held an evening of literary readings and music to assist the families of those imprisoned.[22]

Why Pedro Gandulfo and his friend Rigoberto Soto Rengifo had been freed in October while others remained imprisoned is unclear, although in the case of these two students their release may have been hastened by the words of one deputy on the floor of Parliament the day after Gómez Rojas's death:

> And just like this student [Gómez Rojas], there are many others in similar circumstances. I claim here in the chamber that students Gandulfo and Soto [*sic*] are also ill to the point of becoming victims of this oppression that is inconceivable in a republic with a Constitution and laws to be respected.[23]

Other deputies followed suit, launching repeated critiques at Minister of Justice Montt and demanding that the multitudes arrested—"on mere suspicions"—be released promptly. As they had throughout the previous three months, a number of deputies and senators spoke up on the floor of the Parliament: in defense of Casimiro Barrios, in defense of the right to express one's ideas, in defense of the right to strike, in defense of workers' rights, and in defense of the right to public space. If there is very little to celebrate in a history of repression and persecution, it becomes all the more crucial to remember not only the workers and students who were persecuted, but also the attorneys and politicians who defended them and refused to be silenced or to submit to the coercive power of an unholy trinity: nationalism, elitism, and militarism. Many of these individuals—Senator Agustín Torrealba, attorney Carlos Vicuña Fuentes, and Deputy Pinto Durán, among others—did not share the anarchist or anarcho-communist sensibilities of some of the main protagonists in this history. Even so, they refused—at a dangerous time—to be silent and they refused to let the repugnancies of repression pass.

In the coming months Pedro Gandulfo would have to abandon his law degree for a course of study in dentistry. Because he had been detained on suspicion of subversion, he was prohibited from receiving a degree in law. Not so for the young men who assaulted the FECh club and paraded its bronze plaque through the street. Many of them entered the legal profession. In one of the regular ironies of life in Santiago, at one point Gandulfo found himself taking care of the teeth of a relative of Alfonso Casanova, the young man whose hat was pierced by a bullet fired, by Gandulfo, from a pistol during the attack on the FECh. He would carry the events of 1920 with him in other ways: not only as an experience or memory but also, as so many others would, as a bodily reality. Like his friend Soto Rengifo, who would die in 1924 from a chest wound inflicted by a firework set off amidst celebrations for Alessandri, Gandulfo had contracted tuberculosis while in prison.[24]

Later in life Pedro would recall his youth in a poem to his wife. These are the first two stanzas:

I
In our days of youth, perhaps distant
Together we pursued, his syndicalist ideal
Dear Juan, my brother,
I already loved "the Stirnerian man"

II
Rebellious, happy and proud
We broke chains
And lived a full life
I always dreamed "the Stirnerian man"[25]

These poems were made available to me by Pedro's son, Juan Luis Gandulfo. Raised in the intellectual milieu of Santiago in the 1950s (González Vera was a frequent visitor to his home), Juan Luis would go on to attend Chile's prestigious State Technical University (UTE), whose rector for a time would be Santiago Labarca. Gandulfo would study engineering and perform with the university theater group TEKOS. During Allende's Popular Unity government, he worked as one of the chief engineers at the Chuquicamata mine, the world's largest open-pit mine. During a visit, Allende expressed pleasure at hearing the surname Gandulfo. He took Juan Luis to one side and told him of just how powerful and inspiring a figure his uncle, Juan Gandulfo, had been to him and many of his generation. When the coup d'état came in 1973, TEKOS and the UTE would be savaged by the dictatorship and Pedro, although never detained, would be subjected to unwanted visits from Pinochet's security agents, in large part because of his surname.[26] Juan Luis was in East Germany attempting to negotiate with the government there to get parts for the mine in order to circumvent the blockades strangling Chile's industry and economy. That journey saved his life: he was one of the only senior figures of the mine to survive the coup. He has lived in exile ever since.[27]

DECEMBER 1920

By December, all of those held and accused of sedition and illicit assocation had been released.[28] Some had seen their charges reduced to "public disturbance"; others had no charges at all. Alessandri, meanwhile, had by then been confirmed as the victor in the previous July's elections and was preparing to take office. The administration may have wished, with the release of the prisoners, to put the entire venture behind them. They did not get that wish.

While Pedro Gandulfo had been released from jail sometime in October, his brother Juan remained in the penitentiary until December, tending to the suffering bodies and spirits of the incarcerated but also to the prison guards.[29] Gandulfo would go on to an illustrious career as a surgeon, widely regarded for his compassion, his energy, and his remarkable skill with a scalpel.[30] That skill was akin to artistry, and Gandulfo garnered reknown for his engravings and artwork. He did the engravings for an edition of Pablo Neruda's first collection of poetry, *Crepusculario*, which Neruda dedicated to him. He would also continue to work with the IWW, founding an IWW medical clinic (the Policlínica Obrera) in the heart of the barrio Latino in 1923.[31] The clinic survived through the early 1950s—his brother Pedro provided dental services there—and eventually came to bear his name.

The *proceso* proved ineffective at breaking the IWW. Wobblies began to organize again upon their release from prison in December of 1920 and the union managed to sustain itself through much of the coming decade. Delegates participated in congresses in Chile and in Berlin and continued to organize workers in various industries. By the end of the decade, however, the IWW and anarcho-syndicalist activity and organizing had been eclipsed by the formation of the Communist Party (1922) and then the Socialist Party (1933). Historian Víctor Muñoz has persuasively argued that it was less the repeated repressions—and there were many—that doomed the IWW and anarcho-syndicalism than the growing response on the part of the state to intervene favorably in labor relations, as a result of anarchist and anarcho-syndicalist agitation.[32] "When the state began to intervene, to identify itself as an entity 'defending' the laboring mass, libertarian discourse lost its effectiveness among those thousands of workers who preferred to struggle under the wing of the State, rather than taking the more difficult path of organizing at its margins."[33] Those workers also lost a true organizer "at the margins." The morning of December 27, 1931, a Studebaker traveling from Santiago to Valparaíso flipped on the highway outside of Casablanca. Juan Gandulfo, a passenger in the car, died instantly. He was thirty-six years old.

Many of those involved in events of 1920 recognized the risks they were taking by speaking out and forging the kinds of alliances they forged; their militancy can be measured by their willingness to persist despite the threatening climate of intimidation and violence within which they were forced to live. Police watched as masses of demonstrators beat students and workers or ransacked the premises of their organizations; prison meant confinement, constantly under the jailer's gaze and the shadow of tuberculosis; it meant isolation, deprivation, and uncertainty; it meant being subjected to the whims of unacknowledged gods and masters; it meant a daily confrontation with the arbitrary reality of repression.

Julio Valiente, after six weeks in isolation and another four months in prison, had been through this before: stints of constraint, threats, intimidation, followed by release and a circumspect freedom. Even so, this time had been the most difficult of all. His wife and children struggled to make ends meet and Valiente—his printshop dismantled, his equipment destroyed, the perpetrators walking free—was ruined. Even so, if the multiple arrests and persecutions were intended to cow him, or wear him down, they failed. Upon his release he continued to organize and agitate. He also spoke publicly and vociferously against a fellow comrade, Evaristo Ríos. Valiente exposed him as a Security Section spy, a conclusion he had reached prior to his arrest and had shared with Senator Agustín Torrealba when he visited Valiente in the penitentiary in September.[34] Ríos vigorously denied the charges, but Valiente was insistent. The membership of the POS expelled Ríos, as well as three comrades who defended him during the controversy.[35] Valiente, meanwhile, founded a new press, *Cosmos*, in 1923 and continued to organize for the Left.[36] In the early 1930s he helped found the Revolutionary Socialist Party of Chile.

What became of Valiente later in life is uncertain, although he was working in an office in Santiago in 1960 when historian Marcelo Segall Rosenmann contacted him and asked if he might write a memoir of his life. Segall, one of Chile's most distinguished Marxist historians, sought Valiente's recollections for a history he planned to write on the early Left—by which he meant the libertarian Left—in Chile. Valiente responded but only a few pages exist in Segall's archive. Either Valiente responded only briefly or the full response has been lost. Segall did not finish his history of the early Left. With the coup in 1973 he was arrested, along with a number of his students. The junta's men tortured him in one of their concentration camps. And they forced him to watch his students die. After an international campaign on his behalf Segall traveled to the Netherlands in 1975, where he remained in exile. In Amsterdam he worked in the Latin American desk at the International Institute for Social History. At the IISH he deposited his personal archive, a portion of which served as the evidentiary basis for many parts of this book.

JANUARY 1921

Casimiro Barrios was back in Santiago.[37] Like many immigrants to Chile—whether from Spain, Russia, Italy, or Peru—Barrios had made a life for himself there. He had labored, loved, and agitated in Santiago for all of his adult life. Santiago was his home. It remained so for the next six years. In 1927, under the government of Carlos Ibáñez del Campo, a decree was again issued for his expulsion. This time he was expelled not for being an anarchist, but for being a communist, a label he would not have contested. He had named his son, born in 1925, Santiago Lenin Barrios.[38] His expulsion in 1927 was part of an intensification of expulsions that had begun in 1925, a year of "dark and sad days," wrote exiled attorney Carlos Vicuña Fuentes.[39] Some 1,200 political suspects—anarchists, communists, and homosexual men—were rounded up in early 1927 and either imprisoned or forced in to exile, to Peru, Ecuador, Mexico, the United States, or to Europe.[40] Although most were accused of involvement in some unspecified "communist plot," their expulsions and internments derived from a much more mundane impetus: Ibáñez's efforts to silence his opponents, including Alessandri himself. The US embassy reported at one point that it was to silence Alessandri that the regime had expelled his sons, including one who in 1928 languished on the craggy Pacific outpost of Más Afuera.[41] Even the US Embassy expressed skepticism about the "communist plot," although such skepticism did not prevent US officials from passing along information—names, addresses—on communists in Chile whose identities were uncovered during a raid on a Soviet club in London.[42] Those

Figure E.2
Expelled again. Barrios on the train taking a number of those ordered expelled by then-president Ibáñez out of the country. Courtesy of the Institute for Social History.

harranged, imprisoned, and exiled included an array of political luminaries, including Santiago Labarca and Pedro León Ugalde.

Many were exiled internally to Easter Island and to Isla Más Atierra (the island on which the story for Robinson Crusoe was based). Some 120 union leaders, workers, and intellectuals—including Communist Party founder Elias Lafferte, writer Roberto Meza Fuentes, and writer/anarchist and former president of the FECh Eugenio González Rojas—were exiled to Más Afuera, a small, rocky outcopping west of Más Atierra inhabited mostly by wild goats.[43] They would remain there until the winter of 1929.[44] The Ibáñez government used comprehensive registries of working men's associations in the country—with details regarding purported objectives, composition, and whether they were dedicated to resistance and direct action or "merely" engaged in mutual aid—to track and persecute and expel people. Those registries had been assembled in 1920 under the auspices of José Astorquiza.[45]

Barrios's fate lay elsewhere. Expelled, he made his way to La Paz, Bolivia, where he continued to agitate and organize. Despite having been expelled for his communist sympathies, in La Paz he organized with the city's

«LA RAZON»

Firma del Interesado.

l Sr.

pertenece al personal de

LA RAZON" en calidad de

a Paz. de 192

Administrador Gerente

El Intendente de la Policía de Se-
ridad de La Paz (Bolivia), Certifi-
la autenticidad de la firma que
tecede correspondiente al

La Paz, de 192

Figure E.3
Barrios in Bolivia. While in exile in Bolivia, Barrios found work as a correspondent for the newspaper *La Razón*. Courtesy of Maria Peñaranda Barrios.

anarchists. The capacious Left persisted. He also found work with the newspaper *La Razón*. [46] In the meantime, he wrote extensively to family members and friends in Chile. Whether he continued to sustain contact with his remaining family members in Nieva de Cameros in Spain is unknown, but if he did he would have learned that his father was finishing a term as mayor and his brother Juan was assuming a role on the municipal council. Both would be executed by the fascist forces of Francisco Franco in 1936.[47]

By that time, Casimiro's fate had long been determined. On August 22, 1930, Barrios arrived in Arica on a train from La Paz. His visit had been made possible in part by the Chilean consul in Bolivia, Manuel Bianchi, who not only issued Barrios a visa but also provided him with a letter of introduction testifying to Barrios's support for the Ibáñez government. Security agents, informed of his arrival, detained Barrios on August 23 and held him in the local barracks for the weekend before escorting him to the Bolivian-Chilean border and expelling him to the dusty town of Charaña. Once back in La Paz, Barrios protested vigorously in a letter to Chile's Minister of Foreign Relations, Manuel Barros Castañón, and demanded to be reimbursed for his expenses lest he report his treatment to the Spanish consulates in La Paz and Santiago.[48] Both Barros Castañón and Bianchi balked, uncertain as to how to proceed. Bianchi wrote directly to the minister for guidance.[49] Barros Castañon informed the Governor of Arica that Barrios could indeed travel to the port city.[50] He had to reverse himself in a subsequent telegram two days later.[51] Both, it would seem, had been unaware of how Barrios was perceived by the government. Neither man, one could imagine, was amused by any of this. Even if, as one official claimed, Barrios had caught Bianchi off-guard, the fact that he had managed to get official permission to re-enter the country from which he had been expelled made the Ministry look inept. The specter of insolence returned.

In response, Barrios ratcheted up his revolutionary rhetoric and organizing. In a series of manifestos and editorials, as well as in a letter to one of the senior carabineros in Arica, he sought allies among students and workers, and within the military, in a "war without quarter against Ibáñez and those who keep him in power."[52] In response, officials sought to prevent the circulation of Barrios's manifestos and called for the Ministry of Foreign Relations to lobby their Bolivian counterparts to shut Barrios, and one Carlos Rojo Indo, down.[53] More importantly, senior military officials in the north devised a new strategy for dealing with Barrios. "Because of his anarchist ideas, and because of the influence he has over certain worker elements," wrote a senior military official in October 1930, Barrios was a dangerous individual who should not be permitted to return to the country. However, he continued, in this instance "it would be convenient to allow him to enter in order to detain him and deport him to Easter Island as the most practical method to get him to cease the campaign against the Government, and especially the President, that he has undertaken in the Bolivian press."[54]

Barrios never made it to Easter Island. By December 1930, his family, accustomed to receiving letters regularly from him, began to worry. Letters were no longer arriving. Unbeknownst to his family, Barrios had been expelled by the Bolivian authorities. As he continued to push for journalists and newspaper editors to publish manifestos against Ibáñez, the pressure mounted on the Bolivian government.[55] Bolivia's own residency law was invoked, as was the recent agreement reached among various South American countries with regards to handing over agitators, communists and anarchists, and on the evening of December 18 or 19 Bolivian authorities deposited Barrios in the border town of Charaña, where Chilean carabineros apparently awaited.[56] Barrios boarded a train for Peru but was soon detained by the carabineros, much to the concern of many aboard the train, who then transported him to Arica.[57] Officials there held him for twenty-six days under close guard in solitary confinement. Alberto Rencoret Donoso—at the time a member of the Santiago Investigations unit, soon to be implicated in the disappearing of opposition figures, and later to become a prominent archbishop in Chile—informed his superior that a police offical in Arica had Barrios transferred to the authority of Juan Serrano Ballón.[58] According to some reports, Serrano Ballón worked closely with or for Ventura Maturana, who a decade earlier had helped organize the sting to nab the man with the x-ray eyes. After a stint at the School of Detectives in Paris, where he also spied on Chileans exiled during the first years of Ibáñez's regime, Maturana had returned to Chile to direct the country's detective services and its newly formed secret police.[59] (In the official documentary record Maturana's name appears no where except, tantalizingly enough, on the cover page where someone had scribbled: "Disappearance of Casimiro Barrios. Doc V. Maturana.")

Barrios, rightly fearful for his life, pleaded with an official to instead take him to the border, but to no avail. The official delivered Barrios on January 13, 1931. At 3 a.m. Barrios boarded a car with Serrano Ballón and two other officials. He was never seen again.[60]

MARCH 1921

Six months after the death of Gómez Rojas, an aspiring poet arrived at the University of Chile. Only seventeen at the time, he found a room in a boarding house on Maruri, near the school of medicine, and soon began the poems that would become the basis for his first published collection, *Crepusculario* (1923). He dedicated the book to his friend Juan Gandulfo, who had made the engravings for the collection. He also wrote frequently for *Claridad*, including a front-page editorial accompanied by an image of a man and a woman, clearly workers, seeking shelter from the economic storms, oppressive oligarchs, and cold of a Santiago June. In this editorial, the author is struck mute by the image, at which point the male figure comes to life and speaks:

> "Friend, brother, why do you remain silent? . . . You who have the gift of illuminating words with your fire inside; must you sing and sing of your little pleasures and forget our forsaken hearts, the harsh wound that is our lives, the terror of the cold, the assault of hunger. . . . If you don't speak up, if you don't speak up at every moment of every hour then the land will be filled with lying voices which will only further the evil and silence the protest." . . . The man stops speaking. His compañera looks at me. And I begin to write.[61]

Exceptional for his eloquence, Pablo Neruda was hardly unique in his recognition of the responsibility that students and intellectuals—increasingly radicalized by a world of intolerable social realities, revolutionary possibilities, and international intellectual movements—had to their societies and to rectifying the profound inequalities that characterized them. Yet because they arguably occupied a marginal position of privilege, students like Gómez Rojas, Gandulfo, Meza Fuentes, and their less well-known comrades were at times dismissed as little more than, in one professor's words, "petulant" youths, or spoiled dilettantes, or naïve victims of a youthful idealism out of which they would soon grow.[62] Certainly students had options: the fierce repression they experienced in 1920 led many to moderate their politics and pursue professional paths within the establishment.[63] Others did not. In the wake of the *proceso* and the death of Gómez Rojas, students and former students in the FECh continued to work with the IWW, organize in the barrios of Santiago and Valparaiso, create public forums for critique and opposition, agitate politically, and pursue change.

The seeds of an expanding oppositional—at times, revolutionary—culture had been sown. University students lived in transient states of being but their ideas and experiences were hardly ephemeral. Ideas carried forward; students rarely shed themselves of their accumulated experiences upon graduation. Nor did they let lapse the relationships they forged in the FECh: workers, intellectuals, and former students continued to find an intellectual and political home, and a space of association, in its

El Cartel de Hoy

Frente a mí, el papel blanco en que este cartel debe ser escrito, y, junto a él, el grabado, esta pareja miserable y muda que se aprieta en una contracción desesperada de frío. Pero, ¿por qué no se enciende en mis labios la hoguera de mi rebeldía? ¿Por qué ante estos dos seres anudados en el símbolo mismo de mi dolor, no restalla en mi corazón y en mi boca la palabra roja que azote y que condene? Miro el papel, el grabado, los vuelvo a mirar y... ¡nada! Pero, he aquí que de repente, soltándose de su compañera, el hombre me toma las manos y mirándome a los ojos me dice:

—Amigo, hermano, ¿por qué callas? Si no me hubiera levantado a impedírtelo, ¿es que habría callado una vez más tu boca, es que en el puesto del sufrimiento continuo habrías desdeñado una flor que mañana fructificaría? Tú que sabes la gracia de iluminar las palabras con tu lumbre interior, ¿has de cantar y cantar tus placeres pequeños y olvidar el desamparo de nuestros corazones, la llaga brutal de nuestras vidas, el espanto del frío, el vergajazo del hambre? ¿Sigues en vida para mirar tu sufrimiento, o para elevarte sobre él y gritarlo al mundo con las salivas amargas de tu descontento y tu rebelión? Si tú no lo dices y si no lo dices en cada momento de cada hora se llenará la tierra de voces mentirosas que aumentarán el mal y acallarán la protesta. Sobre los huesos de la canalla actual brotarán sin tregua los que continuarán su obra. Y después otros... Tú, yo, estaremos viejos o muertos, y nuestra vida machacada en tanto yunque de maldición, no podrá decir, no dirá jamás esto que ahora con la frente al viento debes repetir y repetir por todos, contra todos...

Calla el hombre. Me mira su compañera. Y comienzo a escribir...

P. N.

Figure E.4
If you don't speak up . . . : Pablo Neruda's editorial on the front page of the *Claridad*, June 17, 1922.

club. The legacies are myriad: in efforts to protect university autonomy; in the understandings of the political nature of intellectual work; in the forms of alliance and association that refuse classification; in the recognition that education is a right, rather than a privilege; in the demand that students be heard; and in the recognition of one's obligation to speak up.

Gómez Rojas's death nourished a rebellious soil; his friend and comrades tilled it. In 1923, three years after his death, his comrades named a social and intellectual study center in his honor.[64] Shortly thereafter, anarchist Armando Triviño took charge of distributing a third edition of *Rebeldías Líricas*, Gómez Rojas's incendiary collection of poetry first published in 1913.[65] In subsequent years university students in Santiago held annual memorial gatherings honoring him, anarchist lightermen (*lancheros*) in the northern port of Iquique named their theatre group in his honor, and Chile's Popular Front government, elected to power in 1938, invoked his name.[66] In 1941 university students raised a monument to the poet, commemorating the twentieth anniversary of his assassination, with this inscription:

> "José Domingo Gómez Rojas"
> 20 years since his death
> His example continues to be
> The standard-bearer of our labors
> For justice and liberty[67]

In the 1940s and 1950s the poet's friends and collaborators José Santos González Vera and Manuel Rojas, now prominent intellectual and literary figures in their own right, kept his memory alive. Others, such as Enrique Lihn, another of Chile's great poets, were reading and drawing inspiration from his work in the 1950s and 1960s. "This century is hypocritical," one of Lihn's poems began, invoking Gómez Rojas's opening to *Renegación*, before launching into a critique of US imperialism.[68]

In 1982 students at the University of Chile and the Catholic University formed the Grupo José Domingo Gómez Rojas in an effort to find mechanisms through which to change the internal politics of universities under the dictatorship. The founders of the Grupo were in part responding to the creation of the Chilean Federation of Student Centers (FECECh), founded in 1978 as the dictatorship's officially recognized student organization once the FECh had been banned and its juridical status revoked. Students in the Grupo began researching the history of the FECh and encountered the story of José Domingo Gómez Rojas. According to one of the Grupo's founders, Ricardo Brodsky, who currently directs Chile's Museum of Memory and Human Rights, they gravitated toward Gómez Rojas in part because of his close links to the FECh at a time when it had also experienced an intense repression and the revocation of its juridical status; in part because many involved in the movement were students in literature; and in part because of the "tragic air" which seemed to envelope the poet and his history.[69] The recuperation of the fate of Gómez Rojas, and the history of the *proceso de los subversivos*, was crucial in that it resurrected a history of illiberalism and repression, as well as militancy and struggle, in an era in which a dictatorship aimed to obliterate historical memory. It is no coincidence that in his 1993 novel *Nadie Sabe Más que los Muertos* (Nobody Knows More Than the Dead), Ramón Díaz Eterovic has his protagonist, detective Heredia, meditate on precisely this issue through the figure of Gómez Rojas:

> I sat on a bench next to the crumbling monolith of Domingo Gómez Rojas, the poet who died in the decade of the 20s, when the Student Federation shook the streets of Santiago with its cries, and sang "Cielito Lindo" in honor of the populist "Lion of Tarapacá" [Alessandri]. Accused of being a subversive, punished and locked away in an asylum, the poet's will was broken between those walls where he noted the passing of the days and penned some of his most ferocious lines. I think that such a vulgar injustice is repeating itself and the remains of the next monolith could well be in honor of Daniel Cancino, or another of those youngsters who in the last few years have died at the hands of killers with wide smiles who return to anonymity and obscurity once paid the timeless thirty coins by the powerful. But who remembered the poet?[70]

The FECh reemerged in 1984. After the 1988 plebiscite, which denied Pinochet another extended period of control, many from the Grupo José Domingo Gómez Rojas would merge with the University Socialist Convergence, which would dedicate itself to the return of democracy and split from the more militant positions of the Revolutionary Movement of the Left (MIR) and the Communist Party.[71] Gómez Rojas's name and history persisted. More recently his name has been adopted for an online anarchist library and study group. Efforts to rename the Santiago park that bears his name brought an outcry in the 1990s, and it remains as of this writing Parque José Domingo Gómez Rojas. One suspects that the memory of Gómez Rojas has meant also the resurrection of the names of his persecutors. In its August 2008 issue, Chile's richly satirical magazine *The Clinic* assembled a list of the country's most notorious *conchesumadres* ("motherfuckers"). Alongside Augusto Pinochet can be found the names of José Astorquiza and Ventura Maturana.[72]

Chilean students today—both in high school and the university, in the FECh and outside of it—echo the voices of their predecessors from the interwar period, critiquing not only the country's education system but the premises and promises of an economic system rooted in the profit motive and willing to privatize nearly all aspects of social life. What began as a critique of profit in education has expanded in to a broadbased movement deeply opposed to the radical capitalist economic models forcibly imposed by the dictatorship and sustained since. As Chilean journalist Rubén Andino Maldonado has observed, "The student explosion that began in 2011 has been the expression of a lengthy accumulation of discontent shared recently by the majority of Chilean society which observes how the fruits of economic growth are not equally shared in society."[73] Indeed, Andino notes that between 2011 and 2014 public surveys in Chile suggested somewhere between 70 and 80 percent of the population sympathized with student demands.[74] Students have also been at the forefront of a powerful critique of Chile's political class, questioning the claims of representative democracy and of a political model that seems, at best, out of touch with the populace it claims to represent.

Like their predecessors, students are politically capacious. A range of overlapping platforms and positions exist although most share a strong commitment to direct democracy within the movement. Students have a range of affiliations. Some favor actively working with the Congress and government to shape educational and social policy. In 2010 Communist Party militant Camila Vallejo was elected president of the FECh, helped organize the massive student protests that shook the country in 2011, and subseqently stood for, and won, election to the Congress. Her successor as FECh president, Gabriel Boric Font, of the Autonomous Left (IA), is now a Congressional deputy representing the Magallanes region. Others, disparaged as "ultras" by the government, see the entire political system and Chile's political class as morally and politically bankrupt and find little to be gained and much to be lost by working within the existing system. Suspicions of co-optation and manipulation by the traditional political parties understandably run deep and a range of anarchist positions traverse Chile's social movements.[75] Within the student movement more broadly, anarchists are a significant presence. Indeed, it is fair to say that there is a strong, if varied, anarchist orientation among many of the students, one that has only increased in recent years as promises go unfulfilled and the legitimacy of the political and economic system collapses further. In 2013, the FECh membership elected a new president: Melissa Sepúlveda. For the first time since the years of Juan Gandulfo and José Domingo Gómez Rojas, an anarchist led the FECh.

NOTES

INTRODUCTION

1. An editorial in *Claridad*, a magazine founded in late 1920 by and associated with the FECh, put the number in the cortage at some fifty thousand. Even if an exaggerated figure, it points to the remarkable size of the procession. See "En pleno terror blanco: Domingo Gómez Rojas ante la justicia chilena," *Claridad* 1:1 (October 12, 1920), 2.
2. *El Mercurio* (October 2, 1920), 17.
3. For the route, see *El Mercurio* (October 2, 1920,) 17; see also *La Nación* (October 1, 1920), as qtd. in José Domingo Gómez Rojas, *Rebeldías Líricas y otros versos* (Talca: Ediciónes Acéfalo, n.d. [c. 2013]), 98–99; for the machine-gun anecdote, see *Ultima Hora* (October 2, 1920), as qtd. in., Gómez Rojas, *Rebeldías Líricas y otros versos*, 110.
4. "Hasta cuando?" *Claridad* 1:3 (October 26, 1920), front page; "Ultima hora," ibid., 7; and "Otra víctima de la administración Sanfuentes," ibid., 7. Hernández in particular had been repeatedly victimized by the police. In February of 1920 the police had beat him mercilessly during a demonstration, provoking a twenty-four-hour strike by workers in various industries in Valparaíso, Viña del Mar, and Santiago. See Jorge Barría Serón, *Los movimientos sociales desde 1910 hasta 1926* (Santiago: Editorial Universitaria, 1960), 279–280.
5. Manuel Rojas, "José Domingo Gómez Rojas," *Babel: Revista de arte y crítica* 28 (July-August, 1945), 29.
6. Greg Dening, *The Death of William Gooch: A History's Anthropology* (Honolulu: University of Hawai'i Press, 1995), 13.
7. See Rojas, *Manual de Literatura Chilena* and his novel *La oscura vida radiante* (Santiago: Zig-Zag, 1996 [1984]), in which Gómez Rojas appears under his pseudonym Daniel Vázquez; José Santos González Vera, *Cuando era muchacho* (Santiago: Editorial Universitaria, 1996 [1951]). González Vera received the prize in 1950; Rojas in 1957.
8. Pablo Neruda, *Memoirs* (New York: Penguin, 1978 [1974]), 36–37.
9. See for example Andrés Sabella, "Carta a los universitarios," *El Mercurio de Antofagasta* (September 29, 1969); "Homenaje a J.D. Gómez Rojas. Quedó en el camino: Poeta y Luchador," *Puru* (Santiago) (October 1, 1970); José G. Martínez Fernández, "Domingo Gómez Rojas, que en el cielo no estás," *Palabra Escrita* 33 (May 1999), 3; Elisa Cárdenas, "Un héroe del siglo veinte: Hoy la FECh realize homenaje al poeta anarquista José Domingo Gómez Rojas," *La Nación* (October 1, 1997), 79; Virginia Vidal, "Gómez Rojas inédito," *Punto Final*

(Santiago) (November 21, 1997), 18; Virginia Vidal, "Centenario de Domingo Gómez Rojas," *Punto Final* (Santiago) (May 30, 1997), 20; Luis Enrique Délano, "Gómez Rojas a medio siglo I," *Las Noticias de última hora* (Santiago) (October 3, 1970), 14; Délano, "Gómez Rojas a medio siglo II," *Las Noticias de última hora* (Santiago) (October 4, 1970), 2; Délano, "Gómez Rojas a medio siglo III," *Las Noticias de última hora* (Santiago) (October 5, 1970), 6; Rubén Santibáñez, "José Domingo Gómez Rojas," *Líder provincial* (January 5, 6, and 10, 1995); Sergio Muñóz Martínez, "Cuando la 'canalla dorada' asaltó la FECh," *Principios* (July/August 1967), 90–96, in f148, Marcelo Segall Rosenmann collection (hereafter MSR), International Institute for Social History (hereafter IISH). For novels within Chile, see the works in fn7 as well as Ramón Díaz Eterovic's crime novel *Nadie Sabe Más que los Muertos* (Santiago: Planeta, 1993). For outside of Chile, see Thomas Kennedy's remarkable *Greene's Summer*, in which one of the main protagonists is a Chilean exile—Bernardo Greene—living in Copenhagen and seeking treatment for the terrible abuses he suffered under the Pinochet regime. Greene recalls at one point the circumstances of his arrest in Santiago: he was arrested, held, and tortured for teaching the poems of Gómez Rojas to his students. Kennedy, *Greene's Summer* (Galway, Ireland: Wynkin deWorde, 2004), 69. The novel has been republished by Bloomsbury in 2010 as *In the Company of Angels*.

10. Fabio Moraga Valle and Carlos Vega Delgado, *José Domingo Gómez Rojas: Vida y obra* (Punta Arenas: Atelí, 1997).
11. On "the event" and the writing of history, see William Sewell, *Logics of History: Social Theory and Social Transformation* (Chicago: University of Chicago Press, 2005), esp. chap. 8.
12. See, for example, Florencia Mallon, *Courage Tastes of Blood: The Mapuche Community of Nicolás Ailío and the Chilean State, 1906–2001* (Durham, NC: Duke University Press, 2005) and Lessie Jo Frazier, *The Salt in the Sand: Memory, Violence and the Nation-State in Chile, 1890 to the present* (Durham, NC: Duke University Press, 2007).
13. Deputy Pinto Durán, 77th Session (September 29, 1920), 1993.
14. See Charles Maier, *Leviathan 2.0: Inventing Modern Statehood* (Cambridge, MA: Harvard University Press, 2014) for a useful discussion; for the case of Chile in particular, see Barría Serón, *Los movimientos sociales*, esp. 247–249. In neighboring Argentina a series of strikes and insurgencies against the owners of the large sheep estates would rock the Patagonia in 1920 and 1921. See Osvaldo Bayer, *La Patagonia Rebelde* (Buenos Aires: Planeta, 1980). This is the definitive edition put out by Bayer that condensed and completed the earlier multivolume study, published between 1972 and 1976, before he was forced in to exile by the Argentine military dictatorship.
15. See Gabriel Salazar, *La enervante levedad histórica de la clase política civil (Chile, 1900–1973)* (Santiago: Debate, 2015), esp. 756–808.
16. See Leonardo Cisternas Zamora and Claudio Ogass Bilbao, coords, *Archivo Oral del Movimiento Estudiantil: Registrando las memorias de la refundación de la FECh* (Santiago: Archivo y Centro de Documentación FECh, 2014) and José Weinstein and Eduardo Valenzuela, "La FECh de los años veinte: Un movimiento estudiantil con historia," mimeograph, August 1980.
17. There are some exceptions, such as Richard Walter, *Student Politics in Argentina: The University Reform and its Effects, 1918–1964* (New York: Basic Books, 1968); Frank Bonilla and Myron Glazer, *Student Politics in Chile*

(New York: Basic Books, 1970); Andrew Kirkendall, *Class Mates: Male Student Culture and the Making of a Political Class in Nineteenth Century Brazil* (Lincoln: University of Nebraska Press, 2002); and Iván Jaksíc *Academic Rebels in Chile: The Role of Philosophy in Higher Education and Politics* (Albany: SUNY Press, 1989) but in anglophone scholarship the balance is very strongly tipped toward the mid-twentieth century and after. Excellent recent studies include Francisco J. Barbosa, "July 23, 1959: Student Protest and State Violence as Myth and Memory in León, Nicaragua," *Hispanic American Historical Review* 85:2 (May 2005); Lessie Jo Frazier and Deborah Cohen, "Defining the Space of Mexico '68: Heroic Masculinity in the Prison and Women in the Streets," *Hispanic American Historical Review* 83:4 (November 2003); Victoria Langland, "Birth Control Pills and Molotov Cocktails: Reading Sex and Revolution in 1968 Brazil," in Gilbert M. Joseph and Daniela Spenser, eds., *In From the Cold: Latin America's New Encounter with the Cold War* (Durham, NC: Duke University Press, 2008); Langland, *Speaking of Flowers: Student Movements and the Making and Remembering of 1968 in Military Brazil* (Durham, NC: Duke University Press, 2013); Valeria Manzano, *The Age of Youth in Argentina: Culture, Politics and Sexuality from Perón to Videla* (Chapel Hill: University of North Carolina Press, 2014); Elaine Carey, *Plaza of Sacrifices: Gender, Terror and Power in 1968 Mexico* (Albuquerque: University of New Mexico Press, 2005), and Jeffrey L. Gould, "Solidarity Under Siege: The Latin American Left, 1968," *American Historical Review* (April 2009), 348–375. Worth noting here is the degree to which this emphasis on 1968 tends to reify a story young radicals in some places at times told themselves: that the young intelligentsia were now, as if they had not been before, agents of historical change. See the discussion in Saku Pinta and David Berry, "Conclusion," in Alex Prichard, Ruth Kinna, Saku Pinta and David Berry, eds., *Libertarian Socialism: Politics in Black and Red* (London: Palgrave-MacMillan, 2012), 301, as well as, more broadly, Kristin Ross, *May '68 and Its Afterlives* (Chicago: University of Chicago Press, 2002).

18. Mario Garcés, *El "despertar" de la sociedad: Los movimientos sociales en América Latina y Chile* (Santiago: LOM Ediciones, 2012), 7–12. For an overview that situates such movements, at various points in time, in a longer temporal trajectory, see Salazar, *La enervante levedad*, especially the introduction.
19. Carlos Vicuña Fuentes, quoted in Bernardo Subercaseaux, *Historia de las ideas y de la cultura en Chile (tomo 3): El centenario y las vanguardias* (Santiago: Editorial Universitaria, 2004), 70.
20. I have found Kristen Ross's work on May 1968 in France very useful here. See Ross, *May '68*, especially 25 and 60.
21. Perhaps the best definition is a brief anti-definition from Argentine philosopher Nestor Kohan, offered almost in passing: war "against subversion" is another way of saying war against the people. Kohan, *Marx en su (Tercer) Mundo: Hacia un socialismo no colonizado*, 2nd ed. (Buenos Aires: Biblios, 1998), 13.
22. Michael Schmidt and Lucien van der Walt, *Black Flame: The Revolutionary Class Politics of Anarchism and Syndicalism* (Oakland: AK Press, 2013); Carl Levy, "Social Histories of Anarchism," *Journal for the Study of Radicalism* 4:2 (Fall 2010), 1–44; Lucien van der Walt and Steven Hirsch, eds., *Anarchism and Syndicalism in the Colonial and Postcolonial World, 1870–1940: The Praxis of National Liberation, Internationalism, and Social Revolution* (Leiden: Brill, 2010); Ruth Kinna and Alex Prichard, "Introduction," in Prichard, et. al., *Libertarian Socialism*; Andrej Grubačić and David Graeber, "Anarchism or the Revolutionary

Movement of the Twenty-First Century," http://tal.bolo-bolo.co/en/a/ag/andrej-grubacic-david-graeber-anarchism-or-the-revolutionary-movement-of-the-twenty-first-centu.pdf, accessed April 15, 2015; and Andrej Grubačić, "The Anarchist Moment," in Jacob Blumenfield, Chiara Boticci, and Simon Critchley, eds., *The Anarchist Turn* (London: Pluto Books, 2013). Recent historical monographs include Ilham Khuri-Makdisi, *The Eastern Mediterranean in the Making of Global Radicalism, 1860–1914* (Berkeley: University of California Press, 2010); Maia Ramnath, *Decolonizing Anarchism: An Antiauthoritarian History of India's Liberation Struggle* (Oakland: AK Press, 2012); Benedict Anderson, *Under Three Flags: Anarchism and the Anticolonial Imagination* (London: Verso, 2007); Mark Saad Saka, *For God and Revolution: Priest, Peasant and Agrarian Socialism in the Mexican Huasteca* (Albuquerque: University of New Mexico Press, 2013); and Claudio Lomnitz, *The Return of Comrade Flores Magón* (New York: Zone Books, 2014). In a slightly different vein, see James C. Scott's work, especially *Seeing Like a State: How Certain Schemes to Improve the Human Condition Have Failed* (New Haven, CT: Yale University Press, 1998), *The Art of Not Being Governed: An Anarchist History of Upland Southeast Asia* (New Haven, CT: Yale University Press, 2009), and *Two Cheers for Anarchism* (Princeton, NJ: Princeton University Press, 2012). For earlier articulations, see Pierre Clastres, *Society Against the State: Essays in Political Anthropology* (New York: Zone Books, 1989) as well as Miguel Abensour's recent reprise of Clastres in a slightly different vein: *Democracy Against the State: Marx and the Machiavellian Moment* (Cambridge: Polity, 2011), which argues for not fetishizing the divide between Marxism and anarchism. In this vein see the collected essays in Barry Maxwell and Raymond Craib, eds., *No Gods, No Masters, No Peripheries: Global Anarchisms* (Oakland: PM Press, 2015). For a classic study, see Paul Thomas, *Karl Marx and the Anarchists* (London: Routledge and Keegan Paul, 1980).

23. Víctor Muñoz Cortés, "Anarquismo en Chile. Una promesa?" in *Le Monde Diplomatique* (edición chilena), www.lemondediplomatique.cl/article3170,3170.html. See also his *Sin Dios ni Patrones: Historia, diversidad y conflictos del anarquismo en la región chilena (1890–1990)* (Valparaíso: Mar y Tierra, 2014).
24. Even a partial accounting would be long indeed. For a brief, typical treatment, see Alfredo Jocelyn-Holt, "Melissa Sepúlveda y el anarquismo," *La Tercera: Reportajes Especial Anuario* (December 28, 2013), R30. For a succinct and devastating critique of one case—the infamous "caso bombas" of 2010—see Tania Tamayo Grez, *Caso Bombas: La explosión en la Fiscalía Sur* (Santiago: LOM Ediciones, 2014). For succinct overviews, see Hugo Cristian Fernández, *Irrumpe la Capucha: Qué quieren los anarquistas en el Chile de hoy?* (Santiago: OceanSur, 2014); Felipe del Solar and Andrés Pérez, *Anarquistas: Presencia libertaria en Chile* (Santiago: RIL , 2008); and, for a sweeping overview, Muñoz Cortés, *Sin Dios ni Patrones*.
25. See the cogent discussion in James Martel and Jimmy Casas Klausen, "Introduction: How Not to Be Governed," in Casas Klausen and Martel, eds., *How Not to Be Governed: Readings and Interpretations from a Critical Anarchist Left* (Lanham, MD: Lexington Books, 2011).
26. See Kinna and Prichard, "Introduction," in Prichard, et. al., *Libertarian Socialism*. Chilean Marxists at midcentury repeatedly took such a position, seeing in anarchism a kind of revolutionary, but inchoate, precursor to a more theoretical socialism. An excellent succinct summary of that historiography is

offered in Peter DeShazo, *Urban Workers and Labor Unions in Chile, 1902–1927* (Madison: University of Wisconsin Press, 1983), xxiii–xxvii and fn1.

27. Hobsbawm, as quoted in Michael Schmidt, *Cartography of Revolutionary Anarchism* (Oakland: PM Press, 2014), 59; see also Anderson, *Under Three Flags*; Grubačić, "The Anarchist Moment"; and, for a popular rendering, Butterworth, *The World That Never Was: A True Story of Dreamers, Schemers, Anarchists and Secret Agents* (New York: Pantheon, 2010).
28. Kropotkin, *Mutual Aid: A Factor of Evolution* (Boston: Porter Sargent Publishers, 1914); John Clark and Camille Martin, eds., *Anarchy, Geography, Modernity: Selected Writing of Elisée Reclus* (Oakland: PM Press, 2013); Sho Konishi, *Anarchist Modernity: Cooperatism and Japanese-Russian Intellectual Relations in Modern Japan* (Cambridge, MA: Harvard University Press, 2013); Daniel Todes, *Darwin Without Malthus: The Struggle for Existence in Russian Evolutionary Thought* (Oxford: Oxford University Press, 1989); and Butterworth, *The World that Never Was*, xxix.
29. See Ramnath, *Decolonizing Anarchism*; Anderson, *Under Three Flags*; Ziga Vodovnik, *The Living Spirit of Revolt* (Oakland: PM Press, 2013); Khuri-Makdisi, *The Eastern Mediterranean*; and Prichard, et. al., *Libertarian Socialism*.
30. Cited from Colin Ward, *Anarchism: A Very Short Introduction* (Oxford: Oxford University Press, 2004), 8.
31. Rojas, *Sombras contra el muro* (Santiago: Zig-Zag, 1964), 198.
32. See Anderson, "Preface," to van der Walt and Hirsch, eds., *Anarchism and Anarchosyndicalism*; Khuri-Makdisi, *The Eastern Mediterranean*; Craib, "A Foreword," in Maxwell and Craib, eds., *No Gods, No Masters;* and Bosteels, "Neither Proletarian nor Vanguard: On a Certain Underground Current of Anarchist Socialism in Mexico," in Maxwell and Craib, eds., *No Gods, No Masters*. Cf. Thomas, *Karl Marx and the Anarchists*, which draws fairly sharp distinctions between the Marxist and anarchist traditions but largely through the lens of intellectual history and political theory.
33. See Prichard, et. al., *Libertarian Socialism*, and the essays collected in Maxwell and Craib, eds., *No Gods, No Masters*. In some sense this resembles Fernando Tarrida del Mármol's "anarquismo sin adjetivos" (anarchism without adjectives). Having said that, this is not a call for eclecticism, of the kind critiqued by Aijaz Ahmad in his *In Theory: Classes, Nations, Literatures* (London: Verso Press, 1992). "Eclecticism of theoretical and political positions is the common ground on which radical literary theory is, on the whole, constructed." Ahmad, *In Theory*, 5. Ahmad's own strategy of argumentation was itself subjected to withering critique by Benita Parry, who noted in her review the overwhelming need to "register my distaste for the conduct of an argument which, in deploying recrimination as an analytic strategy, misrepresenting the substance of alternative enquiries, and adducing these to retrograde ideological interests, cannot but recall that device of polemical assassination contrived long ago by traditional Communist parties in an attempt to disable other left tendencies." The point in raising this is that it is not only postcolonial theory (the obscure object of Ahmad's ire) but in fact anarchism, more so than any other left tendency, that has been subjected to such repeated accusations of incoherence. Parry, "A Critique Mishandled," *Social Text* 35 (Summer 1993), 121–133.
34. Anderson, *Under Three Flags*; José Moya, "A Continent of Immigrants: Postcolonial Shifts in the Western Hemisphere," *Hispanic American Historical Review* 86:1

(February 2006), 1–28; and Emily Rosenberg, ed., *A World Connecting, 1870–1945* (Cambridge, MA: Harvard University Press, 2012).

35. The relatively recent transnational turn has had the salutory effect of denaturalizing the frame of the nation-state, an artifice for anarchists in particular but for human history more generally. The body of work by this point is substantial. I have found particularly useful Scott, *The Art of Not Being Governed*; Anderson, *Under Three Flags*; Peter Linebaugh and Marcus Rediker, *The Many-Headed Hydra: Sailors, Slaves, Commoners, and the Hidden History of the Revolutionary Atlantic* (Boston: Beacon Press, 2000); Paul Gilroy, *The Black Atlantic: Modernity and Double Consciousness* (Cambridge, MA: Harvard University Press, 1993); Steven Hirsch, "Without Borders: Reflections on Anarchism in Latin America," in *Estudios Interdisciplinarios de América Latina* 22:2 (2011), 6–10; and Davide Turcato, "Italian Anarchism as a Transnational Movement, 1885–1915" *International Review of Social History* 52:3 (2007) 407–444. For a more detailed discussion of the transnational as it relates to Chilean anarchists, see Raymond Craib, "Sedentary Anarchists," in Constance Bantman and Bert Altena, eds., *Reassessing the Transnational Turn: Scales of Analysis in Anarchist and Anarchosindicalist Studies* (London: Routledge, 2014).
36. Peter Kropotkin, "What Geography Ought to Be," *The Nineteenth Century* 18 (1885), 940–956.
37. On militant particularisms, see David Harvey, "Militant Particularism and Global Ambition: The Conceptual Politics of Space, Place and Environment in the Work of Raymond Williams," *Social Text* 42 (Spring, 1995), 69–98. See also Khuri-Makdisi, *The Eastern Mediterranean*, introduction, and Arif Dirlik, "Anarchism and the Question of Place," in van der Walt and Hirsch, eds., *Anarchism and Syndicalism in the Colonial and Postcolonial World.*
38. On translocality, see Ulrich Freitag and Achim von Oppen, "Translocality: An Approach to Connection and Transfer in Area Studies," in Freitag and von Oppen, eds., *Translocality: An Approach to Globalising Processes from a Southern Perspective* (Leiden: Brill, 2010). See also Doreen Massey, "A Global Sense of Place," in Massey, *Space, Place and Gender* (Minneapolis: University of Minnesota Press, 1994), 146–156.
39. See, among others, Henri Lefebvre, *State/Space/World: Selected Essays*, ed. by Neil Brenner and Stuart Elden (Minneapolis: University of Minnesota Press, 2009); Paul Carter, *The Road to Botany Bay: An Exploration of Landscape and History* (Minneapolis: University of Minnesota Press, 2010 [1988]); Edward Soja, *Postmodern Geographies: The Reassertion of Space in Critical Social Theory* (London: Verso Press, 2011, 2nd ed.); David Harvey, *The Condition of Postmodernity: An Enquiry in to the Origins of Cultural Change* (Oxford: Wiley-Blackwell, 1991); and Doreen Massey, *For Space* (London: Sage, 2005).
40. For an excellent effort to appropriate an event from the nationalist grip, see Shahid Amin's *Event, Metaphor, Memory: Chauri Chaura 1922–1992* (Berkeley: University of California Press, 1995). In a similar spirit, see Kristin Ross, *Communal Luxury: The Political Imaginary of the Paris Commune* (London: Verso, 2015).
41. I am indebted to Paulo Drinot for his astute comments here.
42. Jesse Cohn, in an excellent recent work, has pointed out the "intolerable moral bind" in which anarchists find themselves, living as they do in a world dominated by statism and capitalism and yet not wishing to simply escape it—as if that were possible—because the point was (and is) to change it. Thus they

are doomed to participate, and to some degree legitimate, the very society they seek to bring to an end. See Cohn, *Underground Passages: Anarchist Resistance Culture, 1848–2011* (Oakland: AK Press, 2015), 12–14. The protagonists I follow in this book were not hindered nor frozen by such a dilemma, although they were undoubtedly cognizant of it, nor did they resort to a politics of catastrophe, in which they would seek to make things worse in order to hasten the social order's demise. They were too human—and too humanist—for that. They understood the unaccepatable costs and ideological vacuity of such a position. Instead, they organized and struggled, daily. I am reminded of the exchange some years back between an editorialist at the *Wall Street Journal* and anarchist anthropologist David Graeber. When the *Journal* attempted to call Graeber out for some purported hypocrisy—working for a wage when he sought to overthrow the wage system—he responded as follows: "As for the substance of your editorial: I must confess myself confused as to why accepting a job teaching and conducting research for an annual income roughly equivalent to that of a train operator (at roughly twice the hours) qualifies me as a member of the employing class. Or is your real point to assert a more general principle: 'capitalism, love it or leave it'? If so, where exactly am I supposed to go? Outer space?"

43. My approach to anarchism here is inspired by the perspectives of Colin Ward and James C. Scott. See Ward, *Anarchy in Action* and Scott, *Two Cheers for Anarchism*, as well as Ramnath, *Decolonizing Anarchism*.

CHAPTER 1

1. His police record listed his date of birth as March 4, 1890 and his arrival in Chile as May 15, 1906. See Prontuario 130737A, Casimiro Barrios Fernández, Archivo Nacional de la Administración de Chile (hereafter ARNAD), Ministerio del Interior (hereafter MI), v. 8099.
2. David Ringrose, *Spain, Europe and the "Spanish Miracle," 1700–1900* (Cambridge: Cambridge University Press, 1996), 273.
3. Pedro A. Gurría García and Mercedes Lázaro Ruiz, *Tener un Tío en América: La emigración riojana a ultramar (1880–1936)* (Logroño: Instituto de Estudios Riojanos, 2002), 26–29.
4. Juan Antonio García-Cuerdas, "Los almacenes Giménez," *Boletín Informativo de la Asociación Benéfico Cultural Nieva de Cameros y Montemediano*, Año 2008, No. 24 (2009), 65–68.
5. Gurría García and Lázaro Ruiz, *Tener un Tío*, 27, 31.
6. Gurría García and Lázaro Ruiz note that the highest outmigration was among young men, between the ages of thirteen and twenty-one. By the age of thirteen they had completed enough schooling to read and write, and twenty-one was the age for mandatory military service—by 1908, with the war in Morocco, many young men emigrated in part to avoid the war. Gurría García and Lázaro Ruiz, *Tener un Tío*, 39–40.
7. Gurría García and Lázaro Ruiz, *Tener un Tío*, 86. Colonization agents operated in Arnedo, Logroño, Calahorra, Cevera, and Haro.
8. On the Spanish American Iron Company, see Gurría García and Lázaro Ruiz, *Tener un Tío*, 86 n113.
9. On the statistics for migration from La Rioja, see Gurría García and Lázaro Ruiz, *Tener un Tío*, chap. 2.
10. According to an interview with Barrios, in 1919 he had been in Santiago for fourteen years and he was twenty-eight years old. See "Un extremo de la ley de

residencia: Dura lex, sed lex," clipping from the weekly *Zig-Zag*, International Institute for Social History (hereafter IISH), Marcelo Segall Rosenmann collection (hereafter MSR), folder 14 (1919). On emigration to Chile see Javier Fernández Pesquero, "España en Chile: Preliminar," in Fernández Pesquero, *Monografía Estadística de la Colonía Española de Chile en el año 1909* (Cádiz: Talleres Tipográficos de Manuel Alvarez, 1909), 5. For data on the destinations of inhabitants of Nieva de Cameros, see Arrellano, "Aquellos emigrantes," *Boletín 2008 Asociación Benéfico-Cultural Nieva de Cameros*, Año 2007, No. 23 (2008), 58–59. According to Collier and Sater, between 1889 and 1907 over 2 million immigrants arrived in Argentina while the figure for Chile during the same period is around 55,000. See Simon Collier and William Sater, *A History of Chile, 1808–2002*, 2nd ed. (Cambridge: Cambridge University Press, 2004), 172. According to James Morris, the high point of efforts to attract migrants from Spain and Italy to Chile was between 1895 and 1913. See Morris, *Elites, Intellectuals and Consensus: A Study of the Social Question and the Industrial Relations System in Chile* (Ithaca, NY: School of Industrial and Labor Relations, 1966), 85.

11. García-Cuerdas, "Los almacenes Giménez," 66; Ramón Arrellano, "Aquellos emigrantes," 58–59.
12. Juan Antonio García-Cuerdas, "Las desventuras de dos anarquistas cameranos en el norte de Chile," *Análisis* 52, http://dialnet.unirioja.es/servlet/fichero_articulo?codigo=2954359&orden=0, accessed June 30, 2010.
13. Casimiro Barrios, "A mis padres," in Ciriaco Barrios, *Recuerdos: Poesías* (Santiago: Imprenta Franklin, 1912), reproduced in *Boletín 2008 Asociación Benéfico-Cultural Nieva de Cameros*, Año 2007, No. 23 (2008), 73–74.
14. José Angel Barrutieta, "Ciriaco Barrios: Un poeta nevero en ultramar," *Boletín 2007 Asociación Benéfico-Cultural Nieva de Cameros*, Año 2006: No. 22 (2007), 78–79.
15. Barrutieta, "Ciriaco Barrios," 80–81. "Golondrina" was also a slang for migrant laborer and thus the dual meaning here should be noted. See Geoffroy de LaForcade, "Ghosts of Insurgencies Past: Waterfront Labor, Working Class Memory, and the Contentious Emergence of the National-Popular State in Argentina," in Maxwell and Craib, eds., *No Gods, No Masters*. Unless otherwise noted, poetry translations are my own.
16. This excerpt from *La Voz del Obrero* appears in the prologue to Barrios's posthumously published drama *La Patria del Pobre*, 6–8, and reproduced in Barrutieta, "Ciriaco Barrios: Vida y obras de un poeta en el centenario de su muerte," *Boletín 2008: Asociación Benéfico-Cultural Nieva de Cameros*, Año 2007: No. 23 (2008), 69-70.
17. "Un extremo de la ley de residencia." For identification of his workplace, see "Casimiro Barrios: Reclamación por espulsión del territorio según la Lei de Residencia," *Gaceta de los Tribunales, Año 1918: Noviembre i Diciembre* (Santiago: Dirección Jeneral de Talleres Fiscales de Prisiones, 1925), 1990.
18. José Santos González Vera, *Cuando Era Muchacho* (Santiago: Editorial Universitaria, 1996 [1951]), 124.
19. On the ownership of the shop, see Jorge Rojas Flores, "La prensa obrera chilena: El caso de La Federación Obrera y Justicia, 1921–1927," in Olga Ulianova, Manuel Loyola, and Rolando Alvarez, eds., *1912–2012: El siglo de los comunistas chilenos* (Santiago: Instituto de Estudios Avanzados, Universidad de Santiago de Chile, , 2012), 55. The location of the store that employed Barrios comes from the expulsion decree issued against him and which can be found in Decreto 760, December 18, 1920, Archivo Nacional de Chile (hereafter AN), Fondo Intendencia de Santiago (hereafter IS), v. 470.

20. The name of the barrio comes from Rojas, *La oscura vida radiante*, 318.
21. On industries in the area, see *Album Gráfico de la Policía de Santiago* (Santiago: n.p., 1923), 233. On anarchism and spatial politics, see the excellent analysis in Chris Ealham, *Anarchism and the City: Revolution and Counter-Revolution in Barcelona, 1898–1937* (Oakland: AK Press, 2010), esp. chap. 5.
22. Carlos Vicuña Fuentes, *La Tiranía en Chile: Libro escrito en el destierro en 1928* (Santiago: LOM Ediciones, 2002 [1938]), 111.
23. González Vera, *Cuando era muchacho*, 136. See also González Vera, "Los anarquistas," reprinted in Carmen Soria, comp., *Letras Anarquistas: Artículos periodísticas y otros escritos inéditos* (Santiago: Planeta, 2005).
24. On these and other labor laws, see DeShazo, *Urban Workers and Labor Unions*, 40.
25. Vicuña Fuentes, *La Tiranía en Chile*, 111; Unsigned report titled "Asamblea Obrera de Alimentación Nacional" and dated November 11, 1919, AN/IS v. 496. On the passage, and nonenforcement, of the ley of the chair and the ley domenical, see DeShazo, *Urban Workers and Labor Unions*, 39–40. There is more than a little irony in the fact that the article on Barrios was titled "Dura lex sed lex," (which roughly translates as "the law is harsh but it is the law") given that Barrios was fighting in fact to have labor laws enforced. According to Collier and Sater, only two laws were passed prior to 1914 dealing with the social question: a law from 1906 creating the Consejo de Habitaciones Obreras ("which Alejandro Venegas denounced as a paper organization") and one creating the six-day work week but that was not mandatory for all workers. See Collier and Sater, *A History of Chile*, 195. The issue of lending houses was crucial. A National Savings Bank, under the oversight of the Mortgage Bank, had been created in 1910 to encourage saving among nonelites. Even so, through the 1910s much of Chile's urban working class was dependent on smaller lending houses for short-term loans at exorbitant interest rates. See Guillermo Subercaseaux, *Monetary and Banking Policy of Chile* (Oxford: Clarendon Press, 1922), 211–212; and Fernando Silva V., "Expansión y crisis nacional, 1861-1924," in Sergio Villalobos R., Osvaldo Silva G., Fernando Silva V., and Patricio Estellé M., *Historia de Chile* (Santiago: Editorial Universitaria, 1974) 602–603.
26. For Triviño's experience selling alcohol see Juan Gandulfo's introduction to A[rmando] Triviño, *Arengas* (Santiago: Editorial Lux, 1923). At points, workers in the FOCh would refuse to unload wine—in part due to abstinence programs but also because of the power of conservative wine growers in the Parliament. See American Consulate, Arica, to the Secretary of State, April 12, 1921, Records of the Dept. of State Relating to the Internal Affairs of Chile, 1910–1929 (Roll 21; 825.50: Economic Conditions) reporting on a December 1920 proclamation by the FOCh that it would no longer unload wines or liquors from ships.
27. *Paremiología chilena. Discurso leido por don Ramón A. Laval, en su incorporación el 30 de noviembre de 1923 y contestación de don José Toribio Medina* (Santiago de Chile: Imprenta Universitaria, 1923), 48.
28. José Luis Romero, *Latinoamérica: Las ciudades y las ideas* (Medellín: Editorial Universidad de Antioquia, 1999 [1976]), 367; Benjamin Orlove, "Meat and Strength: The Moral Economy of a Chilean Food Riot," *Cultural Anthropology* 12:2 (1997), 1–35; Edward Murphy, *For a Proper Home: Housing Rights in the Margins of Urban Chile, 1960–2010* (Pittsburgh: University of Pittsburgh Press, 2014), chap 1.
29. Rojas, *La oscura vida radiante*, 9–10.
30. Maurice Maeterlinck, *The Blue Bird: A Fairy Play in Five Acts*, trans. by Alexander Teixera de Mattos (New York: Dodd, Mead and Co., 1910), 18–19.

31. *Paremiología chilena*, 41.
32. Vicuña Fuentes, *La Tiranía*, 76; René Millar Carvacho, *La elección presidencial de 1920* (Santiago: Editorial Universitaria, 1982), 12–13.
33. *El Mercurio* (March 11, 1919), as reproduced in "De Hace Medio Siglo," *El Mercurio* (March 11, 1969), IISH/MSR, f13.
34. Richard Walter, *Politics and Urban Growth in Santiago, Chile, 1891–1941* (Redwood City, CA: Stanford University Press, 2005), 20.
35. J. Pablo Silva, "Frustrated Expectations and Social Protest in Post-World War I Chile." Paper presented at the 2013 Latin American Studies Association meeting, Washington, DC.
36. Sergio Grez Toso, *Historia del comunismo en Chile* (Santiago: LOM Ediciones, 2011), 89. See also the statistical evidence provided in Barría Serón, *Los movimientos sociales*, 79–81.
37. Gregory Cushman, *Guano and the Opening of the Pacific World: A Global Ecological History* (Cambridge: Cambridge University Press, 2013), 156–160.
38. "Potpourri," *Sucesos*, IISH/MSR, f13.
39. Deshazo as qtd. in Hugo Alberto Maureira, "Los Culpables de la miseria: Poverty and Public Health during the Spanish Influenza Epidemic in Chile, 1918–1920," (PhD diss., Georgetown University, 2012), 67.
40. "En busca del carne," *Sucesos* (July 22, 1920).
41. Walter, *Politics and Urban Growth*, 68–69.
42. On inflation and critique of monetary policy see the comments of Carlos Silva Vildosola, a long-time writer and editor for *El Mercurio*, as transcribed in American Embassy, Santiago, *Report on General Conditions Prevailing in Chile*, August 20, 1920 to September 3, 1920, in Records of the Department of State Relating to the Internal Affairs of Chile, 1910–1929 (Roll 4. 825.00 Political Affairs). Silva Vildosola was interviewed while in Argentina and was reflecting back on issues of the previous years. See also, more broadly, Morris, *Elites, Intellectuals, and Consensus.*
43. Silva Vildosola, in American Embassy, Santiago, *Report on General Conditions Prevailing in Chile*. Millar Carvacho notes that public sector employees saw no changes from 1912 in their salaries. Millar Carvacho, *La elección presidencial*, 13.
44. DeShazo, *Urban Workers and Labor Unions*, 159–160; Santiago Labarca, "Memorias de Santiago Labarca," *Claridad* 1:9.
45. On the AOAN, see Ignacio Rodríguez Terrazas, "Protesta y soberanía popular: las marchas del hambre en Santiago de Chile 1918–1919," unpublished thesis, Pontífica Universidad Católica de Chile, 2001; DeShazo, *Urban Workers and Labor Unions*, 159–160; and Grez Toso, *Historia del comunismo en Chile*, chap. 6.
46. *Paremiología chilena*, 48.
47. The locations and sizes of these meetings comes from Labarca, "Memorias de Santiago Labarca," *Claridad* 1:9 (1920). See also the discussion in chapter 2.
48. Labarca, "Memorias de Santiago Labarca;" and José Santos González Vera, "Estudiantes del año veinte," *Babel: Revista de arte y crítica* 28 (July–August, 1945), 34–44, esp. 36.
49. Valiente was appointed as an AOAN delegate for the Typesetters' Union of Santiago. See "Sesión de Directorio celebrada el 20 de Febrero de 1919," Sociedad Unión de los Tipógrafos de Santiago, Roll 5, p. 29, IISH.
50. "La carestia de la vida," *El Mercurio* (September 30, 1918), 16. For his leadership role in the Santiago branch of the POS, see Rodríguez Terrazas, "Protesta y soberanía popular," 47.

51. For bringing foodstuffs to market, see Alberto Martínez et. al. to the Minister of the Interior, no date but circa December 1, 1918, AN/IS v. 470. For unjust prices in the Mercado Central and on letting owners sleep in their puestos, see Unsigned report on the AOAN by the Santiago Security Section, December 21, 1918, AN/IS v. 470.
52. Martínez et. al. to the Minister of the Interior, n.d. but circa December 1, 1918, AN/IS v. 470.
53. DeShazo, *Urban Workers and Labor Unions*, 160.
54. Patricio de Diego Maestri, Luis Peña Rojas, and Claudio Peralta Castillo, *La Asamblea Obrera de Alimentación Nacional: Un hito en la historia de Chile* (Santiago: Sociedad Chilena de Sociología, 2002), 74.
55. *El Mercurio* (November 23, 1918), as qtd. in de Diego Maestri et. al., *La Asamblea*, 75.
56. Ibid., 75.
57. 29th Session, November 26, 1918, *Cámara de Diputados: Boletín de las Sesiones Estraordinarias en 1918–1919* (Santiago de Chile: Imprenta Nacional, 1918), 684.
58. De Diego Miestre et. al., *La Asamblea*, 79.
59. DeShazo, *Urban Workers and Labor Unions*, 160–161. Terrazas notes that in the aftermath of the negotiated settlement of the general strike of September 1919, the AOAN lost substantial worker support and began to crumble. More militant workers felt betrayed by the leadership and began to look elsewhere for solidarity and action, including another organization forming at the time: the IWW. Rodríguez Terrazas, "Protesta y soberanía popular," 143–144. On the attacks on the consulates, see William E. Skuban, *Lines in the Sand: Nationalism and Identity on the Peruvian-Chilean Frontier* (Albuquerque: University of New Mexico Press, 2007), 172.
60. On previous calls for the creation of a residency law, see Julio Pinto V. and Verónica Valdívio O., *Revolución proletaria o querida chusma? Socialismo y Alessandrismo en la pugna por la politización pampina (1911–1932)* (Santiago: LOM Ediciones, 2001), 54 and Ignotus, *Los Anarquistas: Vidas que se autoconstruyen* (Santiago: Ediciones Spartacus, 2011), 151 n9.
61. Frank Cain, "The Industrial Workers of the World: Aspects of its Suppression in Australia, 1916–1919," *Labour History* 42 (May 1982), 54–62. The traffic was two-way between Pacific South America and Australia. As a series of strikes shook the northern sugar regions of Peru in 1922, the government expelled some thirty of its own citizens to Australia. Paulo Drinot, *The Allure of Labor: Workers, Race, and the Making of the Peruvian State* (Durham, NC: Duke University Press, 2011), 85. Such concerns of potentially purposeful export of one's radicals persisted. In September 1920, the Chilean government would suspect that a significant number of the crew aboard the German ship the Lucie Woermenn were radicals expelled from parts of Europe looking to settle in Chile. See Pedro García to Minister of Foreign Relations, September 17, 1920; Pedro García to Minister of Foreign Relations, September 23, 1920; and Pedro García to Minister of the Navy, September 22, 1920, all in ARNAD/MI v. 5407.
62. Cited from Cain, "The Industrial Workers of the World," 60.
63. Ley No. 3446: Impide la entrada al país o la residencia en él de elementos indeseables. Published in the Diario Oficial No. 12,243 of December 12, 1918 and reproduced in Brian Loveman and Elizabeth Lira, *Arquitectura política y seguridad interior del Estado: Chile 1811–1990* (Santiago: LOM, 2002), 82–83. The power of expulsion rested with the intendents charged with overseeing particular

regions; they were also given the power to force foreigners to register themselves in special registries which would come under the authority of the police prefects and to obtain personal identity certificates. Foreigners who did not register as ordered within 8 days of the issuance would be sentenced to a term in prison or a fine of 20 pesos each day late.

64. See, for example,the discussions in the *Cámara de Diputados*, 29th session, November 26, 1918.
65. The circumstances of Barrios's arrest and order of expulsion are reviewed in Santiago Intendency to the Minister of the Interior, June 19, 1920, AN/IS v. 497. The actual decree is Decreto 760, Intendency of Santiago, December 18, 1918.
66. Decreto 2, Intendency of Santiago, January 4, 1919, referenced in Santiago Intendency to the Minister of the Interior, June 19, 1920, AN/IS v. 497.
67. Rodríguez Terrazas, "Protesta y soberanía popular," 82.
68. *La Aurora: Organo del Partido Obrero Socialista* 132 (January 10, 1919), 2; on *La Bandera Roja* see Rodríguez Terrazas, "Protesta y soberanía popular," 82.
69. Unsigned report by the Security Section, dated December 20, 1918, on a meeting held the evening December 19, 1920 in AN/IS v. 470.
70. 61st Session, December 20, 1918, in *Cámara de Diputados: Boletín de las Sesiones Estraordinarias en 1918–1919* (Santiago de Chile: Imprenta Nacional, 1918), 1413; Session, December 24, 1918, in *Cámara de Senadores: Boletín de las Sesiones Estraordinarias en 1918* (Santiago de Chile: Imprenta Nacional, 1918), 906–907; Session, January 3, 1919, in *Cámara de Senadores: Boletín de las Sesiones Estraordinarias en 1918*, 1034.
71. See his comments in 69th Session, January 3, 1919, in *Cámara de Diputados . . . 1918–1919*, 1717–1719. The translation here attempts to capture the slang and derision of Pinto Durán's original phrasing: "y yo no meto un brazo al fuego por los procedimientos de la Sección de Seguridad." It could be also translated as "I would not vouch for the procedures of the Security Section" although I have opted for something a bit more derisive.
72. 69th Session, January 3, 1919, *Cámara de Diputados . . . 1918–1919*, 1717–1719, qtd. passage on 1718.
73. Luxemborg, "Social Reform or Revolution?" (London: Militant Publications, 1986 [1900; 1908]). Thanks to Josh Savala for bringing this pamphlet to my attention.
74. See Colin Ward, *Anarchy in Action* (London: Freedom Press, 1982) and *Anarchism*. The qtd. passage comes from *Anarchism*, 74. Ruth Kinna points out that some "anarchists saw Ward's views as inherently reformist and liberal," a point that Ward did not contest as he did not see "anarchy in action" and "revolutionary anarchism" as necessarily mutually exclusive. See Matthew Wilson and Ruth Kinna, "Key Terms," in Kinna, ed., *The Continuum Companion to Anarchism* (London: Continuum, 2012), 352. See also Scott's recent *Two Cheers for Anarchism* which, to my mind, resonates with many of Ward's perspectives.
75. Session, December 24, 1918, in *Cámara de Senadores: Boletín de las Sesiones Estraordinarias en 1918* (Santiago de Chile: Imprenta Nacional, 1918), 907. Torrealba would subsequently direct the Centro de Estudios Sociales and defend, at the Santiago Court of Appeals in November 1920, many of the workers and students arrested as subversives. For Torrealba's lengthy statement to the court of appeals, see Agustín Torrealba Z., *Los subversivos* (Santiago: Imprenta Yara, 1921). He was also, in 1919, appointed by the Middle Class Federation

(Federación de la Clase Media), of which he had been president, to be its delegate to the AOAN.

76. On Torrealba, see Osvaldo López, *Diccionario Biográfico Obrero de Chile* (Santiago: Imprenta Bellavista, 1912), T1–T5.
77. Enacted November 5, 1917, and requiring all employees in all industries to be given one day of rest per week (Sunday). See the summary in L.J. Keena, American consul in Valparaíso, "One day per week established by law," November 20, 1917, in Records of the Dept. of State Relating to the Internal Affairs of Chile, 1910–1929 (Roll 21; 825.50: Economic Conditions)
78. On Triviño, see Juan Gandulfo's introduction in Triviño, *Arengas* as well as Víctor Muñoz C., *Armando Triviño: Wobblie. Hombres, ideas y problemas del anarquismo en los años veinte (Vida y escritos de un libertario criollo)* (Santiago: Quimantú, 2009). On Silva, see Sergio Grez Toso, *Los anarquistas y el movimiento obrero: La alborada de 'la idea' en Chile, 1893–1915* (Santiago: LOM Ediciones, 2007), 188–189. See also Walter, *Politics and Urban Growth*, 84.
79. *Memoria del Ministerio de Justicia* (December 1915—June 1917) (Santiago: Imp. Lit. y Enc. Fiscal de la Penitenciaría, 1917), 87.
80. Ibid., 18; 227–228.
81. Advertisement in *El Mercurio* (September 30, 1920), 20.
82. On government concerns regarding alcohol, and particularly the 'mocking' of laws by corporations with juridical standing, see for example *Memoria del Ministerio de Justicia* (December 1915—June 1917), 9–10.
83. See *Numen* 1:18 (August 16, 1919), front page.
84. See Walter, *Politics and Urban Growth*, 85.
85. Session, December 24, 1918, in *Cámara de Senadores*, 906–907. My emphasis.
86. Ibid., 907.
87. 69th session, January 3, 1919, in *Cámara de Diputados . . . 1918–1919*, 1717–1718.
88. Ibid., 1718.
89. Ibid., 1719.
90. For excellent studies, see Grez Toso, *Los anarquistas*; Muñoz Cortés, *Armando Triviño*; Muñoz Cortés, *Cuando la Patria Mata: La Historia del Anarquista Julio Rebosio (1914–1920)* (Santiago: Editorial USACH, 2011); and Mario Araya Saavedra, "Los Wobblies Criollos," unpublished thesis, Universidad ARCIS, Santiago, 2008.
91. "Un extremo de la ley de residencia," IISH/MSR, f14 (1919).
92. On "misplaced ideas" see the seminal work of Roberto Schwarz. I draw inspiration from Schwarz but do not follow his argument all the way through here. Schwarz, *Misplaced Ideas: Essays on Brazilian Culture* (London: Verso, 1992). For a brief but very productive intervention, see Bosteels, "Neither Proletarian nor Vanguard."
93. Unsigned report by the Security Section, on the AOAN, dated December 21, 1918, regarding a meeting held on December 20, 1918, in AN/IS, v. 470. My emphasis.
94. James Morris long ago pointed out trenchantly the degree to which intellectuals continued to reproduce this kind of importation narrative, or what he termed a discourse of docility. See Morris, *Elites, Intellectuals and Consensus*, 112–114. It is worth seeing here that anarchists were in a particularly good position to offer what were effectively early postcolonial critiques of Eurocentrism. See Craib, "A Foreword," in Maxwell and Craib, eds., *No Gods, No Masters*.

95. Kropotkin, *The Conquest of Bread and Other Writings* (Cambridge: Cambridge University Press, 1995 [1892]), 15.
96. Cited from Ignotus, *Los anarquistas*, 5–6.
97. The original reads: "Lárguese de acá con viento fresco y que no se le ocurra nunca volver por estos lados. Tenga presente que el chileno no aguanta planes, y se va de hacha a las barbas." The final phrase is difficult to translate due to the double entendre. "Irse de hacha a las barbas" is literally to shave or cut away beards with an axe, a clear reference to the bearded anarchist in the image. But its more figurative meaning is to uproot violently and expel. I've translated it here as "cut to the quick" in order to capture the imagery of knives or axes and that of both bodily and emotional harm. Thanks to Leonardo Vargas-Méndez for his help with this phrase.
98. It is difficult to determine what precisely the creators of such images understood by the term "maximalist." I have translated it here in such a way as to capture the association with Russia's revolution and with forms of property and personal violence. In this I am following the entry for "maximalist" in Richard Greeman's glossary for Victor Serge's *Memoirs of a Revolutionary*: the "Party that split from the SOCIAL REVOLUTIONARIES in 1906, advocating the socialization of industry as well as of land, together with a wider application of terrorism (to include pillage and incendiarism of estates, as well as individual assassination." See Serge, *Memoirs of a Revolutionary*, trans. by Peter Sedgwick and George Paizis (New York: New York Review Books, 2012), 480.
99. "Un extremo de la ley de residencia," IISH/MSR, f14 (1919).
100. 71st Session, January 7, 1919, *Cámara de Diputados . . . 1918–1919*, 1845.
101. For an elaboration, see Craib, "Sedentary anarchists."
102. For the Supreme Court verdict, see "Casimiro Barrios: Reclamación por Espulsión del territorio según la Lei de Residencia," *Gaceta de los Tribunales Año 1918: Noviembre y Diciembre* (Santiago: Dirección Jeneral de Talleres Fiscales de Prisiones, 1925), 1988–1991.
103. 70th Session, January 4, 1919, *Cámara de Diputados . . . 1918–1919*, 1751; 71st Session, January 7, 1919, *Cámara de Diputados . . . 1918–1919*, 1840.
104. 71st session, January 7, 1919, *Cámara de Diputados . . . 1918–1919*, 1844; see also the summation in Santiago Intendency to Minister of the Interior, June 19, 1920, AN/IS v. 497 and, for a similar argument in Parliament made by his defenders, 69th session, January 3, 1919, in *Cámara de Diputados . . . 1918–1919*, 1718.
105. 73rd Session, January 8, 1919, *Cámara de Diputados . . . 1918–1919*, 1883; on Blanlot, see Sandra Deutsch, *Las Derechas: The Extreme Right in Argentina, Brazil and Chile, 1890–1939* (Redwood City, CA: Stanford University Press, 1999), 60–62.
106. On "preventive" applications of the law and "thickets" see Sánchez Gárcia de la Huerta, 71st Session, January 7, 1919, *Cámara de Diputados . . . 1918–1919*, 1839.
107. Unsigned report, Santiago Security Section, March 16, 1919, AN/IS v. 476 and Unsigned report, Santiago Security Section, March 17, 1919, AN/IS v. 476.
108. Unsigned report, Santiago Security Section, March 17, 1919, AN/IS v. 476.
109. That such was the case was all too clear to Recabarren who noted that the repression had little to do with fear and everything to do with weakening the labor movement. See Rodríguez Terrazas, "Protesta y soberanía popular," 92.
110. The speech was given on January 16, 1919. Cited from Rodríguez Terrazas, "Protesta y soberanía popular," 87.

111. Ibid., 89–92.
112. *La Opinión*, cited from ibid., 91.
113. Ibid., 84–92 and "El comité de Alimentación Nacional," *Verba Roja* 1:6 (February 1919), 2.
114. Rodríguez Terrazas, "Protesta y soberanía popular," 101.
115. "Un extremo de la ley de residencia," IISH/MSR, folder 14 (1919).
116. González Vera, *Cuando era muchacho*, 105.
117. For the selling of Trotsky's writings, see the July 1920 interrogation of university student Rigoberto Soto Rengifo in Proceso contra Pedro Gandulfo Guerra, et. al., Segundo Juzgado del Crimen de Santiago, AN/JS leg. 1658, f50. For the comments on the Russian Revolution, see "El maximalismo," *Verba Roja* 1:17 (August 29, 1919), 3; "Lenin," *Verba Roja* 1:14 (July 1919), 2; and "La dictadura del proletariado: El Prólogo del comunismo anárquico. Lenin, Trotsky y los maximalistas rusos van hacia él," *Verba Roja* 1:14 (July 1919), 1. As much as this reveals that divisions were not necessarily strong, it also reveals the degree to which, as it unfolded, the Russian revolution had a number of possible paths, some of which appeared agreeable to those with more anarchistic persuasions. It was with the massacre of the Ukranian anarchists and the suppression in Kronstadt that the split began to widen. Even then the divide between communists and anarchists was not all-encompassing. As late as the early 1940s Manuel Rojas, a lifelong anarchist, would pen a beautiful obituary of Trotsky in the intellectual journal *Babel*.
118. See the reports in Sub-Prefect to the Colonel-Prefect (Police of Santiago), June 28, 1920, AN/IS v. 496.
119. See Gandulfo's prologue to "La revolución soviética" (Editorial Lux, 1918), as qtd. in Oscar Ortiz, "La historia de Juan Gandulfo," 42. Gandulfo was not alone in his concerns. Carlos Hermosilla recalled arriving in Santiago in 1920 and being surprised at the hostility directed at the revolution by his father's typesetter colleagues. Letter from Carlos Hermosillo to Carlos Figueroa, May 23, 1980, Archivo del Escritor, Biblioteca Nacional.
120. I thank Mario Araya for sharing this document with me.
121. Rojas, *Sombras contra el muro*, as cited in Dario Cortés, *La narrative anarquista de Manuel Rojas* (Madrid: Pliegos, 1986), 31.
122. *Conferencia Internacional Sudamericana de Policía (Febrero 20/29 de 1920): Convenio y Actas* (Buenos Aires: José Tragant, 1920), 49.
123. *El Mercurio* (February 21, 1919) as reproduced in "De Hace Medio Siglo," *El Mercurio* (February 21, 1969), in IISH/MSR, f14 (1919).
124. *Conferencia Internacional*, 5–18; 84–86; *Album Gráfico de la Policía*, 68; Roberto Hernández Ponce and Jule Salazar González, *De la Policía secreta a la Policía científica* (Santiago: Sección Impr. de la Policía de Investigaciones de Chile, 1994), 147.
125. See Enrique Cuevas (head of the Chilean Legation in Uruguay) to the Minister of Foreign Relations, March 16, 1920, in Ministerio de Relaciones Exteriores (hereafter MRE), Archivo General Histórico (hereafter AGH), vol. 801b. "Social accounting" comes from French sociologist and criminologist Alphonse Bertillon: "From the perspective of social accounting, a Nation is similar to a factory. Whether it is people or things that are produced, the keeping of books is subject to the same rules and obligations: One must record exactly what enters, what exits, establish the balance of this two-way movement and verify, according to the state of the register and the products in the store (inventory

and counting), the accuracy of the account of movements (what comes in and what goes out.)" Bertillon, *Dictionnaire des Sciences Médicales* (1878), as quoted in Mark Neocleous, *Imagining the State* (Milton Keynes: Open University Press, 2003), 115.

126. *Conferencia Internacional*, 39.
127. Ibid., 40.
128. Ibáñez (Chilean legation in Paris) to the Minister of Foreign Relations, October 9/10, 1919, MRE/AGH, vol. 761.
129. See for example Boris Nobel, *El reinado de Lenin*, trans. by Ricardo Cabieses Z. (Santiago: Imp. Fiscal de la Penitenciaría, 1920) and Rafael Calleja, *Bolchevismo y Menchevismo* (Madrid, 1920), reviewed by Omar Emeth in *El Mercurio* (July 18, 1920), 3.
130. José Miguel Varas, *Chacón* (Santiago: Talleres de la Sociedad Impresora Horizonte, 1968), 26–27.
131. Ibid., 27.
132. A. de la Cruz (Consul General de Chile en España) to D. Enrique Bermúdez, Minister of the Interior, October 2, 1919, MRE/AGH, vol. 759.
133. On food shortages—particularly shortages of flour and bread—see Minister of the Interior, first section, to the Minister of Railroads, July 3, 1920, ARNAD, Minister of the Interior (hereafter MI) v. 5407, No. 1295; on the cost of foodstuffs, see "Potpourri," IISH/MSR, f13 (1918) and *El Mercurio* (March 11, 1919) as reproduced in "De Hace Medio Siglo," *El Mercurio* (March 11, 1969), IISH/MSR, f13 (1919). For statistics on increases in the costs of foodstuffs, see "La carestía de la vida," IISH/MSR, f15 (the date of this last publication is unclear but it provides statistics for the period 1913–1925). See also DeShazo, *Urban Workers and Labor Unions*, 159 and 185.
134. The quote from MacIver is from Barría Serón, *Los movimientos sociales*, 371.
135. Morris, *Elites, Intellectuals and Consensus*, 78; Lewis L. Lorwin, *Historia del internacionalismo obrero*, trans. Luis Dávila (Santiago: Biblioteca Ercilla, 1936), 2: 160–161.
136. See the useful discussion in Julio Durán Cerda, "El teatro chileno moderno," *Anales de la Universidad de Chile* Año CXXI: 126 (January–April 1963), 168–203, esp. 177–184; and Acevedo Hernández, "El teatro ácrata en Chile," *Claridad* 12 (January 22, 1921), 6.
137. Report transcribed in Colonel Prefect to the Intendent of the Province, December 30, 1918, AN/IS v. 470.
138. Edwards Bello, *El Roto* (Santiago: Editorial Universitaria, 2006 [1920]), 27.
139. Maureira, "Los culpables de la miseria," 6. Maureira shows the uncertainty that existed regarding the epidemic: was it Spanish influenza or epidemic typhus? He argues that a medical diagnosis of typhus was influenced or predicated upon a social diagnosis of national decay. Maureira, "Los culpables," 4–29.
140. On the day following Gómez Rojas's death, some sixteen infants under the age of one died. This was not a particularly high figure. *El Mercurio* (October 1, 1920), 13.
141. Raquel Bravo G, "Ensayo sobre el índice de morbilidad en Santiago de Chile" (Medical thesis, University of Chile, 1922), 11, as cited in Maureira, "Los culpables," 68.
142. Rinke, *Cultura de Masas: Reforma y nacionalismo en Chile (1910–1931)* (Santiago: Dirección de Bibliotecas, Archivos y Museos, 2002), 98; American Embassy, Santiago, *Report on General Conditions Prevailing in Chile*, August 20,

1920 to September 3, 1920, in Records of the Department of State Relating to the Internal Affairs of Chile, 1910–1929 (Roll 4. 825.00 Political Affairs).

143. González Vera, *Cuando era muchacho*, 53.
144. Subercaseaux, *Historia de las ideas y de la cultura en Chile*, 49. See also Pinto V. and Valdívio O., *Revolución proletaria o querida chusma?*, chap. 1 and the numerous publications noted by Hernández Ponce and Salazar González, *De la policía secreta*, 1: 101–102.
145. *El Mercurio* (August 8, 1919) as reproduced in "De Hace Medio Siglo," *El Mercurio* (August 8, 1969), in IISH/MSR, f14. The AOAN played a role in advocating on behalf of these workers. Many members of the AOAN were targeted during the round-ups in 1919. See Unsigned report titled "Asamblea Obrera de Alimentación Nacional," October 7, 1919, AN/IS v. 496.
146. *El Mercurio* (September 28, 1919) as reproduced in "De Hace Medio Siglo," *El Mercurio* (September 28, 1969) in IISH/MSR f14.
147. Walter, *Politics and Urban Growth*, 83.
148. González Vera, *Cuando era muchacho*, 57.
149. González Vera, "El Conventillo," in González Vera, *Vidas Mínimas* (Santiago: LOM, 1996 [1923]). For a lovely introduction to González Vera's work, one which makes repeated note of his style and its relationship to his experience, see Pascual Brodsky, "Prólogo," in González Vera, *Obras Completas* 2 vols. (Santiago: Cociña, Soria Editores, 2013). For a bureaucratic perspective on conventillos see "Consejo Superior de Habitaciones Obreras: Inspección, Cartilla de Recomendaciones higiénicas a los habitantes de los conventillos," undated, AN/IS v. 476.
150. DeShazo, *Urban Workers and Labor Unions*, 59.
151. See the announcement in *El Mercurio* (September 30, 1920), 10.
152. Collier and Sater note that Alejandro Venegas "denounced" the Consejo de Habitaciones Obreras as a "paper organization." Collier and Sater, *A History of Chile*, 195. For brief background see Maureira, "Los culpables," chap. 2; on deteriorating quality, see DeShazo, *Urban Workers and Labor Unions*, 59; on Alessandri's thesis, see Maureira, "Los Culpables," 65; on affordable housing and anarchism, see the discussion of Carvajal in Walter, *Politics and Urban Growth*, 80–81; for a political history of housing and home, and for discussion of the 1906 law, see Murphy, *For a proper home*.
153. Brian Loveman, *Chile: The Legacy of Hispanic Capitalism* (New York: Oxford University Press, 2001), 170.
154. Arnold McKay, American consul, Antofagasta, to Secretary of State, February 21, 1919, in Records of the Dept. of State Relating to the Internal Affairs of Chile, 1910–1929 (Roll 21; 825.50: Economic Conditions). US companies would, over the course of the 1920s, replace English companies as the dominant foreign presence in nitrate extraction. See Barría Serón, *Los Movimientos Sociales*, 20–30.
155. Statistic provided in American Embassy, Santiago, *Report on General Conditions Prevailing in Chile*, August 20, 1920 to September 3, 1920, in Records of the Department of State Relating to the Internal Affairs of Chile, 1910–1929 (Roll 4. 825.00 Political Affairs).
156. "La crisis en la Pampa," *El Pacífico*, February 18, 1919, IISH/MSR, f13 (1919).
157. *El Mercurio* (December 19, 1919) as reproduced in "De Hace Medio Siglo," *El Mercurio* (December 19, 1969), in IISH/MSR f13; see also the article from *El Mercurio* (August 13, 1919), reproduced in "De Hace Medio Siglo," *El Mercurio*

(August 13, 1969), IISH/MSR, f14, which similarly notes a massive movement of workers and families from the north to the center of the country and comments explicitly on the potentially detrimental impact on wages and the costs of foodstuffs and housing.

158. "La crisis en la Pampa," *El Pacífico*, February 18, 1919, IISH/MSR, f13 (1919). Some five hundred Bolivian workers were also expelled.
159. On the mutual benefits treaty, see Skuban, *Lines in the Sand*, 8.
160. See Sergio González Miranda, *El dios cautivo: Las Ligas Patrióticas en la chilenización compulsiva de Tarapacá (1910–1922)* (Santiaigo: LOM Ediciones, 2004).
161. For details, see *Arbitration Between Peru and Chile. The Case of Peru, In the matter of the controversy arising out of the Question of the Pacific, Before the President of the United States of America* (Washington, DC: National Capital Press, 1923) and the corresponding appendix as well as, more broadly, Skuban, *Lines in the Sand*.
162. *Reports of International Arbitral Awards (Tacna Arica Question (Chile, Peru))*, 4 March 1925, Vol. II: 921–958. On this issue see p. 934, legal.un.org/riaa/cases/vol_II/921-958.pdf, accessed December 14, 2015.
163. On these efforts see Skuban, *Lines in the Sand*, chap. 2 and Skuban, "Civic and Ethnic Conceptions of Nationhood on the Peruvian-Chilean Frontier, 1880–1930," *Studies in Ethincity and Nationalism* 8:3 (December 2008), 386–407.
164. Markos J. Mamalakis, comp., *Historical Statistics of Chile: Demography and Labor Force (vol. 2)* (Westport, CT: Greenwood Press, 1980), 114.
165. On the Chileanization campaign, see among others Note from the Peruvian Minister Chacaltana to the Minister of Foreign Affairs of Chile, November 14, 1900, in *Arbitration Between Peru and Chile. Appendix to the Case of Peru* (Washington, DC: National Capitol Press, 1923), 584–600.
166. On the campaigns see González Miranda, *El dios cautivo*.
167. See Stefanie Gänger, "Conquering the Past: Post-War Archaeology and Nationalism in the Borderlands of Chile and Peru, c. 1880–1920," *Comparative Studies in Society and History* 51:4 (2009), 691–714 and *International Arbitral Awards*, 938.
168. Skuban, *Lines in the Sand*, 172.
169. Ibid., 64.
170. See, e.g., Telegraphic Circular from the Minister of Foreign Affairs of Peru, December 28, 1918, relating to the expulsion of Peruvians from Tarapacá, Tacna, and Arica, in *Arbitration Between Peru and Chile. Appendix to the Case of Peru* (Washington, DC: National Capitol Press, 1923), 724–725.
171. Article 14 of the Law of October 31, 1884, created the province of Tarapacá, which came fully under Chilean sovereignty, and also provided that those Peruvians who wished to do so could maintain their Peruvian nationality by registering in Tarapacá, Iquique or Pisagua. But with respect to Tacna and Arica, citizenship issues remained murky and contested. Article 14 is reproduced in Fernando Albonico Valenzuela, *Derecho internacional privado chileno: leyes y tratados vigentes* (Santiago: Editorial Jurídica de Chile, 1958), 44. For efforts repeatedly to address uncertainty regarding citizenship as well as issues related to obligatory military service, see: Supreme Court case October 6, 1917, reproduced in *Revista de derecho, jurisprudencia y ciencias sociales* XV: 1–10 (March through December 1918) (Santiago: Imprenta Cervantes, 1918), 191–196; *Reports of International Arbitral Awards* (Tacna Arica Question (Chile, Peru)), March 4, 1925, II: 921–958; and Corte Tacna, November 18, 1913,

referenced in *Repertorio de Legislación y Jurisprudencia Chilenas: Constitución Política de la República de Chile, 1980* (Santiago: Editorial Jurídica de Chile, 1993), 14.

172. Investigations Commissioner to the Intendent of the Province, October 24, 1919, ARNAD/MI v. 5375. For Palza's original petition, see Nicanor Palza Morales to the Mayor of Iquique, undated but January 1919, ARNAD/MI, v5375; Libreta de Familia de Nicanor Palza, attachment in Nicanor Palza Morales to the Mayor of Iquique, undated but January 1919, ARNAD/MI, v5375. Palza describes his own background further in Nicanor Palza Morales to the Intendent of Tarapacá, undated but early November, 1919, in ARNAD/MI, v5375.
173. Nicanor Palza Morales to the Intendent of Tarapacá, undated but early November, 1919, ARNAD/MI v. 5375.
174. See for example, Pascual Osega to the Illustrious Municipality, undated but late December 1918, ARNAD/MI v. 5375; Letter from the Superintendent of Locomotives, December 24, 1918, ARNAD/MI v. 5375; and Investigations Commissioner to the Intendent of the Province, October 23, 1919, ARNAD/MI v. 5375. For the case of Abraham González Mantilla in Mantilla to the Mayor of Iquique, no date but January, 1919, ARNAD/MI v. 5375; Commissioner of Investigations (Iquique Police) to the Intendent of the Province, October 22, 1919, ARNAD/MI v. 5375.; Mantilla to the Intendent, undated but circa November, 1919, ARNAD/MI v. 5375.
175. For a work-in-progress that highlights Peruvian-Chilean solidarity, particularly among maritime workers, see Joshua Savala, "The Peruvian-Chilean Pacific World: Maritime Connections, Class, and State formation, 1850s–1930s," PhD dissertation, Cornell University (in progress).
176. Anjel Pacheco to the Illustrious Municipality, no date but January 1919, ARNAD/MI v. 5375.
177. Investigations Commissioner to the Intendent of the Province, October 22, 1919, ARNAD/MI v. 5375. In making this judgment, he referred to the Minister of the Interior's circular No. 3, dated February 24, 1919, which required intendents to do careful checks in to the background and character of any individuals who applied for Chilean citizenship, in particular in order to avoid having foreigners acquire citizenship in order to subvert the order. See Circular 3, February 24, 1919, ARNAD/MI v. 4858.
178. Unsigned report titled "Asamblea Obrera de Alimentación Nacional," November 11, 1919, AN/IS v. 496.
179. On the general strike see Rodríguez Terrazas, "Protesta y soberanía popular," 134–135. The strike in September had again raised the specter of expulsions as an editorial in the leading daily *El Mercurio* pointed to the United States as an exemplar of how to handle undesireables: expulsion. *El Mercurio* (September 17, 1919) as reproduced in "De Hace Medio Siglo," *El Mercurio* (September 17, 1969), IISH/MSR, f14.
180. Santiago Intendent to the Minister of the Interior, June 19, 1920, AN/IS v. 497; see also Fidel Araneda Luco, Investigations Commissioner, to the Intendent of the Province, July 7, 1920, AN/IS v.497.
181. Intendent of Santiago to Fidel Araneda Luco, July 7, 1920, AN/IS v. 505. These are the intendent's words, not Barrios's.
182. Ibid.

183. For examples of foreigners expelled "for being known ruffians and purveyors of prostitution," see the cases discussed in Colonel-Prefect to the Intendent of Santiago, January 20, 1919 and Sub-prefect to the Colonel-Prefect, January 18, 1919, both in AN/IS v. 496.
184. For Paladines see Decree of March 11, 1920, AN/IS v. 504, f72. Nicolás Gutarra, a Wobblie, of Peru was ordered expelled on May 18, and placed on a steamship for Arica and expelled from the country on June 5, 1920. Gutarra had initially been expelled from his native Peru for the same reason: "propagating ideas against the established order." The original expulsion order appears in Decree of May 18, 1920, AN/IS v. 504, Decretos 1920, f178. The actual date of expulsion is in Colonel-Prefect to the Intendent of the Province, June 14, 1920, AN/IS v. 496. On Gutarra's fascinating life—he was expelled from an array of countries and lived his final years in New York and Puerto Rico—see Jake Lagnado, "La inverosímil travesía de Nicolás Gutarra," *Pacarina del Sur: Revista de Pensamiento Crítico Latinoamericano*, www.pacarinadelsur.com/home/huellas-y-voces/1137-la-inverosimil-travesia-de-nicolas-gutarra#_edn1, accessed September 8, 2015. For Gutarra in his Peruvian context, see Drinot, *The Allure of Labor*, 101.
185. Barría Serón, *Los movimientos sociales*, 132–133.
186. Decreto of March 5, 1920, AN/IS v. 504, f60.
187. Intendent of the Province to the Minister of the Interior, July 5, 1920, AN/IS v. 506.
188. Decreto of July 7, 1920, AN/IS v. 504, f290.
189. *El Mercurio* (July 17, 1920), 1.
190. Fidel Araneda Luco, Investigations Commissioner, to the Intendent of the Province, July 7, 1920, AN/IS v. 497.
191. Juan Egaña and Pablo de Rokha, "Sobre el Asunto Barrios," *Numen* 2:65 (July 17, 1920), 3. Cariola was born in 1895 in Santiago and earned a law degree in 1916. He was one of the founders of the Theatrical Society of Chile, editor and owner of the magazine *La Quincena* and *Pchts . . . Pchts*, editorial secretary and literary critic for *La Unión*, and the author of the play *Entre gallos y medianoche*, which had a very long run in Santiago. He was also a member of the conservative party. See William Belmont Parker, ed., *Chileans of Today* (New York: G. P. Putnam's Sons, 1920), 568–569; and Carlos Pinto Durán, ed., *Diccionario Personal de Chile* (Santiago: Claret, 1920), 53. Barrios suggests Cariola is responsible for the Intendent's efforts to expel him in Unsigned report, Santiago Security Section, December 21, 1918, AN/IS v. 470.
192. Intendent of Santiago to the Minister of the Interior, June 19, 1920, AN/IS v. 497.
193. Ibid. The Minister of the Interior confirmed the expulsion on June 28. See Minister of the Interior to the Intendent of Santiago, June 28, 1920, AN/IS v. 496.
194. Intendent of Valparaíso to the Intendent don Francisco Subercaseaux, July 7, 1920, AN/IS v 497.
195. Ibid. See also Telegram from García de la Huerta (Minister of Interior) to Governor of Arica, July 9, 1920, ARNAD/MI v. 5427.
196. Telegram from García de la Huerta (Minister of the Interior) to Governor of Arica, July 9 1920, ARNAD/MI v. 5427 and Telegram from García de la Huerta (Minister of Interior) to Governor of Arica, July 10, 1920, ARNAD/MI v. 5426.

197. Telegram from García de la Huerta to Governor of Arica, July 9, 1920, ARNAD/MI v. 5427; and Certificate, Policía Fiscal, Tacna, July 16, 1920, AN/IS v. 498.
198. Telegram from Fernando Edwards to the Police Prefect, Santiago, July 28, 1920, AN/IS v. 498; on the idea of expelling him to Bolivia see telegram from Fernando Edwards, Intendent of Tacna, to Intendent of Santiago, August 1, 1920, AN/IS v. 498. For details on his expulsion, see Sub-Prefect to Colonel-Prefect, July 30, 1920, AN/IS v. 498 and Telegram from Fernando Edwards to the Police Prefect, Santiago, July 28, 1920, AN/IS v. 498 . A letter from Barrios to comrades in Santiago was published under the title "Desde Lima," in *Claridad* 1:9 (December 11, 1920), 9.

CHAPTER 2

1. The folk wisdom regarding never escaping the Casa de Orates is recounted in Rojas, *La oscura vida radiante*, 175. Details for the July 19 attacks on the FECh recounted in this and subsequent paragraphs come from: Alfredo Demaría, "Manifiesto del Presidente de la Federación de Estudiantes de Chile," *Juventud* 2:11–12 (January–March 1921), 30–35; Juan Gandulfo, "Comienza la farsa," *Juventud* 2:11–12 (January–March 1921), 39–46; Gandulfo, "Juan Gandulfo juzga el momento actual," *Claridad* 1:9 (December 11, 1920); Colonel-Prefect to Intendent of Santiago, July 20, 1920, AN/IS v. 497; *El Mercurio* (July 21, 1920), 17; and José Lafuente Vergara, "Cuarenta años del asalto y destrucción de la FECH," in "Las noticias de Ultima Hora," July 21, 1960, IISH/MSR, f15. On Gandulfo's time as intern at the Casa de Orates see Ricardo Zalaquett S., "*Siembra, juventud! La tierra es propicia, el momento es único.* No es Neruda sino Gandulfo, el cirujano," *Revista Médica de Chile* 133 (2005), 380; see also Moraga, *"Muchachos casi silvestres,"* 266–267. Gandulfo notes that he cared for Balmaceda while he was in the Casa de Orates in his interview with the police, dated July 20, 1920, in Lesiones a Santiago Labarca y Juan Gandulfo, Segundo juzgado del crimen de Santiago, AN/Justicial Santiago (hereafter JS), leg. 1658, f54–55. The figure of one or two hundred I arrived at as an approximation by comparing the numbers given in the above sources.
2. For details on the Olimpia, see Oreste Plath, *El Santiago que se fue: Apuntes de la memoria* (Grijalbo: Santiago, 1997), 65.
3. *El Mercurio* (July 21, 1920), 17; Frank Bonilla and Myron Glazer, *Student Politics in Chile* (New York: Basic Books, 1970) 41; and, for a reiteration of these positions, *Claridad* 1:3 (October 26, 1920).
4. Vicuña Fuentes, *La tiranía*, as cited in Moraga, *"Muchachos casi silvestres,"* 263.
5. The names they called him come from Labarca's testimony to the police on July 20, 1920, in Lesiones, AN/JS, leg. 1658, f54.
6. Gandulfo, "Comienza la farsa."
7. Ibid.
8. Ibid. Moreno claims he could not arrest the assailants—that he estimated to number one hundred—because he was too busy protecting Gandulfo. See the testimony of Moreno, July 20, 1920, in Lesiones, AN/JS, leg. 1658, f56
9. Gandulfo, "Comienza la farsa."
10. Ibid.
11. Ibid.
12. Ibid., 45.
13. Ibid., 46.
14. Ibid., 46.

15. On Labarca's career, see Moraga, *"Muchachos casi silvestres,"* 656 and González le Saux, *De empresarios a empleados: Clase media y estado docente en Chile, 1810–1920* (Santiago: LOM Ediciones, 2011), 353. On Labarca's work in the FOCh, see unsigned report titled "Federación Obrera de Chile: Junta Ejecutiva," September 7, 1919, AN/IS v. 496; unsigned report titled "Federación Obrera: Junta Ejecutiva Federal," June 5, 1920, AN/IS v. 496; unsigned report titled "Federación Obrera de Chile: Junta Ejecutiva," November 26, 1919, AN/IS v. 496; and unsigned report titled "Federación Obrera de Chile: Junta Ejecutiva Federal," January 16, 1920, AN/IS v. 493. On Labarca's position in the AOAN, see unsigned report, February 8, 1919, AN/IS v. 476. The decision to cancel protests due to the imposition of martial law appears in an unsigned report, February 5, 1919, AN/IS v. 476. On Labarca's efforts to bring workers and students together, see the anonymous introdution to Labarca's *Figuras de Agitadores* (Santiago: Cosmos, 1923) as well as chapter 3. The arrest order is recounted in *El Mercurio* (November 5, 1919) as reproduced in "De Hace Medio Siglo," *El Mercurio* (November 5, 1969), IISH/MSR, folder 14.
16. Neruda, *Confieso que he vivido* (Santiago: Pehuen, 2005 [1974]), 55.
17. The details on Salvatore's life and death come from interviews by the author with Juan Luis Gandulfo, July 21, 2011 and October 11, 2011.
18. Rojas, *Sombras contra el muro*, 32.
19. Daniel Schweitzer, "Juan Gandulfo," *Babel: Revista de arte y crítica* 28 (July-August 1945), 18–24; and *Boletín de los Trabajadores Industriales del Mundo* (Santiago, April 1920).
20. "Pedro Gandulfo," in Alfonso Calderón, *Según pasan los años: Entrevistas, retratos, recuerdos* (Santiago: Editorial Andrés Bello, 1990), 45–58.
21. Zalaquett S., *"Siembra, juventud!"* 376–382. See also Ignacio González Ginouves, "El Juan Gandulfo de mis recuerdos," *Anales Chilenos de Historia de la Medicina* 2 (1962), 145–157 and A. Alonso Vial, "Nota biográfica sobre Juan Gandulfo: Lo que he conocido de él," *Revista Médica de Chile* 60 (1932), 99–114.
22. The comment was made by one don Carlos Dávila and is recalled in González Vera, "Un Juan Gandulfo," *Claridad* 9:140 (January 21, 1932), 4.
23. AN/JS, leg. 1658, f110v; Zalaquett S., *"Siembra, juventud!"* 378–380.
24. See the descriptions offered in Rojas, *La oscura vida radiante*, 381 and Sergio Atria, "Nuestro Juan Gandulfo," *Claridad* 9:140 (January 21, 1932), 5.
25. Rojas, *La oscura vida radiante*, 381.
26. Ortíz, "La historia de Juan Gandulfo."
27. This according to González Ginouves, as cited in Zalaquett S., *"Siembra, juventud!"* 379. See also the testimonies provided by various friends and colleagues in *Juan Gandulfo Guerra: Homenaje de sus amigos* (Santiago: Editorial del Pacífico, 1957). I am grateful to Juan Luis Gandulfo for providing me with a copy of this publication.
28. Schweitzer, "Juan Gandulfo," 19.
29. On the Banco de Chile document see Ventura Maturana Barahona, *Mi Ruta* (Buenos Aires: n.p., 1936), 14–15. For "Lucifer or Lenin," see the interview with Pedro Gandulfo in Calderón, *Según pasan los años*, 48.
30. Maturana, *Mi Ruta*, 14–15.
31. On support among the cops, see Maturana, *Mi Ruta*, 14–15.
32. González Vera, "Ideas y críticas," *Numen* (May 22, 1920), 3.
33. José Sepúlveda Ronadelli, *Los radicales ante la historia* (Santiago: Editorial Andrés Bello, 1993), 99–100.
34. Colonel-Prefect to the Intendent of the Province, June 14, 1920, AN/IS v. 496.

35. Intendent of Santiago to the Minister of the Interior, June 19, 1920, AN/IS v. 496.
36. See, e.g., Secretary General of the Conservative Party to the Intendent of Santiago, June 23, 1920, AN/IS v. 496; Interim Commissioner to the Colonel-Prefect, June 26, 1920, AN/IS v. 496.
37. See doc. no. 1295, July 3, 1920, ARNAD/MI v. 5407.
38. See for example Colonel-Prefect to the Intendent of the Province, July 17, 1920, AN/IS v. 497. One author would suggest that some 20,000 people had to be temporarily housed in Santiago during the high point of the crisis. See *Album Gráfico de la Policía*, 34.
39. Colonel-Prefect to Intendent of the Province, July 15, 1920, AN/IS v. 497.
40. 16th Session, July 7, 1920, in *Cámara de Senadores: Boletín de las Sesiones Ordinarias en 1920* (Santiago de Chile: Imprenta Nacional, 1920), 311–314; 19th Session, July 14, 1920, in ibid., 380–382.
41. See Loveman, *Chile*, 170–171.
42. Maturana, *Mi Ruta*, 13.
43. Strikes in the first two weeks of July alone included hundreds of shoe workers across Santiago. Details on these strikes can be found in Colonel-Prefect to Intendent of the Province, July 1, 1920, AN/IS v. 497; Colonel-Prefect to Intendent of the Province, July 8, 1920, AN/IS v. 497; and Colonel-Prefect to the Intendent of the Province, July 14, 1920, AN/IS v. 497. See also Loveman, *Chile*, 171.
44. Sub-Prefect to the 1st Juzgado, July 16, 1920, AN/IS v. 497.
45. Lorenzo Montt, Minister of Justice to the Supreme Court of Justice, July 16, 1920, ARNAD/MJ v. 3044.
46. See the comments of Armando Gutiérrez, a relative of the overthrown president, in a front-page interview titled "La Revolución en Bolivia," *Zig-Zig* (July 17, 1920).
47. Chilean legation to Ministry of War, May 27, 1920, Transcription of telegram No. 139 from La Paz, MRE/AGH vol. 842. For concerns regarding the acquisition of planes, see J. Echaurren (head of Chilean legation in Panama) to Minister of Foreign Relations of Chile, February 24, 1920, MRE/AGH vol. 840. Interestingly France seemed to be the place from which Peru was acquiring much of its materiel. The concerns continued: see, for example, Fernando Edwards, Intendent of Tacna, to the Ministry of Foreign Relations, encl. in Ministry of Foreign Relations to the Ministry of War, July 31, 1920. Transcription of telegram 133 from Tacna (dated July 30, 1920), MRE/AGH vol. 842.
48. On the regiments' support for Alessandri, see Vicuña Fuentes, *La tiranía*, 122–124; Patrick Barr-Melej, *Reforming Chile: Cultural Politics, Nationalism, and the Rise of the Middle Class* (Chapel Hill: University of North Carolina Press, 2000), 180; DeShazo, *Urban Workers and Labor Unions*, 183; and Maturana, *Mi Ruta*, 15–16. Support for Alessandri was not as widespread perhaps as Sanfuentes and others believed: he had his own history of labor suppression. As Minister of the Interior in 1918 he had ordered the army to violently expel settlers on public lands in the south and was not considered a particularly strong advocate of labor. See DeShazo, *Urban Workers and Labor Unions*, 175–177.
49. See for example Villegas (Chilean legation in Rome) to the Ministry of Foreign Relations, July 21/24, 1920, as transcribed in Ministry of Foreign Relations to the Ministry of War, July 26, 1920, MRE/AGH vol. 842; as well as Rivas (Chilean legation in Japan) to Ministry of Foreign Relations, July 31, 1920, as

transcribed in Ministry of Foreign Relations to Ministry of War, August 2, 1920 in MRE/AGH v. 842. See also Friedrich E. Schuler, *Secret Wars and Secret Policies in the Americas, 1842–1929* (Albuquerque: University of New Mexico Press, 2010), 244.

50. As noted in 23rd Session, July 21, 1920, *Cámara de diputados . . . 1920*, 637.
51. Vicuña Fuentes, *La tiranía*, 76; US Consul, Valparaíso, "Chilean Investments in Bolivian Tin and Silver Mines," March 4, 1924, in Records of the Dept. of State Relating to the Internal Affairs of Chile, 1910–1929 (Roll 21; 825.50: Economic Conditions)
52. Vicuña Fuentes, *La Tiranía*, 76. The quoted passage comes from "El aprovisionamiento de las tropas del norte," *Zig Zag* (October 9, 1920). The accusations regarding spoiled foodstuffs were made by, among others, members of the Bolsa de Productores (Grain Markets) and reports from the US Embassy substantiated the claims of unfit soldiers who had arrived without a medical examination and also noted that spoiled beans and potatoes were being sent to the troops. See American Embassy, Santiago, *Report on General Conditions Prevailing in Chile*, August 20, 1920 to September 3, 1920, Records of the Department of State Relating to the Internal Affairs of Chile, 1910–1929 (Roll 4, 825.00 Political Affairs). After the euphoria of July the reality of troop mobilizations had set in, for soldiers and politicians alike. Intendent of Tacna, Fernando Edwards, wrote with some concern to his superiors. "The reservists arriving from the south complain of the lack of uniforms [and] of bad housing," he noted, and many who had been accustomed to earning decent salaries now found themselves without money for even tobacco. Moreover, he claimed, subversive elements were fomenting discontent. Telegram from Fernando Edwards to Ministry of Foreign Relations, August 13, 1920, as transcribed in Ministry of Foreign Relations to Ministry of War, August 18, 1920, MRE/AGH vol. 842. But the largest concern was food. By late August food for the troops was in short supply. Edwards calculated that meat would be gone within fifteen days, in part because no meat could be garnered from Peru and thus had to be brought from the south. Telegram from Fernando Edwards to Ministry of Foreign Relations, August 25, 1920, MRE/AGH vol. 842.
53. See Carlos Tunnermann, *Historia de la Universidad en América Latina: De la época colonial a la Reforma de Córdoba* (San José, Costa Rica: Editorial Universitaria CentroAmericana, 1991), 87–95; and José Luis Romero, "University Reform," in Joseph Maier and Richard W. Weatherhead, eds., *The Latin American University* (Albuquerque: University of New Mexico Press, 1979), 135–146. For the University of Chile, see the discussion in González le Saux, *De empresarios a empleados*, 338–341.
54. Carlos Alborñoz, "Models of the Latin American University," in Maier and Weatherhead, eds., *The Latin American University*, 124.
55. "Manifiesto liminar," June 21, 1918, www.unc.edu.ar/sobre-la-unc/historia/reforma/manifiesto, accessed September 26, 2015.
56. Romero, "University Reform," 136–137; Albornoz, "Models of the Latin American University," 123. For an excellent, succinct overview of university reform movements around the continent, see Romero, "University Reform," as well as Tulio Halperín Donghi, *Historia de la Universidad de Buenos Aires* (Buenos Aires: Editorial Universitaria, 1962), esp. chap. 3.
57. "Manifiesto liminar"; Alborñoz, "Models of the Latin American University," 125–126. As Luis Alberto Sánchez emphatically notes: "Whomever pretends

to reduce the University Reform to the mere ambit of the university . . . would commit a gross error." Cited in Tunnermann, *Historia de la Universidad*, 112. For a collection of documents on the university reform, see *La Reforma Universitaria*, 5 vols. (Buenos Aires: Ferrari Hmnos., 1927).

58. Labarca, "Congreso de la juventud estudiosa," *Juventud* 1:1 (July–August 1918), 4; Jorge Schneider, "Viaje de los delegados chilenos a Buenos Aires," *Juventud* 1:2 (September–October, 1918), n.p.
59. Moraga Valle, *"Muchachos casi silvestres,"* 130–132 and 214; Subercaseaux, *Historia de las ideas*, 70. University reform was much more prominent in Peru and México where, according to Bonilla and Glazer, the universities were still "stronghold[s] of reaction and clericalism." Bonilla and Glazer, *Student Politics*, 54. This would change somewhat in the early 1920s when university reform and educational policy became a more prominent theme, particularly in the pages of the *Claridad*. See Santiago Aránguiz Pinto, "La Reforma Estudiantil en la Universidad de Chile entre 1920–1923 examinada a través de la revista *Claridad* de la Federación de Estudiantes: algunos elementos para su comprensión," *Mapocho: Revista de Humanidades* 58 (segundo semestre, 2005), 111–127. The Córdoba university reform movement has been overly fetishized in the literature, much as May '68 in France has overshadowed so many other student movements as well as the wildcat strikes that overwhelmed France that same year. For a devastating analysis of May '68 in these terms, see Ross, *May '68 and its Afterlives*.
60. For an exhaustive and superb history of the FECh, see Moraga Valle, *"Muchachos casi silvestres."*
61. Collier and Sater, *A History of Chile*, 200.
62. Memorias de Julio Valiente, IISH/MSR, f272.
63. Luis Enrique Délano, *Memorias* (Santiago: RIL, 2004), 30.
64. Délano, *Memorias*, 30–31.
65. An analysis of the 1920 census which appeared in *Los Tiempos* in 1923 revealed that of the 320,000 "students in Chilean institutions, 150,000 are women." As best as I can discern, no women were in the leadership of the FECh and the statistic surely represents women in primary and secondary institutions. The analysis of *Los Tiempos* can be found in a dispatch titled "Miscellaneous," in Records of the Dept. of State Relating to the Internal Affairs of Chile, 1910–1929 (Roll 21; 825.50: Economic Conditions).
66. On the 1921 congress see Alborñoz, "Models of the Latin American University," 127. At the same event students would embrace internationalism, identifying as their enemies the forces of nationalism, militarism, dictatorship and imperialism, and the question of "autonomy" would soon expand to encompass not just the Latin American university but Latin America itself, confronting as it did the spectre of US and British imperialism.
67. Moraga Valle, *"Muchachos casi silvestres,"* 214; on the nationalist aspects of Argentine university reform, see Richard J. Walter, "The Intellectual Background of the 1918 University Reform in Argentina," *Hispanic American Historical Review* 49:2 (May 1969), 233–253, esp. 236–237.
68. Gandulfo, interviewed in Calderón, *Según pasan los años*, 45.
69. Serge, *Memoirs of a Revolutionary*, 187–188.
70. Spengler's influence on students in many parts of Latin America is still to be explored, something noted some forty years ago by Jean Franco in *The Modern Culture of Latin America* (New York: Praeger, 1967), 69–70.

71. In parts of the continent the university reform movement increasingly sought to create "an institution capable of transforming and directing a Latin American culture." Jaime Suchlicki, "Sources of Student Violence in Latin America: An Analysis of the Literature," *Latin American Research Review* 7:3 (Fall 1972), 31–46, qtd. passage on 35–36.
72. For an overview, see Greg Grandin, *Empire's Workshop: Latin America, the United States, and the Rise of the New Imperialism* (New York: Metropolitan Books, 2006). Intellectuals young and old in the 1910s were still influenced by the critiques of North America offered in the essays of Cuban José Martí and, especially, Uruguayan José Enrique Rodó's *Ariel.*
73. On mass culture in Chile see Rinke, *Cultura de masas.* For an overview of transformations in cities, see José Luis Romero, *Latinoamérica: Las ciudades y las ideas* (Medellín: Editorial Universidad de Antioquía, 1999 [1976]), esp. chap. 6.
74. *Guía General de Santiago de Chile, 1918* (Santiago: Imprenta Siglo XX, 1918 [2nd edition]), 93; *Numen* (May 22, 1920), 8; Délano, *El año '20* (Santiago: Piñeda, 1973), 27.
75. See the statement of Soto Rengifo, July 24, 1920, Proceso contra Pedro Gandulfo Guerra, et. al., Segundo juzgado del crimen de Santiago (hereafter "Proceso"), AN/Justicial Santiago (hereafter JS), leg. 1658 and "Pedro Gandulfo," in Calderón, *Según pasan los años*, 51. The English version of Trotsky's book appeared as *The Bolsheviki and World Peace* (NewYork: Boni and Liveright, 1918)
76. On Marx's critique of Stirner and *The German Ideology*, see Paul Thomas, *Karl Marx and the Anarchists* (London: Routledge & Kegan Paul, 1980).
77. "Pedro Gandulfo," in Calderón, *Según pasan los años*, 50.
78. Rinke, *Cultura de Masas*, 34.
79. On university statistics, see Collier and Sater, *History of Chile*, 180.
80. On the middle class and politics, see for example the comments of Deputy Pinto Durán: "The country can no longer be governed like the fiefdom of a few fortunate families. Because now the largest class, the working class, is carefully watching public business. And there is now in the country a numerous and intelligent middle class which will not allow that the country continue to be governed in that way." 77th Session, September 29, 1920, *Cámara de diputados . . . 1920*, 1993.
81. Jeff Gould's comments regarding student movements in 1968 resonate quite strongly here: "In Latin America, the term 'middle class' was geographically and sociologically elastic, including children of low-level government employees, white-collar workers, and shopkeepers, not far removed from the urban working class." Gould, "Solidarity Under Siege," 350. Thus the notion that middle-class students were privileged is misleading and ahistorical, most likely conditioned less by a careful reading of the evidence than by a late-twentieth-century cynicism that sees students as political dilettantes and socially inauthentic. Regardless, in its negation of the very real efforts made, often successfully, to forge links between various social sectors in Santiago, such an interpretation makes for glum history. On university students and the middle class, see González le Saux, *De empresarios a empleados* and Moraga Valle, *"Muchachos casi silvestres."* More broadly on rethinking the middle class, see Robert Johnston, *The Radical Middle Class: Populist Democracy and the Question of Capitalism in Progressive Era Portland, Oregon* (Princeton, NJ: Princeton University Press, 2003) and Louise Walker, *Waking from the Dream: Mexico's Middle Classes After 1968* (Redwood City, CA: Stanford University Press, 2013), esp. chap. 1.

82. "Genteel poverty" comes from Walter, *Politics and Urban Growth*, 13; see also Collier and Sater, *History of Chile*, 172. On the size of the bureaucracy see Murphy, *For a Proper Home*, chap. 1. For further statistical material, see Barría Serón, *Los movimientos sociales*, 87–89.
83. Domingo Silva, Introduction in A. Muñoz Figueroa y Armando Roma Boza, *Crónicas* (Santiago: Imp. Fiscal de la Penitenciaría, 1923), 4–5.
84. Gabriel Salazar and Julio Pinto, *Historia contemporánea de Chile V: Niñez y juventud* (Santiago: LOM Ediciones, 2002), 191; Subercaseaux, *Historia de la ideas y de la cultura en Chile*; Humbert Vera H., *Juventud y Bohemia: Memorial de una generación estudiantil* (Valparaíso: np, 1947), 50–51.
85. See the recollections of Vera H., *Juventud y bohemia*, 51–52.
86. Salazar and Pinto, *Historia contemporánea de Chile V*, 191; González Vera, *Cuando era muchacho*, 58.
87. On students and gambling on Recoleta, see *El Diario Ilustrado*, August 7, 1919, encl. in AN/IS v. 497.
88. On the Centro de Estudios Francisco Ferrer and the Casa del Pueblo, see Moraga Valle and Vega Delgado, *José Domingo Gómez Rojas*, 18–19 and González Vera, *Cuando era muchacho* 112; 133; on Los Inmortales see Délano, *El año 20*; Daniel de la Vega, *Ayer y hoy: antología de escritos* (Santiago: Editorial Universitaria, 1997), 77; and Luis Vitale, "Contribución a una historia del anarquismo en América Latina," www.archivochile.com/Ideas_Autores/html/vitale_l.html, accessed March 2010.
89. Manuel Rojas, *La oscura vida radiante*, 319.
90. 32nd Session, November 28, 1918, in *Cámara de Diputados: Boletín de las Sesiones Estraordinarias en 1918–1919* (Santiago de Chile: Imprenta Nacional, 1918), 764–765 and 41st Session, December 6, 1918, in ibid., 1053–1055. For repeated scrutiny of the FECh and its correspondence with Peruvian students, see, for example, 41st Session, December 6, 1918, in ibid., 1053–1058; and 47th Session, December 12, 1918, in ibid., 1185. For a defense of the FECh's correspondence with Peruvian students from a deputy who had been a former president of the FECh, see Alejandro Rengifo, "La cuestión internacional y la Federación de Estudiantes de Chile," *Juventud* 1:3 (January 1919), 98–108; for a response by students in the FECh to accusations of being unpatriotic, see *Juventud* 1:5 (April–June 1919), 93–94.
91. 28th Session, November 25, 1918, in *Cámara de Diputados . . . 1918–1919*, 664. The debate runs from pp. 659–678. See also 41st Session, December 6, 1918, in ibid., 1054–1055 and 47th Session, December 12, 1918, in ibid., 1185.
92. The quoted comment was offered by Deputy Pinto Durán in the midst of defending the FECh from varied accusations. 47th Session, December 12, 1918, in *Cámara de Diputados . . . 1918–1919*, 1185.
93. 41st Session, December 6, 1918, in *Cámara de Diputados . . . 1918–1919*, 1055.
94. Session, November 27, 1918, *Cámara de Senadores . . . 1918*, 589; Session, December 5, 1918, *Cámara de Senadores . . . 1918*, 677–678.
95. See the discussion between Zañartu and MacIver in Session, July 15, 1919, in *Cámara de Senadores . . . 1919*, 411.
96. Session, November 27, 1918, *Cámara de Senadores . . . 1918*, 590.
97. Ibid., esp. 589–591 and Session, December 5, 1918, *Cámara de Senadores . . . 1918*, 677–680 (qtd. passage on 680).
98. Moraga Valle, *"Muchachos casi silvestres,"* 157–158; on Loyola's time at the Universidad de Chile, see Jaksic, *Academic Rebels in Chile*, 93.

99. Pedro León Loyola to the president of the FECh, September 12, 1919, reproduced in Session, July 21, 1920, *Cámara de Senadores . . . 1920*, 446.
100. Pedro León Loyola to Federico Carvallo, letter dated September 13, 1919, reproduced in Session, July 21, 1920, *Cámara de Senadores . . . 1920*, 446–447.
101. Ibid.
102. Moraga Valle, *"Muchachos casi silvestres,"* 158
103. González Vera, "Estudiantes del año veinte," *Babel* 28 (July–August 1945), 35; Rojas, *La oscura vida radiante*, 392. "Schemers" is my translation for "arbitristas" in the original. It doesn't quite capture the full meaning of the term which, in Spanish, makes reference to a group of seventeenth-century reformers whose ideas for reviving Spain's glory struck many as utopian and impractical.
104. Advertisement, *Juventud* 2:7 (1919), no page.
105. Délano, *El año '20*, 27 and advertisements in issues of *Claridad* 2 (October 16, 1920); *Claridad* 3 (October 26, 1920), and *Claridad* 4 (October 31, 1920), for a sampling.
106. For an excellent discussion, see Carlos Vicuña Fuentes, *La cuestión social ante la Federación de Estudiantes de Chile* (Santiago de Chile: Año 68 de la Era Normal, 1922). The text of the June 1920 document is reproduced in appendix II of that volume. See also Vicuña Fuentes, *La Tiranía*, 122–123 and Campaña de los Estudiantes de Chile (1920), in *La Reforma Universitaria*, vol. VI (Buenos Aires: Ferrari Hmnos., 1927), 36–41.
107. *El Mercurio* (July 21, 1920), 17.
108. "La actitud de la Federación de Estudiantes," *Zig-Zag* (July 24, 1920).
109. González Vera, *Cuando era muchacho*, 85–86.
110. Vicuña Fuentes, *La cuestión social.*
111. "Con el Sr. Alfredo Demaría, Presidente de la Federación de Estudiantes de Chile. La Convención Estddiantil [*sic*]," *Zig Zag*, July 3, 1920 (no page number).
112. Ibid.
113. In Héctor Olivera's 1974 film *La Patagonia Rebelde*, on a worker and anarchist uprising in the Argentine Patagonia in 1921–1922, the perceptive viewer can see police agents in the southern town of Río Gallegos papering over large posters calling for gatherings to commemorate the execution of Ferrer.
114. See Moraga Valle, *"Muchachos casi silvestres,"* 102–103; "Armando Alonso Vial," in Calderón, *Según pasan los años*, 89–90.
115. Moraga Valle, *"Muchachos casi silvestres,"* 204.
116. See Rojas, *La oscura vida radiante*, 133.
117. Unsigned report with the title "Asamblea Obrera de Alimentación Nacional," October 7, 1919, AN/IS v. 496.
118. Unsigned report, February 8, 1919, AN/IS v. 476.
119. "Sobre la prisión de Gandulfo," *Rumbo Nuevo: Organo oficial de la Federación de Empleados de Antofagasta* 1:2 (April 5, 1920), 8.
120. Rojas, *La oscura vida radiante*, 329.
121. González Vera, "Juventud," *Numen* 1:23 (September 20, 1919), 3.
122. "Bajo el imperio del terror," *Verba Roja*, 2:29 (March 1920), 1.
123. "Manifiesto del grupo 'Clarte'" (Claridad): A los trabajadores manuales e intelectuales" *Verba Roja* 2:22 (December, 1919).
124. "Los intelectuales y la Confederación General del Trabajo," *Numen* 2:31 (November 15, 1919), 6–7.
125. González Prada, "El intelectual y el obrero," originally given as a speech to a group of bakers and reproduced in González Prada, *Free Pages and Hard*

Times: Anarchist Musings (New York: Oxford University Press, 2003); Barbusse, "A los intelectuales," *Numen* 2:32 (November 22, 1919), 11.

126. Unsigned brief titled "Federación Obrera de Chile: Junta Ejecutiva," October 2, 1919, AN/IS v. 496.
127. Ibid.
128. Unsigned report for the Santiago Security Section, January 14, 1920, AN/IS v. 493.
129. See, for example, Carlos Vicuña Fuentes who was a lawyer at the time and had four students working with him to defend workers: Unsigned report, "Asamblea Obrera de Alimentación Nacional", March 1, 1919, AN/IS v. 476 and Unsigned report titled "Federación Obrera de Chile: Junta Ejecutiva," October 2, 1919, AN/IS v. 496.
130. Moraga Valle, *"Muchachos casi silvestres,"* 205–206.
131. Unsigned report, February 8, 1919, AN/IS, v. 476. Gath y Chaves was the major department store, located in central Santiago, of the era.
132. *Numen* 2:35 (December 13, 1919), 7; "Pedro Gandulfo," in Calderón, *Según pasan los años*, 52. For reports on students involved in the AOAN, especially Evaristo Molina, see for example Unsigned report by the Santiago Security Section on the AOAN, December 21, 1918, AN/IS v. 470 and Unsigned report, February 5, 1919, AN/IS v. 476. Molina graduated with Pedro Gandulfo with his bachelor's in Law and Political Science in August 29, 1921. See *Anales de la Universidad de Chile* CLXIX: 79 (Santiago: Imprenta Universitaria, 1923), 388.
133. On "space as a terrain of political practice," see Ross, *The Emergence of Social Space*, 8.
134. Useful on this point is Lefebvre's work on the city as discussed in Stanek, *Henri Lefebvre on Space: Architecture, Urban Research and the Production of Theory* (Minneapolis: University of Minnesota Press, 2011), esp. 87.
135. "Manifestaciones Patrióticas: Despedida de las Tropas," *Zig Zag* (July 24, 1920). He was reporting on a demonstration held July 20. For further coverage of the event, see *El Mercurio* (July 21, 1920), 3.
136. See for example Telegram from Luis A. Romo, Copiapó, to the Minister of the Interior, July 21, 1920, ARNAD/MI v. 5375; Telegram from Alfredo del Rio Vidaurre et. al., Liga Patriótica de Viña, to the Minister of the Interior, July 22, 1920, ARNAD/MI v. 5375; as well as the reports in *El Mercurio* (July 19, 1920), 15 and *El Mercurio* (July 21, 1920), 3.
137. As one FECh member would note, regarding the assault, the core of the mass of assailants was composed of "Catholic youth" and he then went on to cite the teachings of the church back to them. Jorge Neut Latour, "A los Estudiantes y Jóvenes Católicos que asaltaron la Federación de Estudiantes el 21 de Julio de 1920," *Juventud* 2:10 (1920), 11–13.
138. Délano, *El año '20*, 75
139. See, for example, the testimony of police agent Horacio Jaramillo, July 28, 1920, in "Proceso," AN/JS, leg. 1658, f66–67.
140. González Vera, *Cuando era muchacho*, 189–190.
141. *El Mercurio* (July 21, 1920), 17.
142. *El Mercurio* (July 21, 1920), 17.
143. Pedro Gandulfo Guerra y Rigoberto Soto Rengifo, "Algunos asaltantes de la Federación" *Juventud* 2:11–12 (January–March 1921), 104; Arancibia Laso, 23rd Session, July 21, 1920, *Cámara de Diputados . . . 1920*, 667; and Moraga Valle, *"Muchachos casi silvestres,"* 665.

144. "Proceso," leg. 1658, f2–67 and f122–191, which include multiple interrogation records of alleged eyewitnesses. See also Gandulfo's recollections in Calderón, *Según pasan los años*, 45–58.
145. Sub-Prefect Horacio Jaramillo claimed that Gandulfo and Soto Rengifo went out on the balcony and incited the crowd below by throwing bottles and that Gandulfo fired shots from his gun—a Browning—in to the air. See testimony included in report of Inspector Moreno González, "Proceso," leg. 1658, f3–4. However, testimony from other officers on the scene as well as other eyewitnesses contradicts Jaramillo's version of the events. See Testimony of Carlos Honorato, July 22, 1920, "Proceso," leg. 1658, f5v–6v and Testimony of Enrique Córdova i Silva, July 22, 1920, in ibid., f7–9.
146. "Pedro Gandulfo," in Calderón, *Según pasan los años*, 48.
147. Testimony of Pedro Gandulfo, July 22, 1920, in "Proceso," leg. 1658, f10–13.
148. See www.genealog.cl/Chile/, accessed July 5, 2012.
149. The various sources for what occurred include: Testimony of Inspector Moreno González, July 22, 1902, f3–4; Testimony of Pedro Gandulfo, July 22, 1920, f10–13; Testimony of Soto Rengifo, July 22, 1920, f13v–15v; Testimony of Zuñiga, July 22, 1920, f15–16; Testimony of Lafuente July 22, 1920, f17–18; Testimony of Edwards, July 23, 1920, f18–22; and Testimony of Armando Rojas, mayordomo of Lyon's house, July 23, 1920, f22–24, all in "Proceso," leg. 1658. See also Sub-Prefect of Order to Prefect, July 21, 1920, enclosure in Colonel-Prefect to the Intendent, July 21, 1920, AN/IS v. 497; Gandulfo, in Calderón, *Según pasan los años*; and González Vera, *Cuando era muchacho*, 191–192.
150. There are a number of sources for the July 21 assault. Not surprisingly, some are contradictory. The sources include the testimonies in f3–67 in "Proceso," leg. 1658; Sub-Prefect to Prefect, July 21, 1920, encl. in Colonel-Prefect to the Santiago Intendent, July 21, 1920, AN/IS v. 497; Roberto Meza Fuentes, "Asalto del club de Estudiantes: 21 de julio de 1920," clipping in IISH/MSR, f.15; Lafuente Vergara, "Cuarenta años del asalto," and González Vera, *Cuando era muchacho*, 189–193. See also the debates in *Cámara de Diputados . . . 1920*, 653–659. I have also found very useful two novels: Manuel Rojas's *La oscura vida radiante* and Enrique Délano's *El año '20*. Rojas was employed as a linotypist with *Numen* at the time of the assault and the events narrated in his novel are based closely on his own experience. Délano's novel builds on the memoirs and recollections of participants to similarly create a very accurate portrait of what happened. Numerous sources make note of police complicity—or apathy—in the assault. See the testimonies of Pizarro, "Proceso," leg. 1658, f.120v–121r; Manuel Helwin Tasso, ibid., f187; and R. Villalón Castillo to Hector Arancibia Laso, July 27, 1920, encl. in Pedro Gandulfo to Special Prosecutor, August 2, 1920, ibid., f106–107.
151. The estimate of 3,000 published volumes is given by Meza Fuentes in "La fiesta de la primavera," *Sucesos* (October 14, 1920).
152. Zuñiga, "La difícil generación del 20," *Ercilla* (June 5, 1968), IISH/MSR, f164.
153. Testimony of Carlos Honorato, July 22, 1920, in "Proceso," leg. 1658, f5v–6v. See also Sergio Pereira Poza, *Antología crítica de la dramaturgía anarquista en Chile* (Santiago: Editorial Universidad de Santiago, 2005), 25–26; and Meza Fuentes, "Asalto del club de Estudiantes: 21 de julio de 1920," IISH/MSR, f.15.
154. The issue of these men too quickly allowing themselves to be photographed is an interesting moment. One suspects they were still themselves coming to terms with the power of photography and did not contemplate the fact that

they could be tagged in a photograph reproduced in one of the country's major dailies.

155. 23rd session, July 21, 1920, *Cámara de Diputados . . . 1920*, 653.
156. Editors of the FECh journal *Claridad* claimed that President Sanfuentes's personal secretary—and a Lieutenant in the Army—participated in the assault, as did a number of policemen. See Moraga, *"Muchachos casi silvestres,"* 665. This was not a rash accusation: congressional deputies, in the wake of the assault, publicly accused the police of participating in the assault and of fabricating their reports to obscure that fact.
157. 23rd session, July 21, 1920, *Cámara de Diputados . . . 1920*, 657–658.
158. Oscar Urzua, 23rd session, July 21, 1920, *Cámara de Diputados . . . 1920*, 659.
159. R. Villalón Castillo to Héctor Arancibia Laso, July 27, 1920, encl. in Pedro Gandulfo to Special Prosecutor (Astorquiza), August 2, 1920, in "Proceso," leg. 1658, f106–107.
160. Horacio Jaramillo, with some 17 years on the force, had recently been promoted to Sub-prefect of the Order section of the police force. See *Album gráfico de la Policía*, 14. Interviewed by Astorquiza, he would claim that he explained to Arancibia that he and his men were outnumbered and could not intervene. Interview dated July 28, 1920, in "Proceso," leg. 1658, f66–67.
161. 23rd session, July 21, 1920, *Cámara de Diputados . . . 1920*, 666–667.
162. Ibid.

CHAPTER 3

1. Arthur Ruhl, "Santiago: The Metropolis of the Andes," *Scribner's Magazine* 43:2 (February 1908), 139 as qtd. in Walter, *Politics and Urban Growth*, 12. See also the quotes in Walter, *Politics and Urban Growth*, 15.
2. Manuel Alejandro Covarrubias had served in various prominent political capacities: mayor of Santiago in 1908; Minister of Public Works and Industry as well as War and the Navy; and was the owner of the El Manzano estate on the outskirts of Santiago. See www.genealog.cl/Chile/C/Covarrubias/, accessed December 31, 2012.
3. "A la memoria de Julio Covarrubias Freire: Sus amigos," in *Coronas fúnebres* (Santiago: Imprenta Cervantes, 1921), 28.
4. Ibid., 41–46.
5. Ibid., 47–73.
6. "Proceso," leg. 1658, f112. He was held for the killing of Covarrubias as well as injuries against Ignacio Alfonso and Augusto Ovalle Rodríguez. Deutsch claims Alfonso is killed also and by a leftist. See Deutsch, *Las Derechas*, 66.
7. *Coronas fúnebres*, 16. It was most likely the case that many of the well-to-do at the time must have recalled with some trepidation the killing 8 years earlier of two young "bourgeois" youths on a downtown street by a young anarchist named Efraín Plaza Olmedo. Plaza Olmedo shot them in retaliation for the deaths of a number of miners at the El Teniente mine. See Alberto Harambour Ross, "Jesto y palabra, idea y acción: La historia de Efraín Plaza Olmedo," in Fernando Purcell et. al., *Arriba quemando el sol. Estudios de Historia Social Chilena: Experiencias populares de trabajo, revuelta y autonomía (1830–1940)* (Santiago: LOM Ediciones, 2004).
8. *Coronas fúnebres*, 122–124.
9. Clipping from *La Libertad*, Talca, Chile, July 25, 1920, ARNAD/MI v. 5375.
10. Deputy Lira, 24th session, July 22, 1920, *Cámara de Diputados . . . 1920*, 687.

11. Urzua, as cited in *Coronas fúnebres*, 88.
12. *Coronas fúnebres*, 115.
13. Deputy O'Ryan, 24th session, July 22, 1920, *Cámara de Diputados . . . 1920*, 692.
14. Deputy Ramírez, 24th session, July 22, 1920, *Cámara de Diputados . . . 1920*, 689. See also the comments of O'Ryan, ibid., 692.
15. Armando de Ramón, *Santiago de Chile*, 249; see also Walter, *Politics and Urban Growth*, 7–9, 12, 74–75, 77.
16. Luis Alberto Romero, *Qúe hacer con los pobres? Elite y sectores populares en Santiago de Chile, 1840–1895* (Buenos Aires: Sudamericana, 1997), 18–19.
17. Ibid., 19–27.
18. Ibid., 19–27. For similar processes in Mexico, see Pablo Piccato, *City of Suspects: Crime in Mexico City, 1900–1931* (Durham, NC: Duke University Press, 2001), esp. part 1.
19. Especially useful here is John Felstiner, *Translating Neruda: The Way to Macchu Picchu* (Redwood City, CA: Stanford University Press, 1980), chapter 3.
20. *Luces de modernidad*, 8.
21. Walter, *Politics and Urban Growth*, 16–17.
22. Subercaseaux, *Historia de las ideas*, 39 (citing Inés Echevarría, in Mónica Echevarría, *Agonía de una irreverente*).
23. Tomás Errázuriz, "El asalto de los motorizados," *Historia* 43:2 (July–December 2010), 371.
24. Ibid., 373–374.
25. Ibid., 374–375.
26. Walter, *Politics and Urban Growth*, 59–60.
27. Ibid., 17.
28. Ibid., 60–61.
29. The first flight over Santiago took place, according to Alfonso Calderón, on August 21, 1910. Calderón, *Memorial de Santiago* (Santiago: RIL , 2005), 208.
30. *Luces de modernidad*, 11. The last parafin and gas lamps were dismantled in 1929.
31. Rinke, *Cultura de masas*, 60.
32. For a good introduction to these changes, see Rinke, *Cultura de masas*, and Subercaseaux, *Historia de las Ideas*, 3:117. On newspapers and navigating the metropolis, I have found very useful Peter Fritzsche, *Reading Berlin 1900* (Cambridge, MA: Harvard University Press, 1996).
33. As qtd. in Paul Virilio, *Speed and Politics* (Los Angeles: Semiotext(e), 2006 [2nd ed.]), 34.
34. See Néstor Ponce, "Alberto Edwards," in Darrell B. Lockhart, *Latin American Mystery Writers: An A-to-Z Guide* (Westport, CT: Greenwood Press, 2004), 72–74.
35. Qtd. passage from Brecht is from Todd Herzog, *Crime Stories: Criminalistic Fantasy and the Culture of Crisis in Weimar Germany* (Oxford: Berghahn Books, 2009), 26. My analysis here is indebted to Herzog's discussion.
36. Ibid., 17.
37. Ibid., 27..
38. Rinke, *Cultura de masas*, 53.
39. This was the opinion offered by Raúl del Pozo, born in Chile of a Paraguayan mother and who would return to Paraguay and work as a journalist and then in the Ministry of Foreign Relations. Del Pozo's advice is quoted in Enrique Gallardo Nieto (head of Chilean Legation in Paraguay) to Ministry of Foreign Relations of Chile, April 20, 1920, MRE/AGH v 840.
40. Walter, *Politics and Urban Growth*, 80–81.

41. See Raúl Cordero R., *Banco del Estado de Chile: Historia de la Caja del Crédito Hipotecario* (Santiago: El Banco de Chile, 1999), esp. chap. 9, www.corporativo.bancoestado.cl/docs/default-source/manuales-y-politicas/historias-de-la-caja-de-credito-hipotecario.pdf?sfvrsn=0, accessed January 19, 2015.
42. Walter, *Politics and Urban Growth*, 80–81.
43. On this point, see Romero, *Latinoamérica*, 359.
44. Walter notes that "while there were few explicit restrictions, many of the so-called public spaces created in these decades [late nineteenth century], including many new parks and plazas, were in practice 'private' or by custom reserved for the elite." Walter, *Politics and Urban Growth*, 12.
45. Ibid., 86.
46. Ibid., 76.
47. Elizabeth Hutchinson, *Labors Appropriate to Their Sex: Gender, Labor and Politics in Urban Chile, 1900–1930* (Durham, NC: Duke University Press, 2001), 48, table 9.
48. For the description of the area around the Estación Central, see Edwards Bello, *El Roto*, 3.
49. Errázuriz, "El asalto de los motorizados," 358. For the case of Mexico, see Piccato, *City of Suspects*, chap. 1.
50. Délano, *Memorias*, 78; Errázuriz, "El asalto de los motorizados," 363.
51. Errázuriz, "El asalto de los motorizados," 367.
52. See Virilio, *Speed and Politics*, 33.
53. Municipal Mayor's Office to the Intendent of the Province, December 9, 1919, AN/IS v. 496.
54. On being appointed delegate to the AOAN for the Sociedad Unión de los Tipógrafos, see "Sesión de Directorio celebrada el 20 de Febrero de 1919," Sociedad Unión de los Tipógrafos de Santiago, IISH, Roll 5, p. 29.
55. Details on Valiente's childhood come from his unpublished memoirs, which he began at the request of historian Marcelo Segall Rosenmann. Memorias de Julio E. Valiente, con epístola de Julio E. Valiente a Marcelo Segall (Enero 25 de 1960), IISH/MSR, folder 272.
56. Memorias de Julio E. Valiente.
57. See the entry for Filidor 2o. Martínez Gajardo in Osvaldo López, *Diccionario Biográfico Obrera de Chile* (Santiago: Imprenta Bellavista, 1912), M10.
58. The poem is *Canción de Venganza*, later to become more popularly known as the *Canto a la Pampa*, published in *La Protesta* 1:3 (Santiago, June 1908). See also Ignotus, "Construcción simbólica y ritualística a raíz de la matanza de Santa María de Iquique (principios del siglo XX)," http://archivohistoricolarevuelta.wordpress.com/2012/12/19/construccion-simbolica-y-ritualistica-a-raiz-de-la-matanza-de-santa-maria-de-iquique/, accessed February 21, 2013.
59. Memorias de Julio E. Valiente.
60. Grez Toso, *Los anarquistas y el movimiento obrero*, 99–100.
61. Ibid., 100; 270; "Lista de los procesados," in "Proceso," leg. 1658, f110–115, provides details on Valiente's arrests in 1911, 1913, and 1920.
62. On ownership see Declaración de Julio Valiente, July 25, 1920, "Proceso," leg. 1658, f93.
63. Rojas, *La oscura vida radiante*, 382.
64. Egaña was in his early twenties when he helped found *Numen* along with Labarca. Born in 1896, he died in 1928. See Raúl Silva Castro, *Panorama Literario de Chile* (Santiago: Editorial Universitaria, 1961), 101.

65. In the United States, the Union of Russian Workers was considered subversive as an organization whereas, in theory, the IWW was not. In other words, membership alone (again, in theory) was not enough to get one expelled or arrested, but if one were caught, say, distributing an IWW song book put together by Elizabeth Gurley Flynn, or the work *Sabotage* by Emile Pouget, or *The IWW: Its History, Structure and Method* by Vincent St. John, then one would be arrested or expelled. The report went on to note that it was one's duty in the IWW to distribute such literature: ergo, while membership alone was not a crime, for all intents and purposes it in fact was a crime. See 66th Congress, 2nd session, House of Representatives, Report 504 (December 16, 1919): Exclusion and Expulsion of Aliens of Anarchistic and Similar Classes, esp. pp. 10–11.
66. *Numen* 1:22 (September 13, 1919), 10; Triviño and Silva, "Desde la cárcel," *Numen* 2:31 (November 15, 1919), 4.
67. Triviño and Silva, "Desde la cárcel," 4.
68. *Numen* 1:22 (September 13, 1919), 2.
69. Barría Serón, *Los Movimientos Sociales en Chile*, as qtd by Manuel Lagos Mieres, *Los 'Subversivos': Las maquinaciones del poder, 'República' de Chile, 1920* (Santiago: Quimantú, 2011), 19.
70. Declaración de Julio Valiente, "Proceso," leg. 1658, f93.
71. Declaración de Julio Valiente, "Proceso," leg. 1658, f93.
72. Torrealba, *Los subversivos*, 39.
73. Paul Brissenden, *The I.W.W.* (New York: n.p., 1919); quote from Melvin Dubofsky, *We Shall Be All: A History of the IWW (The Industrial Workers of the World)* (New York: Quadrangle, 1969), xi.
74. Torrealba, *Los subversivos*, 40. US Embassy officials disagreed among themselves regarding the role of "foreigners" in such organizations. A US consular official in Valparaíso divided Chile's working classes into two categories: on the one hand, "skilled laborers and artisans, the railroad workers, and other groups whose members are comparatively intelligent" and, on the other hand, "the mass of laborers in such industries as the coal mines, the nitrate works, and the handling of merchandise at the ports, are ignorant and improvident to a degree which makes them easily controlled by irresponsible agitators whose main object seems to be to cause labor troubles for their own personal benefit. These agitators are largely foreigners, in many cases connected with the Industrial Workers of the World or similar organizations." American consulate general in Valparaíso, Labor Situation in Chile, March 18, 1921, in Records of the Dept. of State Relating to the Internal Affairs of Chile, 1910–1929 (Roll 21; 825.50: Economic Conditions) In contrast, others suggested that too many Chilean officials were focusing on the IWW "in a vain attempt to deceive themselves into believing that the trouble is imported from abroad by foreigners." Letter of J. Perkins Shanks, encl. in B.C. Matthews, American Vice Consul, Antofagasta, "Labour situation in northern Chile," September 8, 1921, in Records of the Dept. of State Relating to the Internal Affairs of Chile, 1910–1929 (Roll 21; 825.50: Economic Conditions). I describe it as the "chilean region" because Wobblies and anarchist organizations refused the category of the state and thus adopted the language of "the region" in order to define themselves geopolitically. It is for the same reason that I do not capitalize here the first letter in chilean.
75. Rojas, *Antología autobiográfica*, 55; Araya, "Los wobblies criollos," 25–26.

76. See the short history recounted in "Los trabajadores industriales del mundo de la región chilena y el Congreso de Berlin," IISH, Diego Abad de Santillán Collection (hereafter DAS), carpeta 377, f. Chile.
77. DeShazo, *Urban Workers and Labor Unions*, 155.
78. George J. Mills, *Chile*, 113.
79. Romero, *Latinoamérica*, 301.
80. Mills, *Chile*, 119 and George Makinson, American Consul, Valparaíso, December Review of Chilean Conditions, January 7, 1923, in Records of the Dept. of State Relating to the Internal Affairs of Chile, 1910–1929 (Roll 21; 825.50: Economic Conditions).
81. Torrealba, *Los subversivos*, 75.
82. See Anton Rosenthal, "Radical Border Crossers: The Industrial Workers of the World and Their Press in Latin America," *Estudios Interdisciplinarios de América Latina y el Caribe* 22:2 (July/December 2011), 39–70.
83. DeShazo, *Urban Workers and Labor Unions*, 150–151.
84. Parte del Jefe de la Sección de Seguridad No. 2756, in "Proceso," leg. 1658, f85–101. The same document appears in Sub-Prefect to the 2nd Juzgado del Crímen, July 21, 1920, AN/IS v. 497.
85. "Los trabajadores industriales del mundo de la región chilena y el Congreso de Berlin," November 21, 1922, IISH/DAS, carpeta 377, f. Chile.
86. DeShazo, *Urban workers and Labor Unions*, 148–149 and 155.
87. Araya, "Los wobblies criollos," 9.
88. DeShazo, *Urban workers and Labor Unions*, 152. Breadmakers also had organizational successes and were often oriented toward anarchist forms of organizing. See Juan Carlos Yáñez Andrade, "Por una legislación social en Chile," 502–503.
89. DeShazo, *Urban Workers and Labor Unions*, 153.
90. Parte del Jefe de la Sección de Seguridad No. 2756, in "Proceso," leg. 1658, f85–101. This same document appears in Sub-Prefect to the 2nd Juzgado del Crímen, July 21, 1920, AN/IS v. 497.
91. Moraga Valle and Vega Delgado, *José Domingo Gómez Rojas*, 11.
92. Pravda, "Huelga del personal de Telefonistas," *Numen* 2:33 (November 29, 1919), 11.
93. Colonel-Prefect to the Intendent of the Province, March 3, 1920, AN/IS v. 496.
94. Letter (unknown author) to President Sanfuentes, July 2, 1920, AN, Fondo Colecciones y Archivos Particulares (hereafter FCAP), Juan Luis Sanfuentes, v 10, fs. 212–213.
95. Encl. in "Proceso," leg. 1658, f59.
96. Minister of the Interior, 1st Section, Circular reservada 5, July 26, 1920, AN/IS v. 497.
97. On the era and the *attentat*, see the varied perspectives provided in Anderson, *Under Three Flags*; Alexander Berkman, *Prison Memoirs of an Anarchist* (New York: New York Review of Books Classics, 1999 [1912]); John Merriman, *The Dynamite Club: How a Bombing in Fin-de-Siecle Paris Ignited the Age of Modern Terror* (Boston: Houghton Mifflin Harcourt, 2009); and Butterworth, *The World That Never Was*. On the Russian conspirators, see Claudia Verhoeven, *The Odd Man Karakozov: Imperial Russia, Modernity and the Birth of Terrorism* (Ithaca, NY: Cornell University Press, 2011).
98. This according to the judicial report, cited from Harambour Ross, "'Jesto y palabra, idea y acción,'" 137. The designation "anarchist" is made by the interrogator.

99. Bookchin, *The Spanish Anarchists The Heroic Years, 1868–1936* (Oakland, CA: AK Press, 2001), esp. "Saints and Sinners". The point is also made eloquently by Osvaldo Bayer in his *Los anarquistas expropiadores* (Barcelona: Virus, 2003). The quoted passage is from Bookchin, *Social Anarchism or Lifestyle Anarchism?* (San Francisco: AK Press, 1995), 8.
100. Beverly Gage, *The Day Wall Street Exploded: A Story of America in its First Age of Terror* (New York: Oxford University Press, 2009), 7. Importantly, Gage's book shows that the Wall Street bombing of 1920 cannot be presumed to be the actions of anarchists—responsibility was never firmly established.
101. I am paraphrasing here Raymond Williams, *The Country and the City* (New York: Oxford University Press, 1975), 185.
102. See for example the opening sequence of *La oscura vida radiante*, but also the pervasiveness of hunger in *Hijo de Ladrón* and his classic short story "El vaso de leche," in Rojas, *Antología autobiográfica* (Santiago: LOM Ediciones, 1995 [2nd edition]), 47–53. For an astute discussion of anarchism (and hunger) in Rojas's work, see Cortés, *La narrative anarquista de Manuel Rojas*. More generally on revolutionary violence, see Slavoj Žižek, *In Defense of Lost Causes* (London: Verso, 2008), esp. chapter 4.
103. Parte del Jefe de la Sección de Seguridad No. 2756, in "Proceso," leg. 1658, f85–101, esp. f88; Lorenzo Montt to Julio Plaza Ferrand, no. 447, July 20, 1920, ARNAD/MJ v. 3044; Montt to Excma. Corte Suprema de Justicia, no. 451, July 20, 1920, ARNAD/MJ v. 3044. On abolishing the wage system, see for example "Los trabajadores industriales del mundo de la región chilena y el Congreso de Berlin," IISH/DAS, carpeta 377, f. Chile.
104. See Araya, "Los wobblies criollos" and the interview with Santiago Labarca, while he was still in hiding, in *Claridad* 2 (October 16, 1920), 7, where he notes that the IWW "has never been a secret organization. In the "workers' section" of our daily papers you all can find the citations and agreements of that organization. Its declaration of principles is, at its root, absolutely the same as those of all the labor organizations, from the Confederación General del Trabajo of France to the Federación Obrera de Chile. Its foundation is the struggle against the current capitalist system."
105. Vicuña Fuentes, *La tiranía*, 112.
106. See Lorenzo Montt to the Excma. Corte Suprema de Justicia, August 16, 1920 in ARNAD/MJ v. 3045, f576.
107. "Manifiesto," *El Mercurio* (August 4, 1920), as quoted and cited in Moraga Valle and Vega Delgado, *José Domingo Gómez Rojas*, 43.
108. González Vera, *Cuando era muchacho*, 221.
109. For a very good sense of this, see Pereira Poza, *Antología crítica*; González Vera, *Cuando era muchacho*; and Rojas, *La oscura vida radiante*.
110. Triviño, *Arengas*.
111. One of the early scenes in the 1974 film *La Patagonia Rebelde* captures this well with the money expropriated from a local hotel and restaurant owner who employed scabs being used to purchase a printing press.
112. "Los trabajadores industriales del mundo de la región chilena y el Congreso de Berlin," IISH/DAS, carpeta 377, f. Chile. My emphasis.
113. "Tercera convención rejional de los I.W.W. celebrada los días 1-16-17-18 [*sic*] de Marzo de 1924, Santiago, Chile," IISH/DAS, carpeta 367. "Labeling," as explained to the membership by Juan Leighton in 1924, referred to a tactic used in the United States in which producer unions would label or mark a

product they recommended based on the fact that the workers who produced that product were not in conflict with the owners or management. See "Tercera convención."

114. Rudolph Rocker, *Anarcho-Syndicalism* (London: Pluto Press, 1989 [1938]), 116.
115. See Carlos Maldonado Prieto, "Militarización de la policía: Una tendencia histórica chilena," 4–5, www.memoriachilena.cl/archivos2/pdfs/MC0018154.pdf, accessed August 30, 2010; and DeShazo, *Urban Workers and Labor Unions*, 143 and 180. Rather than bombs, if there is a pervasive reality associated with anarchism it is prison. The propagators of a philosophy dedicated to liberty are denied it most intensely. For a valuable discussion see Rodolfo Montes de Oca, *Anarquismo y cárceles: Píxeles para entender la critica antiautoritaria y abolicionista a las Prisiones* (Medellín: CorazónDeFuego, no date), http://corazondefuegorecs.files.wordpress.com/2010/05/anarquismo-y-carceles_web.pdf, accessed August 30, 2010.
116. Deputy Urrejola, 24th session, July 22, 1920, *Cámara de Diputados . . . 1920*, 690.
117. The most visible face of the union was that of Juan Chamorro, who helped a young Manuel Rojas find work on the docks as a stevedore and a "guachiman" (watchman), guarding the various small vessels that filled the harbor. Rojas, *Antología autobiográfica*, 55.
118. Lagos Mieres, *Los "Subversivos,"* 13.
119. Muñoz Cortés, *Armando Triviño*, 25; see also Urrejola, 24th session, July 22, 1920, *Cámara de Diputados . . . 1920*, 690–691.
120. *El Mercurio* (July 23, 1920), 18; Torrealba, *Los Subversivos*, 81. The creation of a special investigator in Santiago paved the way for a similar appointment a few days later, on July 24, in Valparaíso. Lorenzo Montt to the Iltma. Corte Apelaciones, Valparaíso, July 24, 1920, ARNAD/MJ v. 3048. A request soon came from the Minister of Industry and Public Works to make a similar appointment in Coronel and the "región carbonífera" on July 31, 1920. Minister of Industry and Public Works to Minister of Justice, July 31, 1920, ARNAD/MJ v. 3048. See also the request for additional troops to assist with "new detainees of a subversive character." Telegraph from H. Castillo to the Minister of Justice, August 10, 1920, ARNAD/MJ v. 3043.
121. On his parents' background see Pedro Xavier Fernández-Pradel, *Linajes Vascos y Montañeses en Chile* (Santiago: Talleres Gráficos San Rafael, 1930); on his career see "La vida que pasa," *Sucesos: Semanario de Actualidades* 18:933 (August 12, 1920), IISH/MSR f15, (from which the quoted text is taken); Virgilio Figueroa, *Diccionario Histórico, Biográfico y Bibliográfico de Chile* (Santiago: Establecimientos Gráficos Balcells y Co., 1928) 2:28, 30–33; *Anales de la Universidad de Chile* vol. 76 (March–April 1889) (Santiago: Imprenta Nacional, 1889), 112; and *Anuario del Ministerio de Justicia*, 392–393.
122. Properties included Fundo Maica and an unnamed property in Villa Alegre (most likely the Hacienda Lincura) with a taxable value of some 120,000 pesos, making it one of the largest in the Villa Alegre district. *Indice de propietarios rurales y valor de la propiedad rural según los roles de avalúos comunales* (Santiago: Sociedad "Imprenta y Litografía Universo", 1908), 381 and 409. For mention of the Fundo Lincura, see *Boletín de las leyes y decretos del gobierno, segundo semestre de 1888* (Santiago, 1888), 1458. On Eliodoro Astorquiza, see Alfonso M. Escudero, *Eliodoro Astorquiza, el que pudo haber sido nuestro mejor crítico* (Santiago: Nascimento, 1934).

123. Gustavo Opazo Maturana, *Historia de Talca* (Biblioteca Virtual Miguel de Cervantes), chapter xiii, www.cervantesvirtual.com/obra-visor/historia-de-talca--0/html/ff91b0ee-82b1-11df-acc7-002185ce6064_15.html, accessed June 6, 2013.
124. Alexander, *Arturo Alessandri: A Biography* (Ann Arbor: University Microforms, 1977), 138–139; "La vida que pasa," *Sucesos*, clipping in IISH/MSR f15; and Millas, *Hábrase Visto*, 68.
125. Santiago Benadava, *Crímenes y casos célebres* (Santiago: LexisNexis, 2002), 79–90.
126. "La vida que pasa," *Sucesos*, clipping in IISH/MSR f15.
127. Vicuña Fuentes, *La Tiranía*, 113; on the property in Villa Alegre, see *Indice de propietarios rurales y valor de la propiedad rural según los roles de avalúos comunales* (Santiago: Sociedad "Imprenta y Litografía Universo," 1908), 409.
128. "Pedro Gandulfo," in Calderón, *Según pasan los años*, 47.
129. The comment is Paul S. Reinsch's in his "Parliamentary Government in Chile," *American Political Science Review* Vol. III (1908–09), as quoted in Collier and Sater, *A History of Chile*, 193.
130. I am drawing here from Raymond Williams's rich commentary in *The Country and the City*: "There were of course such bailiffs and such agents [who seized the flocks of shephards], but it is idle to isolate them from the social process which they served, and from the engrossing landowners who . . . retained the responsibility for it" (82).
131. *Boletín de los Trabajadores Industriales del Mundo* (Santiago, Abril 1920); *Numen* 2:38 (January 3, 1920), 10. In fact, it was most likely these very lists which the Santiago Security Section forwarded to Astorquiza and which served as the basis for the arrest warrants served that Sunday morning of July 25. The list included Armando Triviño, Eduardo Ranfasto, José Domingo Gómez Rojas, Manuel Antonio Silva, Nicanor Vergara, Adolfo Hernández, Evaristo Lagos, Juan Gandulfo, Manuel Zamorano, Isidoro Santenach, Manuel Montano, José del T. Ibarra and Víctor Garrido. Parte del Jefe de la Sección de Seguridad No. 2756, in "Proceso," leg. 1658, f85–101. The same document can be found in Sub-Prefect to the 2nd Juzgado del Crímen, July 21, 1920, AN/IS v. 497.
132. Parte del Jefe de la Sección de Seguridad No. 2815, in "Proceso," leg. 1658, f94.
133. Ibid.
134. Those arrested were Manuel Zamorano, Ramón Contreras Vargas, Manuel Montano, Luis Cuadry, Luis Soza, José Clota Domenech, Octavio Palmero Martín, José del Tránsito Ibarra, Vicente Amorros, Manuel Figueroa, Isidro Vidal, Luis Blejer, and José Domingo Gómez Rojas.
135. González Vera, *Cuando era muchacho*, 194.
136. Muñoz Cortés, *Armando Triviño*, 25.
137. Police report, July 26, 1920, AN/JS, Caja R13: Exp. Jorge Rosemblatt y Roberto Salinas, por Sedición, f1r–v. Astorquiza's arrest order can be found in ibid., f6r. See also the summary in Sub-Prefect to the Special Prosecutor (Ministro en Visita), August 5, 1920, ibid., f9r.
138. González Vera, *Cuando era muchacho*, 197–200.
139. They found a 7mm pistol in the possession of Ramón Contreras and one in the possession of Luis Soza and a pistol and rifle in the possession of Octavio Palmero. Parte del Jefe de la Sección de Seguridad No. 2815, in "Proceso," leg. 1658, f94–97.
140. Ibid., 94–97; on Gómez Rojas, see ibid., f97.

141. Decree by José Astorquiza, "Proceso," leg. 1658 f92.
142. Ibid., f92.
143. *Coronas fúnebres*, 128.
144. Decree by José Astorquiza, "Proceso," leg. 1658, f92.
145. See 25th session, July 23, 1920, *Cámara de Diputados . . . 1920*, 711 (for traitors) and 710 (for cancer).
146. Federación de Estudiantes de Chile, Proclamation of July 23, 1920, in AN/JS, Caja R21: Unlabeled file on FECh and workers.
147. Too frequently the slightest indication of some kind of national sentiment among anarchists is seen as an obvious contradiction. But such expressions and sentiments need to be understood in their given contexts. In this instance, the writers are attempting as much to accuse the golden youth of cowardice and rhetorical courage as they are embracing a kind of nationalism per se. I am indebted to Geoffroy De Laforcade's comments, regarding the need to distinguish between "national identity" (not "nationalism") and "patriotism," at the European Social Science History Conference in Vienna in 2014.
148. Alfredo Demaría, "Manifiesto del Presidente de la Federación de Estudiantes de Chile," *Juventud* 2:11–12 (January–March 1921), 36.
149. Ricardo Cruz-Coke, *Historia de la medicina en Chile* (Santiago: Andrés Bello, 1995), 508; Salazar and Pinto, *Historia contemporánea de Chile*, 4:188; 30th session, July 30, 1920, *Cámara de Diputados . . . 1920*, 836–840.
150. Pamphlet included in Santiago Security Section to the 3rd Juzgado de Santiago, July 25, 1920, AN/JS, Caja R21: Unlabeled expediente on FECh and workers.
151. Santiago Security Section to 3rd Juzgado de Santiago, July 25, 1920, AN/JS, Caja R21: Unlabeled expediente on FECh and workers; Benavides (Comisario, Santiago Police) to S.J. del C., July 26, 1920, ibid.
152. See the following files for details on the protests and arrests: AN/JS, Caja R8: Exp. Víctor Valderrama; AN/JS, Caja R13: Exp. Jorge Rosemblatt y Roberto Salinas, por Sedición; AN/JS, unlabeled box, Exp. Juan Bautista Aleaux; AN/JS, unlabeled box, exp. Maria Astorga Navarro; AN/JS, Caja R10: Exp. Luis Vergara Keller; AN/JS, Caja 7: Exp. José Rojas Marín; AN/FCAP Juan Luis Sanfuentes, v. 25, f211–212; and Colonel-Prefect to the Intendent, July 28, 1920, AN/IS, v. 497.
153. On women workers and anarchism, see especially Hutchinson, *Labors Appropriate to Their Sex* and Elizabeth Hutchinson, "From 'La mujer esclava' to 'La mujer limón': Anarchism and the Politics of Sexuality in Early Twentieth-Century Chile," *Hispanic American Historical Review* 81:3–4 (2001), 519–553.
154. On Astorga, see Desórdenes Públicos, July 28, 1920, AN/JS, Unlabeled box, Exp. María Astorga Navarro, f1; Reports, Inspector Ortega[?], July 27, 1920, AN/FCAP, Juan Luis Sanfuentes, vol. 25, f211. On the tram incident, see Colonel-Prefect to the Intendent, July 28, 1920; AN/IS v. 497 and Reports, Inspector Ortega[?], July 27, 1920, AN/FCAP, Juan Luis Sanfuentes, vol. 25, f211. The exchange of gunfire led to a heated debate on the floor of the Deputy of Chambers later that day. See 27th session, July 27, 1920, *Cámara de Diputados . . . 1920*, 758–761.
155. Colonel-Prefect to the Intendent of the Province, July 28, 1920, AN/IS v. 497.
156. See the summation of Valderrama's case in AN/JS, Caja R8: Exp. Víctor Valderrama, July 26, 1920, f44–52.

157. See Desórdenes públicos, July 28, 1920, AN/JS, Unlabeled box, Exp. Juan Bautista Aleaux, f1; Reports, Inspector Ortega[?], July 27, 1920, AN/FCAP Juan Luis Sanfuentes, vol. 25, f211.
158. Police report, July 26, 1920, AN/JS, Caja R13: Exp. Jorge Rosemblatt y Roberto Salinas, por Sedición, f1. On Salinas and the communist party, see Ramírez Necochea, *Orígen y formación del Partido Comunista*, 237 and Grez Toso, *Historia del comunismo en Chile*. For Salinas as treasurer of the POS, see *Numen* 2:32 (November 22, 1919), 3.
159. Sub-Inspector to the Commissioner, July 27, 1920, AN/FCAP, Juan Luis Sanfuentes, v. 25, f212.
160. See Comisaría, Santiago Police, July 27, 1920, AN/JS, Caja 7: Exp. José Rojas Marín; Reports, Inspector Ortega[?], July 27, 1920, AN/FCAP, Juan Luis Sanfuentes, vol. 25, f211.
161. AN/JS, Caja R10: Exp. Luis Vergara Keller, July 28 1920, f1–2.
162. AN/JS, Caja R16: Exp. José Romero González por Desórdenes Públicos, July 28, 1920.
163. Quote from Schweitzer, "Juan Gandulfo," 22.
164. Document dated July 22, 1920, in AN/JS, Caja R21: Unlabeled expediente on FECh and workers.
165. 69th session, January 3, 1919, in *Cámara de Diputados . . . 1918–1919*, 1716.
166. "Sesión de Directorio celebrada el 18 de julio de 1920," *Sociedad Unión de los Tipógrafos de Santiago*, Roll 5, p. 99–101, IISH. It could be the case that the records are merely incomplete but the coincidence of dates seems too remarkable.
167. Astorquiza interrogation records, July 26, 1920, AN/JS, Caja R21: Unlabeled expediente on FECh and workers, f9–10.
168. The quotation comes from Federico Carvallo, of the FECh at the time, in a telegram to police officials gathered at an international conference in Buenos Aires, as quoted in Schweitzer, "Juan Gandulfo," 21–22. Deputy Gallardo Nieto argued in the Parliament that members of the FECh can hold whatever ideas they like and such ideas do not allow the police to invade the FECh property without a court order. See 23rd session, July 21, 1920, *Cámara de Diputados . . . 1920*, 662. For the government's defense of seeing words and speeches as subversive, see, for example, Telegram from García de la Huerta to Intendent of San Felipe, July 31, 1920, ARNAD/MI v. 5426. See also Torrealba, *Los subversivos*, 83–84.
169. 27th session, July 27, 1920, *Cámara de Diputados . . . 1920*, 759. Judges however could not be so skeptical: after all, as Manuel Rojas observed, "the judge had to abide by the document and its writer because if he were not to believe the police, who would he believe? If he were to believe the accused, his role would be useless." Rojas, *Hijo de Ladrón*, 164.
170. See for example the statement of Andolia Pizarro, August 11, 1920. Pizarro countered a police agent's claim that she was present in the room when he discovered a large batch of newspapers and documents linking Rojas Marin to the IWW and other anarchist associations. AN/JS, Caja 7: Exp. José Rojas Marín, f23 and f35v–36r.
171. On the size of Santiago's police force, see *Albúm Gráfico de la Policía*, 109.
172. Maldonado Prieto, *Militarización de la policía*, 4.
173. *Numen* 1:21 (September 6, 1919), 10. The article was by Iván, a pseudonym for Juan Gandulfo.
174. Mario, *La corrupción de la Policía Secreta de Santiago*, 21.

175. The reference is to Eugene Francois Vidocq, a criminal turned police detective, who served as a model for Hugo's two main protagonists in *Les Miserables*, among others. Mario, *La corrupción*, 23.
176. Mario, *La corrupción*, 72–75.
177. Vicuña Fuentes, *La Tiranía*, 95–96.
178. This exchange is recounted in Vicuña Fuentes, *La Tiranía*, 96.
179. Lagos Mieres, *Los Subversivos*, 23–24.
180. See for example Edwards, "El despojo sangriento," in Alberto Edwards, *Román Calvo: El Sherlock Holmes Chileno* (Santiago: Editorial del Pacífico, 1953), 49.
181. See the discussion in Colonel-Prefect to the Intendent, June 15, 1920, AN/IS v. 496; on the film see Jacqueline Mouesca and Carlos Orellana, *Cine y memoria del siglo XX* (Santiago: LOM Ediciones, 1998), 92.
182. Report of Sub-Prefect, Comisario Inspector, and Comisario, January 22, 1921, AN/IS v. 506. Noe's original request was sent to the Dean of the Medical School, on November 5, 1920.
183. Hernández Ponce and Salazar González, *De la policía secreta*, 112–113.
184. *Ministerio de Justicia (Diciembre 1915–Junio 1917)* (Santiago: Imp. de la Penitenciaría, 1917), 16.
185. See the biographies provided in *Album gráfico de la Policía*, 34–35. On the militarization of the police see Maldonado Prieto, *Militarización de la policía*, and Hernández Ponce and Salazar González, *De la policía secreta*, 112–114, 128, 131. For Toledo Tagle's appointment, see Maldonado Prieto, *Militarización de la policía*, 7–8.
186. *Album Gráfico de la Policía*, 33. See also René Peri Fegerstrom, *Historia de la Función Policial en Chile: Apuntes y transcripciones, 3a parte (1900–1927)* (Santiago: Carabineros de Chile, 1982), 225–226.
187. *Album Gráfico de la Policía*, 286.
188. Maldonado Prieto, *Militarización de la policía*, 5.
189. *Album Gráfico de la Policía*, 13, 111; Maturana, *Mi Ruta*, 11. Dinator was praised, only a few years later, for his successes at reorganizing the section and at waging war against "undesireable elements." *Album gráfico de la policía*, 13.
190. *Album gráfico de la policía*, 55.
191. For a useful discussion, see Mark Neocleous, *The Fabrication of Social Order: A critical theory of police power* (Sterling, VA; Pluto Press, 2000), x–xi. I am grateful to Guillermina Seri for directing me to Neocleous's work.
192. Sub-Prefect, Santiago Security Section to the 3er Juzgado del Crímen, January 11, 1921, AN/IS v. 506.
193. Ibid. López Martín's assertions for the power of the x-ray were commonplace in the popular press after the revelations regarding the x-ray in the 1890s. Some claimed to have used the x-ray to find the philosopher's stone; others, to help with vivisection or to communicate with the dead. US temperance movement leader Francis Willard claimed the x-ray meant "drunkards and smokers can be shown the steady deterioration in their systems." Otto Glasser, *Wilhelm Conrad Rontgen and the Early History of the Roentgen Rays* (San Francisco: Norman Publishing, 1993 [1934]), 205–206.
194. See file 4455, Tercer Juzgado del Crimen, Valparaíso, December 2, 1914, AN/Fondo Tercer Juzgado del Crimen de Valparaíso, Box 243.
195. Ibid., June 13, 1918, f73.
196. Ibid., f54–66. Rojas, in his semiautobiographical novel *Hijo de Ladrón*, recalled how the police insisted that those arrested provide them with both a name and

an alias ("sobrenombre"), although few complied. The prisoners all claimed to have no aliases to which the officer in charge responded: "No nickname either? Where are you all from? The Ministry of Finance?" Rojas, *Hijo de Ladrón*, 133.

197. *Album gráfico de la policía*, 103.
198. Cristián Palacios Laval, "Entre Bertillon y Vucetich: Las technologías de identificación policial, Santiago de Chile, 1893–1924," in Cristián Palacios and César Leyton, *Industria del Delito: Historias de las ciencias criminológicas en Chile* (Santiago: Ocho Libros, 2014), 95.
199. Decree 2838, July 23, 1920, ARNAD/MI v. 5407; also found in ARNAD/MI v. 5393. The effort to force registration eventually surpassed the infrastructure available. The law proved overwhelming for the police prefects. The registration offices were understaffed and lacking in some of the basic necessities required to do the work, like typewriters: see Colonel-Prefect to the Intendent of the Province, September 3, 1920, AN/IS v. 502 and Colonel-Prefect to the Intendent of the Province, December 21, 1920, AN/IS v. 500. The space within which the Santiago staff worked was so narrow that it not only made working conditions difficult but simply could not accommodate the much-needed increase in staff, a situation that the Prefect suggested was responsible for the limited success at filling the registration rolls, rather than administrative laziness or resistance by foreigners: by the end of November, six months after the new decree, the Santiago office had managed to register only some 17,000 of an estimated 60,000 foreigners. Colonel-Prefect to the Intendent of the Province, December 21, 1920, AN/IS v. 500.
200. See Palacios Laval, "Entre Bertillon y Vucetich," 93–94.
201. Rojas, *Hijo de Ladrón*, 8.
202. This was obviously not the case only for Chile. For Mexico see Pablo Piccato, *City of Suspects*; for Peru, Carlos Aguirre, *The Criminals of Lima and Their Worlds: The Prison Experience, 1850–1935* (Durham, NC: Duke University Press, 2005).
203. See especially Allan Sekula, "The Body and the Archive," *October* 39 (Winter 1986), 3–64.
204. Enrique Prieto Lemm, *Identificación de las personas* (Santiago: Imprenta de la Bolsa, 1923), 8.
205. For a detailed discussion of the possibilities, limits, and applications of identification techniques, see Prieto Lemm, *Identificación de las personas*. On the port strike and the initiation of efforts to develop photograph methods, see Equipo Sombraysén, *Anarquismo y violencia popular en Chile, 1898–1927* (F.U.R.I.A.: Coyhaique, Patagonia, 2008), n.p. For earlier conflicts around the issue, see Eduardo Andrés Godoy Sepúlveda, *La Huelga del Mono: Los anarquistas y las movilizaciones contra el retrato obligatorio (Valparaíso, 1913)* (Santiago: Quimantú, 2014). On Chonofre and photography see Pinto V. and Valdívio O., *Revolución proletaria o querida chusma?*, 53 and DeShazo, *Urban Workers and Labor Unions*, 151; on the strike, and for quoted text, see American consul, Valparaíso, to Secretary of State, August 17, 1917 in *Records of the Dept. of State Relating to the Internal Affairs of Chile, 1910–1929* (Roll 21; 825.50: Economic Conditions). Similar opposition had occurred in Argentina. See Palacios Laval, "Entre Bertillon y Vucetich," esp. 90–91.
206. Victor Serge, *Men in Prison*, trans. by Richard Greeman (London: Readers and Writers Publishing Cooperative, 1977 [1931]), 11–12.
207. Serge, *Men in Prison*, 14. Even an object as simple as a FECh membership card could create problems. On the one hand, the card provided its holder with

numerous benefits, including discounts at some bookstores and clothiers; on the other, in the midst of street sweeps and efforts at quick and easy identification, it could be "a passport to prison," a marker of potential subversion. Délano, *El año '20*, 27–28.

208. Matus and Ducci to Head of the Identification Section, December 30, 1919, included in Colonel-Prefect to the Intendent of the Province, January 24, 1920, AN/IS v. 504. For the creation of the Office of Identification, see Decreto 715 of the Ministry of the Interior, as referenced in Intendent to the Minister of the Interior, July 5, 1920, AN/IS v. 506.
209. Matus and Ducci to Head of the Identification Section, December 30, 1919, included in Colonel-Prefect to the Intendent of the Province, January 24, 1920, AN/IS v. 504. Such passing, of course, had already happened, just not as Matus and Ducci presented it: agents in Santiago's Security Section were passing themselves off as organizers and agitators.
210. Ibid.
211. See for example Minister of Foreign Relations to the Minister of the Interior, December 30, 1921, ARNAD/MI v. 5390.
212. Prieto Lemm, *La identificación*, 3.
213. Prieto Lemm, *La identificación*, 9, 13–14.
214. Prieto Lemm, *La identificación*, 10–11; *Alphonse Bertillon and the Identification of Persons (1880–1914)*, criminocorpus.org/en/museum/alphonse-bertillon-and-identification-persons-1880-1914/.
215. Prieto Lemm, *La identificación*, 12.
216. Julia Rodríguez, "South Atlantic Crossings: Fingerprints, Science and the State in Turn-of-the-Century Argentina," *American Historical Review* 109:2 (April 2004) 387–416 and Palacios Laval, "Entre Bertillon y Vucetich," 108.
217. Prieto Lemm, *La identificación*, 32–35.
218. Rodríguez, "South Atlantic Crossings," 387.
219. Prieto Lemm, *La identificación*, 11–12.
220. For supervision, see Mark Seltzer, *Bodies and Machines* (New York: Routledge, 1992), 100.
221. Prieto Lemm, *La identificación*, 54.
222. A 1919 decree had established a National Institute of Criminology, next to the Penitentiary, overseen by a commission which included noneother than José Ducci (who some in the Parliament would attempt to expel in 1920). See *Memoria del Ministerio de Justicia (1917–1921)*, 108–109. He was appointed at the Institute the head of the laboratory of Experimental Psychology. Ibid., 114.
223. See Seltzer, *Bodies and Machines*, part III. For a similar point, related to photography and the "generalized look," see Sekula, "The Body and the Archive," 7 and John Berger, "Appearances," in Berger, *Understanding a Photograph* (ed. Geoff Dyer) (New York: Aperture, 2013), 55–82. Qtd. text is from Sekula, "The body and the archive," 11.
224. Kristin Ruggiero, "Fingerprinting and the Argentine Plan for Universal Identification in the Late Nineteenth and Early Twentieth Centuries," in *Documenting Individual Identity. The Development of State Practices in the Modern World*, eds. Jane Caplan and John Torpey (Princeton, NJ: Princeton University Press, 2001), 184–196, esp. 189; Rodríguez, "South Atlantic Crossings," 396–397.
225. Sekula, "The Body and the Archive," 11–12.
226. Seltzer, *Bodies and Machines*, 95.

227. *El Mercurio* (August 10, 1920) as reproduced in "De Hace Medio Siglo," *El Mercurio* (August 10, 1970), IISH/MSR f 15.
228. Minister of Justice, Lorenzo Montt to the Jefe de la Oficina Proveedora de Utiles de Escritorio, August 2, 1920, ARNAD/MJ v. 3044, no. 500; for the typewriter, see Jorje Gaete R. to Don José Astorquiza, August 6, 1920, ARNAD/MJ v. 3045, f519.
229. "Los sumarios que se siguen para perseguir a los anarquistas," *El Mercurio* (August 3, 1920), 26. See also the comments of Deputy Ramírez in 39th Session, August 12, 1920, in *Cámara de Diputados: Boletín de las Sesiones Ordinarias en 1920* (Santiago de Chile: Imprenta Nacional, 1920), 1094 and of Deputy Carlos Ruíz, in 42nd Session, August 17, 1920, in *Cámara de Diputados: Boletín de las Sesiones Ordinarias en 1920*, 1155. Grecco was a chauffeur and would at some point become the head of taxi chauffuers union. See Arturo Olivarría Bravo, *Chile entre dos Alessandri: Memorias políticas* (Santiago: Nascimento, 1962–1965 (4 vols.)), 1:82–83 and 39th Session, August 12, 1920, *Cámara de Diputados . . . 1920*, 1094–1095. Labbé's career is mentioned in DeShazo, *Urban Workers and Labor Unions*, 101.
230. 39th Session, August 12, 1920, *Cámara de Diputados . . . 1920*, 1094–1095.
231. 42nd Session, August 17, 1920, *Cámara de Diputados . . . 1920*, 1155.
232. 42nd Session, August 17, 1920, *Cámara de Diputados . . . 1920*, 1156.
233. "Sobre detenciones arbitrarias," *El Mercurio* (August 11, 1920), 21.
234. 39th Session, August 12, 1920, *Cámara de Diputados . . . 1920*, 1096.
235. On the typhus epidemic, see *El Mercurio* (August 10, 1920), as reproduced in "De Hace Medio Siglo," *El Mercurio* (August 10, 1970), IISH/MSR f15 and *El Mercurio* (July 31, 1920), as reproduced in "De Hace Medio Siglo," *El Mercurio* (July 31, 1970), IISH/MSR f15. On the snowfall, see *El Mercurio* (August 13, 1920).
236. "Desenmascarado: Evaristo Ríos Hernández," *Claridad* (December 11, 1920) and "Desenmascarado: Evaristo Ríos Hernández," *Claridad* 10 (December 23, 1920). The full text of Valiente's charge is reproduced in Lagos Mieres, *Los Subversivos*, 176–178.
237. "El allanamiento efectuado antenoche por la policía en el local de la I.W.W.: Se detiene a 121 individuos," *El Mercurio* (August 16, 1920), 5.
238. Vicuña Fuentes, *La Tiranía*, 116, claims that all 118 men on the premises were arrested while wives and children looked on and wept. See also the comments of Deputy Ruíz, 42nd Session, August 17, 1920, *Cámara de Diputados . . . 1920*, 1157.
239. Colonel-Prefect to the Intendent of the Province, August 19, 1920, AN/IS v. 501.
240. Ibid.
241. "El allanamiento efectuado antenoche por la policía en el local de la I.W.W.: Se detiene a 121 individuos," *El Mercurio* (August 16, 1920), 5. One of the few arrested and immediately released was a medical student from a very prominent family from the south, Reinaldo Araneda de la Jara. De la Jara was freed, allegedly because he claimed he went in believing it was a performance of national theatre of some kind, but the likely reason he was released was because he came from a very well-respected family from the south. See "Los sumarios que se siguen contra los subversivos," *El Mercurio* (August 16, 1920), 15.
242. Unsigned report to the Colonel-Prefect titled "Da cuenta del mitin de hoy," August 15, 1920, AN/IS v. 501.
243. 42nd Session, August 17, 1920, *Cámara de Diputados . . . 1920*, 1157.

244. 71st Session, September 10, 1920, *Cámara de Diputados . . . 1920*, 1836.

CHAPTER 4

1. Triviño, *Arengas*, 6.
2. The descriptions of the jail are drawn from the following sources: Vizconde del Palacio, *Historia de la cárcel política: La Bastilla Chilena* (Paris: Imprenta Rochefort, 1893), 10–11; Triviño, *Arengas*, 7–8; "En pleno terror blanco: Domingo Gómez Rojas ante la justicia chilena," *Claridad* 1:1 (October 12, 1920), 3.
3. The most detailed biography is that of Moraga Valle and Vega Delgado, *José Domingo Gómez Rojas*.
4. Oscar Videla, "Los amores del Poeta," *Siembra* (October 1920), 36–38, as quoted in Moraga Valle and Vega Delgado, *José Domingo Gómez Rojas*, 7.
5. See ibid., 8.
6. Ibid., 11.
7. Moraga Valle and Vega Delgado have pointed out the degree to which his many biographers ignore this aspect of his life. Moraga Valle and Vega Delgado, *José Domingo Gómez Rojas*, 8. For recent efforts to rectify this, see Carolina González Varas, "La espiritualidad cristiana en el hablante de Domingo Gómez Rojas," *Literatura y Linguistica* 23 (2011), 15–28, and Benoit Santini, "Intertextualidad Bíblica en *Rebeldías Líricas* (1913) de José Domingo Gómez Rojas: Religión, creación e ideales anarquistas," in Joël Delhom and Daniel Attala, eds., *Cuando las anarquistas citaban la Biblia: Entre mesianismo y propaganda* (Madrid: Catarata, 2014), 171–182.
8. December 29, 1916, Diario de José Domingo Gómez Rojas, as cited in José Domingo Gómez Rojas, *Rebeldías Líricas*, ed. by Andrés Sabella (Santiago: Ercilla, 1940), 139.
9. Moraga Valle and Vega Delgado, *José Domingo Gómez Rojas*, 11. The power of Christian imagery and symbolism in avant-garde and revolutionary poetry of the time is not exclusive to Gómez Rojas. See, for example, Jean Franco's discussion of César Vallejo's work in Franco, *The Modern Culture of Latin America*, 152–153.
10. Rojas, *Sombras contra el muro*, 188–189.
11. See the illuminating discussion in Jesse Cohn, *Underground Passages: Anarchist Resistance Culture, 1848–2011* (Oakland: AK Press, 2014), 11–12.
12. Moraga Valle and Vega Delgado, *José Domingo Gómez Rojas*, 20–23. For the qtd. passage, see 23.
13. On Lillo, and the era more generally, see Gerald Martin, "Literature, music and the visual arts, 1870–1930," in Leslie Bethell, ed., *The Cultural History of Latin America: Literature, Music, and the Visual Arts in the 19th and 20th Centuries* (Cambridge: Cambridge University Press, 1998), 47–130, esp. 99–101. See also Subercaseaux, *Historia de las ideas*, 174–175 and Franco, *The Modern Culture of Latin America*, 62–63.
14. Subercaseaux, *Historia de las ideas*, 75.
15. P.B.G, review in *La Unión* (April 21, 1913), www.sicpoesiachilena.cl/docs/critica_detalle.php?critica_id=93, accessed April 23, 2015.
16. For good overviews see Edwin Williamson, *The Penguin History of Latin America* (London: Penguin, 1992), esp. 513–520; Martin, "Literature, music and the visual arts," 117–120; and Franco, *The Modern Culture*, esp. chap. 5.
17. Subercaseaux, *Historia de las ideas*, 185.
18. Ibid., 186.

19. Ibid., 185.
20. Colonel-Prefect to the Intendent, July 20, 1920, AN/IS v. 497. He posted the bail along with Germán Riesco.
21. Manuel Rojas recalled, "During that period in the State telegraph office there were a few books with the telegram forms. Us young writers, we stole those forms and on the back side we wrote poems, short stories, novels." Qtd. from Naín Nómez and Emmanuel Tornés, eds. *Manuel Rojas: Estudios Críticos* (Santiago: Universidad de Santiago, 2005), 34.
22. See, for example, Antonio Acevedo Hernández, *Memorias de un autor teatral* (Santiago: Editorial Nascimento, 1982), 107; Moraga Valle and Vega Delgado, *José Domingo Gómez Rojas*, 25–26.
23. See Gómez Rojas, Diario íntimo, 1916, Biblioteca Nacional (hereafter BN), Archivo del Escritor (hereafter AE). Recently, these manuscript pages have been digitized and made available online. See www.bncatalogo.cl/escritor/AE0016752.pdf, accessed April 23, 2015.
24. Moraga Valle and Vega Delgado, *José Domingo Gómez Rojas*, 18; Acevedo Hernández, *Memorias*.
25. Moraga Valle and Vega Delgado, *José Domingo Gómez Rojas*, 18.
26. Gómez Rojas, Diario íntimo, 1916, BN/AE, no. 3, f1.
27. Sabella, *Gómez Rojas: Símbolo*, 35–36.
28. Sub-Prefect to the 2o. Juzgado del Crímen, July 21, 1920, AN/IS v. 497; Parte del Jefe de la Sección de Seguridad No. 2756, in "Proceso," leg. 1658, f85–101.
29. *Boletín de los Trabajadores Industriales del Mundo* (Santiago, April 1920). Carlos Vicuña Fuentes argued that Gómez Rojas was not a committed Wobblie but instead accepted the offer of serving on the IWW board due to vanity. Arturo Zuñiga, in an interview many years later, made a similar claim. See Vicuña Fuentes, *La Tiranía*, 115 and Zuñiga, "La dificil generación del '20," *Ercilla* (June 5, 1968), clipping in IISH/MSR f164.
30. González Vera, *Cuando era muchacho*, 209.
31. Vizconde del Palacio, *Historia de la cárcel política*, 2. For "sinister block," see Oliver Brand, "En el reino de la escasez," *Zig-Zag* (c. early August 1920).
32. *Memoria del Ministerio de Justicia* (Diciembre 1915–Junio 1917), 93.
33. Brand, "En el reino de la escasez."
34. Beginning in 1900 all individuals arrested in Santiago had to pass through the Detention Office as part of an effort to centralize identification, criminal, and statistical practices. See Hernández Ponce and Salazar González, *De la policía secreta*, 80–81.
35. "El poeta en la Cárcel," *Juventud* 2:10 (1920), 72–77.
36. "El poeta en la Cárcel," *Juventud* 2:10 (1920), 76. See also González Vera, *Cuando era muchacho*, 209.
37. Decree of José Astorquiza, July 31, 1920, "Proceso," leg. 1658, f100–101 and f112–113; Plaza Ferrand in "Los sumarios que se siguen contra los elementos subversivos," *El Mercurio* (August 11, 1920), 19. The articles were as follows: Article 126—rising up with the intent to interfere with the promulgation or execution of the law, elections, or acts of hatred or vengeance against the persons or property of the authorities or agents of the state; Article 133—crimes included in article 126 but not directed at government officials; Article 292—organizing an association with the intent to attack the social order, moral order, or people or property (the mere fact of organizing such an association constituted a crime); and Article 294—taking part in the association or voluntarily or

knowingly supplying arms, munitions and the like in order to commit crimes, or housing people or hiding them.

38. Examples abound in the documents but see particularly the case of José Rojas Marín, in AN/JS, esp. José Rojas Marín, particularly f15, f21, f24, f30–32, and f36–37, in which an array of conflicting statements are presented. Most issues of *Numen* attracted the attention of the authorities but in this particular instance it was issue 2:44 (February 14, 1920), that raised specific charges of subversion.
39. See the document dated July 31, 1920, in AN/JS, Caja R13: exp. Jorge Rosemblatt y Roberto Salinas, por Sedición, f35.
40. *Memoria del Ministerio de Justicia (1917–1921)*, 127.
41. Aguirre, "Cárcel y sociedad en America Latina," 215; on the creation of the Santiago penitentiary, see F. Ulloa C., *La Penitenciaría de Santiago* (Santiago: Los Tiempos, 1879).
42. Aguirre, "Cárcel y sociedad en America Latina," 214.
43. Ulloa, *La Penitenciaría de Santiago*, 7.
44. Ibid., 75–76.
45. León León, *Encierro y corrección*, 2:414–415.
46. Article XII: Talleres.
47. *Memoria del Ministerio de Justicia* (Diciembre 1915–Junio 1917), 23.
48. Article XI: Trabajo de los reos
49. *Memoria del Ministerio de Justicia* (Diciembre 1915–Junio 1917), 24–26; and Minister of Justice, No. 1379/Secc. P., July 12, 1920, AN/IS v. 497.
50. Victor Serge wrote what to my mind is still the most remarkable work on life in prison, *Men in Prison*. In a letter to a comrade regarding the book, he commented "I had to free myself from that debt, accomplish that task before any other. While I was still in prison, fighting off tuberculosis, insanity, the blues, the spiritual poverty of the men, the brutality of the regulations, I already saw a kind of justfication of that infernal voyage in the possibility of describing it." Serge, *Men in Prison*, trans. Richard Greeman (London: Writers and Readers Publishing Cooperative, 1977 [1931]), xxv. For an official comment on the pervasiveness of tuburculosis in the system, see "Los sistemas carcelarios," *Revista de la Policía de Valparaíso* 2:26 (December 31, 1908), 3, as cited in Maureira, "Los culpables," 70.
51. See León León, *Encierro y corrección*, 2: 510–511.
52. Alejandro Lira, Establecimientos penales, to Ministry of Justice, transcribed in Lorenzo Montt to the Santiago Jail Administrator, September 10, 1920, ARNAD/MJ v. 3049. These issues were widespread and not just exclusive to Santiago: see the complaints regarding food quality in prisons raised by regional authorities in, for example, Telegraph from Governor of Bulnes to the Minister of Justice, September 9, 1920, ARNAD/MJ v. 3043; Telegraph from Governor of Yungay to the Minister of Justice, September 15, 1920, in ARNAD/MJ v. 3043.
53. Lorenzo Montt to the Santiago Jail Administrator, September 10, 1920, ARNAD/MJ v. 3049. On accusations of Matte Eyzaguirre's involvement in the attacks on the FECh, see *Claridad* 1:21 (1921). When Pedro Gandulfo assembled a list of those involved in the attacks on the FECh, he included Matte Eyzaguirre's name followed by the words "muy conocido" ("very well-known"). See Pedro Gandulfo and Rigoberto Soto Rengifo, Denuncian a los delincuentes, in "Proceso," leg. 1658, f246r–v.

54. Office of the Penitentiary, Talca, to the Minister of Justice, July 28, 1920, ARNAD/MJ v. 3049.
55. On typhus, see *Anuario Justicio* (1917–1921), 352. The lack of personnel was apparently even more noticeable in August, September, and October when the jails filled up due to the consequences of independence day celebrations. See Unsigned to Minister of Justice, August 16, 1920, ARNAD/MJ v. 3049.
56. *Memoria del Ministerio de Justicia* (Diciembre 1915–Junio 1917), 19.
57. "Crónica obrera," *Claridad* (November 6, 1920), 9.
58. See Decree of Astorquiza, August 27, 1920; Landa to Astorquiza, August 28, 1920; Decree of Astorquiza, August 28, 1920, all in "Proceso," leg. 1658, f348r, f348r/v, and f349 respectively. For "strict guard," see ibid., f349. More generally on prison conditions and health, see Berkman, *Prison Memoirs*; Serge, *Men in Prison*; Ryan Edwards, "From the Depths of Patagonia: The Ushuaia Penal Colony and the Nature of 'The End of the World,'" *Hispanic American Historical Review* 94:2 (May 2014), 271–302; and Ryan Edwards, "An Ecology of Exile: Earth and Elsewhere in Argentina's Ushuaia Penal Colony (1860–1960)," dissertation in progress, Cornell University.
59. Colonel-Prefect to the Intendent of the Province, November 8, 1920, AN/IS v. 499.
60. Author interview with Juan Luis Gandulfo.
61. Gandulfo, "Las cárceles y los gobernantes cínicos," *Claridad* 2:70 (1922), www.claridad.uchile.cl/index.php/CLR/rt/printerFriendly/9950/10000, accessed October 9, 2015.
62. For details on Lafuente, see his interrogation on July 22, 1920, in "Proceso," leg. 1658, f17–18. On separating minors, see Jorge Rojas, *Moral y prácticas cívicas en los niños chilenos, 1850–1950* (Santiago: LOM Ediciones, 2004), 293–294.
63. Dr. Sabrino Muñóz Labbé to the Minister, August 11, 1920, AN/JS, Caja R21: Unlabeled expediente on FECh and workers, f61.
64. *Memoria del Ministerio de Justicia* (Diciembre 1915–Junio 1917), 96.
65. Gandulfo, "Las cárceles y los gobernantes cínicos." Captured on August 29, he was imprisoned until December 5.
66. Gandulfo, "Las cárceles y los gobernantes cínicos." The Ministry of Justice expressed its own set of concerns regarding the "mixing" of prisoners, from "vicious" criminals to petty thieves. See *Memoria del Ministerio de Justicia* (Diciembre 1915–Junio 1917), 96. The penitentiary was designed for prisoners who had been convicted of a crime, usually a serious one carrying a sentence of more than five years. In the penal code, sentences for "lesser" crimes—carrying a sentence of between sixty days and five years—were to be served in one of the country's presidios. In Santiago efforts had been underway to fold the presidio in to the penitentiary. In the meantime, those arrested, or under indictment, but not yet convicted were theoretically supposed to be held in the jail as well as offered bail, as were those guilty of misdemeanors or serving short stints in lieu of a fine ("condenados por faltas.") See Ministerio de Justicia, *Decreto 2140: Reglamento Cárcelario. Se aprueba para los establecimientos penales* (Santiago, August 1, 1911); for the sentencing guidelines, see Palma and Fernández, "Del delito al encierro," in Sagredo and Gazmuri, *Historia de la vida privada*, 284.
67. "Proceso," leg. 1658, f332 shows that a large number of workers (and a few students, including Lafuente and Hernández) were processed and held at the cárcel; a smaller number and mix of students and workers (including P. Gandulfo,

Gómez Rojas, Soto Rengifo and León Ugalde but also Salinas, Valiente, Zamorano, and Montero) were being processed and held at the penitentiary.

68. "En pleno terror blanco," *Claridad* 1:1 (1920), 3. Carlos Aguirre notes how "traditional" or colonial forms of punishment and detention were still considered appropriate for the "uncivilized and barbarous masses" in the modern era, whereas the penitentiary was for the citizen—redeemable and respectable. Aguirre, "Cárcel y sociedad en America Latina," 214–215.
69. "En pleno terror blanco," *Claridad* 1:1 (October 12, 1920), 3. On Gómez Rojas being in the penitentiary by August 12, see "Proceso" leg. 1658, f332.
70. The details on the visits, the grammar classes, and the reference to "don Pepe" come from Gómez Rojas, Diario íntimo (undated), BN/AE.
71. José Rojas Marín was arrested for purportedly encouraging others to attack and resist the police when they sought to disperse a crowd of "revoltosos" in the Alameda. When he requested release on bail, Astorquiza refused. The file is an impressive example of how persistent purportedly uninformed working people could be in their efforts to get justice. See AN/JS, Caja R7: exp. José Rojas Marín, esp. f38–39; f42r–v; f50–56. Rojas Marín wrote a remarkable letter to Astorquiza in September in which he noted in part: "The accusation against me is not true, and if it were you would not have left me hurt here like a dog but instead the Tribunal, as is its duty, would have begun preliminary proceedings to determine proof of a crime and the appropriate punishment" (f67r–v). He was eventually freed on November 5, 1920 (f97).
72. The cited passage comes from E. P. Thompson, *Whigs and Hunters: The origin of the Black Act* (New York: Pantheon Books, 1975), 267.
73. Pedro Gandulfo Guerra y Rigoberto Soto Rengifo to the Special Prosecutor, August 9, 1920, in "Proceso," leg. 1658, f322–323v.
74. AN/JS, Caja R24, exp. Arturo González.
75. Fidél Araneda Luco, Investigations Commissioner, to the Police Prefect, February 23, 1920, AN/IS v. 496.
76. Pedro Gandulfo to the Special Prosecutor, August 11, 1910, in "Proceso," leg. 1658, f329. The accusations would persist. See "Sanfuentes y su camarilla: La Ultima Cena," *Claridad* 1:10 (December 23, 1920), 7; and Pedro Gandulfo Guerra y Rigoberto Soto Rengifo, "Astorquiza, perseguidor de peruanos, es peruano," *Juventud* 2:11–12 (January–March 1921), 97.
77. See "La obra de los espías peruanos," undated clipping but c. September 1919, IISH/MSR f14 (1919)
78. "Los sumarios que se siguen contra los elementos subversivos," *El Mercurio* (August 11, 1920), 19.
79. "Potpourri," *Sucesos* XVIII: 933 (August 12, 1920), IISH/MSR f15.
80. 24th session, July 22, 1920, *Cámara de Diputados . . . 1920*, 691.
81. Luís Cifuentes, Dirección General de Telégrafos, to the Minister of the Interior, July 15, 1920, ARNAD/MI v. 5375.
82. *El Mercurio* (July 21, 1920), 5.
83. 23rd session, July 21, 1920, *Cámara de Diputados . . . 1920*, 664.
84. A member of the Security Section remarked that "very few had obeyed" the registration order. Colonel-Prefect to the Santiago Intendent, August 10, 1920, AN/IS v. 502.
85. American Embassy, Santiago, *Report on General Conditions Prevailing in Chile*, August 20, 1920 to September 3, 1920, Records of the Department of State

Relating to the Internal Affairs of Chile, 1910–1929 (Roll 4. 825.00 Political Affairs).

86. American Embassy, Santiago, *Report on General Conditions Prevailing in Chile*, August 20, 1920 to September 3, 1920, Records of the Department of State Relating to the Internal Affairs of Chile, 1910–1929 (Roll 4. 825.00 Political Affairs).
87. This according to Arica Governor Renate Valdés, as quoted in American consulate in Tacna to Secretary of State, September 3, 1920. Encl. in American Embassy, Santiago, *Report on General Conditions Prevailing in Chile*, August 20, 1920 to September 3, 1920, Records of the Department of State Relating to the Internal Affairs of Chile, 1910–1929 (Roll 4. 825.00 Political Affairs). In a subsequent report the consular official noted that Tacna-born Peruvian citizens were still being dismissed from positions and that he feared Intendent Fernando Edwards, among others, might provoke a border incident purposefully to exacerbate hostitlities. A Tacna-born Peruvian Alberto Quezada came to see him to let him know he had been ordered expelled by the Police Prefect and that he knew if he did not comply he would be beaten and taken to the border anyway. He also claimed he was being expelled because certain Chileans owed him money. See American consulate in Tacna to Secretary of State, September 11, 1920. Encl. in American Embassy, Santiago, *Report on General Conditions Prevailing in Chile*, August 20, 1920 to September 3, 1920, Records of the Department of State Relating to the Internal Affairs of Chile, 1910–1929 (Roll 4. 825.00 Political Affairs).
88. Pedro García de la Huerta to the Santiago Intendent, August 25, 1920, ARNAD/MI v. 5407.
89. Pedro García de la Huerta to the Santiago Intendent, August 25, 1920, ARNAD/MI v. 5407.
90. "Breve entrevista con el 1er. Alcalde de la Municipalidad, Don Pedro A. Marín," *Zig-Zag* (August 28, 1920).
91. Ibid.
92. Pedro García de la Huerta to the Santiago Intendent, July 31, 1920, ARNAD/MI v. 5407. Molina's personal history is also taken from this document.
93. Telegram from García de la Huerta to Intendente of Iquique, August 20, 1920, ARNAD/MI v. 5426. La Aguada was authorized as an anonymous society in 1901 and had capital of 400,000 pounds sterling, according to *Sinópsis estadística i jerográfica de Chile* (Chile: Dirección de Estadística, 1906), 558.
94. Pedro García de la Huerta to the Santiago Intendent, August 25, 1920, ARNAD/MI v. 5407. Numerous individuals in the northern city of Iquique contacted the minister directly to lobby on their own behalf. Luis Gómez, director of "El Roto," noted that the "patriotic newspaper El Nacional" was calling him Peruvian and that he had proof he was Chilean and wanted guarantees from the Ministry. Telegraph from García de la Huerta to the Iquique Intendent, August 10, 1920, ARNAD/ MI v. 5437.
95. Pedro Gandulfo to Astorquiza, August 11, 1920, and Astorquiza's response, August 12, 1920, both in "Proceso," leg. 1658, f330–331v.
96. For a recapitulation of the material, see Daniel Schweitzer, "La Justicia y los grandes procesos en Chile desde 1905," in *Medio Siglo de Zig-Zag, 1905–1955* (Santiago: n.p., n.d.), 278.
97. "Orientaciones del proceso que se sigue a la asociación denominada IWW" *El Mercurio* (August 12, 1920), 19.

98. "La vida que pasa," *Sucesos* (August 12, 1920), IISH/MSR f15.
99. "Los sumarios de actualidad," *El Mercurio* (August 14, 1920), 19.
100. According to a police report, Soto Rengifo was in an area of the prison with other prisoners for certain judicial procedures when he shouted out "Long live social revolution!" A guard ordered Soto Rengifo and the other prisoners, including Gandulfo, to be placed in isolation. Police report No. 3247, August 17, 1920, in "Proceso," leg. 1658, f203; Pedro Gandulfo to Astorquiza, August 19, 1920, in ibid., f209–210.
101. Pedro Aguirre Cerda to Astorquiza, August 28, 1920, in "Proceso," leg. 1658, f355.
102. Pedro León Ugalde to Astorquiza, August 11, 1920, in "Proceso," leg. 1658, f150–151; "Los sumarios de actualidad," *El Mercurio* (August 14, 1920), 19.
103. Florencio Rozas, Eliodoro Ulloa, y Carlos Salgado to the Special Prosector (Astorquiza), no date but between August 1 and August 5, 1920, AN/JS, Caja R21: Unlabeled expediente on FECh and workers, f49–51.
104. Ibid.
105. Sub-Prefect, Santiago Security Section, to the Special Prosecutor (Astorquiza), August 14, 1920, AN/JS, Caja R21: Unlabeled expediente on FECh and workers, f56–57; "Sumarios de la actualidad," *El Mercurio* (August 15, 1920), 26.
106. A question raised in a letter to Astorquiza by José Rojas Marín. See Rojas Marín to Astorquiza, August 14, 1920, AN/JS Caja 7: exp. José Rojas Marín, f33.
107. Details on Undurraga come from his interrogation in "Proceso," leg. 1658, f142–145.
108. See, for example, the testimony of Nicoimedes Avaria and Luis Henríquez Poblete, "Proceso," leg. 1658, f122–123 and f188v, respectively.
109. "Proceso," leg. 1658, f179–180. The pun does not work particularly well in translation but for those interested, here it is. "Carlos Alarcón es pariente del Kaiser porque es Alarcón Ulloa y el Kaiser, Guillermo de Hohenzollern Ulloa Holanda." Ulloa here is a play on "huyó a" ("fled to") and thus the translation could be "Carlos Alarcón is a relative of the Kaiser because his name is Alarcón Ulloa and the Kaiser's is William of Hohenzollern Fled-to-Holland." See Edwards Bello, *Francisco Miranda y otros personajes* (Santiago: Andrés Bello, 1970), 245.
110. "Proceso," leg. 1658, f148.
111. Teofilio Ruíz Rubio to S. Ministro, Aug 17, 1920, "Proceso," leg. 1658, f200r/v.
112. John F. O'Hara, "A New Form of Pan-Americanism: The Exchange of Students," *Hispanic American Historical Review* 4:1 (1921), 112–113.
113. Kartulovich is identified as an assailant and described by Pedro Gandulfo and Rigoberto Soto Rengifo as a "piloto y sportman" in "Proceso," leg. 1658, 246v. For his relationship with Eva Perón, see Juan José Sebreli, *Comediantes y mártires: Ensayo contra los mitos* (Buenos Aires: Debate, 2008), chap. 4.
114. *Programa oficial del Campeonato Sud-Americano de Box 1927* (Santiago: Imp. Siglo XX, 1927), no pagination.
115. Carlos Maldonado, "La Prusia del América del Sur: Acerca de las relaciones militares Chileno-Germanas (1927–1945)," www.archivochile.com/Poder_Dominante/ffaa_y_orden/Sobre/PDffaasobre0027.pdf, accessed March 2, 2105.
116. Gómez Rojas, Diario íntimo (1920) BN/AE, No. 1, f1.
117. This exchange is recounted in Vicuña Fuentes, *La Tiranía*, 115 and by Zuñiga, "La difícil generación del 20," IISH/MSR f14.

118. See especially James C. Scott, *The Weapons of the Weak: Everyday Forms of Peasant Resistance in Southeast Asia* (New Haven, CT: Yale University Press, 1985), *Domination and the Arts of Resistance: Hidden Transcripts* (New Haven, CT: Yale University Press, 1992), and *Two Cheers for Anarchism*.
119. Quoted from Scott, *Domination and the Arts of Resistance*, in which it appears as an epigraph to the book.
120. See Butterworth, *The World That Never Was*, 126.
121. George Woodcock, *The Paradox of Oscar Wilde*, (London: T. V. Boardman & Co., 1949), 139.
122. González Vera, *Cuando era muchacho*, 116.
123. Roberto Meza Fuentes, "Domingo Gómez Rojas: El poeta martir," in *La Reforma Universitaria* (Vol. VI) (Buenos Aires: Ferrari Hmnos, 1927), 424.
124. *Sucesos* (August 19, 1920)
125. On the meaning of queso de bola, see Ramón Caballero y Rubio, *Diccionario de modismos: (frases y metáforas) primero y único de su género en España* (Madrid: E. García Rico, 1905), 370.
126. Délano, *Memorias*, 42–44; on dropping García de la Huerta's full name, see *Claridad* 1:8 (November 27, 1920), 9.
127. On "quiet revolutions," see Ward, *Anarchism*, chap. 8.
128. Ulloa, *La penitenciaría*, 76–77.
129. Serge, *Men in Prison*, 32.
130. The exact date of his transfer back to the jail is uncertain. Gómez Rojas himself, in his writings, gives conflicting dates for his transfer. As best as I can determine, it occurred at some point between August 26 and August 30. The actual sequence of interactions with Astorquiza is similarly unclear and I have sought here to narrate it according to what the preponderance of the evidence suggests.
131. Vizconde del Palacio, *Historia de la cárcel*, 10–11; Triviño, *Arengas*, 7–8; "En pleno terror blanco: Domingo Gómez Rojas ante la justicia chilena," *Claridad* 1:1 (October 12, 1920), 3.
132. For employment statistics see *Memoria del Ministerio de Justicia (1917–1921)*, 42. On the need for repairs, see Detention Section to Lorenzo Montt, August 27, 1920, ARNAD/MI v. 3049.
133. Brand, "En el reino de la escasez."
134. 69th session, January 3, 1919, *Cámara de Diputados . . . 1918–1919*, 1715, 1720. On Rebosio more generally, see Muñoz Cortés, *Cuando la patria mata*.
135. See Carlos Aguirre, "Cárcel y sociedad en America Latina," 213
136. Lamas, *Desde la cárcel* (Santiago: Imprenta y Litografía Universo, 1905), 20.
137. Ulloa, *La penitenciaría*, 18.
138. Ibid.
139. Lamas, *Desde la cárcel*, 21.
140. Article XIII: Castigos. On the weight of shackles, see the testimony of Pedro Herrera on January 31, 1919, *Cámara de Diputados . . . 1918–1919*, 2674.
141. "El poeta en la cárcel," *Juventud* 2:10 (1920), 75.
142. Gómez Rojas, undated letter, BN/AE, no. 1, f2. Moraga Valle and others assert that the letter was addressed to Santiago Labarca but the copy on microfilm at the Archivo del Escritor shows that it was Alberto Labarca (most likely Santiago's brother). This would make sense given that Santiago Labarca had gone underground by this point. Gómez Rojas signed the letter referring to himself as the Secretario del Centro de Propaganda Radical de la 10a Comisaria

and addressed it to Labarca at the Radical Club located apparently on San Diego Street, only blocks from his home.

143. Gómez Rojas, undated notes, BN/AE, no. 1, f4. On Ducoing, see William Belmont Parker, *Chileans of today* (New York: G.P. Putnam and Sons, 1920), 383–384; on Crenovich, see Vicuña Fuentes, *La Tiranía*, 228, 232, 243.
144. Gómez Rojas, Diario íntimo (1920), BN/AE no. 1, f1.
145. Gómez Rojas, undated letter, BN/AE, no. 1, f5.
146. Serge, *Men in Prison*, 20.
147. Gómez Rojas, letter dated August 27, 1920, BN/AE, No. 1, f3. Although dated August 27, other documents conflict with whether or not he was in the jail at this point.
148. Reproduced in "Una acusación postuma," *Juventud* 2:10 (1920), 98.
149. "Carta de un preso," *Juventud* 2:10 (1920), 80.
150. *El Mercurio* (September 21, 1920), 14.
151. On Gómez Rojas's condition in the jail, prior to his move to the Casa de Orates, see "Carta de un preso," *Juventud* 2:10 (1920), 80 and "El poeta en la Cárcel," *Juventud* 2:10 (1920), 72–77; for an alternative perspective, see *El Mercurio* (September 21, 1920), 14.
152. *El Mercurio* (October 2, 1920), 17.
153. As quoted in Julio Sepúlveda Rondanelli, *Los radicales ante la historia* (Santiago: Editorial Andrés Bello, 1993), 100–101.
154. Gandulfo, "La muerte de Gómez Rojas: Imprecación," October 1920. This was written while Gandulfo was still in the penitentiary. The version cited here is from https://periodicoelsurco.wordpress.com/2011/09/28/documento-la-muerte-de-gomez-rojas-por-juan-gandulfo-1920/, accessed September 7, 2015. The translation does not quite capture the literary sensibility in the piece. I have translated "mordisco en el corazón" as "pierced my heart" but the phrasing comes from Seneca.
155. John Berger, *And Our Faces, My Heart, Brief as Photos* (New York: Vintage, 1992), 21.

EPILOGUE

1. On the weather see "Potpourri," *Sucesos* (October 21, 1920).
2. "Potpourri," *Sucesos* (October 14, 1920).
3. "La fiesta de la primavera," *Sucesos* (Oct 14, 1920).
4. *Album gráfico de la policía*, 233.
5. *El Mercurio* (September 30, 1920), 5. See also the notice of his death in ibid., 21.
6. "Los subversivos de Valparaíso," *Sucesos* (October 14, 1920).
7. "Aquellos comentarios," *Sucesos* (November 4, 1920).
8. See for example, "La Muerte del Sr. Gómez Rojas. Comunicación del director de la Penitenciaría al Ministro de Justicia en la cual desmiente las aseveraciones de un diario," *El Mercurio* (October 3, 1920), 26.
9. The text of these two letters, dated September 20 and 21, 1920, is reproduced in the 1940 edition of Gómez Rojas's *Rebeldías Líricas*, ed. by Andrés Sabella (Santiago: Ediciones Ercilla, 1940), 146.
10. For the petition by Deputy Manuel Barrenechea to see the autopsy report see Lorenzo Montt to the Visiting Minister in the Santiago Criminal Court, Francisco Santapau, October 13, 1920, ARNAD/MJ v. 3045, f716. The negative response his petition receives appears in Lorenzo Montt to the President of the Chamber of Deputies, October 28, 1920, ARNAD/MJ v. 3045, f766. *El Mercurio* claimed the

autopsy was performed the morning of September 30 in the Casa de Orates and that, although the official autopsy had not been released, the verdict was acute diphtheria. "Los funerales del Sr. Gómez Rojas," *El Mercurio* (October 1, 1920), 14.

11. "!Acusamos!" *Claridad* 1:1 (October 12, 1920), front page editorial and page 3. Deputy Bañados made a similar point: "We are returning to the times of the Inquisition during which no one had the right to think." 4th Session, October 14, 1920, *Cámara de Diputados . . . 1920*, 104.
12. I am indebted to Santiago Aránguiz who first suggested to me that the *Claridad* was—in many respects—a continuation of *Numen*.
13. A review of Henri Barbusse's *Le Feu* (*Under Fire*) appeared in *Numen* II: 62 (June 19, 1920), 8. On the movement's membership see Max Eastman, "The Clarté Movement," *The Liberator* 3:4 (April 1920), 40–42, www.marxists.org/archive/eastman/1920/clarte.htm, accessed March 1, 2010. Barbusse has not received the historical attention he deserves. He was an intellectual of significant importance, within and outside of France, in the 1920s. His works were translated in to English and Spanish, and his call for intellectuals to be politically engaged resonated widely. Barbusse's *Le Feu* was immediately translated in to English as *Under Fire: The Story of a Squad* (New York: EP Dutton & Co., 1917), as was his later work *Clarté*, published as *Light* (New York: E. P. Dutton & Co., 1919). *Light* went through five printings in only three months. *Under Fire* has been republished as part of the Penguin Classics series with an introduction by Jay Winter. See *Under Fire*, trans. by Robin Buss (London: Penguin Books, 2003). For a useful biography of Barbusse, see José Mancisador, *Henri Barbusse: Ingeniero de almas* (Mexico: Ediciones Botas, 1945).
14. Serge, *Memoirs of a Revolutionary*, 212, 277.
15. On Barbusse and Mariátegui, see Peter J. Gold, "The Influence of Henri Barbusse in Bolivia," *Bulletin of Latin American Research* 2:2 (May 1983), 117–122. On the *Claridad* generally, see Florencia Ferreira de Cassone, *Claridad y el internacionalismo Americano* (Buenos Aires: Editorial Claridad, 1998) and, for Chile, Santiago Aránguiz Pinto, "Renovarse o morir? La Federación de Estudiantes de Chile y la Revista Claridad," BA thesis, Universidad Finis Terrae (Santiago, 2002), and Moraga Valle, "*Muchachos casi silvestres*."
16. "Potpourri," *Sucesos* (October 28, 1920).
17. Ibid.
18. "Un escrito extraño," *Claridad* 7 (November 20, 1920), 10.
19. The details on the encounter come from Antonio Acevedo Hernández's interview with Gómez Rojas's mother. "Con la madre de Gómez Rojas," *Sucesos* 8/3 (1928), clipping in IISH/MSR, folder 23.
20. *Claridad* 1:5 (November 6, 1920), 5.
21. "Exposición de cuadros de un compañero obrero," *Claridad* 1:4 (October 31, 1920), 8.
22. *Claridad* 1:5 (November 6, 1920), 9.
23. 78th Session, September 30, 1920, *Cámara de Diputados . . . 1920*, 2023.
24. Vicuña Fuentes, *La Tiranía*, 169–170.
25. Pedro Gandulfo, "Solo nací para quererte," manuscript courtesy of Juan Luis Gandulfo.
26. On TEKOS, see Tomás Ireland, *Roquerío* (Toronto: Michael Graphics, 2011). For the assaults during the coup, see ibid., esp. 29–33. The information on Pedro Gandulfo being visited by Pinochet's security agents was provided to me by his daughter Chela to whom I am very grateful.

27. Author interviews with Juan Luis Gandulfo, July and October 2011. See also Tomás Ireland, *Nuestro Cobre: Memorias de la primera administración de la mina El Teniente* (Santiago: Editorial Universidad de Santiago de Chile, 2015) for further discussion.
28. Those released included Luis Jara y Castro, Isolino Norambuena, Ramón Contreras, Evaristo Lagos, Roberto Salinas, Manuel Figueroa, Juan Gómez, Vicente Retamales, Luis Pinto, Ramón Argui[?], Moises Montoya, Oscar Salas, Leónardo Cifuentes, Julio Valiente, Galvarino Troncoso, Lorenzo Loggia, Juan Gandulfo, José del Transito Ibarra, Alberto Baloffet, Adolfo Hernández, Luis Soza, Manuel Montano, Manuel Zamorano, Manuel Silva, Pedro Corail. AN/JS, Caja R13: exp. Jorge Rosemblatt y Roberto Salinas, por Sedición, f38–39.
29. On his caring for prisoners and guards, see Schweitzer, "Juan Gandulfo," 19–20.
30. Manuel Rojas, *La oscura vida radiante*, 176.
31. On the clinic's work, see its publication *La Hoja Sanitaria*.
32. William Miller Collier, US Ambassador to Chile, to Secretary of State, March 17, 1925 in Records of the Dept. of State Relating to the Internal Affairs of Chile, 1910–1929 (Roll 21; 825.50: Economic Conditions)
33. Muñoz Cortés, *Sin dios ni patrones*, 44.
34. The full text of Valiente's claims is reproduced in Lagos Mieres, *Los Subversivos*, 176–178.
35. Grez Toso, *Historia del comunismo*, 110–111.
36. Lagos Mieres, *Los Subversivos*, 178.
37. Colonel-Prefect to the Intendent of the Province, January 6, 1921, AN/IS v. 506. Octavio Palmero in the meantime had been returned and jailed in Valparaíso. Colonel-Prefect to the Intendent of the Province, December 14, 1920, AN/IS v. 500.
38. This according to Barrios's birth certificate, for which I am indebted to Jorge Barrios Pulgar. Barrios too, we should recall, had been a member of the POS in 1918 and 1919 and, as the *proceso de los subversivos* came to its sorry conclusion, in December 1920, the POS sought admission to the Comintern. By 1922 it had become the Communist party of Chile. See Michael M. Hall and Hobart A. Spalding, Jr., "The Urban Working Class and Early Latin American Labour Movements, 1880–1930," in Leslie Bethell, ed., *The Cambridge History of Latin America: vol. 4, c. 1870–1930* (Cambridge: Cambridge University Press, 1986), 364. See also the overview in "Los trabajadores industriales del mundo de la región chilena y el Congreso de Berlin," November 21, 1922, IISH/DAS, carpeta 377, f. Chile.
39. Carlos Vicuña Fuentes, *En las prisiones políticas de Chile: Cuatro evasiones novelescas* (Santiago: Cruz del Sur, 1946), 23.
40. Vicuña Fuentes, *En las prisiones*, 26.
41. American Embassy, Santiago, *Report on General Conditions Prevailing in Chile*, March 7 to April 6, 1928, Records of the Department of State Relating to the Internal Affairs of Chile, 1910–1929 (Roll 9. 825.00 Political Affairs).
42. See Secretary of State Joseph Grew [?] to Honorable William M. Collier, American Ambassador, Santiago (undated but early April 1927); Ambassador Wm. Miller Collier to Secretary of State, May 13, 1927; and Ambassador Wm. Miller Collier to Secretary of State, June 1, 1927; all in Files on Bolshevism, in Records of the Department of State Relating to the Internal Affairs of Chile, 1910–1929 (Roll 9. 825.00 Political Affairs).
43. Meza Fuentes recounts his exile to the Juan Fernández archipelago in his *Los trágicos días de Más Afuera* (Santiago: LOM Ediciones, 2006), originally

published as a series of articles in the daily *Las Ultimas Noticias*, from August 1 to September 23, 1931. Eugenio González Rojas similarly captures the history of being incarcerated on the island in his *Más Afuera* (Santiago: LOM Ediciones, 1997 [1930]). See also Vicuña Fuentes, *En las prisiones*, 26–27.

44. American Embassy, Santiago, *Report on General Conditions Prevailing in Chile*, July 1, 1929 to August 15, 1929, Records of the Department of State Relating to the Internal Affairs of Chile, 1910–1929 (Roll 9. 825.00 Political Affairs).
45. Equipo Sombraysén, *Anarquismo y violencia popular en Chile, 1898–1927* (F.U.R.I.A.: Coyhaique, Patagonia, 2008), n.p.
46. Marcos Burich Parra, Carabrineros de Chile, Prefect of Tarapacá, to the Sub-Prefect of the Carabineros, Arica, September 24, 1930, in Lovemen and Lira, *Los Actos de la Dictadura*, 290–291; Guillermo Lora, *Historia del movimiento obrero boliviano, 1923–1933*, vol. 3, chap. 2.
47. Jesús Vicente Aguirre González, "Nieva: El largo verano del 36," *Boletín Informativo de la Asociación Benéfico-Cultural Nieva de Cameros*, Año 2007, No. 23 (2008), 38–42.
48. Barrios to Barros Castañón, September 1, 1930, ARNAD/MI v. 7668; Major Manuel Castillo Aracena, Subprefect Arica, Carabineros of Chile, to the Prefect of Carabineros in Tarapacá, October 3, 1930, in ARNAD/MI v. 7668.
49. Bianchi to the Minister of Foreign Relations, August 27, 1930, ARNAD/MI v. 7926 (1931).
50. Barros Castañón, Telegram 153, September 11, 1930, ARNAD/MI v. 7926 (1931).
51. Barros Castañón, Telegram 156, September 13, 1930, in ibid.
52. Barrios, "No es verdad que el pueblo chileno está contento con el dictador Carlos Ibáñez," *La República* (September 28, 1930) and Barrios, "Ha sonado la hora de las Revoluciones Libertadoras;" both enclosures in ARNAD/MI v. 7668. Cited text from Carabineros de Chile, Prefecture of Tarapacá, "Informe sobre reclamo de Casimiro Barrios," ARNAD/MI v. 7668; and Marcos Burich Parra, Carabineros de Chile, Prefect of Tarapacá, to the Sub-Prefect of the Carabineros, Arica, September 24, 1930 in Lovemen and Lira, *Los Actos de la Dictadura*, 290. For Barrios's letter, see Barrios to Marcos Burich, Carabineros de Chile, September 21, 1930, ARNAD/MI v. 7926.
53. Luis Troncoso, Intendent of Antofagasta, to the Minister of the Interior, October 14, 1930, Intendencia de Antofagasta v. 85.
54. Ambrosio Viaux, Brigadier General and Director General, Carabineros of Chile, to the Minister of the Interior, "Sobre situación del agitador Casimiro Barrios," No. 428, October 15, 1930 and Viaux to the Minister of the Interior, No. 416, October 10, 1930, both in ARNAD/MI v. 7668.
55. See, for example, Barrios to the Administrator of the Arica Mail Office (Correos de Arica), November 23, 1930, ARNAD/MI v. 7926 and Barrios to the Administrator of La Unión, November 27, 1930, ARNAD/MI v. 7926.
56. Fra Moreale, "Casimiro Barrios," *La República* (December 21, 1930), ARNAD/MI v. 7926; Bianchi to the Minister of Foreign Relations, December 26, 1930, ARNAD/MI v. 7926.
57. Townsend y Onel, *La inquisición chilena* (Valparaíso: Talleres Graficas "Augusto", 1932), 47–48.
58. Rencoret Donoso to the Prefect of Investigations, May 25, 1931, ARNAD/MI v. 7926.

59. 36th Session, August 5, 1931, *Cámara de diputados*, 1279. On Ventura Maturana, see, among others, "Efemérides." www.investigaciones.cl/paginas/mision/histo/efemerides/efemerides.htm. On his position in 1930, see Maturana, *Mi Ruta*, 123.
60. Maturana wrote a response to Townsend y Onel's many accusations: he remained silent regarding Casimiro Barrios. See Maturana, *Mi Ruta*. According to Townsend y Onel, Barrios was most likely murdered by the officials in Las Maitas in the Azapa valley. Townsend y Onel, *La inquisición chilena*, 48. His widow, Rosario Riveros Martínez, was paid reparations by the government in 1931, as part of the political investigations regarding the Ibáñez dictatorship. Elizabeth Lira and Brian Lovemen, *Políticas de reparación: Chile 1990–2004* (Santiago: LOM Ediciones, 2005), 25.
61. *Claridad* (June 17, 1922). The editorial is signed P.N. That Neruda was the author is confirmed in Hernán Loyola, ed., *Pablo Neruda: Obras Completas* (5 vols.) (Barcelona: Galaxia Gutenberg y Círculo de Lectores, 2001), 4: 263–264.
62. The professor was Guillermo Subercaseaux, as quoted in Barr-Melej, *Reforming Chile*, 184; for another example, see the comments of Oscar Chanks, in "Un diputado obrero," undated clipping in IISH/MSR, folder 16, (1921).
63. Gabriel Salazar Vergara, *Del poder constituyente de asalariados e intelectuales: Chile, siglo XX y XXI* (Santiago: LOM, 2009), 71.
64. *Verba Roja* 5:47 (June 1923), 1.
65. *La Voz del Mar* 2:33 (November 11, 1926), 6.
66. Manuel Rojas, *Manual de Literatura Chilena* (Mexico City: Universidad Nacional Autónoma de México, 1964), 93; *Araucaria de Chile* (1982), 17–18; Sergio González Miranda, comp., *La sociedad del salitre: Protagonistas, migraciones, cultura urbana y espacios públicos* (Santiago: RIL Editores, 2013), 278.
67. See "La tumba de José Domingo Gómez Rojas," photograph by Patricia Alfaro Insunza, in Museo de la Memoria y los Derechos Humanos, Archivo de Fondos y Colecciones, 309-000001-000342.
68. Enrique Lihn, notes on Domingo Gómez Rojas, Enrique Lihn Papers, 1941–1988, Getty Research Institute, Special Collections, Series II. Notebooks, circa 1960s–1980s, Box 12, folder 7, Carrasco [51].
69. See the interview with Brodsky in Leonardo Cisternas Zamora and Claudio Ogass Bilbao, coords, *Archivo Oral del Movimiento Estudiantil: Registrando las memorias de la refundación de la FECh* (Santiago: Archivo y Centro de Documentación FECh, 2014) and his "Prólogo" in the same volume as well as José Weinstein and Eduardo Valenzuela, "La FECh de los años veinte."
70. Díaz Eterovic, *Nadie Sabe Más que los Muertos* (Santiago: Planeta, 1993), 117–118.
71. Interview with Ricardo Brodsky, March 2015.
72. *The Clinic* (August 16, 2008), http://theclinicsemanal.blogspot.com/2008/08/grandes-conchesumadres.html, accessed June 6, 2013.
73. Andino Maldonado, "Introducción," in Rubén Andino Maldonado, *La rebelión estudiantil en Chile: Una generación con voz propia* (Santiago: OceanSur, 2014).
74. Ibid., 7.
75. For an excellent discussion and set of interviews, see Hugo Cristian Fernández, *Irrumpe la Capucha: ¿Qué quieren los anarquistas en el Chile de hoy?* (Santiago: OceanSur, 2014).

BIBLIOGRAPHY

ARCHIVES

Archivo Nacional de Chile
- Intendente de Santiago
- Fondo Colecciones y Archivos Particulares
- Judicial de Santiago, Criminal

Archivo Nacional de la Administración de Chile
- Ministerio del Interior
- Ministerio de Justicia

Biblioteca Nacional de Chile
- Archivo del Escritor

Getty Research Institute, Special Collections (US)
- Enrique Lihn Papers

International Institute for Social History (The Netherlands)
- Marcelo Segall Rosenmann collection
- Diego Abad de Santillán collection
- Unión Sociedad de los Tipógrafos de Santiago, Chile

Ministerio de Relaciones Exteriores de Chile
- Archivo General Histórico

PERIODICALS

Araucaria de Chile
Babel: Revista de arte y crítica
Boletín de los Trabajadores Industriales del Mundo
Bulletin of the Pan-American Union
Claridad: Periódico Semanal de Sociología, Arte y Actualidades
El Mercurio (Santiago)
El Mercurio (Antofagasta)
Ercilla
Juventud
La Nación
Las Noticias del Ultima Hora
Lider Provincial
Numen: Seminario de Arte, Sociología, Actualidades y Comercio
Palabra Escrita

Principios
Punto Final
Puru
Revista de la Policía de Valparaíso
Rumbo Nuevo: Organo oficial de la Federación de Empleados de Antofagasta
Sucesos: Revista Ilustrada de Actualidades
Verba Roja
Zig-Zag

WORKS CITED

Abensour, Miguel. *Democracy Against the State: Marx and the Machiavellian Moment.* Cambridge: Polity, 2011.

Acevedo Hernández, Antonio. *Memorias de un autor teatral.* Santiago: Editorial Nascimento, 1982.

Aguirre González, Jesús Vicente. "Nieva: El largo verano del '36," *Boletín Informativo de la Asociación Benéfico-Cultural Nieva de Cameros*, año 2006, no. 22 (2007), 38–42.

Aguirre, Carlos. *The Criminals of Lima and Their Worlds: The Prison Experience, 1850–1935.* Durham, NC: Duke University Press, 2005.

Aguirre, Carlos. "Carcel y sociedad en America Latina," in Eduardo Klingman Garcés, ed., *Historia social urbana: Espacios y flujos*, 209–252. Quito: Facultad Latinoamericana de Ciencias Sociales, 2009.

Ahmad, Aijaz. *In Theory: Classes, Nations, Literatures.* London: Verso, 1992.

Albonico Valenzuela, Fernando. *Derecho internacional privado chileno: leyes y tratados vigentes.* Santiago: Editorial Jurídica de Chile, 1958.

Alborñoz, Carlos. "Models of the Latin American University," in Joseph Maier and Richard W. Weatherhead, eds., *The Latin American University*, 123–134. Albuquerque: University of New Mexico Press, 1979.

Album gráfico de la Policía de Santiago. Santiago: n.p., 1923.

Aleinikoff, Thomas Alexander. *Semblances of Sovereignty: The Constitution, the State, and American Citizenship.* Cambridge, MA: Harvard University Press, 2009.

Alexander, Robert. *Arturo Alessandri: A Biography.* Ann Arbor: University of Michigan Microforms, 1977.

Alphonse Bertillon and the Identification of Persons (1880–1914).criminocorpus.org/en/museum/alphonse-bertillon-and-identification-persons-1880-1914/.

Altena, Bert, and Constance Bantman. "Introduction," in Constance Bantman and Bert Altena, eds., *Reassessing the Transnational Turn: Scales of Analysis in Anarchist and Syndicalist Studies*, 3–22. London: Routledge, 2014.

Amin, Shahid. *Event, Metaphor, Memory: Chauri Chaura 1922–1992.* Berkeley: University of California Press, 1995.

Anales de la Universidad de Chile 76 (March–April, 1889). Santiago: Imprenta Nacional, 1889.

Anderson, Benedict. *Under Three Flags: Anarchism and the Anti-Colonial Imagination.* London: Verso, 2007.

Andino Maldonado, Rubén. *La rebelión estudiantil en Chile: Una generación con voz propia.* Santiago: OceanSur, 2014.

Aránguiz Pinto, Santiago. "La Reforma Estudiantil en la Universidad de Chile entre 1920–1923 examinada a través de la revista *Claridad* de la Federación de Estudiantes: algunos elementos para su comprensión," *Mapocho: Revista de Humanidades* 58 (segundo semestre, 2005), 111–127.

Aránguiz Pinto, Santiago. "Renovarse o morir? La Federación de Estudiantes de Chile y la revista *Claridad*." BA thesis, Universidad Finis Terrae (Santiago), 2002.

Araya Saavedra, Mario. "Los Wobblies Criollos: Fundación e ideología en la Región chilena de la Industrial Workers of the World (1919–1927)," BA thesis, Universidad ARCIS (Santiago), 2008.

Arbitration Between Peru and Chile. The Case of Peru, In the matter of the controversy arising out of the Question of the Pacific, Before the President of the United States of America. Washington, DC: National Capital Press, 1923.

Arrellano, Ramón. "Aquellos emigrantes," *Boletín 2008 Asociación Benéfico-Cultural Nieva de Cameros*, año 2007, no. 23 (2008), 58–65.

Bantman, Constance and Bert Altena, eds. *Reassessing the Transnational Turn: Scales of Analysis in Anarchist and Syndicalist Studies*. London: Routledge, 2014.

Barbosa, Francisco J. "July 23, 1959: Student Protest and State Violence as Myth and Memory in León, Nicaragua," *Hispanic American Historical Review* 85:2 (May 2005), 187–222.

Barbusse, Henri. *Light*. New York: E. P. Dutton & Co., 1919.

Barbusse, Henri. *Under Fire: The Story of a Squad*. New York: E. P. Dutton & Co., 1917.

Barría Serón, Jorge. *Los movimientos sociales desde 1910 hasta 1926*. Santiago: Editorial Universitaria, 1960.

Barrios, Ciriaco. *La Patria del Pobre*. Santiago: Imprenta i Encuadranación Galvez, 1911.

Barrios, Ciriaco. *Recuerdos: Poesías*. Santiago: Imprenta Franklin, 1912.

Barr-Melej, Patrick. *Reforming Chile: Cultural Politics, Nationalism, and the Rise of the Middle Class*. Chapel Hill: University of North Carolina Press, 2000.

Barrutieta, José Angel. "Ciriaco Barrios: Un poeta nevero en ultramar," *Boletín Informativo Asociación Benéfico-Cultural Nieva de Cameros*, año 2006, no. 22 (2007), 78–79.

Barrutieta, José Angel. "Ciriaco Barrios: Vida y obras de un poeta en el centenario de su muerte," *Boletín 2008 Asociación Benéfico-Cultural Nieva de Cameros*, año 2007, no. 23 (2008), 66–75.

Bayer, Osvaldo. *La Patagonia Rebelde*. Buenos Aires: Planeta, 1980.

Bayer, Osvaldo. *Los anarquistas expropiadores*. Barcelona: Virus, 2003.

Benadava, Santiago. *Crímenes y casos célebres*. Santiago: LexisNexis, 2002.

Berger, John. *And Our Faces, My Heart, Brief as Photos*. New York: Vintage, 1992.

Berger, John. *Understanding a Photograph* (ed. Geoff Dyer). New York: Aperture, 2013.

Berkman, Alexander. *Prison Memoirs of an Anarchist*. New York: New York Review of Books Classics, 1999 [1912].

Bethell, Leslie, ed. *The Cultural History of Latin America: Literature, Music, and the Visual Arts in the 19th and 20th Centuries*. Cambridge: Cambridge University Press, 1998.

Bey, Hakim. *T.A.Z. The Temporary Autonomous Zone, Ontological Anarchy, Poetic Terrorism*. 2nd ed. Brooklyn: Autonomedia, 2003.

Boletín de las leyes y decretos del gobierno, segundo semestre de 1888. Santiago, 1888.

Bonilla, Frank, and Myron Glazer. *Student Politics in Chile*. New York: Basic Books, 1970.

Bookchin, Murray. *Social Anarchism or Lifestyle Anarchism: An Unbridgeable Chasm*. Oakland, CA: AK Press, 2001.

Bookchin, Murray. *The Spanish Anarchists: The Heroic Years, 1868–1936*. Oakland, CA: AK Press, 2001.

Bosteels, Bruno. "Neither Proletarian nor Vanguard: On a Certain Underground Current of Anarchist Socialism in Mexico," in Barry Maxwell and Raymond Craib, eds., *No Gods, No Masters, No Peripheries: Global Anarchisms*, 336–347. Oakland: PM Press, 2015.

Briggs, Laura, Gladys McCormick, and J. T. Way. "Transnationalism: A Category of Analysis," *American Quarterly* 60:3 (September 2008), 625–648.

Brissenden, Paul. *The I.W.W.* New York: n.p., 1919.

Brodsky, Pascual. "Prólogo," in José Santos González Vera, *Obras Completas* (2 vols.). Santiago: Cociña, Soria Editores, 2013.

Butterworth, Alex. *The World That Never Was: A True Story of Dreamers, Schemers, Anarchists and Secret Agents*. New York: Pantheon, 2010.

Caballero y Rubio, Ramón. *Diccionario de modismos: (frases y metáforas) primero y único de su género en España*. Madrid: E. García Rico, 1905.

Cain, Frank. "The Industrial Workers of the World: Aspects of its Suppression in Australia, 1916–1919," *Labour History* 42 (May 1982), 54–62.

Calderón, Alfonso. *Memorial de Santiago*. Santiago: RIL, 2005.

Calderón, Alfonso. *Según pasan los años: entrevistas, retratos, recuerdos*. Santiago: Editorial Andrés Bello, 1990.

Cámara de Diputados: Boletín de las Sesiones Estraordinarias en 1918–1919. Santiago de Chile: Imprenta Nacional, 1918.

Cámara de Diputados: Boletín de las Sesiones Ordinarias en 1920. Santiago: Imprenta Nacional, 1920.

Cámara de Senadores: Boletín de las Sesiones Estraordinarias en 1918. Santiago: Imprenta Nacional, 1918.

Cámara de Senadores: Boletín de las Sesiones Ordinarias en 1919. Santiago: Imprenta Nacional, 1919.

Cámara de Senadores: Boletín de las Sesiones Ordinarias en 1920. Santiago: Imprenta Nacional, 1920.

Carey, Elaine. *Plaza of Sacrifices: Gender, Terror and Power in 1968 Mexico*. Albuquerque: University of New Mexico Press, 2005.

Carter, Paul. *The Road to Botany Bay: An Exploration of Landscape and History*. Minneapolis: University of Minnesota Press, 2010 [1988].

Ciccariello-Maher, George. "An Anarchism That Is Not Anarchism," in Jimmy Casas Klausen and James Martel, eds., *How Not to Be Governed: Readings and Interpretations from a Critical Anarchist Left*, 19–46. Lanham, MD: Lexington Books, 2011.

Clark, John, and Camille Martin, eds. *Anarchy, Geography, Modernity: Selected Writing of Elisée Reclus*. Oakland: PM Press, 2013.

Clastres, Pierre. *Society Against the State: Essays in Political Anthropology*. New York: Zone Books, 1989.

Cohn, Jesse. *Underground Passages: Anarchist Resistance Culture, 1848–2011*. Oakland: AK Press, 2014.

Collier, Simon, and William Sater, *A History of Chile, 1808–2002*, 2nd ed. Cambridge: Cambridge University Press, 2004.

Conferencia Internacional Sudamericana de Policía (Febrero 20/29 de 1920): Convenio y Actas. Buenos Aires: José Tragant, 1920.

Cordero R., Raúl. *Banco del Estado de Chile: Historia de la Caja del Crédito Hipotecario*. Santiago: El Banco de Chile, 1999.

Coronas fúnebres. Santiago: Imprenta Cervantes, 1921.

Cortés, Dario. *La narrativa anarquista de Manuel Rojas*. Madrid: Pliegos, 1986.

Craib, Raymond B. "Students, Anarchists and Categories of Persecution in Chile, 1920," *A Contracorriente* 8:1 (Fall 2010), 22–60.

Craib, Raymond B. "A Foreword," in Barry Maxwell and Raymond Craib, eds., *No Gods, No Masters, No Peripheries: Global Anarchisms*, 1–8. Oakland: PM Press, 2015.

Craib, Raymond B. "Sedentary Anarchists," in Constance Bantman and Bert Altena, eds., *Reassessing the Transnational Turn: Scales of Analysis in Anarchist and Syndicalist Studies*, 139–156. London: Routledge, 2014.

Craib, Raymond B. "The Firecracker Poet: Three poems of José Domingo Gómez Rojas," *New Letters: A Magazine of Writing & Art* 78:1 (Fall 2011), 71–79.

Cruz-Coke, Ricardo. *Historia de la medicina en Chile*. Santiago: Andrés Bello, 1995.

Cushman, Gregory. *Guano and the Opening of the Pacific World: A Global Ecological History*. Cambridge: Cambridge University Press, 2013.

De Diego Maestri, Patricio Luis Peña Rojas, and Claudio Peralta Castillo, *La Asamblea Obrera de Alimentación Nacional: Un hito en la historia de Chile*. Santiago: Sociedad Chilena de Sociología, 2002.

De la Vega, Daniel. *Ayer y hoy: antología de escritos*. Santiago: Editorial Universitaria, 1997.

De LaForcade, Geoffroy. "Ghosts of Insurgencies Past: Waterfront Labor, Working Class Memory, and the Contentious Emergence of the National-Popular State in Argentina," in Barry Maxwell and Raymond Craib, eds., *No Gods, No Masters, No Peripheries: Global Anarchisms*, 180–214. Oakland: PM Press, 2015.

Del Mazo, Gabriel, ed. *La Reforma Universitaria*, 5 vols. Buenos Aires: Ferrari Hmnos., 1927.

Del Solar, Felipe and Andrés Pérez. *Anarquistas: Presencia libertaria en Chile*. Santiago: RIL, 2008.

Délano, Luis Enrique. *El Año 20*. Santiago: Piñeda Libros, 1973.

Délano, Luis Enrique. *Memorias*. Santiago: RIL, 2004.

Dening, Greg. *The Death of William Gooch: A History's Anthropology*. Honolulu: University of Hawai'i Press, 1995.

DeShazo, Peter. *Urban Workers and Labor Unions in Chile, 1902–1927*. Madison: University of Wisconsin Press, 1983.

Deutsch, Sandra. *Las Derechas: The Extreme Right in Argentina, Brazil and Chile, 1890–1939*. Redwood City, CA: Stanford University Press, 1999.

Díaz Eterovic, Ramón. *Nadie Sabe Más que los Muertos*. Santiago: Planeta, 1993.

Dirlik, Arif. "Anarchism and the Question of Place," in Lucien van der Walt and Steven Hirsch, eds., *Anarchism and Syndicalism in the Colonial and Postcolonial World, 1870–1940: The Praxis of National Liberation, Internationalism, and Social Revolution*, 131–146. Leiden: Brill, 2010.

Dostoevsky, Fyodor. *The Brothers Karamazov*, trans. by Constance Garnett. Pennsylvania: The Franklin Library, 1977.

Drinot, Paulo. *The Allure of Labor: Workers, Race, and the Making of the Peruvian State*. Durham, NC: Duke University Press, 2011.

Dubovsky, Melvin. *We Shall Be All: A History of the Industrial Workers of the World*. New York: Quadrangle Books, 1969.

Duffy Burnett, Christina, and Burke Marshall,eds., *Foreign in a Domestic Sense: Puerto Rico, American Expansion, and the Constitution*. Durham, NC: Duke University Press, 2001.

Durán Cerda, Julio. "El teatro chileno moderno," *Anales de la Universidad de Chile* Año CXXI: 126 (January–April, 1963), 168–203.

Ealham, Chris. *Anarchism and the City: Revolution and Counter-Revolution in Barcelona, 1898–1937.* Oakland: AK Press, 2010.

Eastman, Max. "The Clarté Movement," *The Liberator* 3:4 (April 1920), 40–42.

Edwards, Alberto. *Román Calvo: El Sherlock Holmes Chileno*. Santiago: Editorial del Pacífico, 1953.

Edwards Bello, Joaquín. *El Roto*. Santiago: Editorial Universitaria, 2006 [1920].

Edwards Bello, Joaquín. *Francisco Miranda y otros personajes*. Santiago: Andrés Bello, 1970.

Edwards, Ryan. "From the Depths of Patagonia: The Ushuaia Penal Colony and the Nature of 'The End of the World,'" *Hispanic American Historical Review* 94:2 (May 2014), 271–302.

Edwards, Ryan. "An Ecology of Exile: Earth and Elsewhere in Argentina's Ushuaia Penal Colony (1860–1960)," Ph.D. dissertation in progress, Cornell University.

En la tumba del estudiante poeta, Domingo Gómez Rojas. s.n. 1921.

Equipo Sombraysén, *Anarquismo y violencia popular en Chile, 1898–1927.* Coyhaique, Patagonia: F.U.R.I.A., 2008.

Errázuriz, Tomás. "El asalto de los motorizados: El transporte moderno y la crisis del tránsito público en Santiago, 1900-1927," *Historia* 43:2 (July–December 2010), 357–411.

Escudero, Alfonso M. *Eliodoro Astorquiza, el que pudo haber sido nuestro mejor crítico.* Santiago: Nascimento, 1934.

Fegerstrom, René Peri. *Historia de la Función Policial en Chile: Apuntes y transcripciones, 3a parte (1900–1927)*. Santiago: Carabineros de Chile, 1982.

Felstiner, John. *Translating Neruda: The Way to Macchu Picchu*. Redwood City, CA: Stanford University Press, 1980.

Fernández Pesquero, Javier. *Monografía Estadística de la Colonia Española de Chile en el año 1909*. Cádiz: Talleres Tipográficos de Manuel Alvarez, 1909.

Fernández, Hugo Cristián. *Irrumpe la Capucha: ¿Qué quieren los anarquistas en el Chile de hoy?* Santiago: OceanSur, 2014.

Fernández-Pradel, Pedro Xavier. *Linajes Vascos y Montañeses en Chile*. Santiago: Talleres Gráficos San Rafael, 1930.

Ferreira de Cassone, Florencia. *Claridad y el internacionalismo Americano*. Buenos Aires: Editorial Claridad, 1998.

Figueroa, Virgilio. *Diccionario Histórico, Biográfico y Bibliográfico de Chile.* Santiago: Establecimientos Gráficos Balcells y Co., 1928.

Franco, Jean. *The Modern Culture of Latin America*. New York: Praeger, 1967.

Frazier, Lessie Jo, and Deborah Cohen. "Defining the Space of Mexico '68: Heroic Masculinity in the Prison and "Women" in the Streets," *Hispanic American Historical Review* 83:4 (November 2003), 617–660.

Frazier, Lessie Jo. *The Salt in the Sand: Memory, Violence and the Nation-State in Chile, 1890 to the Present*. Durham, NC: Duke University Press, 2007.

Freitag, Ulrich, and Achim von Oppen. "Translocality: An Approach to Connection and Transfer in Area Studies," in Ulrich Freitag and Achim von Oppen, eds., *Translocality: An Approach to Globalising Processes from a Southern Perspective*, 1–22. Leiden: Brill, 2010.

Fritzsche, Peter. *Reading Berlin 1900*. Cambridge, MA: Harvard University Press, 1996.

Gaceta de los Tribunales Año 1918: Noviembre y Diciembre. Santiago: Dirección Jeneral de Talleres Fiscales de Prisiones, 1925.

Gage, Beverly. *The Day Wall Street Exploded: A Story of America in its First Age of Terror*. New York: Oxford University Press, 2009.

Gamarra Romero, Juan Manuel. *La Reforma Universitaria: El movimiento estudiantil de los años veinte en el Perú*. Lima: Okura, 1987.

Gänger, Stefanie. "Conquering the Past: Post-War Archaeology and Nationalism in the Borderlands of Chile and Peru, c. 1880–1920," *Comparative Studies in Society and History* 51:4 (2009), 691–714.

Garcés, Mario. *El "despertar" de la sociedad: Los movimientos sociales en América Latina y Chile*. Santiago: LOM Ediciones, 2012.

García-Cuerdas, Juan Antonio. "Las desventuras de dos anarquistas cameranos en el norte de Chile," *Análisis* 52, http://dialnet.unirioja.es/servlet/fichero_articulo?codigo=2954359&orden=0.

García-Cuerdas, Juan Antonio. "Los almacenes Giménez," *Boletín Informativo de la Asociación Benéfico Cultural Nieva de Cameros y Montemediano*, año 2008, no. 24 (2009), 65–69.

Gelvin, James. "Al-Qaeda and Anarchism: A Historian's Reply to Terrorology," *Terrorism and Political Violence* 20:4 (2008), 563–581.

Gilroy, Paul. *The Black Atlantic: Modernity and Double Consciousness*. Cambridge, MA: Harvard University Press, 1993.

Glasser, Otto. *Wilhelm Conrad Roentgen and the Early History of the Roentgen Rays*. San Francisco: Norman Publishing, 1993 [1934].

Goicovic Donoso, Igor. "Del control social a la política social: La conflictiva relación entre los jóvenes populares y el Estado de Chile," *Ultima Década* 12 (marzo, 2000), 103–123.

Godoy Sepúlveda, Eduardo Andrés. *La Huelga del Mono: Los anarquistas y las movilizaciones contra el retrato obligatorio (Valparaíso, 1913)*. Santiago: Quimantú, 2014.

Gold, Peter J. "The Influence of Henri Barbusse in Bolivia," *Bulletin of Latin American Research* 2:2 (May 1983), 117–122.

Gómez Rojas, José Domingo. *Rebeldías Líricas y otros versos*. Talca: Ediciónes Acéfalo, n.d. [c. 2013].

Gómez Rojas, José Domingo. *Rebeldías Líricas*, ed. by Andrés Sabella. Santiago: Ediciones Ercilla, 1940.

González Ginouves, Ignacio. "El Juan Gandulfo de mis recuerdos," *Anales Chilenos de Historia de la Medicina* 2 (1962), 145–157.

González le Saux, Marianne. *De empresarios a empleados: Clase media y estado docente en Chile, 1810–1920*. Santiago: LOM Ediciones, 2011.

González Miranda, Sergio. *El dios cautivo: Las Ligas Patrióticas en la chilenización compulsiva de Tarapacá (1910–1922)*. Santiaigo: LOM Ediciones, 2004.

González Miranda, Sergio, comp., *La sociedad del salitre: Protagonistas, migraciones, cultura urbana y espacios públicos*. Santiago: RIL, 2013.

González Prada, Manuel. *Free Pages and Hard Times: Anarchist Musings*. New York: Oxford University Press, 2003.

González Varas, Carolina. "La espiritualidad cristiana en el hablante de Domingo Gómez Rojas," *Literatura y Linguistica* 23 (2011), 15–28.

González Vera, José Santos. "Estudiantes del año veinte," *Babel: Revista de arte y crítica* año XI, vol. 7, no. 28 (julio–agosto 1945), 34–44.

González Vera, José Santos. *Cuando era muchacho*. Santiago: Editorial Universitaria, 1996 [1951].

González Vera, José Santos. *Obras Completas* (2 vols.). Santiago: Cociña, Soria Editores, 2013.

González Vera, José Santos. *Vidas Mínimas*. Santiago: LOM Ediciones, 1996 [1923].

González Vera, José Santos. "Los anarquistas," in Carmen Soria, ed., *Letras Anarquistas: José Santos González Vera y Manuel Rojas: Artículos periodísticas y otros escritos inéditos*, 245–263. Santiago: Planeta, 2005.

González Rojas, Eugenio. *Más Afuera*. Santiago: LOM Ediciones, 1997 [1930].

Gould, Jeffrey L. "Solidarity Under Siege: The Latin American Left, 1968," *American Historical Review* 114: 2 (April 2009), 348–375.

Graeber, David. *Fragments of an Anarchist Anthropology*. Chicago: Prickly Pear Press, 2003.

Graeber, David. "The New Anarchists," *New Left Review* 13 (January/February 2002), 61–73.

Grandin, Greg. *Empire's Workshop: Latin America, the United States, and the Rise of the New Imperialism*. New York: Metropolitan Books, 2006.

Grez Toso, Sergio. *Historia del comunismo en Chile: La era de Recabarren (1912–1924)*. Santiago: LOM Ediciones, 2011.

Grez Toso, Sergio. *Los anarquistas y el movimiento obrero: La alborada de "la idea" en Chile, 1893–1915*. Santiago: LOM Ediciones, 2007.

Grubačić, Andrej, and David Graeber, "Anarchism or the Revolutionary Movement of the Twenty-First Century," http://tal.bolo-bolo.co/en/a/ag/andrej-grubacic-david-graeber-anarchism-or-the-revolutionary-movement-of-the-twenty-first-centu.pdf.

Grubačić, Andrej. "The Anarchist Moment," in Jacob Blumenfield, Chiara Boticci, and Simon Critchley, eds., *The Anarchist Turn*, 187–202. London: Pluto Books, 2013.

Guerin, Daniel. *No Gods, No Masters: An Anthology of Anarchism*. Oakland, CA: AK Press, 2005.

Guía General de Santiago de Chile, 1918. 2nd ed. Santiago: Imprenta Siglo XX, 1918.

Gurría García, Pedro A., and Mercedes Lázaro Ruiz. *Tener un Tío en América: La emigración riojana a ultramar (1880–1936)*. Logroño: Instituto de Estudios Riojanos, 2002.

Hall, Michael M., and Hobart A. Spalding, Jr. "The Urban Working Class and early Latin American Labour Movements, 1880–1930," in Leslie Bethell, ed., *The Cambridge History of Latin America: vol. 4, c. 1870–1930*, 325–366. Cambridge: Cambridge University Press, 1986.

Halperín Donghi, Tulio. *Historia de la Universidad de Buenos Aires*. Buenos Aires: Editorial Universitaria, 1962.

Harambour Ross, Alberto. "'Jesto y palabra, idea y acción': La historia de Efraín Plaza Olmedo," in Marcos Fernández et. al., *Arriba quemando el sol: Estudios de Historia Social Chilena: Experiencias populares de trabajo, revuelta y autonomía (1830–1940)*, 137–193. Santiago: LOM Ediciones, 2004.

Harvey, David. "Cosmopolitanism and the Banality of Geographical Evils," *Public Culture* 12:2 (2000), 529–564.

Harvey, David. "Militant Particularism and Global Ambition: The Conceptual Politics of Space, Place and Environment in the Work of Raymond Williams," *Social Text* 42 (Spring, 1995), 69–98.

Harvey, David. *The Condition of Postmodernity: An Enquiry in to the Origins of Cultural Change*. Oxford: Wiley-Blackwell, 1991.

Hebdige, Dick. *Subculture: The Meaning of Style*. London: Routledge, 1979.

Hernández Ponce, Roberto and Jule Salazar González. *De la policía secreta a la policía científica*. Santiago: Sección Impr. de la Policía de Investigaciones de Chile, 1994.

Herzog, Todd. *Crime Stories: Criminalistic Fantasy and the Crisis of Culture in Weimar Germany*. Oxford: Berghahn Books, 2009.

Hidalgo Dattwyler, Rodrigo. *La vivienda social en Chile y la construcción del espacio urbano en el Santiago del siglo XX*. Santiago: Dirección de Bibliotecas, Archivos, y Museos de Chile, 2005.

Hirsch, Steven. "Without Borders: Reflections on Anarchism in Latin America," *Estudios Interdisciplinarios de América Latina* 22:2 (2011), 6–10.

Hutchinson, Elizabeth. *Labors Appropriate to Their Sex: Gender, Labor and Politics in Urban Chile, 1900–1930*. Durham, NC: Duke University Press, 2001.

Hutchinson, Elizabeth. "From 'La mujer esclava' to 'La mujer limón': Anarchism and the Politics of Sexuality in Early Twentieth-Century Chile," *Hispanic American Historical Review* 81:3–4 (2001), 519–553.

Ignotus. "Construcción simbólica y ritualística a raíz de la matanza de Santa María de Iquique (principios del siglo XX)," http://archivohistoricolarevuelta.wordpress.com/2012/12/19/construccion-simbolica-y-ritualistica-a-raiz-de-la-matanza-de-santa-maria-de-iquique/.

Ignotus. *Los Anarquistas: Vidas que se autoconstruyen*. Santiago: Ediciones Spartacus, 2011.

Indice de propietarios rurales y valor de la propiedad rural según los roles de avalúos comunales. Santiago: Sociedad Imprenta y Litografía Universo, 1908.

Ireland, Tomás. *Nuestro Cobre: Memorias de la primera administración de la mina El Teniente*. Santiago: Editorial Universidad de Santiago de Chile, 2015.

Ireland, Tomás. *Roquerío*. Toronto: Michael Graphics, 2011.

Jaksíc, Iván. *Academic Rebels in Chile: The Role of Philosophy in Higher Education and Politics*. Albany: SUNY Press, 1989.

Johnston, Robert. *The Radical Middle Class: Populist Democracy and the Question of Capitalism in Progressive Era Portland, Oregon*. Princeton, NJ: Princeton University Press, 2003.

Juan Gandulfo Guerra: Homenaje de sus amigos. Santiago: Editorial del Pacífico, 1957.

Kennedy, Thomas. *Greene's Summer*. Galway: Wynkin deWorde, 2004.

Kennedy, Thomas. *In the Company of Angels*. New York: Bloomsbury, 2012.

Khuri-Makdisi, Ilham. *The Eastern Mediterranean and the Making of Global Radicalism, 1860–1914*. Berkeley: University of California Press, 2010.

Kinna, Ruth, ed., *The Continuum Companion to Anarchism*. London: Continuum, 2012.

Kirkendall, Andrew. *Class Mates: Male Student Culture and the Making of a Political Class in Nineteenth Century Brazil*. Lincoln: University of Nebraska Press, 2002.

Klausen, Jimmy Casas, and James Martel, eds. *How Not to Be Governed: Readings and Interpretations from a Critical Anarchist Left*. Lanham, MD: Lexington Books, 2011.

Kohan, Néstor. *Marx en su (Tercer) Mundo: Hacia un socialismo no colonizado*, 2nd ed. Buenos Aires: Biblios, 1998.

Konishi, Sho. *Anarchist Modernity: Cooperatism and Japanese-Russian Intellectual Relations in Modern Japan*. Cambridge, MA: Harvard University Press, 2013.

Kropotkin, Peter. "What Geography Ought to Be," *The Nineteenth Century* 18 (1885), 940–956.

Kropotkin, Peter. *Mutual Aid: A Factor of Evolution*. Boston: Porter Sargent Publishers, 1914.

Kropotkin, Peter. *The Conquest of Bread and Other Writings.* Cambridge: Cambridge University Press, 1995 [1892].

Labarca, Santiago. *Figuras de Agitadores.* Santiago: Cosmos, 1923.

Lagnado, Jake. "La inverosímil travesía de Nicolás Gutarra," *Pacarina del Sur: Revista de Pensamiento Crítico Latinoamericano,* www.pacarinadelsur.com/home/huellas-y-voces/1137-la-inverosimil-travesia-de-nicolas-gutarra#_edn1.

Lagos Mieres, Manuel. *Los "Subversivos": Las maquinaciones del poder, "República" de Chile, 1920.* Santiago: Quimantú, 2011.

Lamas, Alvaro. *Desde la cárcel.* Santiago: Imprenta y Litografía Universo, 1905.

Langland, Victoria. *Speaking of Flowers: Student Movements and the Making and Remembering of 1968 in Military Brazil.* Durham, NC: Duke University Press, 2013.

Langland, Victoria. "Birth Control Pills and Molotov Cocktails: Reading Sex and Revolution in 1968 Brazil," in Gilbert M. Joseph and Daniela Spenser, eds., *In From the Cold: Latin America's New Encounter with the Cold War,* 308–349. Durham, NC: Duke University Press, 2008.

Langland, Victoria. "La casa de la memoria en Praia de Flamengo 132: memorias estudiantiles y nacionales en Brasil, 1964–1980," in Elizabeth Jelin and Victoria Langland, comps., *Monumentos, memoriales y marcas territoriales,* 57–96 Buenos Aires: Siglo XXI Editores, 2003.

Larsen, Neil. *Determinations: Essays on Theory, Narrative and Nation in the Americas.* London: Verso, 2001.

Larsen, Neil. *Reading North by South: On Latin American Literature, Culture and Politics.* Minneapolis: University of Minnesota Press, 1995.

Latour, Bruno. *We Have Never Been Modern.* Trans. Catherine Porter. Cambridge, MA: Harvard University Press, 2003.

Laval, Ramón A. *Paremiología chilena. Discurso leido por don Ramón A. Laval, en su incorporación el 30 de noviembre de 1923 y contestación de don José Toribio Medina.* Santiago de Chile: Imprenta Universitaria, 1923.

Lefebvre, Henri. *State/Space/World: Selected Essays,* ed. Neil Brenner and Stuart Elden. Minneapolis: University of Minnesota Press, 2009.

León León, Marco Antonio. *Encierro y corrección: la configuración de un sistema de prisiones en Chile: 1800-1911* (3 vols.) Santiago: Universidad Central de Chile, Facultad de Ciencias Jurídicas y Sociales, 2003.

Levy, Carl. "Social Histories of Anarchism," *Journal for the Study of Radicalism* 4:2 (Fall 2010), 1–44.

Linebaugh, Peter, and Marcus Rediker. *The Many-Headed Hydra: Sailors, Slaves, Commoners, and the Hidden History of the Revolutionary Atlantic.* Boston: Beacon Press, 2000.

Lira, Elizabeth, and Brian Lovemen. *Políticas de reparación: Chile 1990–2004.* Santiago: LOM Ediciones, 2005.

Lomnitz, Claudio. *The Return of Comrade Flores Magón.* New York: Zone Books, 2014.

López, Osvaldo. *Diccionario Biográfico Obrero de Chile.* Santiago: Imprenta Bellavista, 1912.

Lora, Guillermo. *Historia del movimiento obrero boliviano (1923–1933)* (3 vols.) La Paz: Editorial Los Amigos del Libro, 1967–1970.

Lorwin, Lewis L. *Historia del internacionalismo obrero,* trans. Luis Dávila. Santiago: Biblioteca Ercilla, 1936.

Losurdo, Domenico. *Liberalism: A Counter-History.* London: Verso Press, 2011.

Loveman, Brian, and Elizabeth Lira. *Los Actos de la Dictadura*. Santiago: LOM Ediciones, 2006.

Loveman, Brian, and Elizabeth Lira. *Arquitectura política y seguridad interior del Estado: Chile 1811–1990*. Santiago: LOM Ediciones, 2002.

Loveman, Brian. *Chile: The Legacy of Hispanic Capitalism*. 3rd ed. New York: Oxford University Press, 2001.

Loyola, Hernán ed., *Pablo Neruda: Obras Completas* (5 vols.) Barcelona: Galaxia Gutenberg y Círculo de Lectores, 2001.

Luxemburg, Rosa. *Social Reform or Revolution?* London: Militant Publications, 1986 [1900; 1908].

Maeterlinck, Maurice. *The Blue Bird: A Fairy Play in Five Acts*, trans. Alexander Teixera de Mattos. New York: Dodd, Mead and Co., 1910.

Maier, Charles. *Leviathan 2.0: Inventing Modern Statehood*. Cambridge, MA: Harvard University Press, 2014.

Maldonado Prieto, Carlos. "Militarización de la policía: Una tendencia histórica chilena," www.memoriachilena.cl/archivos2/pdfs/MC0018154.pdf.

Maldonado Prieto, Carlos. "La Prusia del América del Sur: Acerca de las relaciones militares Chileno-Germanas (1927–1945)," www.archivochile.com/Poder_Dominante/ffaa_y_orden/Sobre/PDffaasobre0027.pdf.

Mallon, Florencia. *Courage Tastes of Blood: The Mapuche Community of Nicolás Ailío and the Chilean State, 1906–2001*. Durham, NC: Duke University Press, 2005.

Mamalakis, Markos J. comp., *Historical Statistics of Chile: Demography and Labor Force (vol. 2)* Westport, CT: Greenwood Press, 1980.

Mancisador, José, *Henri Barbusse: Ingeniero de almas*. Mexico: Ediciones Botas, 1945.

Manzano, Valeria. *The Age of Youth in Argentina: Culture, Politics and Sexuality from Perón to Videla*. Chapel Hill: University of North Carolina Press, 2014.

Martel, James and Jimmy Casas Klausen, "Introduction: How Not to Be Governed," in Klausen and Martel, eds., *How Not to Be Governed: Readings and Interpretations from a Critical Anarchist Left*. Lanham, MD: Lexington Books, 2011.

Massey, Doreen. "A Global Sense of Place," in Doreen Massey, *Space, Place and Gender*, 146–156. Minneapolis: University of Minnesota Press, 1994.

Massey, Doreen. "Places and their Pasts," *History Workshop Journal* 39: 1 (1995), 182–192.

Massey, Doreen. *For Space*. Thousand Oaks, CA: Sage, 2005.

Maturana Barahona, Ventura. *Mi Ruta*. Buenos Aires: n.p., 1936.

Maureira, Hugo Alberto. "Los culpables de la miseria: Poverty and Public Health during the Spanish Influenza Epidemic in Chile, 1918–1920," PhD diss., Georgetown University, 2012.

Maxwell, Barry, and Raymond Craib, eds., *No Gods, No Masters, No Peripheries: Global Anarchisms*. Oakland: PM Press, 2015.

May, Todd. *The Political Thought of Jacques Ranciere: Creating Equality*. University Park: Pennsylvania State University Press, 2008.

Memoria del Ministerio de Justicia (1917–1921). Santiago: Imp. Fiscal de la Penitenciaría, 1921.

Memoria del Ministerio de Justicia (Diciembre 1915–Junio 1917). Santiago: Imp. Lit. y Enc. Fiscal de la Penitenciaría, 1917.

Merriman, John. *The Dynamite Club: How a Bombing in Fin-de-Siecle Paris Ignited the Age of Modern Terror*. Boston: Houghton Mifflin Harcourt, 2009.

Meza Fuentes, Roberto. "Domingo Gómez Rojas: El poeta mártir," in Gabriel del Mazo, *La Reforma Universitaria* (Vol. VI). Buenos Aires: Ferrari Hmnos, 1927.

Meza Fuentes, Roberto. *Los trágicos días de Más Afuera*. Santiago: LOM Ediciones, 2006.

Millar Carvacho, René. *La elección presidencial de 1920*. Santiago: Editorial Universitaria, 1982.

Montes de Oca, Rodolfo. *Anarquismo y cárceles: Píxeles para entender la critica antiautoritaria y abolicionista a las Prisiones*. Medellín: CorazónDeFuego, s/f., http://corazondefuegorecs.files.wordpress.com/2010/05/anarquismo-y-carceles_web.pdf.

Moraga Valle, Fabio and Carlos Vega Delgado. *José Domingo Gómez Rojas: Vida y obra*. Punta Arenas: Atelí, 1997.

Moraga Valle, Fabio. *"Muchachos casi silvestres": La Federación de Estudiantes y el movimiento estudiantil chileno, 1906–1936*. Santiago: Universidad de Chile, 2007.

Morris, James O. *Elites, Intellectuals and Consensus: A Study of the Social Question and the Industrial Relations System in Chile*. Ithaca, NY: Cornell University School of Industrial Relations, 1966.

Mouesca, Jacqueline and Carlos Orellana. *Cine y memoria del siglo XX*. Santiago: LOM Ediciones, 1998.

Moya, José. "A Continent of Immigrants: Postcolonial Shifts in the Western Hemisphere," *Hispanic American Historical Review* 86:1 (February 2006), 1–28.

Moya, José. "Italians in Buenos Aires' Anarchist Movement: Gender Ideology and Women's Participation," in Donna R. Gabaccia and Franca Iacovetta, eds., *Women, Gender and Transnational Lives: Italian Workers of the World*, 189–216. Toronto: University of Toronto Press, 2002.

Muñoz Cortés, Víctor. "Anarquismo en Chile. Una promesa?" in *Le Monde Diplomatique* (edición chilena), www.lemondediplomatique.cl/article3170,3170.html.

Muñoz Cortés, Víctor. *Armando Triviño, Wobblie: Hombres, ideas y problemas del anarquismo en los años '20. Vida y escritos de un libertario criollo*. Santiago: Editorial Quimantú, 2007.

Muñoz Cortés, Víctor. *Cuando la patria mata: La historia del anarquista Julio Rebosio*. Santiago: Editorial USACH, 2011.

Muñoz Cortés, Víctor. *Sin Dios ni Patrones: Historia, diversidad y conflictos del anarquismo en la región chilena*. Valparaíso: Mar y Tierra, 2014.

Muñoz, Diego *Memorias: Recuerdos de la bohemia nerudiana*. Santiago: Mosquito Editores, 1999.

Murphy, Edward. *For a Proper Home: Housing Rights in the Margins of Urban Chile, 1960–2010*. Pittsburgh: University of Pittsburgh Press, 2014.

Neocleous, Mark. *The Fabrication of Social Order: A Critical Theory of Police Power*. Sterling, VA: Pluto Press, 2000.

Neruda, Pablo. *Confieso que he vivido*. Santiago: Pehuén, 2005 [1974].

Neruda, Pablo. *Memoirs*. New York: Penguin, 1978 [1974].

Nobel, Boris. *El reinado de Lenin*, trans. Ricardo Cabieses Z. Santiago: Imp. Fiscal de la Penitenciaría, 1920.

Nómez, Naín, and Emmanuel Tornés, eds. *Manuel Rojas: Estudios Críticos*. Santiago: Universidad de Santiago, 2005.

O'Hara, John F. "A New Form of Pan-Americanism: The Exchange of Students," *Hispanic American Historical Review* 4 (1921), 112–116.

Olavarría Bravo, Arturo. *Chile entre dos Alessandri: memorias políticas*. (4 vols.) Santiago: Editorial Nascimento, 1962–1965.

Opazo Maturana, Gustavo. *Historia de Talca* (Biblioteca Virtual Miguel de Cervantes), chapter xiii, www.cervantesvirtual.com/obra-visor/historia-de-talca--0/html/ff91b0ee-82b1-11df-acc7-002185ce6064_15.html.

Orlove, Benjamin. "Meat and Strength: The Moral Economy of a Chilean Food Riot," *Cultural Anthropology* 12:2 (1997), 1–35.

Ortner, Sherry. "Resistance and Ethnographic Refusal," *Comparative Studies in Society and History* 37:1 (1995), 173–193.

Palacios Laval, Cristián "Entre Bertillon y Vucetich: Las technologías de identificación policial, Santiago de Chile, 1893–1924," in Cristián Palacios and César Leyton, *Industria del Delito: Historias de las ciencias criminológicas en Chile*, 89–121. Santiago: Ocho Libros, 2014.

Palti, Elías José. "The Problem of 'Misplaced Ideas' Revisited: Beyond the 'History of Ideas' in Latin America," *Journal of the History of Ideas* 67:1 (January 2006), 149–179.

Parker, William Belmont. *Chileans of Today*. New York: G. P. Putnam and Sons, 1920.

Parry, Benita. "A Critique Mishandled," *Social Text* 35 (Summer 1993), 121–133.

Pereira Poza, Sergio. *Antología crítica de la dramaturgía anarquista en Chile*. Santiago: Editorial Universidad de Santiago, 2005.

Piccato, Pablo. *City of Suspects: Crime in Mexico City, 1900–1931*. Durham, NC: Duke University Press, 2001.

Pinta, Saku and David Berry, "Conclusion," in Alex Prichard, Ruth Kinna, Saku Pinta, and David Barry, eds., *Libertarian Socialism: Politics in Black and Red*, 294–303. London: Palgrave-MacMillan, 2012.

Pinto Durán, Carlos, ed., *Diccionario Personal de Chile*. Santiago: Claret, 1920.

Pinto V., Julio, and Verónica Valdívio O. *Revolución proletaria o querida chusma? Socialismo y Alessandrismo en la pugna por la politización pampina (1911–1932)*. Santiago: LOM Ediciones, 2001.

Plath, Oreste. *El Santiago que se fue: Apuntes de la memoria*. Santiago: Grijalbo, 1997.

Ponce, Néstor. "Alberto Edwards," in Darrell B. Lockhart, *Latin American Mystery Writers: An A-to-Z Guide*, 72–74. Westport, CT: Greenwood Press, 2004.

Pratt, Mary Louise. *Imperial Eyes: Travel Writing and Transculturation*. London: Routledge, 1993.

Prichard, Alex, Ruth Kinna, Saku Pinta, and David Berry, eds., *Libertarian Socialism: Politics in Black and Red*. London: Palgrave-MacMillan, 2012.

Prieto Lemm, Enrique. *La identificación de las personas*. Santiago: Imprenta de la Bolsa, 1923.

Programa oficial del Campeonato Sud-Americano de Box 1927. Santiago: Imp. Siglo XX, 1927.

Raj, Kapil. *Relocating Modern Science: Circulation and the Construction of Knowledge in South Asia and Europe, 1650–1900*. Basingstoke: Palgrave McMillan, 2006.

Ramírez Necochea, Hernán. *Orígen y formación del partido comunista: Ensayo de historia del Partido*. Austral, 1965.

Ramnath, Maia. *Decolonizing Anarchism: An Antiauthoritarian History of India's Liberation Struggle*. Oakland: AK Press, 2012.

Ranciere, Jacques. *On the Shores of Politics*. London: Verso, 1995.

Repertorio de Legislación y Jurisprudencia Chilenas: Constitución Política de la República de Chile, 1980. Santiago: Editorial Jurídica de Chile, 1993.

Reports of International Arbitral Awards (Tacna Arica Question (Chile, Peru)), March 4, 1925, Vol. II: 921–958.

Revista de derecho, jurisprudencia y ciencias sociales XV: 1–10 (March–December, 1918). Santiago: Imprenta Cervantes, 1918.

Ringrose, David. *Spain, Europe and the Spanish Miracle, 1700–1900*. Cambridge: Cambridge University Press, 1996.

Rinke, Stefan. *Cultura de masas: Reforma y nacionalismo en Chile 1910–1931*. Santiago: Ediciones de la Dirección de Bibliotecas, 2002.

Rocker, Rudolph. *Anarcho-Syndicalism*. London: Pluto Press, 1989 [1938].

Rodríguez Terrazas, Ignacio. "Protesta y soberanía popular: Las marchas del hambre en Santiago de Chile, 1918–1919," BA thesis, Pontífica Universidad Católica de Chile, (Santiago), 2001.

Rodríguez, Julia. "South Atlantic Crossings: Fingerprints, Science and the State in Turn-of-the-Century Argentina," *American Historical Review* 109:2 (April 2004), 387–416.

Rojas Flores, Jorge. "La prensa obrera chilena: El caso de La Federación Obrera y Justicia, 1921–1927," in Olga Ulianova, Manuel Loyola, and Rolando Alvarez, eds., *1912–2012: El siglo de los comunistas chilenos*, 23–80. Santiago: Instituto de Estudios Avanzados, 2012.

Rojas, Jorge. *Moral y prácticas cívicas en los niños chilenos, 1850–1950*. Santiago: LOM Ediciones, 2004.

Rojas, Manuel. *Antología autobiográfica*. Santiago: LOM Ediciones, 1995 [1962].

Rojas, Manuel. *La oscura vida radiante*. Santiago: Zig-Zag, 1996 [1971].

Rojas, Manuel. *Sombras contra el muro*. Santiago: Zig-Zag, 1964.

Rojas, Manuel. *Hijo de ladrón*. Madrid: Cátedra, 2001 [1951].

Rojas, Manuel. *Manual de Literatura Chilena*. Mexico City: Universidad Nacional Autónoma de México, 1964.

Romero, José Luis. "University Reform," in Joseph Maier and Richard W. Weatherhead, eds., *The Latin American University*, 135–146. Albuquerque: University of New Mexico Press, 1979.

Romero, José Luis. *Latinoamérica: Las ciudades y las ideas*. Medellín: Editorial Universidad de Antioquia, 1999 [1976].

Romero, Luis Alberto. *¿Qúe hacer con los pobres? Elite y sectores populares en Santiago de Chile, 1840–1895*. Buenos Aires: Sudamericana, 1997.

Rosenberg, Emily, ed., *A World Connecting, 1870–1945*. Cambridge, MA: Harvard University Press, 2012.

Rosenthal, Anton. "Radical Border Crossers: The Industrial Workers of the World and Their Press in Latin America," *Estudios Interdisciplinarios de América Latina y el Caribe* 22:2 (July/December 2011), 39–70.

Ross, Kristin. *May '68 and Its Afterlives*. Chicago: University of Chicago Press, 2002.

Ross, Kristin. *The Emergence of Social Space: Rimbaud and the Paris Commune*. Minneapolis: University of Minnesota Press, 1988.

Ross, Kristin. *Communal Luxury: The Political Imagination of the Paris Commune*. London: Verso, 2015.

Ruggiero, Kristin. "Fingerprinting and the Argentine Plan for Universal Identification in the Late Nineteenth and Early Twentieth Centuries," in *Documenting Individual Identity. The Development of State Practices in the Modern World*, eds. Jane Caplan and John Torpey, 184–196. Princeton, NJ: Princeton University Press, 2001.

Saad Saka, Mark. *For God and Revolution: Priest, Peasant and Agrarian Socialism in the Mexican Huasteca*. Albuquerque: University of New Mexico Press, 2013.

Sagredo, Rafael, and Cristián Gazmuri. *Historia de la vida privada en Chile (vol. 2): el Chile Moderno (1840–1925)*. Santiago: Taurus, 2006.

Salazar Vergara, Gabriel. *Del poder constituyente de asalariados e intelectuales: Chile, siglo XX y XXI*. Santiago: LOM Ediciones, 2009.

Salazar Vergara, Gabriel. *La enervante levedad histórica de la clase política civil (Chile, 1900–1973)*. Santiago: Debate, 2015.

Salazar Vergara, Gabriel, and Julio Pinto. *Historia contemporánea de Chile V: Niñez y juventud*. Santiago: LOM Ediciones, 2002.

Santini, Benoit. "Intertextualidad Bíblica en *Rebeldías Líricas* (1913) de José Domingo Gómez Rojas: Religión, creación e ideales anarquistas," in Joël Delhom and Daniel Attala, eds., *Cuando las anarquistas citaban la Biblia: Entre mesianismo y propaganda*, 171–182. Madrid: Catarata, 2014.

Schmidt, Michael and Lucien van der Walt, *Black Flame: The Revolutionary Class Politics of Anarchism and Syndicalism*. Oakland: AK Press, 2013.

Schmidt, Michael. *Cartography of Revolutionary Anarchism*. Oakland: AK Press, 2014.

Schuler, Friedrich E. *Secret Wars and Secret Policies in the Americas, 1842–1929*. Albuquerque: University of New Mexico Press, 2010.

Schwarz, Roberto. *Misplaced Ideas: Essays on Brazilian Culture*. London: Verso, 1992.

Schweitzer, Daniel. "Juan Gandulfo," *Babel: Revista de arte y crítica*, año XI, vol. 7, no.28 (julio–agosto 1945), 18–24.

Schweitzer, Daniel. "La Justicia y los grandes procesos en Chile desde 1905," *Medio Siglo de Zig-Zag, 1905–1955*. Santiago: n.p., n.d.

Scott, James C. *The Weapons of the Weak: Everyday Forms of Peasant Resistance in Southeast Asia*. New Haven, CT: Yale University Press, 1985.

Scott, James C. *Domination and the Arts of Resistance: Hidden Transcripts*. New Haven, CT: Yale University Press, 1992.

Scott, James C. *Seeing Like a State: How Certain Schemes to Improve the Human Condition Have Failed*. New Haven, CT: Yale University Press, 1998.

Scott, James C. *The Art of Not Being Governed: An Anarchist History of Upland Southeast Asia*. New Haven, CT: Yale University Press, 2009.

Scott, James C. *Two Cheers for Anarchism*. Princeton, NJ: Princeton University Press, 2012.

Sebreli, Juan José. *Comediantes y mártires: Ensayo contra los mitos*. Buenos Aires: Debate, 2008.

Sekula, Allan. "The Body and the Archive," *October* 39 (Winter 1986), 3–64.

Seltzer, Mark. *Bodies and Machines*. New York: Routledge, 1992.

Sepúlveda Rondanelli, José. *Los radicales ante la historia*. Santiago: Editorial Andrés Bello, 1993.

Serge, Victor. *Unforgiving Years*, trans. Richard Greeman. New York: New York Review of Books, 2008.

Serge, Victor. *Memoirs of a Revolutionary*, trans. Peter Sedgwick and George Paizis. New York: New York Review Books, 2012.

Serge, Victor. *Men in Prison*, trans. Richard Greeman. London: Writers and Readers Publishing Cooperative, 1977 [1931].

Sewell, William. *Logics of History: Social Theory and Social Transformation*. Chicago: University of Chicago Press, 2005.

Shaffer, Kirwin. *Anarchism and Countercultural Politics in Early Twentieth-Century Cuba*. Gainesville: University Press of Florida, 2005.

Silva Castro, Raúl. *Panorama Literario de Chile*. Santiago: Editorial Universitaria, 1961.

Silva, Víctor Domingo. "Prólogo," in Alberto Muñoz Figueroa and Armando Roma Boza, *Crónicas*. Santiago: Imp. Fiscal de la Penitenciaria, 1923.

Silva, J. Pablo. "Frustrated Expectations and Social Protest in Post-World War I Chile." Paper presented at the 2013 Latin American Studies Association meeting, Washington, DC.

Silva V., Fernando. "Expansión y crisis nacional, 1861–1924," in Sergio Villalobos R., Osvaldo Silva G., Fernando Silva V., and Patricio Estellé M., *Historia de Chile*, 563–750. Santiago: Editorial Universitaria, 1974.

Sinópsis estadística i jerográfica de Chile. Santiago: Dirección de Estadística, 1906.

Skuban, William E. *Lines in the Sand: Nationalism and Identity on the Peruvian-Chilean Frontier*. Albuquerque: University of New Mexico Press, 2007.

Skuban, William E. "Civic and Ethnic Conceptions of Nationhood on the Peruvian-Chilean Frontier, 1880–1930," *Studies in Ethincity and Nationalism* 8:3 (December 2008), 386–407.

Soja, Edward. *Postmodern Geographies: The Reassertion of Space in Critical Social Theory*, 2nd ed. London: Verso Press, 2011.

Soria, Carmen, comp. *Letras Anarquistas: José Santos González Vera y Manuel Rojas: Artículos periodísticas y otros escritos inéditos*. Santiago: Planeta, 2005.

Stanek, Lukasz. *Henri Lefebvre on Space: Architecture, Urban Research and the Production of Theory*. Minneapolis: University of Minnesota Press, 2011.

Subercaseaux, Bernardo. *Historia de las ideas y de la cultura en Chile (tomo 3): El centenario y las vanguardias*. Santiago: Editorial Universitaria, 2004.

Subercaseaux, Guillermo. *Monetary and Banking Policy of Chile*. Oxford: Clarendon Press, 1922.

Suchlicki, Jaime. "Sources of Student Violence in Latin America: An Analysis of the Literature," *Latin American Research Review* 7:3 (Fall 1972), 31–46.

Tamayo Grez, Tania. *Caso Bombas: La explosión en la Fiscalía Sur*. Santiago: LOM Ediciones, 2014.

Thomas, Paul. *Karl Marx and the Anarchists*. London: Routledge and Keegan Paul, 1980.

Thompson, E. P. *Whigs and Hunters: The Origin of the Black Act*. New York: Pantheon Books, 1975.

Thompson, E. P. *The Poverty of Theory & Other Essays*. London: Merlin Press, 1978.

Todes, Daniel. *Darwin Without Malthus: The Struggle for Existence in Russian Evolutionary Thought*. Oxford: Oxford University Press, 1989.

Torrealba Zenón, Agustín. *Los subversivos: Alegato del abogado señor Agustín Torrealba Z. ante la Iltma. Corte de Apelaciones de Santiago, en el proceso contra la sociedad Industrial Workers of the World (Trabajadores Industriales del Mundo) I.W.W.* Santiago: Imp. Yara, 1921.

Townsend y Onel. *La inquisición chilena*. Valparaíso: Talleres Gráficas Augusto, 1932.

Triviño, A[rmando]. *Arengas*. Santiago: Editorial Lux, c. 1923.

Trotsky, Leon. *The Bolsheviki and World Peace*. New York: Boni and Liveright, 1918.

Tunnermann, Carlos. *Historia de la Universidad en América Latina: De la época colonial a la Reforma de Córdoba*. San José, Costa Rica: Editorial Universitaria CentroAmericana, 1991.

Turcato, Davide. "Italian Anarchism as a Transnational Movement," *International Review of Social History* 52:3 (2007), 407–444.

Ulloa C., F. *La Penitenciaría de Santiago*. Santiago: Los Tiempos, 1879.

Van der Walt, Lucien, and Steven Hirsch, eds., *Anarchism and Syndicalism and the Colonial and Postcolonial World, 1870–1940: The Praxis of National Liberation, Internationalism, and Social Revolution*. Leiden: Brill, 2010.

Varas, José Miguel. *Chacón*. Santiago: Talleres de la Sociedad Impresora Horizonte, 1968.

Venegas Salas, Rodolfo. *Lo que ví en la carcel pública de Santiago de Chile*. Santiago: Imp. y Enc. La Economía, 1925.
Vera H., Humbert. *Juventud y Bohemia: Memorial de una generación estudiantil*. Valparaíso: n.p., 1947.
Verhoeven, Claudia. *The Odd Man Karakozov: Imperial Russia, Modernity and the Birth of Terrorism*. Ithaca, NY: Cornell University Press, 2011.
Vial, A. Alonso "Nota biográfica sobre Juan Gandulfo: Lo que he conocido de él," *Revista Médica de Chile* 60 (1932), 99–114.
Vicuña Fuentes, Carlos. *La cuestión social ante la Federación de Estudiantes de Chile*. Santiago: Año 68 de la Era Normal, 1922.
Vicuña Fuentes, Carlos. *En las prisiones políticas de Chile: Cuatro evasiones novelescas*. Santiago: Cruz del Sur, 1946.
Vicuña Fuentes, Carlos. *La Tiranía en Chile: Libro escrito en el destierro en 1928*. Santiago: LOM Ediciones, 2002 [1938].
Viotti da Costa, Emilia. *The Brazilian Empire: Myths and Histories*, rev. ed. Chapel Hill: University of North Carolina Press, 2000.
Virilio, Paul. *Speed and Politics*. 2nd ed. Los Angeles: Semiotext(e), 2006.
Vitale, Luis. "Contribución a una historia del anarquismo en América Latina." Centro de Estudios "Miguel Enríquez," www.archivochile.com/Ideas_Autores/vitalel/2lvc/02lvchistsocal0027.pdf.
Vizconde del Palacio, *Historia de la cárcel política: La Bastilla Chilena*. Paris: Imprenta Rochefort, 1893.
Vodovnik, Ziga. *The Living Spirit of Revolt*. Oakland: PM Press, 2013.
Walker, Louise *Waking from the Dream: Mexico's Middle Classes After 1968*. Redwood City, CA: Stanford University Press, 2013.
Walter, Richard J. "The Intellectual Background of the 1918 University Reform in Argentina," *Hispanic American Historical Review* 49:2 (May 1969), 233–253.
Walter, Richard J. *Student Politics in Argentina: The University Reform and its Effects, 1918–1964*. New York: Basic Books, 1968.
Walter, Richard J. *Politics and Urban Growth in Santiago, Chile, 1891–1941*. Redwood City, CA: Stanford University Press, 2005.
Ward, Colin. *Anarchism: A Very Short Introduction*. Oxford: Oxford University Press, 2004.
Ward, Colin. *Anarchy in Action*. London: Freedom Press, 1982.
Weinstein, José, and Eduardo Valenzuela. "La FECh de los años veinte: Un movimiento estudiantil con historia." Mimeograph, August 1980.
Williams, Raymond. *The Country and the City*. New York: Oxford University Press, 1975.
Williamson, Edwin. *The Penguin History of Latin America*. London: Penguin, 1992.
Wood, Andrew Grant. *Revolution in the Street: Women, Workers, and Urban Protest in Veracruz, 1870–1927*. Wilmington, DE: SR Books, 2001.
Woodcock, George. *The Paradox of Oscar Wilde*. London: T. V. Boardman & Co., 1949.
Zalaquett S., Ricardo. "*Siembra, juventud! La tierra es propicia, el momento es único.* No es Neruda sino Gandulfo, el cirujano," *Revista Médica de Chile* 133 (2005), 376–382.
Žižek, Slavoj. *In Defense of Lost Causes*. London: Verso, 2008.

INDEX

Note: Page numbers in italics refer to illustrations, maps, and photographs. Endnotes follow page number with and "n" and note number.

CPSIA information can be obtained
at www.ICGtesting.com
Printed in the USA
BVHW030016210319
543286BV00004B/5/P

9 780190 053789